Kim Il Sung

On Juche in Our Revolution

Volume I

**Dedicated to the Great Leader
President Kim Il Sung
on his 65th Birthday**

**Weekly Guardian Associates, Inc.
New York, N.Y.**

Printed in the United States of America by Faculty Press, Inc.,
    Brooklyn, N.Y.

Library of Congress Cataloging in Publication Data

Kim Il Sung, 1912-
On Juche in our Revolution

Selection from the author's writings, speeches and reports,
    1931-1966
Library of Congress catalogue number 77-72756

ISBN 0-917654-30-7 (paperback)
ISBN 0-917654-31-5 (hardcover)

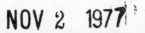

CONTENTS

PREFACE

*Of all the socialist countries in the world today, it is doubtful
any stress the idea of independence and self-reliance in all
spheres more emphatically than the Democratic People's
Republic of Korea [DRPK].*

*They have a word for it—Juche. As formulated and
developed by President Kim Il Sung, the concept of Juche is
one of the DPRK's major contributions to world revolution.*

*The Juche idea means, in essence, that the masters of the
revolution and the work of construction are the masses of the
people and that they are also the motive forces of the revolution
and the work of construction. In other words, one is responsible
for shaping one's destiny.*

President Kim Il Sung has said:

*"The Juche idea is based on a philosophical theory that man
is master of everything and decides everything."*

*On the basis of this theory, the DPRK has developed from an
oppressed semifeudal country into a modern socialist society,
completely rebuilding in the process from the destruction*

wrought by U.S. imperialism during the Korean War.

Among modern revolutionary leaders in the world today, President Kim Il Sung—who has led the Korean people to national independence, the building of a modern socialist state and to the front lines of the worldwide struggle against imperialism—is among the most profound thinkers and prolific writers.

His voluminous "Selected Works," compiled over decades of revolutionary war and socialist construction, make many important theoretical contributions to the science of Marxism-Leninism. As with much else about remarkable socialist Korea, the writings and ideas of President Kim Il Sung are not yet well-known in the U.S. The "Selected Works" are not available here so far. This situation is slowly changing, however, as more and more progressive people take an interest in socialism.

The present volume, soon to be followed by a second, consists of President Kim Il Sung's writings about Juche, its importance in the Korean revolution and as a general idea in socialist development. The writings included here contain selections from the years 1931—at the very start of the guerrilla war against the Japanese army of occupation—to 1966. They deal with such diverse subjects as establishing guerrilla bases, enhancing the role of social sciences, revolutionary literature and art, and improving higher education and combating dogmatism and revisionism. In each article, President Kim Il Sung stresses the need for Korean solutions to Korean problems.

Although these 32 articles deal specifically with Korea, they have international significance. All are examples of how to apply Marxism-Leninism to the concrete conditions of one's own country, avoiding dogmatism and subservience in the process.

Virtually none of the essays published here has been printed before in the West. As such, this volume constutues a wealth of material for all progressive Americans.

We take particular pleasure in publishing this volume on April 15, 1977, as it marks the 65th birthday of the great Korean leader.

Weekly Guardian Associates

LET US REPUDIATE THE "LEFT" ADVENTURIST LINE AND FOLLOW THE REVOLUTONARY ORGANIZATIONAL LINE

Speech Delivered at the Meeting of Party and Young Communist League Cadres Held at Mingyuehkou, Yenchi County, *May 20, 1931*

Comrades,

The chaotic world economic crisis which started in 1929 stirred up the frantic arms race among the imperialist powers and added fuel to the fire of their wild ambitions of foreign aggression.

The Japanese imperialists are seeking a way out of the economic crisis in the war of continental aggression. They are openly preparing for the invasion of the vast land of China with its inexhaustible underground resources and huge labor force, infringing upon the vested interest of the British, US and French imperialist powers. The Japanese imperialist aggressors, hell-bent on war preparations for the continental aggression, are further strengthening their colonial suppression and exploitation of the Korean people for the "security of the rear."

With the strengthening of Japanese imperialist colonial rule the plight of the Korean people is getting worse and the contradictions between the Japanese imperialists and the Korean people become sharper daily. The Korean people's resistance against the colonial rule of the Japanese imperialists is growing stronger and the people themselves are becoming involved in a more active mass struggle against Japanese imperialism.

The struggle of the workers, peasants, students and other young people against the colonial oppression of Japanese imperialism is growing fiercer in all parts of our country; it is beginning to take the form of mass violence.

The present situation and the high revolutionary spirit of our workers and peasants, students and other young people call for the Korean Communists to lead the anti-Japanese national-liberation struggle on to a higher plane.

Armed struggle is the only way to advance the anti-Japanese national-liberation struggle to a higher stage. This is in conformity with the requirements of the present subjective and objective revolutionary situation in our country.

The Japanese imperialists, the robbers, are ruling our country and imposing colonial slavery upon the Korean people by dint of the counterrevolutionary armed forces. Without weapons we cannot defeat the Japanese imperialists, who are armed to the teeth, nor can we achieve the liberation and independence of the country.

However, we cannot launch an armed struggle right now when we are unprepared. No revolutionary struggle is won without adequate preparation of the revolutionary forces.

Only when the revolutionary forces are fully prepared is it possible to wage an armed struggle and defeat the Japanese imperialists.

We must gather our own revolutionary forces and go on increasing them if we are to wage an energetic struggle against the Japanese imperialist aggressors. A blind and badly prepared revolt is useless; instead of strengthening the revolutionary forces, it does the revolution untold harm.

Today we are drawing serious lessons from the May 30 Uprising. This is because we must take a decisive move in the preparation of the revolutionary forces to develop the anti-Japanese national liberation struggle to a higher stage.

The sectarian-flunkeys rose in reckless revolt on May 30 in east Manchuria to serve only their factional ends. They had neither a detailed plan nor organizational preparation for the revolt; they only set up the "Uprising Headquarters," rousing peasants in every village to attack towns. As a result, a violent struggle began on May 30, 1930. In the important towns of east Manchuria such as Lungching, Toutaokou, Erhtaokou, Nanyangping, Chiemantung, Yenchi, and Tungfossu they destroyed or set fire to the Japanese consulate, the office of the Korean Residents Association, the Financial Agency of the Oriental Development Company, public schools, power stations, and railway bridges and liquidated the Japanese fellow-travellers, landlords and capitalists.

In the streets there were bloody struggles between the Japanese army and police forces and unarmed rioters. Our numerous comrades were killed and the masses bled under the bayonets of the enemy. Meanwhile, the Japanese imperialist policemen and their minions ransacked every village, rounded up many Korean youths, jailed them and subjected them to cruel torture, and murdered them barbarously.

The reactionary Chinese warlords, hoodwinked by the national estrangement policy of the Japanese imperialist aggressors and at their instigation, massacred many people under the pretext of "arresting Korean Communists." The Kirin provincial government appointed Wang Shiu-tang, the Commander of the 7th Regiment stationed in Tunhwa, the commander of the punitive force, and sent out thousands of troops to arrest, imprison and kill innocent Korean peasants indiscriminately.

The number of young and middle-aged Koreans arrested and imprisoned by the Japanese imperialists and Kuomintang warlords during the past year alone amounted to hundreds of thousands, of whom those shot on the spot numbered hundreds. Hundreds of Korean Communists arrested were transferred to Sodaemun Prison in Seoul. The total casualties of young and middle-aged Koreans, if those killed in action on the day of revolt, those who died by enemy torture and the wounded are combined, number several thousands.

As a result, today in east Manchuria the Korean villages are stricken with terror. Revolutionary organizations have been destroyed, some comrades who could have made a narrow escape are at their wits' end, and the peasant masses shrink under the enemy's terrorism.

We must save this critical situation promptly, restore the revolutionary organizations and heighten the revolutionary

spirit of the masses so as to revitalize the Korean revolution.
To this end, it is important to analyse and sum up correctly the
rash and adventurous May 30 Uprising, and to draw correct
lessons from it.

What, then, is the main reason for the failure of the May 30
Uprising?

First, it lies in the dogmatism and petty-bourgeois heroism
of the sectarian-flunkeys.

The sectarians demolished the Korean Communist Party
founded in 1925, by indulging in factional strife. Instead of
learning the right lessons, they hung out the signboard of
"party reconstruction" even in Manchuria, and have been engrossed in the mere expansion of their own factions only to
split the revolutionary forces. When their factional activities
were criticized by the Comintern, they rose in the adventurous
and foolhardy May 30 Uprising with the preposterous thought
of fostering trust through what they called struggle and thus
joining the Chinese Communist Party on the principle of one
party for one nation. The sectarian-flunkeys who had wormed
their way into the leadership of this movement did not care
whether the revolution would fail or the masses die, but attempted to win trust from the Comintern and guarantee their
factions' hegemony, acquiring the fame of individuals or their
own groups in the uprising.

Blinded by fame-seeking and flunkeyism, the sectarians
unavoidably fell into the dogmatic error of dancing to others'
tunes.

They had seen the temporary predominance within the party
of another country of the "Left" adventurist line of the revolt,
and without a clear idea as to whether the line was correct or
relevant to the specific reality of our revolution, they incited a
great number of the revolutionary masses to revolt, thus causing useless sacrifices and harming the revolution greatly.

Second, the uprising progressed in an ultra-"Leftist" way.

The sectarian-flunkeys had neither a correct understanding
of the present stage of the Korean revolution nor any scientific
strategy and tactics. But out of a mere subjective desire, they
started the revolt under an unfeasible ultra-"Leftist" slogan of
struggle. Regardless of the anti-imperialist, anti-feudal,
democratic character of the Korean revolution, the organizers
of the revolt used the ultra-"Leftist" slogans,"Let us build a

worker-peasant Soviet power!" and "Down with the Chongui-bu, the branches of the Singan-hoe Association of the Kunu-hoe Association!" and forced the masses to smash all the landlords and capitalists, whether they were pro- or anti-Japanese. In some areas the "Leftist" error was committed of setting fire at random to the grain stacks of those who were landlords and rich peasants only by name, and liquidating even the waverers who could have been won over, labelling them as minions.

These "Leftist" acts prevented the masses in revolt from displaying their revolutionary enthusiasm and participating voluntarily in the struggle. These acts caused unrest particularly among many of the anti-Japanese masses who could have been won over to the side of revolution, and instead made them waver.

Third the uprising was an adventure, inadequately prepared without scientific calculation.

The revolt only wins when the subjective and objective situations mature and the revolutionary forces are sufficiently prepared for a determined attack with an elaborate plan and correct strategy and tactics. However, the organizers of the May 30 Uprising did it in a risky and reckless way, without correct analysis and judgment of the revolutionary situation; without taking proper account of the balance of forces between friends and foes and without correct plans and adequate arrangements.

At that time, the revolutionary organizations in east Manchuria were young and still weak; the masses lacked organizational training. Moreover, the masses were forced to revolt without sufficient revolutionary education. Therefore, some of them, who were not awakened, joined in the revolt without a clear understanding of its purpose and significance. Even in some areas the revolt did not enjoy positive support from the revolutionary masses since mass organizations had just been formed and the uprising was organized through intimidation or threat. In these areas, therefore, the uprising organizations could not counter the enemy's trifling white terrorism and were soon dissolved. Thus the reckless "Leftist" May 30 Uprising ended in failure, causing numerous deaths, under the armed suppression by thousands of allied crack troops of Japanese imperialism and the reactionary Kuomintang warlords.

What, then, are the consequences of the May 30 Uprising?

First of all, it weakened the relations between revolutionary organizations and the masses and separated the latter from the former.

As the revolt was put down and the enemy intensified suppression and widespread massacres, the rioters who lacked organizational training and had insufficient ideological preparation, lost confidence in victory and regretted having been involved in the struggle. Some of them had even gone so far as to believe "the Communist Party is to blame for our ruin" as the enemy's pillage of innocent people became intolerable. This degraded the dignity of Communists among the masses and produced such a serious effect that quite a few people, seized with fear, quitted the revolutionary organizations.

Furthermore, as the struggle was waged in a "Leftist" way, large sections of the masses who could have been involved in the anti-Japanese national-liberation revolution to fight side by side with us, went over to the enemy.

Next, it resulted in the collapse of fledgling revolutionary cadres, especially of the revolutionary leadership cadres in different regions.

In east Manchuria revolutionary organizations emerged and young Communists were brought up amidst the mass struggles of various forms against Japanese imperialism and its lackeys. On this basis, the revolutionary leadership cadres began to emerge in every region.

It was just then that the reckless revolt was organized. As a result, tens of fine young Communists, the leadership cadres of revolution, were killed and hundreds of our revolutionary comrades and thousands of the anti-Japanese masses were arrested and put into prison. Because of this loss of a number of Communists, particularly revolutionary leadership cadres, the revolutionary organizations in east Manchuria found it difficult to regroup the wrecked revolutionary forces, extend the revolutionary organizations to untouched areas and revive the revolutionary struggle. No less serious was the loss to the revolution of many revolutionary leadership cadres brought up in the many years of the socialist enlightenment movement and struggle.

Another consequence was that most of the local revolutionary organizations were destroyed.

In all parts of east Manchuria the socialist enlightenment movement had developed earlier, so that many revolutionary vanguard and other mass organizations were formed and grew in scope and strength. However, since the uprising led the revolutionary organizations here to their destruction or exposure, they suffered tremendous losses from enemy suppression. Thus the organized masses have lost their organizations and tremble with fear, not knowing which way to go.

Moreover, the May 30 Uprising gave the enemy the pretext for an evil propaganda campaign and bestial suppression, and particularly, it benefited the Japanese imperialist policy of national estrangement. The ultra-"Leftist" organizers of the uprising incited people to set fire to schools run by the Japanese imperialist aggressors and to grain stacks belonging to the landlords. These rash acts caused the enemy to intensify its propaganda: "The Korean Communists are murderers and arsonists," and "The Korean Communists are burglars setting fire to the grain stacks of the Chinese." The Japanese imperialists had thus found a good excuse to urge the Kuomintang warlords to kill the Koreans mercilessly.

Meanwhile, under the plea of protecting the Japanese citizens and ruling the Koreans in Manchuria, the Japanese imperialists are carrying on the "movement for dispatching the Japanese troops to Manchuria."

The reactionary Kuomintang warlords, fooled by the Japanese imperialists' national estrangement policy, killed the Korean people at random, slanderously accusing them, saying: "The Koreans are the cat's-paws of the Japanese imperialists." This worsened the relations between the Korean and Chinese peoples.

Comrades,

The "Leftist", risky and blind May 30 Uprising brought extremely grave consequences to our revolution. However, we must never be defeatists swaying or giving way in the face of these temporary difficulties. On the road of revolution there may be turns and twists, temporary failures and sacrifices.

Though our revolutionary struggle now faces a bitter trial owing to the "Leftist", risky and misguided May 30 Uprising in east Manchuria, if we draw up a correct line and policies and rely on them in our struggle, then the revolutionary organizations will be restored and the revolutionary forces will be stronger and the revolutionary struggle will lead to a new up-surge.

Then, what line and policies must we take in our struggle?

Above all, we must prepare ourselves to meet a forthcoming greater event by opposing the "Leftist", blind adventurism of the sectarian-flunkeys and strengthening our mass organiza-tional and political work. In other words, we must make better preparations for advancing the anti-Japanese national-libera-tion struggle to a new stage based on an armed struggle.

Success in revolution is dependent upon the preparation of one's own strong revolutionary forces.

It now appears that Japanese imperialism is strong and the revolutionary forces of the Korean people are sadly insignifi-cant. However, our homeland will certainly be liberated if we the Communists, steadily boost and strengthen our revolu-tionary forces, if we take advantage of the contradictions be-tween Japanese imperialism and the Soviet Union, between Japanese imperialism and colonial countries and between Japanese imperialism and the rest of the imperialist powers to drive the Japanese imperialists into a tight corner, and deal a decisive blow to them through an armed struggle with the sup-port of the working class and of the oppressed nations all over the world.

The most important task for the Korean Communists at present is to follow out the revolutionary organizational line which makes it possible to unite the main masses of the revolu-tion firmly, and around them, the anti-Japanese forces from all walks of life, thereby building up the whole nation into a political force.

To this end, we must form, first of all, strong revolutionary leadership cadres and strengthen their independent roles.

For the skillful organization and development of revolu-tionary struggles in keeping with the demand of the ever-changing situation, there must be in every region leading cadres who are conversant with the local conditions, politically prepared, and having organizational abilities. What is more, since our revolutionary activities have to be done underground and our work carried on almost independently to fit in with the characteristics of each respective region, it is imperative to have revolutionary leadership cadres. If we have at least one or two capable leadership cadres in every region we shall guarantee success in educating and rallying workers and peasants and thus laying the mass foundation of revolution.

Therefore, we must form leadership cadres in every region with competent comrades who have high class consciousness, a revolutionary fighting spirit, organizing ability, popularity among the masses, and enterprising spirit.

It is important in shaping leadership cores to arm them firmly with the Marxist-Leninist revolutionary ideas.

Only when they are fully equipped with these ideas can the core elements fight consistently for the revolution in any distress and adversity and infiltrate deep into the worker and peasant masses to share the sweet and bitter life with them, and train them as ardent revolutionary fighters by arming them with revolutionary ideas. Leadership cadres must be active in the work and spearhead any difficult and dangerous work for the benefit of revolution, so that they can educate the masses by practical examples.

The revolutionary leadership cadres must correct all the Rightist and "Leftist" tendencies revealed in the past work of organizing and guiding the masses and thoroughly implement a new revolutionary organizational line and thus bring about a great change in preparing the revolutionary forces. They should discover and register on the list of core elements men of high class consciousness and strong will to fight, train them and rely firmly on them in their energetic organization and guidance of the masses. The ranks of core elements should be firmly built up with those comrades who have fought bravely in the past years' struggle, especially those who strictly kept the organization's secret recently in defiance of arrest, imprisonment and cruel torture.

At the same time, it is particularly important in developing our revolutionary movement to extend and strengthen the YCL ranks with the young Communists tested in revolutionary practices. There are now large numbers of Korean peasants in east Manchuria. The young people form the majority of peasant activists who are politically awakened and have a high degree of anti-Japanese revolutionary enthusiasm. In actual fact, the YCL organizations composed of the select young people are developing the countryside in a revolutionary way and revolutionizing it. Only when these organizations carry out their work properly can a sound basis be laid for establishing party organizations in the future.

Attention should, therefore, be paid first to expounding and strengthening the YCL organizations, in which many fine, enterprising, revolutionary and sensitive young men and women should be enlisted. In particular, we must absorb in these organizations the young activists working in the Anti-Imperialist League, the Peasants' Association and the Women's Association, who have done well in their assignments defying the enemy's recent savage suppression and turning the legal possibilities to good account.

Secondly, we must restore and put in order the wrecked mass organizations, educate and rally the broad masses so as to lay a solid mass basis for the revolution.

No revolution can be made by a few Communists alone, without the active support and participation of the majority. For the masses to be involved in the revolutionary struggle and to be turned into a strong political force, they should be armed with a revolutionary consciousness and organized in large numbers in mass organizations. Therefore, we should restore the mass organizations quickly, expand and strengthen them still further and enhance their role. This is very important today in educating and uniting the broad anti-Japanese masses and thus consolidating a mass basis for the revolution.

The enemy's wholesale roundup has now led to the destruction of mass organizations and made the masses shrink. In this situation we must organize and carry on more energetic political work among the masses to raise their dampened spirits and range them in the revolutionary organizations in a big way.

In order to restore, readjust, extend and strengthen the mass organizations, competent leadership cadres should above all be dispatched to every region. There they must have a good grasp of the excellent core elements among the workers and poor peasants and rely on them to restore the broken Peasants' Association, the Anti-Imperialist League, the Women's Association and the Children's Corps, and to expand their ranks.

At the same time, many best leading cadres must be sent to the untapped areas where no organization exists, to form various anti-Japanese mass organizations—the Peasants' Association, the Anti-Imperialist League (AIL), the Revolutionary Mutual Aid Society (RMAS), the Women's Association and the Children's Corps. Peasants, with both hired and poor at the core, should be enlisted in the Peasant's Association; the men of strong national consciousness among the former participants in the Independence Army and the nationalist movement incorporated in the AIL; those who are friendly toward us and maintain neutrality, the revolutionary sympathizers and the aged in the RMAS; women in the Women's Association; and children in the communist Children's Corps. In this way all the anti-Japanese masses can be made members of revolutionary organizations. Besides, in order to defend the revolutionary organizations and the revolutionary masses against the enemy's incursion, the Red Guards, a paramilitary organization, should be formed with the young and middle-aged who have got organizational training through mass organizational life, and who are brave and have a strong will to fight. The Red Guardsmen should be progressively trained in military knowledge in preparation for a revolutionary armed force.

Thirdly, it is important in building up a strong revolutionary force, to temper the masses in the struggle, to say nothing of organizing them. Revolutionary practices only foster the revolutionary cores and train the revolutionary forces militantly. However, it is too dangerous to drive the masses to a reckless, "Leftist" and adventurous riot as was the case with the May 30 Uprising. A revolutionary struggle should be based on a correct understanding of the balance of forces between enemies and friends and should be based on scientific strategy and tactics. This alone can mature the revolutionary situation, develop the revolutionary leadership cores and train the broad masses organizationally and revolutionally.

The principles we are to abide by in our tactics are gradually to develop a struggle from a small to a big operation and from an economic struggle to a political one, and skillfully combine the legal struggle with semi-legal and illegal ones.

You must strictly keep the secrets of revolutionary organizations and maintain a high revolutionary vigilance in your activities to safeguard the organizations from the enemy's suppression, subversion and sabotage, and protect the revolutionary masses.

Today the Japanese imperialist aggressors are making every desperate effort to stifle the anti-Japanese revolutionary forces of the Korean people growing under the impact of the communist idea. They are smuggling their minions into our ranks and trying to take advantage of our possible indolence and unwatchfulness to discover the secret of the organizations. The enemy is wicked and sly. There could be serious consequences in our revolutionary work if the secret leaks out because of the slightest indolence or unwatchfulness of a few people.

The secret of the organization is worth the life of a revolutionary and it is his first and foremost duty to keep the secret. We are waging a hard struggle to rally the masses around the revolutionary organizations by educating and awakening them, and lay a mass basis for the revolution by steadily enlarging the organizations in defiance of the enemy's barbarous repression. So we must always be highly vigilant and work flexibly so that the secret will not be let out. Particularly, the members of the YCL and other revolutionary organizations ought to keep at the cost of their lives the secret of their organizations without submitting to the enemy's appeasement, deception, menace and blackmail.

Fourthly, energetic endeavor should be made to expose the national estrangement policy of the Japanese imperialist aggressors and to strengthen militant friendship and revolutionary solidarity between the Korean and Chinese peoples.

The Japanese imperialists are following their stereotyped national estrangement policy while encouraging by hook or by crook the discord and enmity between the Korean and Chinese peoples caused by the "Leftist", adventurous and misguided May 30 Uprising. They are seeking to realize their aggressive ambitions more easily by keeping the anti-Japanese forces of the two peoples apart and pitting them against each other.

We must reveal and condemn before the Korean and Chinese worker and peasant masses the harmfulness of the "Leftist", adventurous May 30 Uprising and the diabolical murders perpetrated by the reactionary Kuomintang warlords, and thoroughly expose the Japanese imperialists' underhand nation-provoking plots through which they are busy furthering a temporary antagonism between the two peoples. Particularly we must get them to know clearly genuine friends and foes so that they can firmly unite in the struggle against the Japanese imperialist and their puppets, the common enemies of the two peoples.

Since the enemy is running into a more furious white terrorism against the revolutionary forces and large sectors of the masses are still to be awakened, we expect to meet many difficulties and hardships in our work. However, with wholehearted determination to save our country and nation from the tyranny of the Japanese imperialist colonial rulers, we must overcome all difficulties, trials and dangers, and exert every ounce of our strength to implement the new organizational line.

We must thoroughly put the revolutionary organizational line into effect and thus build a solid foundation for leading the revolution to an upsurge within a short space of time in east Manchuria and, further, in the whole of Korea and developing the anti-Japanese national-liberation struggle into an organized armed struggle.

ON ORGANIZING AND WAGING ARMED STRUGGLE AGAINST JAPANESE IMPERIALISM

Speech Delivered at the Meeting of Party and Young Communist League Cadres Held at Mingyuehkou, Yenchi County, *December 16, 1931*

Comrades,

The present situation demands that we immediately organize and wage armed struggle against Japanese imperialism.

While they are starting aggression against the continent, the Japanese imperialists are intensifying their all-round reactionary offensive against the Korean people for the "security of the rear." These scoundrels are now suppressing the Korean people's revolutionary advance by force of arms, they are wantonly arresting, imprisoning and murdering our innocent people in every part of the country. This greatly aggravates the national and class contradictions between Japanese imperialism and the Korean people.

The anti-Japanese struggle of workers, peasants and the remaining broad masses to resist the Japanese imperialists' barbarous suppression grows stronger, and is gradually developing into violent conflict.

The general strike of dockers at Wonsan, the strikes by workers at the Sinhung Coal Mine and the Pyongyang Rubber Factory, the peasant uprising in Tanchon, and the peasant struggle on the Fuji farm of Ryongchon—all these show that the workers and peasants in our country began with violent opposition to Japanese imperialism armed to the teeth. A youth and student resistance is also rapidly developing with the Kwangju Student Incident as a driving force.

In keeping with the violent advance of the people in the homeland, the Korean peasants' struggle is rapidly gaining momentum in east Manchuria, too. Under the leadership of the Korean Communists, a large-scale, well-organized autumn struggle took place involving more than 100,000 peasants in east Manchuria; and this developed into a violent struggle and struck a great blow against Japanese imperialism and reactionary landlords, thus winning a brilliant victory.

It became obvious to the Korean working class, peasants, youths and students and other patriotic-minded people, that they could not escape the destiny of a ruined people nor meet the simple needs of their lives without resorting to revolutionary violence.

Under these conditions, it is vital for the anti-Japanese national-liberation struggle to organize the surging violence of the masses and to develop it into armed struggle.

To organize and launch armed struggle is the only correct method of restoring the country and liberating the people from Japanese imperialist colonial enslavement.

The Japanese imperialists, the burglars, have occupied our country by force of arms, and employed counterrevolutionary forces to maintain their colonial rule in Korea. In order to violently suppress every patriotic struggle of the Korean people, they permanently station armed forces of more than two divisions, and have set up at least 2,000 police stations and military police institutions, and dozens of prison houses in our country. They have passed all kinds of evil fascist laws, whereby they deprive the Korean people of the freedom of speech, of the press, assembly, association and demonstration, and prohibit them from all political activities.

The Japanese imperialist aggressors are using all possible means and methods to reduce the Korean people to permanent colonial slavery. They will not retreat even one step until their aggressive forces are crushed.

It is a naive illusion to expect the Japanese imperialist scoundrels to leave our country meekly. This fact is confirmed by the experience of the past twenty-odd years of the anti-Japanese national liberation movement.

From around the time when the Japanese imperialists occupied Korea to this day, our people have continued to develop all forms of anti-Japanese struggle. But each time, Japanese imperialism mobilized its armed forces and barbarously suppressed these protests. Patriots grieved over the ruin of the country and fervently appealed for independence, but in vain. Foolishly enough, the bigoted nationalists tried to attain independence by means of "petition," disregarding the people's will, and Japanese imperialism answered this with bloody suppression.

There were also the armed uprisings of the Righteous Volunteers' Army and of the Independence Army. But these struggles were foiled one by one by the counterrevolutionary forces of Japanese imperialism because they, too, failed to be guided by Marxist-Leninist strategy and tactics and were sporadic.

Experience clearly shows that our national desire for the liberation of the country can never be achieved without crushing the aggressive forces of Japanese imperialism.

In order to smash these forces and liberate the country, it is imperative that we launch an organized armed struggle based on the strategy and tactics of Marxism-Leninism.

It is self-evident that we cannot depend upon nor beg to anyone for our country's liberation.

We must achieve the liberation of our country and nation by our own efforts through an active armed struggle.

Comrades,

The present tense revolutionary situation, which has been brought about by the Japanese imperialist occupation of Manchuria, urgently demands that we take up arms.

Now is the best time to undertake an anti-Japanese war on a mass scale by waging an armed struggle. First, because the whole of Manchuria is in a state of anarchy, as the Kuomintang rule has disintegrated and the Japanese imperialist ruling machinery is not yet established; second, because the Chinese people have risen up en masse in their anti-Japanese struggle,

thus opening up a great era of stormy revolution. The broad
sectors of the Chinese people are launching an anti-Japanese
save-the-nation movement throughout their country against
the imperialist occupation of Manchuria. Among the armed
units engaged in that movement, the progressive sector, led by
the Chinese Communist Party, is small as yet. But we can
develop it into a more vigorous struggle when we fight in unity
with all the anti-Japanese armed units.

The time has come when everyone should come out, weapons
in hand, in the dedicated struggle to restore their country. Let
us fully mobilize all the patriotic forces opposed to Japanese
imperialism irrespective of wealth or poverty, partisanship
and religion, whether nobles or commoners. We must
guarantee that the whole nation participate in the anti-
Japanese armed conflict in full force, those who possess
weapons offering weapons, those who have money donating
money and those who have strength dedicating strength.

We must support the national-liberation struggle of the
Chinese people fighting Japanese imperialism, the common
enemy, and for a united front with them, thus enjoying mass
support from not only the Korean people but broad sectors of
the Chinese people in Manchuria.

In this way we shall successfully develop the anti-Japanese
armed struggle, enjoying the active support and encouragement of the two peoples.

From now on we must begin to organize armed units and expand and develop our own armed forces, taking weapons away
from the enemy to arm ourselves. If we use to our advantage
the nature and terrain of Korea's border and the wide expanse
of Manchuria, we can win a final victory, weakening and
smashing the enemy forces progressively even with small
forces.

This means that we must organize and wage armed struggle
with guerrilla warfare as our major tactic.

Guerrilla warfare is a method of armed struggle which will
enable us to deal heavy political and military blows to the
enemy while preserving our own forces, and to defeat the
numerically or technically superior enemy even with small
forces. Only when we organize and launch armed struggle using guerrilla warfare, while relying on the active support and
encouragement of the masses of the people and the favorable

conditions of nature and terrain, are we fully capable of defeating the piratical Japanese imperialist aggressive forces.

1. On Organizing the Anti-Japanese People's Guerrilla Army

Comrades,

If we want to organize and wage armed conflict, we must found our own revolutionary armed forces sufficiently to smash the enemy's counterrevolutionary armed forces. In order to win the fight against the Japanese imperialist robbers it is essential that we have revolutionary armed forces which are fully capable of preserving and expanding our own forces, continuously weakening and destroying the enemy's forces in the long-drawn-out struggle. We must organize such revolutionary armed forces as an Anti-Japanese People's Guerrilla Army.

The Anti-Japanese People's Guerrilla Army must be fundamentally different from the nationalist armed forces, the Righteous Volunteers' Army or the Independence Army which advocated Korea's independence. It must become a genuine people's army, made up of the fine sons and daughters of workers and peasants; it must become a genuine revolutionary army equipped with Marxist-Leninist ideas, and fighting for the country's liberation, the people's freedom and happiness. The guerrilla army must become a political army which not only fights for the people's interests but educates, organizes and mobilizes them in the revolutionary struggle; and it must become a working-class army which is true not only to the Korean revolution but to the world revolution.

We are not starting from scratch in organizing revolutionary armed forces now.

In the past we brought up the Communists of the new generation in the organizations of the Young Communist League of Korea and the Anti-Imperialist Youth League. Thus we provided the core from which we can organize the revolutionary armed forces.

Furthermore, last year we gained some experience and learned some lessons by organizing the Korean Revolutionary Army and by carrying on political and military action.

On the basis of these successes and experiences we must, first, push ahead actively with the work of organizing an Anti-Japanese People's Guerrilla Army with a core of fine young Communists seasoned and tested in the crucible of the hard-fought underground revolutionary struggle. By closely combining the organization of the guerrilla army with the masses' revolutionary advance, we shall admit progressive workers and peasants as well as patriotic youth, trained and tested in the practical revolutionary struggle, and strive to continue to reinforce the ranks.

In order to guarantee that the Anti-Japanese People's Guerrilla Army properly discharges its mission as a genuine people's army, a revolutionary army, we should intensify the struggle to consolidate its ranks politically and militarily while fully ensuring the Communists' leadership in it.

Obtaining arms is another important task to be carried out at the same time as the organization of the guerrilla army.

Men and weapons are the two elements of the armed forces. Arming is one of the basic factors in the success of the armed struggle.

How, then, should we equip the guerrilla army?

We have no source of weapons, nor anyone to give them to us. Therefore we have no alternative but to get them by our own efforts.

The only way is to capture them from the enemy and to arm ourselves. True, this is a dangerous and difficult task. But if we actively attack the enemy, displaying bravery and a self-sacrificing spirit with a high degree of revolutionary determination and if, at the same time, we surprise them, skillfully utilizing and intensifying their weaknesses, then we are fully capable of seizing their weapons and arming ourselves. "Weapons are our life and soul! Oppose armed force with armed force!"—this must become our fighting slogan at present.

Under this slogan we are required to display a revolutionary spirit of self-reliance. Thus, we shall take weapons from the Japanese imperialist aggressive army, the Chinese Northeastern Army which surrendered to Japanese imperialism, Japanese and Chinese northeast police, evil reactionary landlords and bureaucrats, and so obtain arms for the Anti-Japanese People's Guerrilla Army soon to be organized.

While seizing enemy weapons and arming ourselves, we

must not neglect to make spears, swords, clubs and the like, for without even these primitive weapons, it is impossible to capture enemy weapons.

We have to begin by organizing small guerrilla units in different areas and arming them, and then gradually expand them into revolutionary armed forces of large units.

When we organize the Anti-Japanese People's Guerrilla Army with the fine sons and daughters of workers and peasants, we young Communists at the core, and give repeated political and military blows to Japanese imperialism by waging swift and flexible guerrilla warfare everywhere, the scoundrels will be rendered powerless and will surely be driven out of Korea and Manchuria.

2. On Establishing a Guerrilla Base

To organize and develop the armed struggle through guerrilla warfare, a guerrilla base must be set up. A solid guerrilla base will make it possible to continually expand the armed ranks and wage protracted guerrilla warfare even when besieged by the formidable enemy. It will also make it possible for us to protect the revolutionary masses from the cold-blooded murder and barbarity of the enemy. In particular, as we fight the armed struggle with no state backing and no aid from outside, we badly need our own firm military base, a rear base. Furthermore, this base is absolutely necessary in order to progress with preparations for the founding of the Communist Party and the revolutionary movement as a whole, while waging armed struggle.

A guerrilla base can take different forms according to the prevailing subjective and objective situation, the environment and conditions of struggle or the degree of preparation of armed forces.

Our present conditions demand the establishment of guerrilla zones—bases in the form of liberated base areas. Only when guerrilla zones, completely beyond the enemy's ruling system, are set up, will it be possible to protect the young revolutionary armed forces and the revolutionary masses and make successful military and political preparations which will enable us to develop the anti-Japanese national-liberation struggle as a whole, concentrating on armed struggle.

To establish guerrilla zones we should, in the initial stage, struggle to revolutionize the broad rural areas.

The revolutionized rural area will, on the one hand, serve as the provisional center from which the guerrilla army can conduct its operations until the guerrilla zones are established, and, on the other hand, it will serve as a firm basis for establishing them. Moreover, in the course of revolutionizing the countryside, valuable experience will be gained for founding such zones.

From now on, therefore, we must force the revolutionization of rural areas so that the Anti-Japanese People's Guerrilla Army, the moment it is organized, can rely on these areas to carry on guerrilla warfare and constantly expand its own military and political force. We will have to set up firm guerrilla bases or liberated areas in the favorable zones of revolutionized rural areas, as the conditions develop in time.

The establishment of a guerrilla base or liberated area must presuppose the following three basic conditions: first, there must be an economic base and a mass foundation to enlist protection and support from the revolutionary masses; second, it must be geographically advantageous for the guerrilla army to defend itself even with small armed forces and the site should be such that it would be difficult for the enemy to attack the guerrilla army even though he has up-to-date weapons; third, it must have armed forces of its own which should at least be capable of self-defense.

The mountainous area along the Tuman-gang River, the northern border area of our country, satisfies these conditions fairly well.

This is the area where more than 80 per cent of the population is composed of poverty-stricken peasants who immigrated from Korea, unable to endure the oppression and exploitation of Japanese imperialism and where the socialist enlightenment developed from early days, and so the national and class awareness of the masses is comparatively high.

In particular, it is here that revolutionary organizations rapidly expanded and a great many followers were united around them after the Mingyuehkou Meeting of last spring, and that the mass movement swiftly developed through the recent autumn struggle.

In addition, this area is covered with steep mountains and valleys as well as dense forests and so forms a natural fortress difficult for the enemies to attack even with their modern weapons, but easy for the guerrilla army to defend.

Also, as it immediately adjoins the Hamgyong and the Rangnim Mountains of our country, this area is conveniently placed for an advance into our homeland for the future revolutionary movement.

For these reasons we must set up guerrilla zones—guerrilla bases in the form of liberated areas—right in the mountainous and the revolutionized rural areas along the Tuman-gang River.

In the guerrilla zone we must not only develop the guerrilla army politically and militarily; we must also expand and reinforce paramilitary organizations such as the Red Guards and the Children's Vanguard and arm everyone in defense of the guerrilla base. At the same time we must actively train qualified cadres for the Korean revolution and unite the broad masses into a single revolutionary force through the intensified work of all the revolutionary organizations, thus energetically organizing and mobilizing them for victory in the armed conflict. In this zone we must also establish a revolutionary government, enforce democratic reforms, build a school, a hospital, an armory, a publishing house, etc. and bring about a new revolutionary order.

Only by accomplishing these tasks can the guerrilla zone creditably perform its part as a base for the armed struggle, a base for the Korean revolution.

A guerrilla zone can only be consolidated when it is closely adjacent to the revolutionized rural areas. If not, it will fail to be in contact with the broad masses in the enemy-held area and will consequently be isolated, hemmed in by the enemy.

Therefore, we must concentrate on revolutionizing the rural areas even after the establishment of the guerrilla zone. To this end we must deploy the revolutionary organizations in the rural areas around it, and educate the masses in revolution. We must also make sure that our comrades hold the positions of village head and hsiang (township) head, working at the lowest levels of the enemy's ruling institutions. If the broad masses are revolutionized and our men take these posts, then such an area is under enemy control only in name, but in actuality, it is, like the guerrilla zone, under the jurisdiction of the revolutionary government. When these revolutionary areas expand they will clearly favor the establishment, consolidation and development of the guerrilla zones, and will also guarantee very advantageous conditions for guerrilla operation.

For the purpose of stifling by arms the Korean people's national-liberation struggle, which is daily intensifying all over the northern border area of our country, the Japanese imperialists are now harshly suppressing revolutionary organizations, even massacring the Korean people, especially revolutionaries.

Therefore, unless we rapidly expand the revolutionized rural areas and successfully establish the guerrilla zones, there is a risk of losing the revolutionary masses.

So, we have to push ahead energetically with the work of setting up the guerrilla bases in close combination with the organization of the Anti-Japanese People's Guerrilla Army.

3. On Laying the Mass Foundation for the Armed Struggle

In order to organize and proceed with armed struggle there must be a solid mass foundation on which the guerrilla army can depend in its operations.

Guerrilla warfare is, in essence, a people's warfare that presupposes the active participation of the masses. The energetic participation and support and encouragement of the people is the basic condition that guarantees the constant reinforcement of the guerrilla army and the success of guerrilla warfare. Only when there is a solid mass foundation and close ties of kinship with the masses can the guerrilla army break bottlenecks, overcome difficulties and win a final victory however protracted and arduous the struggle.

Therefore, we must firmly unite the broad sectors of the people under the banner of the anti-Japanese armed struggle by strengthening the organizational and political activity among them.

The present situation favors the promotion of the movement for the anti-Japanese national united front embracing all sectors of our people.

With the Japanese imperialist invasion of Manchuria, the anti-Japanese sentiments of Korean people in all social strata have risen higher than ever before and the anti-Japanese struggle of the masses is rapidly gaining momentum.

In the homeland violent protest by workers, peasants, youth and students is increasing, and the anti-Japanese movement of conscientious nationalists and patriotic religious men is developing rapidly. In particular, the revolutionary spirit of the Korean peasants in east Manchuria is higher than ever before.

When we give full play to this mounting revolutionary spirit and the anti-Japanese sentiments of the masses and organize and mobilize them properly, we can form the anti-Japanese national united front on a nationwide scale and lay a solid mass foundation for the armed struggle.

In the past we infiltrated workers, peasants and all other sectors of the Korean people in central and east Manchuria, formed the mass organizations such as the Labor Union, the Peasants' Association and the Anti-Imperialist League, and carried on active mass political work, uniting the broad masses under them. In the course of this, mass foundation for the armed struggle was gradually built up, and we accumulated rich experiences in mass political work.

In particular, we brought about radical change in the mass political work in accordance with the correct organizational line laid down at the Mingyuehkou Meeting last Spring. As a result, we revolutionized many rural districts all over the northern border area of our country and east Manchuria and, basing ourselves on this success, led the recent autumn struggle to victory.

On the basis of the successes and experiences in mass political work we must, in future, go among the broad sectors of anti-Japanese masses—workers, peasants, youth and students, intellectuals, petty bourgeoisie, national capitalists, religious men—and strengthen the work of educating, awakening and uniting them in the revolutionary organizations. In this way we shall lay a solid mass foundation for the anti-Japanese armed struggle.

In order to lay a firm mass foundation for the armed struggle it is of great importance to get the majority of the people from all walks of life to join the Anti-Imperialist Youth League, the

Peasants' Association, the Revolutionary Mutual Aid Society and various other revolutionary organizations, and strengthen their revolutionary education. To do this educational work well, we must first arm ourselves firmly with the revolutionary ideas of the working class and adopt the revolutionary work attitude of relying on the masses. If we fail to do so we cannot enjoy the trust of the majority of working people nor develop the mass movement. First of all, we must go among the basic masses of revolution—workers and peasants—and carry on active propaganda by speech and pamphlets to suit the given situation and people. In due course we must bring the progressive elements among them class awareness and train them to be revolutionaries. And we must ensure that they revolutionize their families and villages and further wide rural areas.

While developing the revolutionary leading core elements in each district and continuously raising their leadership role, we must form basic party organizations on an experimental basis, reinforce the YCL organizations and expand and strengthen numerous mass organizations. In the rural areas, in particular, it is necessary to strengthen the Peasants' Association, the Revolutionary Mutual Aid Society and the Anti-Imperialist League, actively receive the peasant masses into the organizations and give them organizational training.

To lay the firm mass foundation for the armed struggle we must also continue forming, training and expanding the revolutionary forces in revolutionary practice in a militant way.

While continuously encouraging the revolutionary advance of the masses we must, in the course of this, expand the revolutionary organizations and develop and train the revolutionary forces so as to lay a more solid mass foundation for the anti-Japanese armed struggle.

4. On Forming the Anti-Japanese United Front of the Korean and Chinese Peoples

A successful armed struggle against Japanese imperialism also requires the formation of the broad anti-Japanese united front of the Korean and Chinese peoples.

The Japanese imperialists' occupation of Manchuria has

stirred up the Chinese people's indignation. The mass of the Chinese people started with the anti-Japanese save-the-nation movement and some units of the Chinese Northeastern Army have risen in mutiny under the anti-Japanese banner.

It is a matter of urgency which brooks no delay to form the anti-Japanese united front of the Korean and Chinese peoples in the struggle against the common enemy, the Japanese imperialists.

Only when we form the united front with the anti-Japanese forces of the majority of the Chinese people will it be possible to combine the efforts of the Korean and Chinese peoples to the utmost and deal greater political and military blows against the Japanese imperialist aggressors.

Today, the most urgent need in organizing the anti-Japanese united front of the Korean and Chinese peoples, is to form a united front with the soldiers of the Chinese Northeastern Army who rose up holding the anti-Japanese save-the-nation banner against the Japanese imperialist invasion of Manchuria.

Overawed by the Japanese imperialist aggression in Manchuria, the Chinese northeast warlords wavered, did not resist and have ultimately escaped to China proper or surrendered to the Japanese imperialist aggressors. Chief of the northeast warlords, Chang Hsueh-liang, fled to Chinchou the moment the Japanese made inroads and then, in October, left Manchuria and went through Shanhaikuan over to China proper. Many other warlords in the military areas under the control of the Chinese Northeastern Army knelt down before the Japanese imperialist aggressors without even fighting and became their puppets, so betraying their homeland.

But many soldiers and some officers of national conscience in the Chinese Northeastern Army have mutinied against their warlords' attempt to surrender and have gone into the mountains.

In east Manchuria alone there is a growing tendency to refuse to surrender to Japanese imperialism among the units of the Chinese Northeastern Army stationed in Holung and Yenchi; thousands of soldiers, in groups or individually, have already risen up against Japanese imperialism in Wangching, Antu and other districts.

We, therefore, should form a united front with the Chinese nationalist anti-Japanese units that separated from the

Chinese Northeastern Army after mutinies under the banner of anti-Japanese national salvation. Then the anti-Japanese armed forces will rapidly grow in scope and strength and deal greater political and military blows to the Japanese imperialist aggressive forces.

Although they have rallied under the anti-Japanese banner, some units of the Chinese Anti-Japanese National-Salvation Army and the peasants' armed units now in mutiny are duped by the Japanese imperialists' false propaganda and by attempts to set the nations against each other; and they take a hostile attitude toward the Korean people, Communists in particular, saying that they are the "puppets of Japanese imperialism," and that they are going to "communize Manchuria."

Unless we make them realize their mistake and lead them in the right direction, it will be very difficult to unite the anti-Japanese forces and it will be impossible to concentrate our efforts on the struggle against Japanese imperialism.

Therefore, in order to expose the Japanese imperialists' deceptive propaganda against the Korean Communists and their trick of making the nations oppose each other, and to cement the militant unity of the Korean and Chinese peoples, we must do our utmost to form the united front with the Chinese nationalist anti-Japanese units.

To form this united front, we must, first of all, make bold approaches to the Chinese anti-Japanese units and strengthen the work among their soldiers.

Though the Chinese anti-Japanese units, a nationalist army, are not steadfast because of the vacillation and class limitations of the upper crust, they are big anti-Japanese forces. We must overcome their vacillation and dual characters through struggle, while actively encouraging their anti-Japanese element. At the same time, we must bring the rank and file, the basic masses in the anti-Japanese units, to the national and class awareness and thus actively lead them in the anti-Japanese struggle.

In forming the united front with the Chinese nationalist anti-Japanese units, the basic principle to which to adhere must be to form a united front among the rank and file and, firmly relying on it, the united front at the top level. The top level of the anti-Japanese units consists of warlords of landlord and capitalist origin, and so they constantly waver in the anti-

Japanese struggle, whereas the absolute majority of the rank and file are the basic masses of worker and peasant origin who can actively participate in that struggle. Therefore, we must first direct our serious attention to going boldly among the masses of anti-Japanese soldiers and forming the united front with them. Only when we base ourselves on the united front among the rank and file to form the united front at the top level can we easily overcome the latter's vacillation and irresolution and soundly develop the movement for an anti-Japanese united front as a whole.

However, we should not neglect to have contacts at the top level. An army is a group of strong esprit de corps, commanded by the superiors. So, if we make bold contacts with the high-ranking officers of the anti-Japanese units and win them over first, it will be a great help in forming the anti-Japanese united front.

As an organizational step for actively winning over the Chinese nationalist anti-Japanese units we must organize detached columns in Wangching and Antu where they gather. The detached columns must strive to win over the anti-Japanese units to expand our armed forces, and at the same time, increase organizational and political activity so that they may take an active part in the anti-Japanese struggle.

As mentioned above, we must strive to achieve the formation of the united front with the Chinese anti-Japanese units, simultaneously with organizing the Anti-Japanese People's Guerrilla Army in each county. By doing so, we shall forge ahead with the armed struggle against Japanese imperialism, the common enemy of the Korean and Chinese peoples.

5. On Strengthening the Work of the Party Organizations and Young Communist League

Comrades,
The successful implementation of our important tasks makes it imperative to establish basic party organizations in all areas and strengthen the work of the YCL organizations.

We achieved no small successes in improving and strengthening the leadership of the work of the YCL and other mass organizations in accordance with the decisions of the Mingyuehkou Meeting held last May.

On the basis of these successes we must continue to pay careful attention to forming party organizations and strengthening the work of the YCL.

Only when the vanguard role of party organization is enhanced and the work of the YCL further strengthened, can we successfully carry out all the tasks that will arise in organizing and waging the armed struggle and make sound organizational and ideological preparations for founding a unified Marxist-Leninist party.

To establish the leadership elite of the guerrilla army and the organizational backbone of the Korean Communist Party to be founded in the future we must strengthen the life of Party organizations.

The organizational backbone of the revolution can only be formed through hard organizational training in the practical struggle. Therefore, we must accept into the party at grassroots level those fine workers and peasants and progressive intellectuals who have been tempered in the mass political struggle, and give them even harder party training. In this way we shall bring them up to be the communist elite who establish the revolutionary world outlook, know no vacillation in any adversity and can be equal to any revolutionary task.

At present it is a very important task to strengthen the work of the YCL together with that of party organizations.

Since party organizations are still weak it is imperative to do good YCL work and keep on expanding its ranks. Only then can we form a group of pure new young Communists who are not poisoned by factionalism and the filths of various kinds of opportunism and establish the organizational backbone of Party building more soundly. Not only that, but only when we reinforce these ranks can we found the Anti-Japanese People's Guerrilla Army with fine young Communists at the core and briskly organize and launch a mass movement for supporting and helping the guerrilla army.

To enlarge the YCL ranks we need a good knowledge of the characteristics of young workers and peasants and all other sectors of youth and to strengthen the organizational and political work to suit them.

Some YCL functionaries, who have little knowledge of the

specific features of youth from all walks of life, do poor work with the young workers and peasants and other youths of basic class origin, saying that they cannot play a vanguard role because of their poor education and that they cannot keep secrets; they also keep them away instead of educating them, and fail to actively enlist them in the YCL ranks. As a result, the staunch young workers and peasants with strong class hatred and high fighting spirit stand outside the ranks for one reason or another.

If we are careless about influencing the working youth and peasant youth and do not actively accept them into the YCL ranks, we will be unable to create young Communists of basic class origin.

The YCL must attach the highest importance to work among the young workers and peasants.

Being young proletarians the working youth have a stronger revolutionary spirit, esprit de corps and sense of unity than their counterparts of any other class. Moreover, owing to their wretched plight—the absence of political rights and unbearable hunger and poverty, they have a vital interest in the revolution and naturally take the lead in the revolutionary struggle to overthrow the old society.

For this reason, even if they lack knowledge they can all be brought up as staunch young Communists when they are educated in revolution and recruited into the YCL ranks.

Peasant youth, who account for the majority of our youth, are suffering from the most outrageous oppression and harsh feudal exploitation under the torture of the Japanese imperialists and landlords.

Therefore, even though they are still backward politically and do not have enough organizational training, when they are brought to class awakening and admitted to the YCL and other revolutionary organizations where they receive a good political education, they will go hand in hand with the working youth and creditably discharge their duties as the main force of the revolution.

It is of importance in YCL work to rally progressive students in the YCL organizations by working effectively amongst them.

They not only have a strong sense of justice and are sensitive to the progressive ideas and the trends of the time; they also have a very strong idea of social reform and anti-feudalism which will do away with the shackles of the old society and build a new one.

In particular, since the students of our country are subjected to the Japanese imperialists' suppression and discrimination against the Korean nation, their anti-Japanese sentiments are strong and their national awareness high. So, if they are given a good education and organizational training they will successfully play the role of pioneer by disseminating progressive socialist ideas, and educating and awakening the majority of workers and peasants, thus guiding them to the revolutionary movement.

In reinforcing the YCL ranks it is important to form many leadership core elements among the most progressive of the young workers and peasants in each locality. As the enemy's suppression becomes intensified only these elements in different areas can educate the majority of young people well, expand and develop the YCL organizations to suit the demand of the development of revolution and lead them to play the vanguard role creditably.

The YCL members must be pioneers in educating the masses and organizing and mobilizing them.

Revolutionary work always begins with mass political work, and to follow the political method of work is a revolutionary's basic duty. The YCL cadres must acquire the revolutionary method of work—they put confidence in the masses' strength and rely thoroughly on them and activate them in carrying on the revolutionary struggle.

Comrades,

Whether or not we can realize the historical cause of the country's restoration by organizing and waging the armed struggle and wiping out Japanese imperialism depends entirely upon how we discharge our assigned revolutionary tasks.

We are the revolutionaries who are determined to devote our very lives to the country's restoration and to the victory of the cause of socialism and communism.

Whatever ordeals and difficulties stand in our way, we will fulfill the duty of the Communists as revolutionaries by finally accomplishing our revolutionary tasks.

Let us all pool our strength and come out in the armed struggle to destroy Japanese imperialism.

Victory will surely be ours and the country's liberation achieved without fail.

THE TEN-POINT PROGRAM OF THE ASSOCIATION FOR THE RESTORATION OF THE FATHERLAND

May 5, 1936

1. To mobilize the entire Korean nation and realize a broad-based anti-Japanese united front in order to overthrow the piratical Japanese imperialist rule and establish a genuine people's government in Korea;

2. To defeat Japan and overthrow its puppet state "Manchukuo" by the Koreans resident in Manchuria through a close alliance between the Korean and Chinese people, and to effect full autonomy for the Korean people residing in Chinese territory;

3. To disarm the Japanese armed forces, gendarmes, police and their agents and organize a revolutionary army truly fighting for the independence of Korea;

4. To confiscate all enterprises, railways, banks, shipping, farms and irrigation systems owned by Japan and Japanese and all property and estates owned by pro-Japanese traitors, to raise funds for the independence movement, and to use part of these funds for the relief of the poor;

5. To cancel all loans made to people by Japan and its agents and abolish all taxes and monopoly systems; to improve the living conditions of the masses and promote the smooth development of national industries, agriculture and commerce;

6. To win the freedom of the press, publications, assembly and association, oppose terrorist rule and the fostering of feudal ideas by the Japanese imperialists, and to release all political prisoners;

7. To abolish the caste system which divides the *ryangban* (nobles) and the common people, and other inequalities; to ensure equality based on humanity irrespective of sex, nationality or religion; to improve the social position of women and respect their personalities;

8. To abolish slave labor and slavish education; to oppose forced military service and military training of young people; to educate people in our national language, and to enforce free compulsory education;

9. To enforce an eight-hour day, improve working conditions and raise wages; to formulate labor laws; to enforce state insurance laws for the workers, and to extend state relief to the unemployed;

10. To form a close alliance with nations and states which treat the Koreans as equals and to maintain comradely relations of friendship with states and nations which express goodwill and maintain neutrality towards our national-liberation movement.

THE TASKS OF
KOREAN COMMUNISTS

Treatise Published in *Sogwang*, Organ of the Korean People's Revolutionary Army, *November 10, 1937*

Twenty-seven years have elapsed since the Japanese imperialists occupied Korea.

During this period they have made our country a source of raw materials and labor, a market for their commodities and a military base for aggression against the continent.

Owing to their ferocious colonial policy, the Korean people have been deprived of their national rights and freedom and are suffering great sorrow as a ruined people. Our people are not only subjected to double and treble oppression and exploitation by the Japanese imperialists and their lackeys in a manner reminiscent of medieval times, but are threatened with the danger of being deprived of their beautiful written and spoken language.

The Sino-Japanese War unleashed by the Japanese imperialists is driving our people into an even more terrible plight. With an eye to ensuring safety in the rear, the Japanese imperialists have greatly expanded their fascist, colonial repressive machinery—troops, police, prisons, gallows and all—and concocted a new set of Draconian laws. Thus, they have turned our beautiful land of 3,000 *ri* into a living hell on earth. They are cracking down on the revolutionary forces with fury, while suppressing and slaughtering innocent people as never before. Since last summer those hangmen have destroyed the lower echelons of the Association for the Restoration of the Fatherland and atrociously arrested and imprisoned a large number of underground political workers and members of the ARF in the northern border area of our country. In all parts of Korea they have seized and imprisoned countless innocent people and are wantonly slaughtering them. They have openly forced conscription and grain delivery in order to meet the ever-increasing demand for manpower and materials in their aggressive war against the continent. Thus, our precious young and middle-aged people are being forcibly rounded up to become bullet-shields for the Japanese imperialists and our country's abundant natural wealth is being ruthlessly plundered.

Our people, known for their history of 5,000 years and brilliant culture, are now standing at the crossroads of life and death, and the dark clouds of national calamity are hanging over our land.

In these grim days of national suffering, all kinds of renegades from the revolution—national reformists, Right and "Left" opportunists and sectarian-flunkeys—have cast off their masks and are openly colluding with the Japanese imperialist aggressors.

Time has proved that we, the Communists, are the only pivotal force of the revolution capable of guiding the destiny of the country and the people to the end, and it has set before us a heavier and more difficult task.

Severe trials and difficulties stand in the way of the Korean revolution, but the situation continues to develop in favor of the revolution.

The frantic war policy and the savage fascist suppression of the Japanese imperialists are not a sign of their might but reflect the last-minute desperation of those who are on the brink of ruin. The Sino-Japanese War ignited by Japanese imperialism is intensifying the contradictions between the imperialist powers and weakening the imperialist camp as a whole. The more the Japanese imperialists expand the war, the deeper they will fall into a bottomless pit. In the end, the flames of war will engulf those who ignited them.

Today the national and class contradictions between the Japanese imperialists and the Korean people are becoming extremely acute. Workers, peasants, youth, students, intellectuals, national capitalists, traders, men of religion and, indeed, the entire Korean people, cursing Japanese imperialism as their sworn enemy, are waiting impatiently for the day when the enemy is defeated and are waging anti-Japanese struggles in different parts of the country.

From ancient times the Korean people have been known as a valiant and resourceful people who would rather die fighting than surrender. Following the occupation of Korea by Japanese imperialism, there took place in our country various forms of stout anti-Japanese struggles such as the Righteous Volunteers' Army Movement, the Independence Army Movement, riots by workers and peasants and the anti-Japanese movement of youth and students.

Now, in the 1930's, the anti-Japanese armed struggle, organized and led by us Communists, is dealing Japanese imperialism a telling blow and has raised the anti-Japanese national liberation struggle to a new stage. The path traversed by our people since the Japanese imperialist occupation is the path of national salvation, one attended by bloody struggles.

We Korean Communists must take advantage of all favorable internal and external circumstances and take up the brilliant patriotic traditions of our people, and we must properly organize and mobilize the masses in the struggle to fulfill the solemn task of defeating Japanese imperialism and regaining our lost country.

1. The Nature of the Korean Revolution at the Present Stage

To define the nature of the revolution correctly is of very great significance for organizing and leading the revolutionary struggle properly and hastening the victory of the revolution. Only by correctly defining the nature of the revolution is it possible to map out scientific strategy and tactics and, on this basis, confidently organize and mobilize the masses of the people for the revolutionary struggle.

Formerly, some people asserted that the Korean revolution at the present stage is a "socialist revolution," and others that it is a "bourgeois revolution." Both are wrong.

The nature of a revolution is decided by the basic tasks of the revolution and by the socio-class relations at each stage. The view that the revolution in our country is a "socialist revolution," and the view that it is a "bourgeois revolution" are Right and "Left" deviations resulting from an incorrect understanding of the basic tasks of the Korean revolution and the actual socio-class relations at the present stage in our country. These views are hostile to the revolution and aim to hinder the close unity of the revolutionary forces and divert spearhead of struggle.

Our country is a semi-feudal, colonial society where because of Japanese imperialist colonial rule, capitalist development is extremely retarded and feudal relations of production are predominant.

Under these circumstances, the basic tasks of the Korean revolution at the present stage are to carry out the task of the anti-imperialist national-liberation revolution to overthrow Japanese imperialist colonial rule and regain our lost country and, at the same time, to fulfill the task of the anti-feudal, democratic revolution to eliminate feudal relations and pave the way for the country's development on democratic lines. These two tasks are closely interrelated. This is seen in the fact that the Japanese imperialist aggressors—the colonial rulers on the one hand, and the landlords and the former feudal bureaucrats—the champions of feudal relations on the other— are in collusion with each other.

Japanese imperialism maintains its colonial system of rule in Korea with the help of its agents, the comprador capitalists and the feudal landlords, and the landlords retain the feudal relations of exploitation under its patronage. Therefore, the struggle against Japanese imperialism and the struggle against feudalism must be waged as an integral whole.

Hence, our revolution at the present stage is an anti-imperialist, anti-feudal, democratic revolution.

What, then, are the concrete targets of our revolution at the present stage?

In the Korean revolution the main target is the aggressive forces of Japanese imperialism. Colonial rule by Japanese imperialism is at the very root of all the misery the Korean people are suffering and the buttress of all social fetters in this country. The Japanese imperialists have done everything possible to turn our country into a permanent colony and enslave our people for all time. They are wantonly obliterating everything unique to the Korean nation and are fiercely checking the revolutionary advance of the Korean working class and the rest of the working masses. They have no scruples about introducing into Korea all the decadence and corruption which they think helpful to their colonial rule.

The overthrow of Japanese imperialist colonial rule and the restoration of the country's independence are prerequisites for the national and class liberation of our people and for social progress in our country. Our people's struggle against Japanese imperialism is aimed at regaining their lost country and restoring their national rights in all spheres of politics, the economy and culture and, at the same time, at removing all the obstacles which stand in the way of national and social progress so as to pave the way for national prosperity.

So, the first and foremost revolutionary task confronting Korean Communists and the revolutionary people is to organize and mobilize all the revolutionary forces for the anti-Japanese national-liberation struggle.

Other targets of the Korean revolution are pro-Japanese landlords, comprador capitalists, traitors to the nation and the pro-Japanese bureaucrats who put themselves at the beck and call of the Japanese imperialists and serve them as faithful pawns.

They all actively help the colonial rule of Japanese imperialism in Korea and, in tandem with it, oppress and exploit the people. They most viciously hamper the people in their anti-Japanese struggle. In the countryside they use feudal methods based on the feudal ownership of land, to oppress and exploit the peasants savagely with the backing of Japanese imperialism, and in towns they cruelly exploit the workers in a capitalist as well as a feudal way. They also play the role of transmitters of obsolete feudal customs and slavish mentality and of guides helping Japanese imperialism to stretch out its claws of colonial rule deep into all fields.

Consequently, if they are left untouched, the anti-Japanese national-liberation struggle can never be successful nor can the way be paved for the democratic development of the country. Therefore, we must fight against Japanese imperialism and, at the same time, wage a resolute struggle against the pro-Japanese landlords, comprador capitalists, traitors to the nation and pro-Japanese bureaucrats.

To be successful in the revolutionary struggle we must have a correct understanding not only of the nature and targets of the revolution but also of its motive force. In any revolution an important guarantee of victory is the involvement of people of all classes and strata who are interested in the revolution.

The motive force of the Korean revolution at the present stage comprises the broad anti-imperialist, democratic forces such as the workers, peasants, youth, students, intellectuals and petty bourgeois. National capitalists and religious people with a conscience can also join in the anti-imperialist struggle.

The working class is the leading class in the anti-imperialist, anti-feudal, democratic revolution, not to mention the future socialist revolution and the period of building socialism and communism. This is because it is the working class alone that champions the fundamental interests of the working masses, that is the most advanced class with the strongest revolutionary spirit and sense of organization and that is able to organize and lead all working masses to victory in the revolution.

Our working class has a more vital interest in the anti-imperialist national-liberation revolution than any other class.

Under Japanese imperialist colonial rule, the Korean working class is in abject misery. The Japanese imperialists have on the one hand retarded the growth of our national economy to the extreme and, on the other, have almost all industries in their grip. They are exploiting the Korean workers with unheard-of cruelty. In pursuit of their aim of grinding down our workers more ruthlessly, they are using every possible method to intensify labor to the maximum and extending the working day to as much as 12-18 hours. Even with such terrible conditions, not all workers are provided with jobs. The Japanese imperialists are pursuing the most wicked colonial predatory policy—employing cheap juvenile and female labor and continually dismissing adult workers—to secure the maximum colonial super-profits. Thus, many workers are thrown out of work to form an industrial reserve army, deprived even of the elementary right to live.

The Japanese imperialists pay the Korean workers less than half the wages of the Japanese workers for the same work. Worse still, they take back the greater part of this in the name of "defense contribution," "government bonds," "fines" and so on. Thus Korean workers have been reduced to such a state that they can hardly eke out a living in spite of their indescribable hard toil.

The living conditions of our workers have worsened since the beginning of the Sino-Japanese War. The Japanese imperialists forcibly drag our workers to military construction sites for slave labor and do not pay them even starvation wages. Finally, they kill them in cold blood under the pretext of protecting "secrets."

This intolerably unfair and wretched situation our workers find themselves in has not only roused their revolutionary spirit, but also made them move forward toward organizing and tempering themselves as a class in actual struggles and stand in the forefront of the anti-Japanese national-liberation struggle.

An analysis of this struggle which has gone on for more than 20 years in our country reveals that it is only the working class that can lead the anti-imperialist, anti-feudal, democratic revolution.

The bourgeois and petty-bourgeois intellectuals in our country have always vacillated in face of the difficulties which have cropped up in the course of the anti-Japanese national-liberation struggle because of the weakness inherent in their class position, and they have attempted to attain the independence of Korea not in a revolutionary way but in an easy way. The "Incentive Production Association," the "Yonjong-hoe Association" and the "Singan-hoe Assocaiation" and so on which they created allegedly for Korean independence were all national reformist groupings which wanted reform and compromise instead of revolution and struggle.

Therefore, if we are to complete the anti-imperialist, anti-feudal, democratic revolution, it is of primary importance to ensure the leading role of the working class, the class that is vitally interested in this revolution and struggling dauntlessly in defiance of difficulties.

Together with the working class, the peasantry also occupies an important place in the Korean revolution. The peasantry is a dependable ally of the working class and, like the working class, constitutes a main force of the revolution.

In countries like ours, where the peasantry accounts for the overwhelming majority of the population, special importance should be attached to their postition in the revolution. Peasants comprise more than 80 per cent of our population. In such circumstances, winning them over is a key to the success of the revolution. If we neglect to involve the peasants in the revolution in such a country as ours, the end result will be that the working class will be isolated, its leading role weakened and, furthermore, the overwhelming majority of the population will be left to the influence of the enemy.

The numerical preponderence of our peasantry is one reason why they hold an important place in the revolution. Another reason is that they also have a vital interest in the anti-imperialist, anti-feudal, democratic revolution.

The colonial rule of Japanese imperialism has condemned our peasants to awful poverty and starvation. In the country-side the Japanese imperialists exploit the peasants, keeping feudal landownership intact and using the landlords as their agents. At the same time, they expropriate their fertile land in the name of "land surveys," the organization of the "Oriental Development Company," and so on and so forth.

In 1914, shortly after the Japanese imperialist occupation of Korea, more than 60 per cent of Korean peasants tilled their own land, with tenant farmers and hired hands accounting for only 35 per cent. But today, the proportion of tenant farmers and hired hands has jumped to over 70 per cent, while that of peasants tilling their own land has fallen below 18 per cent. Thus the overwhelming majority of the Korean peasants have been reduced to the status of the rural proletariat. Driven from their hereditary farmlands, innumerable peasants are tramping alien countries begging for food or are eking out a mere existence subjected to inhuman treatment under the lash of the Japanese gangsters, the landlords and the capitalists. As for those peasants who are still lucky enough to work on their own land, most of them are living on the bark of trees or on grass roots, being unable to secure the food required for existence because of the imposition of heavy taxation, and they live in constant anxiety lest they be evicted.

To meet their war demands, the Japanese imperialists are press-ganging rural young people and middle-aged men indiscriminately for military duties or as labor for the construction of military installations. Every year they plunder millions of *sok* of rice, which they ship to Japan. This military burden imposed on the peasants has made their plight absolutely intolerable.

Thus our countryside has been turned into a shocking famine area, the like of which has scarcely been seen anywhere in the world at any time in history.

This dire distress has triggered off the bitter wrath of our peasants against the Japanese imperialists and the feudal landlords, and they have stepped out with determination onto the road of anti-imperialist, anti-feudal struggle, realizing that revolution is the only thing that will make life possible for them.

Disregarding this situation, the "Left" opportunists and sectarian-flunkeys have underestimated the revolutionary spirit of the Korean peasantry, alleging that the peasants are "two-faced" and that "the peasantry can hardly make the revolution to the end because they are a small-propertied class and so vacillate easily."

This conflicts with the realities and is in total opposition to the stand that must be taken to strengthen the revolutionary forces.

Korean Communists should repudiate all the prejudices against and wrong attitudes toward our peasants and strive to win them over, so that the main forces of the revolution will be built up on a solid basis.

Because of its anti-imperialist, anti-feudal, democratic nature, our revolution requires that not only workers and peasants, but also youth, students, intellectuals, members of the small-propertied classes, national capitalists and honest religious believers be enlisted on the side of the revolution. The fascist colonial rule of the Japanese imperialists inevitably fills the youth, students, intellectuals, members of the small-propertied classes, national capitalists and honest religious believers with hatred against Japanese imperialism and leads them to fling themselves into the fight for the independence of the country and the liberation of the people.

The youth, students and intellectuals generally have a strong sense of justice and are responsive to progressive ideas and the trend of the times because they are searching for science and truth. Therefore, the progressive elements among them are the first to learn Marxism-Leninism, awaken and enlighten the workers and peasants and thus play the role of pioneer leading them into the revolutionary movement.

Moreover, our youth, students and intellectuals are not only directly subjected to national oppression and discrimination by Japanese imperialism but suffer the hard fate common to the whole nation caused by Japanese imperialist colonial rule, and they are more keenly aware than anyone else of the irrationality of our present-day society.

This is why they have developed a national consciousness faster than others and have stronger anti-imperialist sentiments. They are participating actively in the national- liberation revolution, impelled by the progressive spirit to fight for justice and inspired by the anti-imperialist, anti-feudal, democratic revolution to drive out the foreign imperialist aggressor forces and make our backward country as prosperous as others.

Many of them have been struggling resolutely against the Japanese imperialists since the first days of their occupation of Korea and have made great contributions in rousing workers and peasants and other broad masses who are against Japanese imperialism to revolutionary struggle. In the period of preparing the anti-Japanese armed struggle, too, revolutionary youth, students and intellectuals played a great role in cementing the revolutionary ranks organizationally and ideologically and in laying the mass base of the struggle. Joining the ranks of the anti-Japanese guerrillas and the underground revolutionary organizations, they are now fighting unyieldingly.

All this testifies to the fact that they are playing an important role in the revolutionary struggle.

But they cannot themselves become a political force or perform a decisive role in the revolutionary struggle because of their weakness, vacillation and "do-it-only-halfway" nature. Only under the leadership of the Communists and the working class can they play a revolutionary role in the anti-imperialist, anti-feudal, democratic revolution.

As for the national capitalists, their question should also be analytically viewed. National capitalists in colonial and semi-colonial countries have certain characteristics different from the bourgeoisie of the capitalist countries.

From the class point of view, the national capitalists come under the category of the exploiting class but their economic activities are repressed by foreign imperialists and their comprador capitalist allies and they are always exposed to the threat of bankruptcy. Therefore, they have an anti- imperialist spirit, though not steadfast, and a desire for national independence.

In particular, national capitalists in our country are slipping rapidly towards bankruptcy as a result of the fascist colonial terrorist rule of the Japanese imperialists and the subsequent large-scale infiltration of Japanese monopoly capital. The proportion of total industrial output value held by Korean capital in 1928 represented over 26 per cent. But the figure today is less than 10 per cent. Even this barely maintains its existence by sticking to such extrememly secondary branches as rice cleaning, cotton-willowing and so on.

Since they are destined to ruin under Japanese imperialist colonial rule they have an interest in the anti-Japanese national-liberation revolution and are impelled to join it.

The comprador capitalists are more afraid of the people's anti-imperialist revolutionary struggle than of imperialist aggression. The national capitalists, however, resist imperialist aggression and support the people's anti-imperialist revolutionary struggle. To define the national capitalists as reactionaries because of the acts of treachery to the country and the people perpetrated by the handful of comprador capitalists would mean weakening the anti-imperialist national-liberation revolutionary forces. Drawing them into the anti-imperialist national-liberation struggle is of great importance for isolating the enemy to the maximum and strengthening the revolutionary forces.

As you see, at the present stage of the Korean revolution its motive force consists of the anti-Japanese forces from broad sections of society. We should assume a principled and magnanimous attitude toward all classes and strata which can join the revolution. We should accept, rally and organize them and thus mobilize all the anti-Japanese forces to the anti-imperialist national-liberation struggle.

What then are the tasks of the anti-imperialist, anti-feudal, democratic revolution in our country?

Needless to say, the primary and fundamental task is to overthrow the Japanese imperialist aggressors and all the reactionary forces—pro-Japanese landlords, comprador capitalists and so on—who ally themselves with the aggressors. But when this task has been fulfilled it does not mean that the anti-imperialist, anti-feudal, democratic revolution will have been completed. It should be followed up by abolishing the social and economic relations on which the Japanese imperialists and their accomplices—the reactionary forces—rely in all branches of politics, the economy and culture and by firmly establishing a new, progressive democratic system so as to make sure that the old system will never be revived.

Our foremost task following the defeat of the Japanese imperialist aggressors is to set up a democratic government.

The question of power is the fundamental question of the revolution. The seizure of power is indispensable for our people's complete national and class liberation and for the building of a prosperous, sovereign, independent state in our country. Through their bitter experience as slaves in a ruined nation, the Korean people have come to the keen realization of what fate a people will suffer as long as they are without state power of their own. Indeed, there is no more important task facing us than that of establishing a state power genuinely our own.

In solving the question of power it is very important to decide the form it should take to fit in with the nature and tasks of the revolution and the class relationships in a given period.

Then what form of democratic power should we set up?

There can be two forms of democratic power. One belongs to the category of bourgeois power, i.e., democratic power led by the propertied classes, and the other comes under the category of proletarian power, i.e., democratic power led by the working class.

The former champions the interests of an extremely limited section of the population, comprising the bourgeoisie and the petty bourgeoisie. It always vacillates and is not steadfast, and therefore, cannot lead the people to socialism and communism, the ultimate goal of the workers and poor peasants.

In contrast, democratic power led by the working class defends the fundamental interests of the workers and peasants, carries out the tasks of the anti-imperialist, anti-feudal, democratic revolution in a thoroughgoing way and can lead the masses to socialism and communism.

Therefore, the power we will establish after the overthrow of Japanese imperialism is popular democratic power, coming under the category of proletarian power, i.e., democratic power led by the working class.

After the establishment of this power we must firmly rely on it in introducing agrarian reform and other democratic reforms. The most important thing here is to wipe out the remnant forces of Japanese imperialism root and branch.

Even after the destruction of the colonial ruling machine of Japanese imperialism, this is essential in all branches of politics, the economy and culture for ensuring the successful fulfillment of the tasks of the anti-imperialist national-liberation revolution, the complete political independence of the country and its development on democratic lines after the elimination of all feudal forces.

To do away with the remnant forces of Japanese imperialism, we should first eliminate all the reactionary landlords, pro-Japanese elements and traitors to the nation who constitute the mainstay of the colonial rule of Japanese imperialism and actively defend its ruling machine, and leave no room for them to maneuver.

Furthermore, all the laws and rules concocted by the Japanese imperialists must be declared invalid and new ones safeguarding the interests of the broad masses formulated to establish a new order in state building. Survivals of ideology and way of life introduced by Japanese imperialism should be abolished, public education developed in our own speech and letters and our own national culture restored.

Unless we destroy the economic base of the Japanese imperialists and comprador capitalists, we cannot pave the way for the independent development of the economy, nor can we consolidate the political independence of the country. We must nationalize the major industries—the mines, factories, railways, transport, banks, communications, home and foreign trade—

held by the Japanese state and by Japanese and comprador capitalists and make them the property of the whole people. In this way, we will see to it that the major means of production are effectively used to promote the independence and prosperity of the country and the people's welfare, and that the economic base is laid for building a new society, free from exploitation and oppression.

Along with these anti-imperialist revolutionary tasks, we must carry out the tasks of the anti-feudal, democratic revolution in a thoroughgoing way.

Top priority here is to solve the land problem correctly. The solution of this problem constitutes the basic content of the anti-feudal, democratic revolution. This is because it can deliver the peasantry, the overwhelming majority of the population, from the feudal fetters and feudal exploitation, radically improve their social and political status and open up a wide avenue for social progress and the development of the productive forces.

We must confiscate the land held by the Japanese state and the Japanese and pro-Japanese landlords and distribute it among the peasants who till it, and put an end to all aspects of feudal landownership, such as tenancy and the purchase and sale of land. The economic base of the feudal forces should be so completely eliminated that it will never be able to revive again.

Furthermore, we must see to it that the people are emancipated from all kinds of social discrimination and inequalities, and, especially that women, who make up half the population, are completely freed from feudal subjugation.

Along with this, the working people must be assured political freedom and democratic rights in all respects. Various social measures, such as the introduction of the eight-hour working day, labor protection and state insurance, must be taken to protect the working people, and conditions must be provided for all working people to participate in labor freely and work to their hearts' content under the protection of the state and society.

The introduction of all these social and economic reforms will constitute a deep-going social revolution aimed at removing the consequences of the monstrous colonial rule of Japanese imperialism and all the social evils and fetters that have existed for thousands of years.

The Communists should realize at the earliest possible date the centuries-old desire of broad sections of the working masses to rid themselves of all social oppression and exploitation and thus make them actively participate in the revolutionary struggle with a high degree of political enthusiasm and lead them constantly along the road of revolution.

When we have fulfilled the tasks of the anti-imperialist, antifeudal revolution it does not mean that we will have completed the revolution. Having carried out the anti-imperialist, antifeudal, democratic revolution, we Communists must continue the revolution and build a veritable paradise of socialism and communism in this country, free from oppression and exploitation.

2. Immediate Tasks of Korean Communists

What are the immediate tasks of the Korean Communists for carrying the Korean revolution to victory?

To begin with, Korean Communists must broaden and step up the anti-Japanese armed struggle and lead it to victory, thus splendidly accomplishing the sacred task of regaining our country.

In order to drive out the imperialist aggressors and carry the national-liberation revolution to completion, we must wage armed struggle resolutely. Imperialism relies on the military power of counterrevolution to establish its class rule and dominate its colonies and it will never give up aggression and war until its counterrevolutionary military power is totally defeated.

Nobody can expect the Japanese imperialists, the most shameless and piratical aggressors, who have tasted the sweat and blood of the colonial people and boast of the "might of great Imperial Japan," to withdraw from Korea meekly before their counterrevolutionary military power is routed.

That is why we Korean Communists have organized and waged armed struggle against the Japanese imperialist robbers since the beginning of the 1930's, delivering heavy blows at their counterrevolutionary military power.

The need to broaden and step up the anti-Japanese armed

struggle has become a matter of pressing urgency today.

After igniting the Sino-Japanese War, the Japanese imperialists sent a large force to the front in the Hwapei region of
China, aiming to win their war of aggression against the continent by blitz warfare tactics. Meanwhile, to make their "home
front safe," they are desperately carrying out "mopping-up
campaigns" against our revolutionary armed forces and intensifying the suppression and plunder of the Korean people.

Frantic expansion of the Japanese imperialists' aggressive
war only accelerates their ruin and creates favorable conditions for the struggle of the Korean Communists to hasten the
liberation of our country.

Under these conditions, we must decisively broaden and
step up the anti-Japanese armed struggle to defeat the ram-
paging Japanese imperialists and realize the noble historic
cause of regaining our lost country at the earliest possible
date.

This is also necessary to ensure the continued upsurge of the
overall Korean revolution.

The anti-Japanese armed struggle is the main stream of the
anti-Japanese national-liberation struggle in our country and
the highest form of this struggle. Stepping it up is essential for
the successful development of the various forms of anti-
Japanese struggle being waged by all sections of the people, including workers, peasants, youth and students.

Therefore, the Korean Communists must do this to bring
about a new upswing in the overall Korean revolution.

To broaden and develop the anti-Japanese armed struggle,
we must first increase the strength of the Korean People's
Revolutionary Army and intensify its military and political
activities.

The KPRA is not only a revolutionary armed force directly
engaged in the anti-Japanese armed struggle, but also a
revolutionary army of organizers and propagandists whose
task is to educate and organize broad masses and thus expand
and further the Korean revolution as a whole.

Strengthening the KPRA politically and militarily is a
decisive guarantee for stepping up the anti-Japanese armed
struggle and increasing its influence in every way.

The most important thing in strengthening the KPRA is to
raise the political and ideological level of all the commanders

and soldiers.

The source of the revolutionary army's invincible might lies in its political and ideological superiority. Because of its commanders' and soldiers' intense loyalty to their country and class, the KPRA is invincible and is capable of annihilating any army of the exploiter classes. However, we cannot give full scope to the essential superiority of a revolutionary army unless we make continuous efforts to raise the political and ideological level of the officers and men. Therefore, we must steadily arm all commanders and soldiers with a revolutionary world outlook, so that they will be able to persist in the arduous and prolonged revolutionary struggle with an indomitable fighting spirit.

All the commanders and soldiers of the KPRA are revolutionary fighters who are ready to give their all for the restoration of the motherland and the emancipation of the people. However, if we do not continue to increase their confidence in the victory of the revolution under present conditions in which our struggle is becoming more difficult and the enemy is stepping up his ideological offensive, we cannot increase the KPRA's political and ideological might.

This sets up the task of continuing to strengthen political and ideological education among them. First we must teach them Marxist-Leninist principles. At the same time, we must firmly arm them with the lines, strategy and tactics of the Korean revolution. This will help them establish a firm revolutionary world outlook. Furthermore, we should get them to adopt the revolutionary mass viewpoint, the revolutionary style of work, a sense of revolutionary comradeship and voluntary discipline. This is the way to turn all of them into dauntless revolutionary fighters convinced of victory in the revolution and filled with the lofty revolutionary spirit to devote their youth and lives wholly to the sacred task of restoring the country. And this is the way to turn them into true educators of the people and skillful organizers of the mass movement.

The political and ideological superiority of the KPRA can become even greater when it is combined with powerful military technical might. The Japanese imperialist aggressor troops are the most savage and crafty invaders, armed to the teeth with modern military hardware. If we are to defeat such an enemy we must get the KPRA thoroughly prepared politically and ideologically. We must also arm them with excellent military technique and superb guerrilla tactics.

While constantly expanding and strengthening the units of the KPRA, we must avail ourselves of all possible opportunities to intensify military education and training, so that all military cadres and soldiers will become expert in handling weapons and equipment and well versed in guerrilla tactics.

By strengthening the KPRA politically and militarily in this way, we will be able to train it to become a revolutionary force to crush the numerical superiority of the enemy with our political and ideological superiority, and his military and technical superiority with our superiority in guerrilla tactics.

Strengthening the KPRA politically and militarily must go hand in hand with its increasing military and political activities.

Units of our army should launch a large-scale offensive behind the lines of the Japanese imperialist aggressor troops, who are intent on their war of aggression against China proper, put them in a passive position and create a situation decisively favorable to the Korean revolution.

To this end, we should closely and actively combine large and small unit operations in keeping with the balance of forces between the enemy and our side and the changes in the situation; extend the scope of our armed struggle to make it go deeper into our homeland; and in combination with this, organize a nationwide war of resistance. When the vigorous military and political activities of the KPRA and the nationwide war of resistance are combined, the Japanese imperialist robbers will be defeated and the country's independence will certainly be restored.

Second, Korean Communists must more vigorously organize and conduct the anti-Japanese national united front movement and unite closely a wider segment of the anti-Japanese patriotic forces on a nationwide scale so that the revolutionary forces secure superiority over the counterrevolutionary forces.

This is a powerful political movement aiming at rallying all the patriotic forces of Korea opposing Japanese imperialism around the Communists so as to turn the balance of forces decisively in favor of the revolution. It occupies a very important place in our anti-Japanese national-liberation struggle.

Revolution is for the sake of the masses and it emerges victorious only when broad sections of the people participate in it. Winning over the masses, uniting them into a political force and relying on their inexhaustible strength is therefore a fundamental principle Communists and revolutionaries must abide by in their revolutionary struggle.

Winning over the anti-Japanese forces in all walks of life and forming them into an organized body has been an important task of the Korean Communists from the beginning of the anti-Japanese national-liberation struggle.

On the basis of scientific assessment of the subjective and objective conditions created in the development of our revolution, we set forth the line on forming an anti-Japanese national united front already at the beginning of the 1930's and strove consistently to implement it. And at last, in May 1936, we formed the Association for the Restoration of the Fatherland, the first organization of the anti-Japanese national united front in our country.

Within a short space of time, the ARF has grown in scope and strength to become a powerful underground revolutionary organization and a very broad-based mass organization, drawing a good many of the anti-Japanese masses under its wing.

The masses with anti-Japanese leanings, including workers and peasants and patriotic personages of all strata in Manchuria and the homeland who are widely embraced in the anti-Japanese national united front, are now vigorously waging a revolutionary struggle, upholding the Ten-Point Program of the ARF.

Its lower bodies have been formed and are active over a vast area of Manchuria and in major cities and villages at home, including those in North and South Hamgyong, North and South Pyongan and Kangwon Provinces. Thus a ramified organizational network is being formed to cover the whole country.

In our country today, not only workers and peasants, but also many patriotic youths, students and intellectuals support the Ten-Point Program and are launching into determined action against Japanese imperialism. Meanwhile, they are volunteering for our army by scores. All forces who love the country and nation and aspire to democracy, including small and middle entrepreneurs, small tradesmen, handicraftsmen and nationalists, are blended into a single stream of anti-Japanese struggle under communist leadership.

Particular mention should be made here of the Korean Independence Army, a nationalist armed force. This army, caught in the snare of conservatism, long rejected alliance with the Communists. But upon learning the Declaration and Program of the ARF it earnestly supported them and expressed its readiness to form an alliance with us. Some of its units have already participated in joint operation with our units. This concerted action helps to strengthen unity and affords the prospects of a more solid united front.

In addition, many progressive followers of the Chondo Religion in the homeland, opposing pro-Japanese activities of the reactionary Choe Rin clique, have also joined the struggle for the nation's common cause. Upholding the Ten-Point Program of the ARF and responding to its appeal, they are actively supporting and encouraging our anti-Japanese armed struggle. Dozens of their representatives came to see us on the same front to win back our country. They are now offering us aid, both moral and material. The ARF has succeeded in winning over a great many Chondo believers in a number of counties in the northern part of Korea and its influence among progressive believers across the country is increasing daily.

Thus, today the Korean people see a bright dawn of national liberation in the anti-Japanese armed struggle and in the ARF movement which is growing under the immediate influence of this struggle. They are rising bravely in the anti-Japanese revolutionary struggle, certain that victory will be theirs.

The present internal and external situation urgently demands that we Korean Communists expand and develop the anti-Japanese national united front movement.

Confronted with the crisis in which their colonial rule might collapse through our people's anti-Japanese national-salvation war of resistance, the Japanese imperialist aggressors are intensifying the colonial suppression and exploitation of the Korean people to an unprecedented degree. A huge military force and every conceivable means of repression are geared to this end. As the enemy's suppression intensifies, the anti-Japanese spirit of the Korean people surges ever higher and their revolutionary advance becomes very active.

To cope with this situation, the Korean Communists must keep abreast with the upsurge of anti-Japanese spirit in the masses and strive to mobilize all the anti-Japanese patriotic forces of the people for the national-liberation struggle.

Pushing the anti-Japanese national united front movement forward is also an important task for the development of the world revolution.

In imperialist countries such as Japan, Germany and Italy which have embarked upon full-scale fascistization, fascist dictatorship deprived people of democratic freedoms and all political rights and the revolutionary movement is undergoing a severe trial. The danger of fascistization is daily growing on a worldwide scale. Communists are countering this situation with an anti-fascist popular front movement and making positive efforts to organize and mobilize broad masses in it.

In this situation, strengthening our anti-Japanese national united front movement is the way we can contribute to weakening the allied international fascist forces and hastening the victory of all the international democratic forces, and help turn the international climate in favor of our own revolution.

Korean Communists must struggle energetically to deepen and advance this movement in conformity with the new demands of the revolution.

The most important thing here is to make the organizations of the Association for the Restoration of the Fatherland more militant and expand and strengthen its ranks.

The ARF is a united front organization formed by the Communists in a situation where a Marxist-Leninist party is still absent in our country. At the same time, it is a powerful underground revolutionary organization.

Therefore, by making its organizations militant and expanding and strengthening its ranks it will be possible to rally the anti-Japanese patriotic forces across the country in a unified way and, at the same time, to provide the Korean revolutionary movement with communist leadership.

In order to strengthen the anti-Japanese national united front movement we must expand the ARF's organizational network deep into the homeland and actively organize the broad anti-Japanese masses in it.

We must also intensify its organizational and political activities in every way, while making its organizations militant and skillfully employing flexible methods of work suitable to underground activities. Under the severe conditions in which the enemy is stepping up his suppressive measures, we should not give every organization the same name, but give them various names according to the actual conditions in each locality and the characteristics and political level of the people in all walks of life. Each organization should adopt various forms of activity in accordance with the actual conditions. This will make the ARF a more powerful revolutionary underground organization of a mass character which is active and deeply rooted among broad masses.

In order to further expand and develop the ARF movement, communist leadership must be established over the entire movement. Only when this leadership is firmly ensured can the anti-Japanese national united front movement be consistently pushed forward in conformity with the interests of all the people, including the working class, and develop successfully in accordance with revolutionary strategy and tactics. We Communists, therefore, should firmly establish ourselves in leading positions in the organizations of the ARF and give them revolutionary leadership.

In leading the movement, Communists should clearly recognize the Right and "Left" tendencies and thoroughly overcome them.

If we are to unite the people of all strata we must properly combine the revolutionary mass line with the class line. We must guard against both "Left" and Right tendencies—such as establishing contacts only with the workers and peasants, getting caught in the snare of class prejudice or, in the name of united front, joining hands with anyone unconditionally. If we draw only workers and peasants into the ARF organizations and exclude the rest of the anti-Japanese patriotic forces, we may lose a great many anti-Japanese masses. On the other hand, if we accept everybody who comes along, regardless of political considerations, alien elements of different colors will sneak in.

We should therefore stick firmly to the principle of winning over as many of the patriotic, democratic forces opposing Japanese imperialism as we can and, at the same time, of thoroughly isolating the pro-Japanese elements, traitors to the nation and all other alien and hostile elements.

In leading the anti-Japanese national united front move-ment it is also important for us to properly combine solidarity with struggle within its ranks.

Proceeding from their own class interests, the anti-Japanese masses of various strata take different positions and attitudes in the struggle against Japanese imperialism. Because of their class limitations many of them are irresolute and waver in the anti-Japanese struggle, even though they hate Japanese im-perialism. If we do not help them to discard their vacillating nature they will be unable to overcome the difficulties that crop up in the course of the struggle and to keep a firm anti-Japanese position and, in the end, will become turncoats and cause grave harm to the revolution.

Communists must therefore strengthen solidarity with them while unfolding a principled struggle to overcome their vacil-lating nature and weaknesses. This will preserve the ranks of the united front and bring its strength into full play even under conditions in which the enemy is intensifying its military and ideological offensives.

Third, Korean Communists should strive to strengthen solidarity with the international revolutionary forces.

This is the proletarian internationalist duty of the Korean Communists and an important guarantee for strengthening the world's revolutionary forces, isolating the Japanese imper-ialists internationally and consolidating our own revolutionary forces.

Particularly now when the Japanese imperialists have occu-pied Manchuria, are conducting a large-scale aggressive war against China and desperately making preparations for a war against the Soviet Union, it is a matter of urgency to safe-guard the Soviet Union and strengthen solidarity with the Chinese revolutionary forces for the advance of both the world revolution and the Korean revolution.

Japanese imperialism is the enemy not only of the Korean people but also of the Chinese people. Only when the militant solidarity between the peoples of Korea and China is strength-ened and the anti-Japanese united front cemented in their struggle against Japanese imperialism, the common enemy, can we deal it heavier political and military blows and hasten the victory of the Korean and Chinese revolutions.

It is on this principle that we Korean Communists have

fought together on the common battlefront in firm unity with the anti-Japanese forces of the Chinese people from the early period of the anti-Japanese armed struggle and, moreover, we have made great efforts to unite with all Chinese anti-Japanese units that could possibly add up to a big force in the war against Japan.

There are various Chinese anti-Japanese units. Among them are those under the influence of the Chinese Communist Party, and remnants of the former Northeastern Army under the Kuomintang which, impelled by the "Manchurian Incident," rose to fight under an anti-Japanese save-the-nation banner. There are also anti-Japanese armed units formed by peasant rebels such as the "Red Spear Society" and "Broad Sword Society."

The Korean Communists long ago formed an Allied Anti-Japanese Army with the anti-Japanese guerrilla units led by the Chinese Communists and have waged a dynamic joint anti-Japanese struggle.

Moreover, we have striven to form an anti-Japanese united front with the "National-Salvation Army" and "Self-Defense Army" formed out of the remnant units of the former North-eastern Army and with all other anti-Japanese units organized by peasant rebels. Right after the September 18 incident we organized and perseveringly waged an active and self-sacrificing struggle, forming anti-Japanese soldiers' committees and task forces, dispatching political workers to these units and helping the task forces increase their role in every way. These steps helped to overcome their obstinacy in views, vacillating nature and political ignorance and to form a united front.

The KPRA has fought shoulder to shoulder with these anti-Japanese units in many successful joint operations such as the attack on Tungning county seat, inflicting powerful blows on Japanese imperialism. These battles demonstrated the united strength of the peoples of Korea and China and laid a firm foundation for all-round alliance and unity of action with the anti-Japanese units.

In the second half of the 1930's when the main units of the KPRA advanced to the Paekdu-san guerrilla base, we also persuaded many anti-Japanese units which were discouraged by the enemy's punitive operations to join the Allied Anti-Japanese Army through revolutionary education or successful large-scale joint operations. (We not only sent political cadres to them but supplied them with provisions, clothes and weapons though we ourselves were in need.) This raised their morale and inspired them with confidence in victory, leading them to fight actively on the anti-Japanese front.

There are some among us, however, who are not successful in forming a united front with other anti-Japanese units because of their narrow outlook. If we do not do effective work with these units, they will be unable to withstand the enemy's relentless punitive operations and are liable to waver, surrender and turn traitor or take the backward step of becoming local bandits. Therefore, we must not ignore anti-Japanese units but strengthen our united front with all of them, even if they do waver and are not steadfast in their stand; we must give them positive leadership, and continue to expand the anti-Japanese war so that we will isolate Japanese imperialism to the maximum and add muscle to our anti-Japanese armed forces.

In our work with the Chinese anti-Japanese units the principle we should continue to follow is that we lead them not to surrender to Japanese imperialism but to fight, holding aloft the anti-Japanese save-the-nation banner, and not to encroach upon the interests of the people but to confiscate the property of the Japanese, their lackeys and pro-Japanese Chinese landlords and use it to obtain military supplies.

On the basis of steadily consolidating unity with the Chinese Communists, we must unite with all anti-Japanese units and all revolutionary forces in China, thus forming a broader Korean-Chinese anti-Japanese united front.

In strengthening solidarity with the international revolutionary forces, it is also important to defend the Soviet Union, the motherland of the proletariat of the world.

The Soviet Union, founded by Lenin, is the first socialist state and the first state of the proletarian dictatorship which genuinely champions the interests of the workers and peasants. It affords the first example of the victory of Marxism-Leninism and stands as the great bulwark of the international working class.

It is the internationalist obligation of the working class of all countries to protect the great Soviet Union. Revolution in each country develops and is defended on the basis of the militant unity and solidarity of the international working class. The growth of the might of the Soviet Union, the socialist state, is a source of great inspiration to the working class of the world and to the oppressed peoples struggling against foreign imperialism and their own ruling classes. Therefore, we must struggle to defend the Soviet Union, the only state of the proletariat and the first of its kind in the world, thereby defending the world revolution and creating a more favorable international climate for the Korean revolution.

Under the slogan "Defend the Soviet Union with arms!" we must ceaselessly attack the Japanese imperialists in the rear to strike constant terror into the hearts of these bandits and frustrate their aggressive machinations against the Soviet Union at every step.

In the future, too, in keeping with the requirements of the newly created situation and raising the banner of proletarian internationalism, we must be active in defending the Soviet Union, consolidate the anti-Japanese united front with the Chinese people and strengthen solidarity with the international working class and all oppressed colonial peoples. Thus, we must direct the spearhead of attack upon the Japanese imperialist aggressors, the chief enemy of the Korean people, and shatter their ambition to dominate Asia.

Fourth, Korean Communists must struggle vigorously to found a revolutionary, Marxist-Leninist party in our country.

A Marxist-Leninist party is the vanguard of the working class and the General Staff in revolution. Only when we have a party of the working class can we rally broad masses who are interested in the revolution, successfully organize and mobilize them for revolutionary struggle and lead them to victory with correct strategy and tactics.

Under the influence of the October Socialist Revolution, the communist movement began early in our country. Our first Communist Party was founded in 1925.

Our working masses, who have long languished under Japanese imperialist colonial rule and feudal oppression, hailed the founding of the Communist Party of Korea whose mission was to struggle to defend the interests of the have-nots, and they put their expectations and hopes in it. However, due to fundamental weaknesses and limitations, it could not satisfy these expectations and hopes.

The Party failed to take root among the working class and other broad sections of the people. It consisted mainly of bourgeois and petty-bourgeois intellectuals and show-off Marxists with a shaky class position. To make matters worse, it could not achieve unity of its ranks owing to the scramble for "hegemony" among the sectarians who had wormed their way to the top. Consequently, unable to overcome the Japanese imperialist suppression and the subversive activities of the sectarians, it was dissolved three years after it was founded.

Under these circumstances, the Korean Communists are confronted with the urgent task of founding a revolutionary, Marxist-Leninist party, drawing serious lessons from the communist movement in the 1920's.

But we cannot create a revolutionary party the way sectarians did in the past, in which a small number of Communists got together, without any organizational and ideological preparation, set up a "party center" and proclaimed the founding of the party.

To found a revolutionary, Marxist-Leninist party, solid organizational and ideological groundwork must be laid before anything else.

We have achieved great success in this respect through a strenuous struggle.

Although we have not announced the party center yet, we have set up party organizations and underground revolutionary organizations of various kinds in the units of the Korean People's Revolutionary Army and among workers and peasants at home and abroad, and provided them with a unified leadership. In the KPRA units a system of leading party organizations based on the principle of democratic centralism is now established and party organizational life is functioning regularly. In the areas along the Tuman-gang and Amnok-gang Rivers, party organizations have also been formed among broad masses of workers and peasants and a unified leadership is ensured for them. In particular, an active struggle has been waged to form Communist Party organizations in the homeland in line with the policy of making preparations independently for founding a party, and significant success has been registered.

In the flames of the armed struggle and in the course of the underground revolutionary struggle over the past few years we have also reared the finest sons and daughters of the workers, peasants and other working people as Communists, thereby building up the organizational core for founding a party.

At the same time, we have waged an energetic struggle to overcome the sectarianism left over from the communist movement of the 1920's, with the result that the sects have now been basically removed from our ranks and that unity of ideology and purpose has been brought about and solidarity achieved within the revolutionary ranks.

The Korean Communists, basing themselves on the successes achieved so far, should endeavor to found a Marxist-Leninist party as soon as possible. To this end, we should more vigorously advance organizational and ideological preparations on a nationwide scale.

The important tasks of the Korean Communists in this work are:

First, to expand party organizations in the units of the KPRA and in the revolutionary mass organizations, including the ARF and the Anti-Japanese Youth League, in the homeland and in the areas along the Tuman-gang and Amnok-gang Rivers, rally Communists under a unified organizational system and steel them in militancy through party organizational life.

Now that a sound center of leadership has been formed for the Korean revolution, many Communists of new generation have been brought up, and the ARF and various other revolutionary organizations have taken root among the broad masses, it is an urgent task for us to expand party organizations and unite the Communists. The successful fulfillment of this task will enable party organizations to take deep root among the masses including workers and peasants and, on this basis, guarantee a firm unified leadership for the Korean revolution.

In strict accordance with the principle of independence in our preparations for the founding of a party, we must form party cells and groups wherever possible in units and regions and unite all Communists organizationally. In particular, we should foster a revolutionary leading core in the main industrial areas and in farming and fishing villages in the homeland and expand the network of the ARF organizations by ourselves. On this basis, we should form party groups and cells among the workers and peasants and put them under a unified organizational system.

In view of the historical lessons of the early communist movement, we should strictly adhere to the policy of building party organizations from the bottom. Only then can we draw on the class consciousness of the broad working masses and accept into the party those progressive elements of worker and peasant origin who have been steeled and prepared in action and establish a most revolutionary and militant party with a sound mass base.

The party organizations in the KPRA units and in the different regions should strictly abide by the principle of democratic centralism in all their activities and increase both their fighting capacity and their vanguard role.

Every party member should be faithful in his organizational life and steel himself in actual struggle to become an indefatigable revolutionary fighter, a Communist.

Secondly, to train large numbers of best elements of worker and peasant origin in the revolutionary struggle to become the revolutionary core and thus build up a sound organizational backbone for founding a party.

In the light of the bitter lessons of the early communist movement in our country, this is vital for the consolidation and development of the party we are going to create.

We must do active work in recruiting the finest sons and daughters of the workers and peasants into the People's Revolutionary Army and, in the flames of the armed struggle, bring them up to be communist core elements boundlessly faithful to the revolution, to be the organizational backbone of the party. We must accept into the party those people made politically aware and steeled in militancy in the underground revolutionary struggle and train them to become revolutionary core elements.

Furthermore, we must unite revolutionary workers, peasants and other broad masses with anti-Japanese sentiments in mass organizations, such as the Association for the Restoration of the Fatherland, the Anti-Japanese Youth League, the Anti-Japanese Association and the Women's Association, and train them to become ardent Communists through the actual struggle against Japanese imperialism.

Thirdly, to continue the all-out struggle against sectarianism, prevent it from penetrating party and other revolutionary organizations and thus firmly ensure the purity of the communist ranks and unity in ideology and purpose.

Unless sectarianism is completely overcome it is impossible to guarantee firm unity among the Communists, achieve community of ideology, purpose and action based on the unified line, strategy and tactics of the Korean revolution and accomplish the historical task of founding a party.

Sectarianism in our country rose with intellectuals of bourgeois, petty-bourgeois and ruined gentry origin who, taking advantage of the revolutionary tide rising under the impact of the October Socialist Revolution, wormed their way into the ranks of the working-class movement under the cloak of Marxism.

Although they talked about communism and the emancipation of the working class, the sectarians utilized the labor movement as a means of gaining fame and high position and realizing careerist, political ambitions.

As soon as they had sneaked into the working-class movement, they split off into parties of five or groups of three for sectarian purposes and formed sects such as the Tuesday group, the M-L group and the Seoul-Shanghai group. Without any political views or theoretical basis, they continued sectarian feuds to spread the influence of their own particular group and obtain "hegemony." In the end, they destroyed the Party.

Even after the Party was dissolved, they continued their sectarian feuds here in Manchuria under the slogan of "Reconstruct the Party."

Driven by the desire to spread their groups' influence and gain fame and high position, the sectarians organized the adventurist and misguided "May 30 Uprising." This incident resulted in exposing the revolutionary underground organizations, caused the death of many Communists and other revolutionary people and did great harm to our communist movement. Moreover, the sectarian-flunkeys, with the backing of the national chauvinists, used the anti-"Minsaengdan" struggle for their own evil sectarian purpose and committed grave criminal acts—sacrificing many fine Communists and revolutionaries and creating alienation, enmity and distrust within the revolutionary ranks, thereby weakening their unity and solidarity.

If we had not promptly corrected the "Left" error in the anti-"Minsaengdan" struggle through a principled struggle against the sectarian-flunkeys and national chauvinists, things would have come to a serious pass beyond remedy in the communist and revolutionary movement.

Sects have now been removed from our ranks in the main. But former sectarians who backslid to become national reformists and even spies for Japanese imperialism are now engaged in all manner of schemes to disrupt the communist ranks from within.

Therefore we should first make party members, soldiers of the KPRA and the broad revolutionary masses thoroughly aware of the crimes committed by the sectarian-flunkeys who have done tremendous harm to our communist and revolutionary movement. By so doing, we will get them to maintain a constant and high degree of vigilance and hatred for the class enemy, to prevent the penetration of sectarianism and to detect and smash the sectarian-flunkeys' subversive and wrecking activities in good time.

In addition to this, we must arm all party members and soldiers of the KPRA with Marxism-Leninism and with the line, strategy and tactics for the Korean revolution and thus ensure community of ideology, will and action in the entire ranks.

This is a prerequisite for fully guaranteeing the purity as well as the unity of ideology and will of the communist ranks, and for preparing a sound organizational and ideological groundwork for the founding of a party.

The Korean Communists should faithfully carry out these main tasks in making preparations for founding a party and thus accomplish the historical cause of establishing a revolutionary, Marxist-Leninist party at the earliest possible date.

*   *   *

The Korean Communists should, above all, stick to a firm independent position in order to carry their revolutionary tasks to success.

An independent position means the fundamental stand of the Communists—having confidence in the strength of their

own people and responsibly carrying through the revolution in
their country with their own efforts. Only when they maintain
a firm independent position in the revolutionary struggle can
they formulate revolutionary lines and policies corresponding
to the actual conditions in their country, safeguard and implement them thoroughly and fight to the last for their country's
revolution no matter what the difficulties and hardships.

The masters of the Korean revolution are the Korean people
and the Korean Communists. The Korean revolution must be
carried out by the Korean people under the leadership of the
Korean Communists.

We should never forget the bitter lesson of the past when the
communist and revolutionary movement in our country suffered severe damage and went through many twists and turns
because the sectarians took to flunkeyism.

The Korean Communists must carry on revolutionary struggle by their own faith and build up their own strong revolutionary forces and firmly rely on them in leading the Korean
revolution to victory.

Revolution in each country is a link in the chain of world
revolution and a component part of it. It is carried on with
powerful assistance from the world revolutionary forces. It is
the internationalist duty of the Communists of each country to
fight energetically for the triumph of the world revolution.

Powerful assistance from the world anti-imperialist forces is
very important in our national-liberation struggle against the
military-feudal Japanese imperialist aggressors who are allied
with world imperialism.

But no matter how great the assistance of the international
revolutionary forces may be, the Korean Communists cannot
lead the Korean revolution to victory if they fail to map out the
line, strategy and tactics for the revolution to fit the realities
of their country and, on this basis, solidly build up their own
revolutionary forces.

The Korean Communists will continue to strengthen
solidarity with the international revolutionary forces, reject
flunkeyism and Right and "Left" opportunism, take a firm independent stand in leading the Korean revolution, and fulfill
the historical cause of national liberation without fail.

Victory and glory belong to the Korean Communists who are
fighting unyieldingly under the unfurled banner of the Korean

revolution.

Long live the Korean revolution!
Long live the world revolution!

THE KOREAN REVOLUTIONARIES MUST KNOW KOREA WELL

Speech Addressed to the Political Cadres and Political Instructors of the Korean People's Revolutionary Army, *September 15, 1943*

Today when the great event of national liberation is at hand I am going to talk to you about the need to intensify the study of the homeland and also about some urgent tasks.

The world situation is rapidly turning in favor of the revolution, and the great event of national liberation is now the order of the day.

The fascist nations—Japan, Germany and Italy—that unleashed World War II with the object of dominating the world are going downhill step by step as time goes on.

Backed stealthily by the US and British imperialists, fascist Germany treacherously surprised the Soviet Union with a huge force of 170 divisions, reinforced by aircraft and tanks. They boasted that they would defeat the Soviet Union within a few months. But the Soviet people and the Red Army led by great Comrade Stalin gradually resolved the unfavorable situation that prevailed in the first stage of the war. Single-handedly they checked fascist Germany in her frantic attack for which she had mobilized all internal forces as well as the military force, manpower and resources of the 14 European countries already under her occupation, and they took the counteroffensive.

Early this year at Stalingrad, the incomparably brave Red Army crushed fascist Germany's 30 crack panzer divisions equipped with the latest weapons, marking a new turning point in the Soviet-Germany war. It is evident that the fate of the fascist German army was decisively sealed at Stalingrad.

The Red Army has now driven the German aggressors back to the vicinity of the Dnieper, and before long will destroy all the aggressors on Soviet territory and win a great victory.

Firmly believing Germany's victory over the Soviet Union a fait accompli, the Japanese imperialists had started an adventurous Pacific War. But they are also suffering one defeat after another on the vast fronts of China, Southeast Asia and the Pacific.

On the Chinese front, the Japanese imperialists are gradually getting into hot water owing to the counterattack of the Eighth Route Army and the New Fourth Army led by the Chinese Communist Party. The greater part of their armed forces sent out to the Chinese front along with the puppet army were directed into operations calculated to "wipe out" the Eighth Route Army and the New Fourth Army, but one after another their "punitive operations" have come to grief. In north China the Eighth Route Army is gradually expanding its liberated area.

The Japanese imperialists planned to surprise the Americans in Pearl Harbor of Hawaii and administer a mortal blow to the US Pacific Fleet and then, before the United States could recover, seize a wide area of Southeast Asia. They then planned to plunder the rich natural resources such as oil and rubber, so that they would meet their shortage of strategic materials and cope with the protracted war. Their daydream was that this would enable them to defeat the US and British forces in Southeast Asia and in the Pacific together with Germany's victory over the Soviet Union. But they have already completely lost balance in the Pacific and are suffering defeat after defeat.

Italy has surrendered and Germany and Japan have begun to retreat hastily.

When we analyze World War II, there is no doubt that the fall of the Japanese imperialists is inevitable and that the great event of national liberation is at hand.

1. On the Need to Study the Homeland Well

Today, with the great event of national liberation almost in sight, one of our most important tasks is to study the homeland well.

A good knowledge of our country and our people is essential for us to discharge our duties successfully as patriots and Communists and carry out the Korean revolution with honor.

In order to carry the responsibility for the Korean revolution we must be well versed in the history and geography of the homeland and be well informed about its brilliant cultural traditions. This is indispensable to us in fostering ardent patriotism, increasing our readiness to serve the country and the people with devotion, and in educating our people by understanding their preferences and so persuading them to become actively involved in the revolutionary struggle.

At the same time, a good knowledge of our history, geography, economy and culture is essential for us Communists to apply Marxist-Leninist principles creatively to the realities of our country, take an independent attitude and form our own views in regard to the revolution in our country.

Also, for the purpose of saving our fine national traditions and national riches from the Japanese imperialist colonial rulers' policy of national eradication, we must know well about our history, geography and culture.

Not only are the Japanese imperialists now intensifying their cruel colonial plunder of our people in order to make up for their successive ignominious setbacks in the war, but also, with the object of erasing our country off the map forever, they are openly pursuing the national assimilation policy, raving about the "same ancestry" and "oneness of Japan and Korea." Distorting or deleting our time-honored brilliant history and cultural traditions and widely propagating the *"samurai* spirit" of the "Empire's subjects," these colonial rulers of Japanese imperialism are trying to stamp out all that is Korean. In order to prevent Korea's resurrection, they forbade the use of our language, spoken and written. Furthermore, they prohibit the Koreans from using their proper names, forcing them to change their names according to Japanese fashion, such as "Ushichiro" and "Umasaburo."

Now that the Japanese imperialists are making a frenzied attempt to erase the history and culture of our nation and Korea forever, we, the true patriots of Korea, must study our homeland well. This is one of our most important revolutionary tasks.

We must study our country hard in order to reconstruct our liberated country well in the future.

The commanding officers and soldiers of the Korean People's Revolutionary Army are all fighters who have taken the road of revolution from a burning desire to restore the Japanese-imperialists-ridden homeland and build a new society of happiness in a liberated country. Even amidst the difficult conditions of hard battles being waged against the Japanese imperialist army of aggression, we have been working to instill a sound, revolutionary world outlook into the commanding officers and soldiers of the KPRA, with particular stress on an intensified study of Marxist-Leninist principles and the lines, strategy and tactics of the Korean revolution.

The current situation with the great event of national liberation fast approaching makes it imperative that while studying Marxism-Leninism we acquire a deep knowledge needed for the build-up of the economy and culture in a liberated homeland.

As Communists of Korea, how can we expect to cope adequately with the Korean revolution without being well versed in the history, culture, nature and geography of Korea and the good ethics and customs of its people?

Korean Communists must know well, boast of and love ardently the 5,000 years of our people's history and brilliant culture and the physical aspects and rich resources of the homeland. They must hold to the lofty ideal and firm resolve to build a communist society, a paradise for the people, in their beautiful country.

In the first place, we must make a thorough study of our history.

When we say we must study the history, we mean that we must be acquainted with the history of our people's struggle and creative activities, not the history of kings or other feudal rulers.

A solid knowledge of this history is indispensable to us in order to develop an ardent feeling of patriotism and foster both national pride and revolutionary self-respect.

From olden times our people waged an unyielding struggle against the tyranny of the feudal rulers and foreign invaders, and developed science and culture by their own creative labor and wisdom, thus making Korea famous in the East.

Our people are brave and resourceful, industrious and peace-loving. In particular, our people are highly patriotic and fight indefatigably against foreign invaders in defence of the dignity of the nation.

The invasion of our country by foreign aggressors has been ceaseless since ancient times, and it has been more rampant especially during the latter part of the 19th century, and after.

From olden times the Korean people rose as one man in a holy war to defend their country and they repulsed the aggressors each time an invasion occurred. They defended their country heroically as recorded in 5,000 years of honored history.

The history of our people in ancient times and in the Middle Ages was a history of struggle against aggression in defence of the homeland—repulsing the invasions of Sui and Tang and those of Khitan and Yuan to the north and curbing the invasion of the Japanese to the south. In modern times it has been a history of anti-imperialist struggle, a history of national-liberation struggle, fought against the invasion of the Japanese and US imperialists.

Foreign aggressors invaded our country ceaselessly for ages, but were unable to break the patriotic loyalty and valor of our people at all, failing to bring them to their knees.

The people of Koguryo were not only resourceful and intrepid, but they regarded it as the most honorable thing to defend their country with all their devotion. It was considered to be men's duty to learn military arts and from childhood they were trained in running, riding, archery and fencing. The military arts were the basis of all folk games and sporting contests. There is a story about Ondal, a man of obscure birth, who was taken into service after winning a hunting game and performed great feats in defending the country. This eloquently shows that in evaluating people in Koguryo importance was attached to their military accomplishments and their wisdom and bravery.

Because the people of Koguryo were educated in patriotism, received military training and were disciplined to be brave from an early age, they acquired a high sense of national pride and a stout heart and safeguarded the country's honor and the nation's dignity by repulsing the three-million-strong invading army of Sui, the largest country on the Asian continent.

The peoples of Silla and Paekje living in the southern part of our country firmly defended their territories with great fortitude so that no foreign enemy dared to intrude.

If in the period of the Three Kingdoms those three countries: Koguryo, Silla and Paekje had unitedly repelled the foreign invaders, our homeland would have been further developed.

When hundreds of thousands of Khitan troops invaded our country the people of Koryo under the command of General Kang Gam Chan dealt them a crushing blow at the Amnokgang River and at Kusong, thus saving the country.

Under the Li Dynasty, too, our people fought courageously against the foreign invaders. The feudal rulers, however, instead of taking measures to cope with alien aggression by strengthening the national defence and training the army, only sang the praises of peace and indulged in a life of ease. Taking advantage of this, the vicious Japanese *samurai* invaded in great force in 1592. The feudal rulers who had been easy-going, neglecting the necessary day-to-day build-up of defence, found themselves powerless to check the invasion. So they ran away to Uiju with the king, abandoning the country and people to the mercy of the Japanese intruders.

The sagacious and intrepid people of Korea, however, fought the aggressors with valor everywhere—Namhae, Chinju, Yonan, Pyongyang and other places. Admiral Li Sun Sin in command of a meager naval force defended the sea off the coast of Cholla Province and stopped the advance of Japanese invaders. They won a great victory through annihilating the Japanese naval force off the Island of Hansan-do. The patriots, including Kwak Jae U, raised armies of volunteers, defeating the Japanese invaders everywhere. Peasants, lower-grade officials and even monks living in seclusion in mountains raised volunteer armies and even the women fought with them.

The people fought for seven years with a "do-or-die" spirit against the atrocious and heinous Japanese *samurai* and at last drove the enemies out of their territory and thus defended national honor and dignity.

In the middle of the 19th century when our country was invaded by the capitalist powers from Europe and America, the incompetent and bigoted feudal rulers indulged themselves in factional strife, greedy only for power and pleasure without any regard for the country and people, but our people unyieldingly fought against the aggressors.

In 1866 the people of Pyongyang sank the US pirate ship *General Sherman* which intruded into the Taedong-gang River. Our people and soldiers also repulsed an invading French ship.

In 1894 the peasants of Cholla Province started a peasant war directed against the misgovernment of the feudal rulers. At that time, too, the peasants and patriotic soldiers and scholars not only fought the rulers, but also waged a bloody struggle against the Japanese army of aggression that had made inroads into our country by taking advantage of its internal confusion.

As you can see, over a long period of 5,000 years the people of Korea fought unflinchingly against the foreign aggressors and defended their country, demonstrating their ardent patriotism, courage and indomitable spirit to the whole world.

But the feudal rulers did not try to reject the foreign forces and foster the national resources to preserve the integrity of the country. Instead, they acted as flunkeys to the great powers and indulged in factional strife, fawning upon foreign forces and backed by them, and ended by committing the never-to-be-pardoned treachery of selling the country over to the Japanese imperialist aggressors.

After the country was seized by the Japanese imperialists in 1910, our people unremittingly launched the Righteous Volunteers' Army Movement, the Independence Army Movement, the anti-Japanese movement of workers, peasants and youths and students, and so on. And in the latter part of the 1920's they waged a violent struggle against Japanese imperialism and its lackeys.

Particularly in the early 1930's, we, the Communists who are true patriots, organized and pursued a heroic anti-Japanese armed struggle. We thus advanced the national-liberation struggle of Korea to a higher stage, and over ten long years we dealt heavy political and military blows to our enemy, Japanese imperialism, pushing it towards its doom.

The intelligent and brave people of Korea will never succumb and the Korean spirit will remain alive forever. The anti-Japanese national-liberation struggle of the Korean people guided by the all-conquering revolutionary ideas of Marxism-Leninism is bound to win and our homeland will certainly be liberated. The day is not far off when the Korean spirit will be demonstrated to the whole world.

By intensely studying the glorious history of the struggle of the Korean people, we must cultivate even further ardent patriotism, national pride and burning hatred for the enemy.

The Korean people is a talented, sagacious and civilized people who also developed brilliant traditions in science and culture.

Our forefathers in ancient times created a resplendent culture which contributed to the flowering of the civilization of the East.

From olden times our people began to produce iron. In the period of the Three Kingdoms they made and used ironware widely in their daily life and displayed a high degree of craftsmanship in gold, silver and bronze.

In the first half of the 7th century our ancestors already built Chomsongdae, the world-famous astronomical observatory, thus greatly contributing to the development of meteorology and astronomy.

Architecture was a well developed art in the period of the Three Kingdoms. The nine-storied pagoda of the Hwangryongsa Temple was built in the 7th century and the Tabo-tap and Sokga-tap pagodas of the Pulguk-sa Temple have preserved their original appearance intact until today, over a thousand and several hundred years later. All this proves eloquently the development of architecture in those days. The mural paintings of the ancient tombs of Koguryo which are not discolored though thousands of years have passed, and the stone statues and reliefs of Sokguram (a rocky cavern) of Silla also display the high level of the ancient art of our country.

Our country also saw music and dance highly developed in ancient times. Our ancestors promoted music with the production of excellent national instruments such as *kayagum* and *komungo* and developed a folk dance which was outstanding in its graceful, rhythmical movement.

Our advanced culture, metallurgy and ceramics had already been spread abroad during the period of the Three Kingdoms and become famous. At the same time the artisans, architects, painters and scholars sailed across the sea to Japan and spread knowledge of our literature and crafts, thus strongly influencing Japanese cultural development.

The people of Koryo greatly developed the printing industry by inventing metal type for the first time in the world and manufactured the Koryo ceramics which the world values as treasures because of their distinctive colors, patterns and models. All these made our country famous.

Our people who had used *ridu* characters for writing ever since the period of the Three Kingdoms produced the *Hunminjongum* (Korean script), the most advanced characters, in the year 1444, and thus greatly helped to develop our culture.

Even when the feudal rulers who had fallen prey to flunkeyism were idling their time away, reciting the Confucian scriptures and chanting poems about the beauties of nature, the people were putting their distinguished talents to use and produced works of art worthy of world praise. And, together with technicians, they invented the original mighty "Turtle Boat," the world's first iron-clad warship.

Through the quoted examples, we can realize clearly how talented and wise our people are and how greatly our nation has assisted mankind's development of science and culture.

We Communists must know more about, and learn to value, the traditions of science and culture established by our ancestors. By doing so, we will be able to develop science that genuinely serves the people and helps to build a new society, and will be able to create a national culture, democratic and socialist, in a liberated country. A new socialist national culture never arises out of nothing. It is created by critically inheriting and developing the excellent traditions of our national culture handed down from generation to generation. In order to create a new socialist national culture we must be well aware of the fine traditions of our national culture, and critically analyze and appreciate them.

Ours is a single nation with 5,000 years of history; it is a valorous, ambitious nation that has been vigorously fighting against foreign invaders and successive reactionary rulers from olden times; and it is a talented nation that has contributed greatly to mankind's development of science and culture.

We are Communists who love the homeland and the people more ardently than anybody else. We must further heighten our national self-respect and pride as Koreans and have the revolutionary self-confidence and pride as fighters who have been waging the ten or more years of bloody struggle for the liberation and independence of the country. Without such feelings one becomes a pitiable and servile national nihilist, that is, a flunkey. Flunkeyism and national nihilism are, in the long run, bound to lead one to betray and ruin one's country and nation. Being most ardent lovers of the country and the people, we Communists must resolutely fight against national nihilism and flunkeyism which ignore our nation and the history of our country.

If we had lacked that intense patriotism which defends the dignity of our country and loves our nation, we would not have become true patriots and Communists faithful to the revolution of our country. As we had the ardent spirit of loving and valuing the country and nation more than anyone else, we could begin the struggle to liberate the Japanese-imperialists-ridden homeland and people and become today's fine Communists who have been firmly armed with the revolutionary world outlook of Marxism-Leninism and tested in the prolonged revolutionary struggle.

We must have a good knowledge not only of the country's history but also of its geography.

The ultimate goal of our revolution is to make our country rich and mighty so that our people will lead a full and happy life. In other words, it is to build a paradise of socialism and communism in our country. Who builds this paradise? We must do it by ourselves. We must defeat the Japanese imperialists and then construct in the homeland a socialist state like that of the Soviet Union with an advanced industry and agriculture. To this end we must exploit our abundant natural resources to reconstruct and develop all fields of the economy including industry, agriculture and fisheries.

Our country has every condition to build a rich, strong, independent and sovereign state, whether from the viewpoint of area or population or resources.

Situated in the east of the Asian continent, our country borders the continent on the north, and its three sides—east, west and south—face on the sea. It covers an area of more than 220,000 square kilometres with a population of 23 million—neither too big nor too small. Among those countries known as being powerful or civilized in the world there are many far smaller than our country both in area and in population. As regards natural resources, few countries are richer than ours.

It has huge deposits of hundreds of kinds of valuable and useful minerals including iron ore, a veritable treasure house with gold, silver and jewels.

Over the Paekmu Plateau, the northern region of our country, an inexhaustible deposit of magnetic iron ore is buried and the western plain areas abound in good-quality limonite. The estimated iron ore deposits already amount to thousands of millions of tons and the figure is expected to increase.

High-caloric bituminous coal abounds in the northern region, and anthracite in South Pyongan Province and in the Taebaek-san range of central Korea. Coal supplies are inexhaustible, more than our people can consume for many generations.

And our country is so rich in gold, silver, copper, lead, zinc, black lead, molybdenum, magnesite and other valuable metals and ores that the world might well be envious. Moreover, quantities of limestone can be found everywhere.

We have rich power resources, particularly hydroelectric power. In the northern region including the Kaema Plateau which is called the roof of the country there are hydro-power resources enough to produce several million kw of electricity. If we turn the flow of water to the East Sea from the Kaema and Pujon Plateaus, we can find many places suitable for building power stations, thanks to its great falls. In fact the Hochon-gang, Changjin-gang and Pujon-gang Power Stations are situated there, and the Supung Power Station with a generating capacity of 700,000 kw, the biggest in the East, also relies on the northern hydro-power resources. If we make better use of these resources, we would turn out millions more kw of electricity. This will make our country rich in electricity.

Our country produces the most nutritious rice in the world.

In the south there are the Mangyong Plain of Kimje, the Ryongnam and Kyonggi Plains where millions of *sok* of good-quality rice are produced every year and in the north are the Yonbaek, Namuri and Pura Plains. Over 15 million *sok* of rice are annually turned out in more than one million *chongbo* of paddyfields. If we establish a people's state some day and reclaim the tideland along the west coast, we would obtain hundreds of thousands of *chongbo* of fertile lands to produce several million *sok* of rice. Our hills are suitable for fruit growing. So Korea is famous for all sorts of fruits—the apples of Hwangju, Taegu, Anbyon and Pukchong; the oranges and persimmons of the south coast; the pears of Haeju and Tokwon; and the sweet chestnuts of Pyongyang and Chungsan.

Our country is surrounded by the sea on three sides and therefore abounds in marine resources. Adjoining one of the world's three major fishing grounds, the East Sea has various kinds of fish, and yields an abundant catch. In spring shoals of mackerel and anchovy come up from the south while shoals of herring come from the north. In summer sardines come up just off our coast and in winter *myongtae*, Korea's special product, come in swarms. Once these cruising fish are netted, the catch could reach millions of tons. The East Sea is rich in tasty fishes such as trout and yellowtail, and the South Sea and the West Sea also have plentiful marine resources.

The natural resources of our country are really abundant. But our people do not enjoy the benefits of these rich resources. Today the Japanese imperialists, in an attempt to secure the huge military supplies needed for the aggressive war against China and for the Pacific War, annually plunder Korea of 8,000 million kwh of electricity, over three million tons of iron ore, over five million tons of coal, and over 800,000 tons of cement. They ship to Japan more than ten million *sok* of rice, or over two-thirds of total annual output, over 100,000 head of cattle and the seafoods produced in the East, West and South Seas. Their piratic plunder has rapidly exhausted the natural resources of our country. So that these rich resources can truly serve the people's welfare, we must defeat the Japanese imperialists and establish a people's state owned by the workers and peasants. If we establish a people's state and then develop power, coal, metal and chemical industries and agriculture and fisheries, using our abundant resources, our country would become wealthy, powerful and civilized, with advanced industries, and our people would live on rice and meat, a dream cherished by them for thousands of years. By then as many as a hundred million population, not just the present 23 million, will be well-off.

Our country is not only abundant in natural resources, but in beautiful natural scenery. Everywhere we can see hills and mountains and clear rivers, presenting a picturesque view. Beautiful mountain ranges—the sky-kissing Mt. Paekdu-san in the north, then Mt. Kumgang-san and Mt. Taebaek-san and Mt. Halla-san in Cheju-do Island! Vast plains stretch endlessly, drained by the rivers of Amnok-gang, Tuman-gang, Taedong-gang, Han-gang, Rakdong-gang, Kum-gang and many others that wind their way to the east, the west and the south! And the wonderful landscape along thousands of miles of coastal lines! Korea is, indeed, a beautiful land of 3,000 *ri*. Moreover, there are many hot springs including those in Chuul and Yangdok, and spas are found in Sambang, Kangso and all the other parts of the country.

Our country will become a happy land if the beautiful mountains, crystal waters and picturesque scenery all serve the people to promote their health and recreation! We must liberate our country as soon as possible, build rest centers for the working people in scenic spots, and erect sanatoria where there is clear water and fresh air to promote the health of our people.

There are many countries on the globe, but those as beautiful and good to live in as our homeland are rare. A country with picturesque mountains and rivers, its fertile land producing various cereals and fruits and its underground deposits of gold, silver and other treasures, the country where an intelligent, gallant and civilized people are living—what a proud and precious homeland it is!

Today, however, our people are leading the worst life in the world and our brilliant national culture with its 5,000 years of traditions is losing its color. They have no right to eat at will the rice produced by themselves, nor the freedom to travel about their own territory. Numerous compatriots, brothers and sisters are on the brink of starvation. Unless we defeat the enemy, Japanese imperialism, and establish a people's state whose power belongs to workers and peasants, a beautiful land of Korea would not bring us joy, nor would gold, silver and other valuables, even if they were boundless, make our people well-off.

We Communists, the revolutionaries of Korea, must drive out the Japanese imperialists and achieve the age-long dream of national liberation, thus building on our territory of 3,000 *ri* a paradise of communism which the world might well envy. For the realization of this historical cause we have been fighting indefatigably for 10-odd years, and we will continue to fight in the future, too.

2. On Some Pressing Tasks

Today, in World War II, the Japanese imperialists find themselves in a tight corner and are becoming more desperate as their days are numbered.

Their oppression and plunder of the Korean people have reached their zenith since the Pacific War. They have over three divisions of their army permanently stationed in Korea, while largely extending the machinery of fascist repression including police and gendarmes. The enemy is engrossed in the bestial suppression of Koreans, arresting and imprisoning them without any reason under the name of "rebellious Koreans" whenever they act suspiciously.

The Japanese imperialist policemen are beating indiscriminately even the aged under the pretext of "unpatriotic persons" if they fail to learn by heart the "Oath of the Empire's Subjects" in Japanese, and severely punishing the children on the "charge" of speaking their mother tongue.

The Japanese imperialists are not only making a desperate effort to erase everything Korean but also plundering a huge amount of labor forces and materials under the signboard of the "successful conclusion of war". They are forcing a number of Korean youths into the battlefields as conscripts and "student soldiers", only to use them as cannon fodder. Besides, they have drafted almost all the able-bodied young and middle-aged Koreans for forced labor without pay in coal mines and construction sites for military establishments in Japan.

Those who escaped labor requisition have been forcibly dragged into the "national service brigade" and are worked cruelly and endlessly for nothing. Young pupils, too, have to undertake backbreaking labor under the pretext of "working service" all the year round.

In order to meet the increasing demands of the war, the Japanese imperialists are intensifying their economic plunder more than ever before, thus depriving the Koreans of even brass vessels, spoons and chopsticks.

Greatly inspired by the military and political activities of our People's Revolutionary Army, the Korean people are intensifying the anti-Japanese struggle under difficult circumstances seeing that the enemy's fascist suppression has reached its climax. The workers continue to go on with various forms of struggle including strikes, sabotage and mass escape at the factories, the important construction sites, ports and munitions plants in Seoul, Pyongyang, Chongjin, Hungnam, Pusan and other principal industrial cities. The peasants are unyieldingly fighting against the forced delivery of produce, murderous war burdens and coercive mobilization. The ideological movements and school strikes by teachers and students are frequent. The young and middle-aged people combat military service, drafting and forced labor. Particularly, in response to the anti-Japanese armed struggle, the masses show an ever-increasing trend towards hand-to-hand fighting with weapons, and many youths and students are trying to get in touch with the Korean People's Revolutionary Army.

In defiance of the tight cordon of the Japanese imperialists posted along the border line with the permanent marshalling of their armed forces hundreds of thousands strong, detachments of the Korean People's Revolutionary Army have marched deep into the homeland and attained great victories by their smart action. The main unit is now making successful political and military preparations for the great event of national liberation.

Although the Japanese imperialists are desperate in their attempt to escape their doom, the internal and external situations are changing decidedly in favor of the revolution.

However, no matter how mature the revolutionary situation at home and abroad may be, a decisive victory in the revolution cannot be won unless the Korean Communists, the leading force of the Korean revolution, act as the host to organize and mobilize the masses successfully.

We must put all our energies and talents into the struggle

to hasten the great event of national liberation as soon as possible.

In order to meet this great event with full preparation, we must further strengthen the military and political activities of the Korean People's Revolutionary Army to reinforce our own revolutionary forces and thus get the whole nation ready for the general mobilization for the final battle with the Japanese imperialists.

Firstly, for this purpose, we must step up the anti-Japanese national united front movement on a nationwide scale and firmly unite all patriotic forces of the country, thus, laying a solid mass basis for fighting it out with the burglar, Japanese imperialism.

The anti-Japanese national united front movement in our country has made a rapid advance since the founding of the Association for the Restoration of the Fatherland in May, 1936.

The lower organizations of the association have become widespread in the areas along the rivers of Amnok-gang and Tuman-gang and its networks spread deep into the homeland, uniting the people from all walks of life around this united front.

Since 1939 the united front has branched out over the northeast part of Mt. Paekdu-san and many other places of the homeland, despite the harsh suppression of the Japanese imperialists.

However, all the anti-Japanese patriotic forces throughout the country are not yet fully involved in the anti-Japanese national united front. If we fail to firmly organize and unite all forces opposing Japanese imperialism, we cannot have a solid mass base for a decisive battle with the enemy, which will break out at home in the near future. Therefore, we must expand and strengthen the united front organizations all over the country, and organize and rally all forces that can join hands with us. This is a key factor in deciding the fate of our last battle. We must form the lower organizations of the front in various places by sending many more competent political workers to the homeland and unite all the anti-Japanese forces—youths and students, intellectuals, conscientious national capitalists and patriotic men of religion, with workers and peasants as their core. This organizational and political work must be done energetically.

The objective situation in the homeland is now un-precedentedly favorable for strengthening and developing the anti-Japanese national united front. The last-ditch suppression and plunder by the Japanese imperialists have placed all the Koreans in a dreadful predicament, irrespective of their political views, property, knowledge and religious beliefs. Workers are either drafted or forced to hard toil at munitions factories, equal to a life behind bars. They have to slave endlessly, eating only 100 grams of Manchurian bean dregs for each meal.

It is needless to mention their low wages and the inadequate labor protection.

The peasants are in a much worse plight. The crop has been sharply decreased because they till devastated lands without the young men. Still worse, most of their harvests are plundered by the Japanese imperialists, the landlords and officials, with the result that the peasants find it very difficult to make a living.

Curtailed statistics issued by the Japanese imperialists show that more than 50 per cent of peasant households have run out of provisions in spring dearth. In fact, all of the peasants live on arrowroots unearthed from under the snow in winter and grassroots in spring. What is more, the enemies bleed the poor countryside of Korea dry by imposing upon the peasants all sorts of war burdens such as the "national defence donation", the "arms contribution" and the "lottery ticket".

The students and intellectuals are also in the worst state of misery. The war has forced the closure of schools. All the university and college students, whose number could be counted on our fingers, have been conscripted under the name of "student soldiers" and the secondary schools have been turned into military training camps. Even the pupils of primary schools have to do military training and the days spent for the forced labor are more than the actual school days.

The situation of workers, peasants and all other sectors of the Korean people today is at its lowest ebb. Therefore, every Korean bitterly laments over the state of this world by saying "When will it come to an end?" and thirsts for the day when the Korean People's Revolutionary Army will defeat the Japanese imperialists and liberate our nation.

Under these circumstances, if we actively promote the anti-Japanese national united front movement, the broad masses of all strata except a handful of Japanese fellow-travellers and traitors to the nation, would vie with each other in joining it. So today, when the enemy's repression and murder is at its peak and a tight cordon is placed around us, we must acquire a proficient method of political work and underground activities and make our energetic endeavors to organize and mobilize successfully the masses for the final battle.

Secondly, we must build revolutionary bases as strong, organizational centers in the homeland. The main units of the Korean People's Revolutionary Army must have strong bases from which they may fight a last battle with the thieving Japanese imperialists. Without such bases we can neither rapidly reinforce the ranks of the Korean People's Revolutionary Army with the youths at home, nor train them in a short period, nor deal a decisive blow to the enemy.

The building of revolutionary bases in the home country can be fully realized when the prevailing situation and the balance of forces between friend and foe are taken into consideration. As days go by, the Japanese imperialists will be further isolated and their forces dispersed, finding themselves very vulnerable in our homeland. Then we will be able to set up the revolutionary bases deep in the mountains in all parts of the country and, relying on them, expand and reinforce the armed ranks, and lay the mass foundation.

The mass foundation for building the revolutionary bases is very good. We have already established the underground revolutionary organizations in the homeland. A number of young people have evaded the forced labor and conscription by the Japanese imperialists and hidden themselves in the mountains. And the youths in different areas have formed secret organizations, have prepared weapons, and are ready to join the revolutionary army the moment it advances. Some of them have already got in touch with the Korean People's Revolutionary Army and others, to this end, are coming to our units, breaking through the death line. Therefore, if we set up the revolutionary bases in the ranges of Rangnim and Taebaek and other deep mountains in the country and call for the Korean youths, many would flock together from all quarters. If we rapidly reinforce our armed ranks with the rallied youths and train them, with those who have been tested and brought up through the anti-Japanese armed struggle over ten years as their core, and wage a decisive battle against the Japanese imperialists, we would certainly drive them out of our land and achieve the cause of national liberation by our own efforts.

Our main units should get ready for an advance into the homeland promptly if the situation arises. Then they should occupy the mountains of various regions in North and South Hamgyong Provinces, North and South Pyongan Provinces, Kangwon Province and Hwanghae Province. Establishing contacts with the local leadership cadres we have already trained, we should enroll many patriotic youths including those who have escaped conscription and forced labor and are wandering about in the mountains in quest of our units, and we should arm and train them in preparation for an impending decisive battle.

To this end, we should form the main units beforehand according to the regions, organize the reserve units and prepare necessary weapons.

We have ample opportunity to arm the revolutionary people at home, in case of emergency. There is a considerable stock of arms seized from the enemy in the past period and we have every possibility of capturing his weapons and arming many more people when the great event takes place. Therefore, it is quite possible to arm our rapidly increasing ranks, as over ten years of our combat experience shows.

Meanwhile, we should see to it that some of our units set up new guerrilla bases in east and south Manchuria and further escalate the armed struggle so as to hold in check the Kwantung Army of Japan and assist the main units that may operate in the homeland.

We have already trained our own leading cadres to liberate the country. We have not only the commanding officers with combat skills and rich experiences in military and political activities obtained during the fierce battles and in different circumstances for ten-odd years, but we have also the political workers possessed with the excellent art of leadership and revolutionary work method whereby they are united as one with the people, to organize and lead them.

These revolutionary leading cadres are, indeed, a priceless treasure of the Korean revolution. If we form the whole nation into a combat unit with them as a framework in time of need and launch a decisive battle against the Japanese imperialists, we shall be able to defeat these burglars.

Thirdly, the entire force of commanding officers and soldiers of the Korean People's Revolutionary Army should have everything in full readiness politically and militarily in order to meet the great event of national liberation.

Victory in the revolutionary struggle depends largely on the political and ideological preparedness of the participants and mainly on the political and theoretical level and the art of leadership of the commanding officers who organize and lead the struggle. However, even though the situation is favorable and the conditions are mature, these commanding officers will never lead the masses to victory without correct strategy and tactics and scientific leadership based on the accurate judgment on the balance of forces between friend and foe. Therefore, in order to meet the great event in readiness, it is most important for us, the commanders of the revolution, to firmly arm ourselves with Marxist-Leninist revolutionary theory and possess correct strategy and tactics and the refined art of leadership. This is a pressing issue that arises before us not only to win a decisive battle for national liberation but also to build a new country after defeating the Japanese imperialists and thus liberating the homeland.

Our task does not come to the end with national liberation. We should build a people's state in our liberated homeland and make it rich, mighty and independent. If we are ignorant of the revolutionary theories and the practical problems of state building, we will never carry out this honorable task successfully. So, the members of the Korean People's Revolutionary Army should study more than ever before to raise their political and theoretical level.

All the commanding officers and soldiers should, first of all, study more profoundly the strategic and tactical lines of the Korean revolution and be well informed about Korea including her history and geography.

Also, they should raise their military technique to a higher level.

All of them are national treasures, who have gained rich fighting experiences in the fierce flames of guerrilla warfare for more than ten years. But the guerrilla warfare alone will not win the coming decisive battle against the thieving Japanese imperialists. We will have to make a showdown with the strong Japanese army equipped with modern military techniques. Accordingly, if we fail in the application of various modern tactics—offensive, landing and air-borne operations—we cannot expect a successful battle with the aggressive troops of Japanese imperialism. Therefore, we must combine up-to-date military techniques with our wealthy experiences of guerrilla warfare, and modern tactics with the swift and peerless guerrilla tactics, and then annihilate the enemy, overwhelming him by strategy and tactics.

For this purpose, it is essential for us to study and master the offensive and defensive tactics of a regular army and intensify tactical training, practicing modern tactics such as amphibious and air-borne operations.

It is, of course, not an easy job to finish in a short span of time the political and theoretical studies and the military studies equivalent to the several years' courses of study in a regular college and military academy.

However, we are not mere students going to school but revolutionary fighters carrying on the bloody revolutionary struggle. Our study is not a private affair for improving merely our own qualifications. It is our duty as those responsible for national liberation and the future destiny of the country, a militant task assigned to us by the beloved fatherland and the revolution. Revolutionaries are the iron-willed people who can do anything if necessary for the revolution. We are the revolutionary fighters who have overcome all difficulties and ordeals and won one victory after another, by displaying the lofty revolutionary spirit of self-reliance in any adversity whenever the revolution demanded.

The present commanding officers must be prepared to command tens of thousands of officers and soldiers in the several higher ranks in the future and the present soldiers must be determined to become political or military cadres capable of commanding thousands of troops.

You comrades must study for the day when the dreams of the comrades-in-arms fallen in the sacred struggle for national liberation, so longing for the future homeland, the people's country and the future society of socialism and communism, would have come true. If we study and train in a revolutionary

and militant way with great stamina and mental attitude as
becoming revolutionaries, we can surely master any difficult
theories and techniques in a short span of time.

The dark clouded homeland and people are anxiously waiting
for us and the acute situation is urging us forward. Let us meet
the great event of national liberation in full readiness by
studying and training hard with all our efforts!

ON BUILDING THE PARTY, STATE AND ARMED FORCES IN THE LIBERATED HOMELAND

Speech Delivered to Military and Political Cadres, *August 20, 1945*

Comrades,

Thanks to the decisive role played by the Soviet army the aggressive army of the Japanese imperialists was routed and our people accomplished their historic cause of national liberation. This great victory is stained with the precious blood of hundreds of thousands of fine sons and daughters of Korea. They fought bravely in the arduous struggle against the Japanese imperialist aggressors to recover the country, bring freedom and happiness to the people and build a paradise of socialism and communism free from exploitation and oppression.

Our people have finally succeeded in putting an end to nearly half a century of Japanese imperialist colonial rule and won their freedom and liberation. They have a bright future with the possibility of building a new Korea, independent and prosperous.

With the accomplishment of the historic cause of national

liberation we are now faced with a fresh struggle. On the basis of our triumphant success we must continue to advance the Korean revolution and build a rich, powerful, sovereign and independent state through our own efforts.

What should we do to fulfill this great task?

We must first found a Marxist-Leninist party which will be able to steadily guide the Korean revolution to victory. At the same time, we must establish a people's government to solve the question of power, the fundamental question in the revolution, and build the people's armed forces which will defend our country, people and revolutionary gains. These three immediate tasks are a revolutionary duty, the fulfillment of which brooks not a moment's delay in our revolution's rapid advance through the liberated homeland.

We must push ahead dynamically with the building of a party, state and army relying on the invaluable revolutionary achievements and rich experiences gained in the course of the anti-Japanese armed struggle. Thus we will without doubt creditably fulfill the historic task of building a new Korea.

1

At the present stage the most important and historic task before the Korean Communists is that of founding the Korean Communist Party, which will be the General Staff of the Korean revolution and the vanguard detachment of the working class.

Without a revolutionary working-class party, the General Staff of revolution, we will not be able to rally together the working people and broad sectors of other democratic forces on the side of the revolution. Nor will we be able to successfully establish a people's government and build the people's armed forces by organizing and mobilizing the masses.

We have already laid the foundations of a unified Marxist-Leninist party in our country. At the height of the anti-Japanese armed struggle we fought hard battles to frustrate the conspiratorial maneuvers and subversive activities of internal and external enemies of all colors. Thus we overcame the fundamental weaknesses manifested in the early years of the Korean communist movement, and laid the firm organizational and ideological groundwork for the building of a party.

In the first place, we developed a new communist core of elements tried and tested in the actual course of the arduous revolutionary struggle, so as to lay solid foundations for building our Party now.

In the early 1930's when the destiny of our nation was at stake, our finest sons and daughters took up arms for the country's liberation and the people's honor, fighting indefatigably for 15 years. In this bloody struggle they became ardent revolutionaries, a dependable nucleus of Communists.

We Communists who grew up in the flames of the anti-Japanese armed struggle are the staunchest revolutionaries. We not only overcame completely sectarianism—the cancer of our 1920's communist movement—but also equipped ourselves with the progressive ideas and theories of Marxism-Leninism. We fought fiercely any adversity, unhesitatingly offering our youth and our lives to implement the correct line for the Korean revolution. That is why we have enjoyed the absolute support and love of the popular masses and in us lies their great hope. We communist core elements, tested and trained in the actual revolutionary struggle, enjoying the people's unreserved support and love, must now serve as the main force and organizational backbone in the construction of a Marxist-Leninist party in the liberated homeland.

During the anti-Japanese armed struggle the sectarian-flunkeys and the narrow-minded national chauvinists maneuvered feverishly to undermine the revolutionary ranks from within, taking advantage of the Japanese imperialists' conspiratorial machinations. We opportunely overcame their counterrevolutionary plots and subversive activities, and closely united and cemented the revolutionary ranks with one idea and will, making sure of the Marxist-Leninist purity of the communist ranks.

This provides the important guarantee for our future Party to promptly expose and crush any factional activities or subversive and sabotaging maneuvers on the part of the class enemies and all kinds of opportunists. It also guarantees that the Party will firmly defend the unity and cohesion of the ideology and will of its ranks, the life blood of a Marxist-Leninist party.

Moreover, we established a firm mass foundation for the

building of a party. To do this, during the anti-Japanese armed struggle we patiently conducted political work among workers, peasants and many other working people despite the Japanese imperialists' rigid surveillance and brutal suppression. This was effective in equipping them with the revolutionary ideas of the working class and training them through actual mass struggles against Japanese imperialism.

We can thus have total faith in the development of our Party, as the true defender and representative of the Korean people's interests. It will develop on a sound basis, having struck deep roots among the working masses, maintaining kindred ties with the people. In this way our Party is now being built not on sand but on the foundations of the organizational and ideological preparations made during the long and arduous anti-Japanese armed struggle.

However, we must never rest content on these assets. We should expect that our struggle to found, consolidate and develop the Party in the liberated homeland will face no less difficult and complicated problems than those we previously had to solve.

The vast majority of our workers are not fully prepared, either organizationally or ideologically, to be the leading class, because they have not undergone organizational training and ideological education by their revolutionary vanguards. In addition, because of nearly half a century of Japanese imperialist colonial rule, our workers, peasants and other strata of the people are still considerably infected with all sorts of obsolete ideas implanted by the Japanese imperialists. What is worse, the absurd calumnies and slanders and demagogy heaped up by the Japanese imperialists and their lackeys against the Korean Communists made many of our people distrust communism and prejudiced them against it. This will be a great obstacle in the way of our Party's efforts to take deep root in the majority of the working masses, win their support and trust and strengthen itself organizationally and ideologically in close contact with them.

We must also expect that the sectarians and renegades of the revolution who, thirsty for hegemony, were engrossed in their partisan strife, finally destroying the Korean revolution, will again disguise themselves as revolutionaries and try to deceive and toy with our honest working masses. What is more, the US imperialist armed forces of aggression will be stationed in the southern half of the country, south of the 38th parallel. Taking this into consideration, there will be many difficulties in our future activities.

It is in this context that we must build a party, establish a people's government and carry out an anti-imperialist, anti-feudal, democratic revolution and thus build a rich, powerful sovereign and independent state.

How then must we build a Marxist-Leninist party in our country?

We must first build the Korean Communist Party, a unified working-class party, as soon as possible. This will center around the core of Communists fostered and tempered in the harsh anti-Japanese armed struggle. It is true that some of the Communists who worked at home may be lacking in organizational training and may not yet be free from the ideological after-effects of sectarians. But we have a reliable core detachment prepared for the Korean revolution, the detachment born and bred in the long armed struggle. If we put all our trust in them and work with them broad-mindedly, they will take the correct path of revolution. Only in this way, will we be able to prevent a split in our communist ranks, defend the unity and cohesion of the revolutionary ranks, and closely rally the working class and broad sectors of other revolutionary forces around the Party.

The Korean Communist Party must in no way be an organization for only a few Communists. It must be a mass political party which is deeply rooted in the workers, peasantry and other working masses. It must become the experienced General Staff of revolution which organizes and leads the construction of a new Korea. Therefore, we must rapidly expand the Party ranks with those excellent people from among the workers, peasants and progressive intellectuals. They will fight devotedly in the interests of the working masses and will play a most positive, vanguard role in establishing a democratic, sovereign and independent state.

Furthermore, on the basis of the organizational principle of a Marxist-Leninist party we must ensure the identity of ideology, purpose and action of all our ranks. There must be no factions. We will arm all the Party members with Marxist-Leninist ideology and theory, establish voluntary iron discipline and hold fast to the principle of democratic centralism. In forming Party organizations particularly we must maintain high revolutionary vigilance against the subversive machinations and factional activities of political speculators and sectarians. We must promptly expose and smash them.

In order that our Party may fulfill its mission and role as the General Staff of the Korean revolution, we must firmly prepare, politically and ideologically, the cadres of the Party. They are its nucleus. They will be the most influential force in determining the destiny of the Korean revolution. Unless we organize and steadily expand the fine communist ranks of political cadres, we cannot raise the Party's leadership role. Nor can we repulse all our enemies within and without, or successfully build a rich, powerful, sovereign and independent state. Therefore, our urgent task is to found the Party and, at the same time, develop well-qualified Party cadres who are armed with Marxist-Leninist ideology and theory and are capable of defending and implementing the Party's lines and policies. For this purpose we must first set up a training center for Party cadres.

If our Party is to rally the broad masses around itself and establish its position of leadership, we must also work to form mass organizations for different trades and strata. Without maintaining kindred ties with broad masses, the Party cannot become a genuine revolutionary organization. Without their protection and support, it cannot play its part as the vanguard of the working class. Whether or not we win the masses over to the fold of the Party and the revolution is the vital question decisive to the destiny of the Party and the outcome of the revolution. Therefore, revolutionary organizational activity should always begin with mass organizational and political work.

Even in the darkest period of Japanese imperialist colonial rule we sowed the seeds of revolution among the people. We tended the seeds carefully despite all our difficulties and hardships and saw them bear fruit; we relied on the strength of the masses and led the revolution to victory. In other words, the leading nuclear forces of the Korean Communists were also born of the organized masses and developed with active popular support and protection.

Therefore, the formation of mass organizations, the transmission belts that link the Party with the masses, will be of great significance. They will aid in consolidating and developing the Party organizationally and ideologically, building up the revolutionary forces and enhancing its leadership role.

In instituting mass organizations, we must above all organize the youth, reserve forces of the Party and the hope of the revolution.

A vital problem, decisive in our country's destiny, will be rallying around the Party youth, who are masters of a new society and who can be depended upon to build a rich and strong country. That is why we quickly and dearly marked their role in the development of the revolutionary movement and paid deep attention to the youth work throughout our armed struggle. Both the preparation of the organizational nucleus for Party building and the founding and reinforcement of the Anti-Japanese Guerrilla Army were started with the activities of the Young Communist League. We trained many youths as devoted revolutionary fighters by intensifying the work of the Young Communist League and other youth organizations.

On the basis of this experience we must now unite the working youth and youth in other sectors such as youth in the rural areas and students into a democratic youth organization forming an organized political detachment; we must develop it into a vanguard which will fight heroically in the fore of the struggle to build a new country, into invincible revolutionary ranks with iron discipline.

To unite and organize the women, who account for one half of the entire membership of our society, is important in expanding and strengthening the revolutionary forces and accelerating the construction of a rich and powerful new state.

From our experience gained in women's activities during the anti-Japanese armed struggle, we know we must organize a women's union embracing the broad sections of working women in conformity with the specific conditions of our country and the demands of the new situation.

The revolutionary consciousness of our women is very high, as they were subjects of multiple maltreatment and repression under the barbarous colonial rule of Japanese imperialism and the shackles of feudalism. During the anti-Japanese armed struggle, in particular, the fine working women of Korea fought as bravely as men for the country's liberation and the people's honor, and for their social emancipation and freedom. The women revolutionaries who were firmly equipped with the communist world outlook and matured in hard ordeals took up arms and fought heroically, negotiating rugged snow-covered mountains. Even the forests of bayonets behind enemy lines, the cruel tortures or the gallows did not daunt them. They held fast to their revolutionary principles and defended the honor of the Communists.

We must carry forward this brilliant tradition of our resourceful and brave women fighters, so that all our women will play an important role in establishing a new country.

In building mass organizations we must also push ahead with the formation of trade unions. The role of the working class is very important in building a new Korea. It must always take the lead both in defending the revolutionary gains against the subversive and sabotaging maneuvers of all enemies within and without, and in constructing a prosperous, powerful, sovereign and independent state. It should guide the masses by setting a practical example. To do this we must unite the workers into trade unions as soon as possible, and give them organizational and ideological training, enabling the working class to fulfill its historic mission with honor in building a new democratic Korea.

To rally and organize the peasants, who account for more then 80 per cent of our population, and rouse them to the revolutionary struggle is one of the most important tasks now before our Communists.

Owing to the Japanese imperialists' predatory colonial policy in our countryside, and their obscurantist policy towards our nation, our peasants lived a subhuman life, far behind modern civilization.

The sagacious Korean people have a brilliant civilization of their own over five thousand years old; they should develop it and join the advanced countries of the world in all spheres of politics, economy and culture as soon as possible. Before this can happen we must completely emancipate the peasants, who form the major part of our population, but who are the most backward, from the ideological remnants of Japanese imperialism and feudal customs. It is vital that we heighten their class awareness and educate them in patriotism and collectivism, so that they will be the main force in the construction of a new homeland, with the working class. To do this we must form a peasants' union and firmly unite all of them within it.

2

The fundamental question in the revolution is that of power. We Communists, true patriots of Korea, and the revolutionary people organized and waged the protracted anti-Japanese armed struggle to destroy Japanese imperialism, establish a genuine people's government in the liberated homeland and build a prosperous new Korea. In the days of fierce and bloody battle we fought all hardships, without fear of death, in order to establish the government which would bring freedom and happiness to the people in the liberated country.

Our desire to build a rich, powerful, sovereign and independent state which would be governed by the people came true at last when we accomplished our sacred task of national liberation.

So, what kind of government should we establish in the liberated homeland?

Because of the barbarous colonial rule of Japanese imperialism the development of capitalism was hampered in our country. It remained a colonial semi-feudal society for a long time. Because of this, the Korean people are still confronted with the task of carrying out an anti-imperialist, anti-feudal, democratic revolution. As far as the question of power is concerned, in the light of the character and goal of our revolution at the present stage, we should establish a Democratic People's Republic which represents the interests of the entire Korean people.

The Democratic People's Republic must be founded by the Koreans themselves. The Korean people are capable of setting up their own government and we have rich experience of organizing popular power.

In the early days of the anti-Japanese armed struggle, we shattered the "Leftist" line of the sectarian-flunkeys on establishing a Soviet power and set up a people's revolutionary government, a true people's power, in the guerrilla bases or liberated areas. We stipulated the need for establishing a people's government in Article 1 of the Program of the Association for the Restoration of the Fatherland and fought for a long time to fulfill it. If we now use this experience and maintain and implement the line of establishing a people's government, we will succeed in setting up a people's government of a new type in the liberated country.

To build a Democratic People's Republic we must first organize, under the leadership of the working class, a democratic national united front. This will embrace various strata of the democratic forces such as the broad masses of peasants, intellectuals and conscientious national capitalists. On this basis, we will establish a people's government. Ours is a united front to build a Democratic People's Republic, so it must include the patriotic, democratic forces of all spheres and levels — workers and peasants who are the real masters of the country, working intellectuals, urban petty bourgeoisie, and conscientious national capitalists — who want to construct a democratic independent state, and we must see to it that no reactionary forces such as pro-Japanese elements and traitors to the nation infiltrate this front.

Furthermore, we must build a people's government around a selected core of fine patriots who will work devotedly for the fatherland and people.

We will ensure that our people's government, under the leadership of the working-class party, will rally around itself as closely as possible the workers, peasants and all other patriotic, democratic forces affiliated with the democratic national united front. It should isolate all the counterrevolutionary forces such as the pro-Japanese elements, traitors to the nation, reactionary landlords and comprador capitalists and serve as a powerful weapon in the class struggle against them.

In establishing a government, we Communists should neither take a passive stand nor act in a conservative way. In forming a democratic national united front or establishing a people's government, the Communists must always take the initiative and perform an active leadership role, as front-rankers and organizers leading various sectors of the popular masses. We cannot neglect even in the slightest the work of establishing power in our homeland, liberated at the cost of the precious blood of our revolutionary comrades-in-arms. Neglect would amount to betraying the wishes of the dead comrades and the long-cherished national aspiration of the Korean people. Therefore, we must do everything in our power to establish a people's government, as early as possible in our land of 3,000 *ri* where darkness prevailed for nearly half a century. This government will be a banner of freedom and liberation for our people and will open up the road ahead to the prosperity of the fatherland and the well-being of future generations.

The struggle for the establishment of power is a class struggle, a serious question of who will conquer whom.

We must remember that some will take advantage of the complicated situation created in the liberated homeland. The sectarians who destroyed the revolution disguised as Communists, the nationalists who degenerated into the servants of Japanese imperialism and even the pro-Japanese agents will make frantic efforts to seize power and satisfy their brazen political ambitions disguising themselves as patriots. Therefore, we must keep sharpest revolutionary vigilance and expose and smash every attempt by the enemy to conspire and subvert.

What then is the program of action for the people's government at the present stage? It is as follows:

1. To form a democratic national united front embracing all the patriotic, democratic forces of our country such as the workers, peasants, progressive intellectuals, conscientious national capitalists and conscientious men of religion and, on this basis, to establish a Democratic People's Republic.

2. To ensure the freedom of speech, the press, assembly, association and religious belief and guarantee citizens over seventeen years of age and of both sexes the rights to vote and to be elected.

3. To confiscate and nationalize all the factories, enterprises, railways, banks, ships, farms, irrigation facilities and all the properties owned by the Japanese imperialists, pro-Japanese Koreans and traitors to the nation.

4. To confiscate the land of the Japanese nationals and reactionary pro-Japanese Korean landlords and distribute it free of charge to the landless or near-landless peasants.

5. To completely liquidate the remnants of Japanese imperialism and all the elements left over by it.

6. To introduce an eight-hour day and a minimum wage system to ensure the workers' living and provide the unemployed

with jobs.

7. To make sure that men in both the cultural and technical spheres are well treated in public life and improve their living conditions.

8. To revitalize the time-honored, brilliant national culture of the Korean people, develop our spoken and written language and gradually introduce a system of compulsory education.

9. To enforce progressive income tax system based upon the incomes and living standards of the people.

10. To abolish the financial agencies of Japanese imperialism and cancel all its usuries and credits.

11. To establish sexual equality in all spheres of political, economic and cultural life and pay equal wages for equal work.

12. To prohibit infringement upon human rights and any type of inhumane punishment.

13. To promote friendship with peoples and states that have dealings with the liberated Korean people and our independent country on an equal footing.

3

For our country to become a fully independent sovereign state we must found our own powerful national army capable of defending the country and people and safeguarding the advances made in the revolution.

A country without its own national army can hardly be called a fully independent sovereign state. We did not use to have a powerful national army of our own. This was one of the main reasons why our country was occupied by the Japanese imperialist aggressors. In the past the feudal rulers of the Li dynasty kept some armed forces merely to repress the people, but they were powerless and insignificant. With these forces it was impossible to repel the Japanese imperialist regular army of aggression equipped as it was with modern weapons.

If we do not found a powerful revolutionary army at the same time as establishing a people's government in the liberated homeland, we will not be able to safeguard the revolutionary gains won at the cost of our blood against the armed invasion of foreign imperialists. We will again suffer the bitter experiences of a ruined nation.

At present our country is in an extremely complex situation. Though the Japanese imperialists were defeated, it is reported that the armed forces of US imperialism are to occupy Korea south of the 38th parallel. Of course the US imperialists formally sided with the Allies in fighting against the Japanese, German and Italian fascists in World War II and directly participated in the war against Japan.

But we know well how the United States came into being and has expanded. US imperialism started stretching its tentacles of aggression to our country toward the end of the 19th century. In 1905 it helped the Japanese imperialists to occupy Korea through the conclusion of a secret agreement between Katsura and Taft.

The aggressive army of US imperialism which has long been watching for a chance to invade our country is going to be stationed in the southern half of Korea. This political situation demands us to sharpen our revolutionary vigilance. It also poses as a most urgent task the founding of our own powerful national army to defend the country and people against foreign imperialist aggressors.

We must build a revolutionary regular army through our own efforts whatever the obstacles.

We have solid assets for building a revolutionary regular army. In the gloomiest days of Japanese imperialist colonial rule the Korean Communists organized the Korean People's Revolutionary Army, the first revolutionary people's armed force in our country, with advanced workers, peasants and patriotic youth. The members of the People's Revolutionary Army united as one man and fought bravely for the liberation of the homeland and the honor of the nation. Through the trying ordeals of the 15-year-long anti-Japanese armed struggle for national independence and social emancipation, the Korean People's Revolutionary Army matured to become an army of invincible iron ranks, an army of cadres prepared politically and militarily. This means that firm foundations have already been laid for us, so that we can build revolutionary regular armed forces, without any delay.

We must form a revolutionary army with the sons and daughters of the workers, peasants and other working people, around the revolutionary fighters experienced in the trials of the anti-Japanese armed struggle. In building these new

armed forces we must instill in our soldiers a fervent love for
their country and people, a burning hatred for the enemy,
revolutionary spirit to overcome any hardships and to stand
on their own feet. They must also learn the traditions of unity
between men and officers and between the army and people,
revolutionary comradeship, the popular style of work, voluntary military discipline and a revolutionary way of life. All
these were characteristics of the personnel of the People's
Revolutionary Army during the anti-Japanese armed struggle.

The foundation of revolutionary armed forces is a very important problem decisive in the destinies of the state and people. We who are the cadres forming the leading core must participate directly in this work and take the initiative in it. We
must do all we can to build as soon as possible in the liberated
homeland a revolutionary regular army, invincible people's
armed forces thoroughly equipped with Marxist-Leninist
ideology.

* * *

Comrades,

It depends largely on our role as the leading core of Communists whether or not the three major tasks—those of
building the Party, state and armed forces—in the liberated
country are successfully carried out.

In order to satisfactorily fulfill these tasks we must first
educate the workers and peasants and all other sectors of the
broad patriotic forces and unite them firmly on the side of the
revolution; and we must actively organize and mobilize the
masses of the people, whose political enthusiasm has increased
with the joy of liberation, in our efforts to build the nation. Only on the basis of this work and with the active support and
participation of the broad masses of the people will it be possible to accomplish these three major tasks.

True, our struggle to fulfill these tasks will encounter numerous difficulties and obstacles which we can hardly foresee, and
we will have to tackle many complex problems. But we Communists do not fear difficulty; we are revolutionary optimists
who believe in final victory under any adversity. We have the
revolutionary trait of carrying through our tasks to the end
however difficult they may be. In the days of the harsh anti-

Japanese armed struggle we fought for victory solely for the independence of the country and the liberation of the people, and we were undaunted by hardship and death, sleeping in the open air. If we work with the same indomitable spirit, we will be able to carry out successfully any difficult task.

We Communists do not look to revolution for high rank, individual fame and career or wealth and pomp. We are fighting for the sovereignty and independence of the country and the freedom and happiness of the people. We are fighting for socialism and communism. Whatever work we may do and wherever we may do it, the question of rank or status must be irrelevant to us. We must conscientiously fulfill our assignments, regarding them as honorable. We must single-heartedly dedicate all our energy and talents to the interests of the country and people, to the interests of the revolution.

We must work, always believing in and relying on the strength of the masses at any time and at any place. To do this we must go truly among the people and teach them and actively endeavor to learn from them. We will have to grasp and satisfy their demands and desires without hesitation and share life and death, sweets and bitters with them, thus winning their support and trust.

We have much more to learn in order to build the Party, government and people's armed forces. We cannot succeed in these tasks with revolutionary zeal alone. We must have a thorough preparation politically, theoretically and practically. To this end, we must patiently study the advanced ideology and theory of Marxism-Leninism, make a deep study of the experiences of the advanced state, the Soviet Union, while at the same time, accumulating one experience after another in the course of our actual work.

True, it cannot be said that we are young when the experience we gained in our revolutionary activities is considered. But no matter what long experience we have in revolution, if we do not constantly prepare and train ourselves politically, we will become arrogant and indolent and fall behind the developing reality. We will thus be unable to play our part as revolutionary cadres and become stragglers in the revolution. Therefore, we must at every opportunity seek and remedy defects in the actual revolutionary work, strengthen comradely criticism and self-criticism, examining ourselves regularly. In this way we will constantly prepare and train ourselves politically.

Not only must we take the utmost care that we develop in the right direction but we must actively endeavor to prevent the emergence of careerists and bureaucrats among the cadres of new Korea who will be engaged in all spheres of Party and state activity.

Experience shows that careerists ultimately degenerate into factionalists.

We must also nip in the bud any negative elements such as arrogance, bureaucratism, subjectivism and liberalism. We must mercilessly combat all the leftovers of Japanese imperialism.

In this way we will found our Communist Party, the vanguard detachment of the working class, and develop it into a powerful Marxist-Leninist party as early as possible. We must steadily push forward, with all the power we have, the establishment of a people's government and the building of revolutionary regular armed forces.

CLOSING UP THE CONGRESS OF THE PROVINCIAL, CITY AND COUNTY PEOPLE'S COMMITTEES OF NORTH KOREA

Concluding Speech Delivered at a Congress of the Provincial, City and County People's Committees of North Korea, *February 20, 1947*

Delegates,

At this congress we have triumphantly accomplished another work which will shine forth forever in our history.

The present congress has clearly shown that all the delegates present here are true representatives of the people, qualified to stand at the head of the people, bearing the destiny of the nation on their shoulders.

The congress has vividly demonstrated that our people are firmly united around the people's committee, their own power organ, and that they are fully able to build an independent, sovereign state by their own hands.

The democratic reforms carried out last year and the historic victory in the democratic election of November 3 and then the resolutions adopted by the present congress have proved that our people earnestly desire a democratic life in all domains of politics, economy and culture and that they have sufficient ability to materialize it for themselves. Now no one can deny the ability of the Korean nation to build an independent and sovereign democratic state. If the reactionary clique of Syngman Rhee, Kim Song Su and the like in Seoul had not dusrupted the unity of our nation and if the entire people of North and South Korea had fought united as one in mind and purpose, we would have already established a unified government and achieved the complete independence and sovereignty of the nation after tearing down the 38th parallel.

The congress has brought us the profound realization that the unity of our people has been further consolidated and that their strength has grown remarkably, and it has convinced us that we can overcome all difficulties and obstacles lying in our way of building the country and achieve a new, greater victory.

Delegates,

We have done a really great work at this congress. We have sanctioned all our democratic laws in the name of the entire people at the congress. Thus, all our laws have taken on a perfectly democratic form and the democratic reforms carried out under these laws have been legally approved by the entire people. This is another severe blow at the reactionary clique that attempts to hinder the democratic construction by our people.

The reactionaries have propagated that all the laws including the Agrarian Reform Law were provisional because they were promulgated by the Provisional People's Committee. They have noised abroad that once a reactionary regime is set up, these laws will be repealed and that the democratic reforms effected under these laws will also be invalidated. Last year when the Agrarian Reform Law was proclaimed and the agrarian reform was carried out, the reactionary elements prattled: "Don't be overjoyed that you have got land," and "Don't be grieved that you have lost your land." By this it was meant that though people who received land were glad of it now, they would be deprived of the land in the future, and those who lost their land could take it back. But now this jargon-like wild story of the reactionary clique cannot fool anyone. Our laws are not provisional ones but are permanent laws of the people sanctioned by the entire people. We declare: "Those who have received land, rejoice for all time; the land belongs forever to the peasants who till it."

One of the most important matters decided upon at the

present congress is that a national economic plan has been adopted.

To build an independent democratic state, the basis of an independent economy of one's own nation should be built without fail, and to lay the basis of an independent economy, the national economy should be developed rapidly. Without the basis of an independent economy we can neither achieve independence, nor can we build a state or maintain our existence.

That we have entered upon the road of planned development of our national economy on the basis of the successes achieved in the democratic reforms in one year after liberation, means that we have taken the first step in the great work of laying the economic basis for the building of an independent and sovereign state, and it acquires a tremendous historic importance. We should exert every effort for the successful carrying out of the 1947 Plan for Development of the National Economy.

At the present congress we have created the People's Assembly, the supreme organ of state power of our people. This is a truly popular form of power required by our people. At the People's Assembly the deputies elected directly by the people, representing their will, institute all laws which safeguard the interests of the people, and organize the People's Committee, the power organ of the people capable of executing these laws faithfully. After we close this congress today, the deputies to the People's Assembly will sit together and reorganize the Provisional People's Committee of North Korea into the People's Committee of North Korea. The People's Committee of North Korea will be the legally established central power organ in north Korea.

In this way our people will fight more vigorously to further consolidate the central power organ of north Korea and win at the earliest possible date the complete independence and sovereignty of our nation under the guidance of the People's Committee of North Korea. Our people will certainly fulfill the 1947 Plan for Development of the National Economy and further consolidate the material basis for a happy life of the people and the building of an independent, sovereign state. The People's Committee of North Korea will guarantee democratic liberties and rights more securely for the people and will wage an unremitting struggle to build a unified independent and sovereign state and to elevate the international position of our country.

With the successes of last year and the victory of the present congress, we have opened up the road to a yet greater victory in the future. Our nation and country will certainly achieve independence, prosperity and development. For our people have patriotic sentiments unsparingly to devote everything to the building of their state and a strong fighting spirit to break through any difficulties, and are firmly united around the people's power.

Also, we receive fraternal assistance from the great Soviet people. The Soviet people are giving us material and moral aid so that our nation can build an independent, sovereign state. We are convinced that the Soviet Union, the most advanced and democratic state, will render an active support to our people in their just struggle in future as well and will stand by our people for all time.

Delegates,

We held the election of November 3 last year with success to consolidate the provincial, city and county people's committees and have now successfully accomplished the work of the Congress of the Provincial, City and County People's Committees of North Korea to strengthen the People's Committee of North Korea, our central power organ, and to create the People's Assembly, the supreme organ of state power. This represents a historic victory of our people in their struggle to build an independent, sovereign state.

Now we have before us the immediate task of successfully conducting the election to the myon and ri (dong) people's committees which constitute the basis of our people's power organ. We should all take an active part in the election to the myon and ri (dong) people's committees and assure the complete triumph of the election. In this way we will legally consolidate the people's committees, the organs of genuine people's power, from the center down to the lowest terminal units. Victory belongs to us.

Long live the victorious Congress of the Provincial, City and County People's Committees of North Korea!

Long live the People's Assembly, the supreme organ of state power of north Korea!

Long live the People's Committee of North Korea!

Long live the establishment of a unified government of the Korean people!

Long live the independence and sovereignty of the Korean people!

WHAT SHOULD WE DO AND HOW SHOULD WE WORK THIS YEAR?

Speech Delivered at a Meeting of Activists of the Political Parties and Social Organizations in Kanggye County, *January 12, 1948*

I extend my warm congratulations to you for your enthusiastic participation in the struggle for carrying out the democratic reforms after liberation and, particularly, for your victorious fulfillment of last year's national economic plan, the first of its kind in the history of our country, and I present my whole-hearted respects to you for your firm determination to score ever greater victories in this year of 1948.

As all of you know, the achievements our people have scored in north Korea are really tremendous. We made a great success especially in economic construction in 1947. Last year we drew up a national economic plan for the first time in order to further consolidate the victories of the democratic reforms and lay the basis for an independent national economy of the country and successfully fulfilled it, and we are making a continued headway for newer victories.

In the short period of slightly over two years after liberation, our people have done what other countries had failed to do in scores of years. The victories of the democratic reforms and the brilliant successes our people have registered in building a new life in north Korea are widely known to the whole world and furnish an inspiring example to the peoples of many Eastern countries. We have thus demonstrated at home and abroad that the Korean nation is a nation who is quite capable of building a politically and economically independent, rich and strong country with a brilliant culture by its own efforts and of advancing proudly shoulder to shoulder with the peoples of all the advanced countries of the world.

This proves that the Korean nation was not dead but remained alive, did not forget its country nor abandoned its history even under the 36-year long tyrannical rule of Japanese imperialism. This also shows that our nation is entirely capable of attaining its independence and sovereignty and will never be overridden by any aggressor if it wages an active struggle with such fine national traits and patriotism.

As you know well, what a cruel rule the Japanese imperialists bore over Korea! They oppressed the Korean people at will and robbed them of everything as they pleased, tried to obliterate the history of our country and exterminate our culture and our language and, to top it all, went so far as to force the Korean people to change their surnames, desecrating our ancestors. And they deprived the Koreans of the opportunities for education and prevented them from learning science and technology. An ordinary nation would probably have perished forever in the face of such persecution and oppression.

The Korean people, however, did not give in; they carefully preserved the history of their country and their national sagacity, loved their culture and did not abandon their language. The Koreans tried hard to lose no opportunity to learn even a thing more and fought through all difficulties for the day of our national regeneration. That is why our people set about building a genuinely independent and democratic state in north Korea without the slightest confusion from the first days of liberation. We use our own language to creditably conduct radio broadcasting and publish newspapers, books and textbooks, and teach Korean history to the younger generation, and even run the institutions of higher learning on our own, training large numbers of native cadres.

As they were driven out of Korea, the Japanese imperialists declared cynically that without them Korea's industry and transport would all be paralyzed. But we soon started operating factories and set trains running. The 17-18 years old stokers who barely shoveled coals under the Japs in the days of Japanese imperialism, have now become engine drivers and are running express trains. Big factories and enterprises such as the Hungnam Fertilizer Factory, Nampo Smeltery, Hwanghae Iron Works, Songjin Steel Plant and Supung Hydroelectric Power Station have been rehabilitated and are in normal operation, and all of them fulfilled their plans brilliantly last year.

Needless to say, all this did not come as a gracious gift. These successes have been made possible entirely by the united strength of our liberated people, their lofty patriotic zeal, their indomitable perseverance in overcoming all difficulties, their ability of investigation and creative initiative.

The reactionaries mocked at our plan as an idle dream which would never be realized, and among us, too, there were some who were distrustful of the plan. But our people, displaying a high degree of patriotic zeal and creative activity, have creditably accomplished the things they once chose to. This is really something to boast about. This is the strongest answer and counterblow to the US imperialists including Hoover and their lackeys who prattled that the Korean people should be placed under an international trusteeship for 25 years because they were incapable of self-government. This has convinced us more deeply, and imbued us with boundless national pride, that the Korean nation is a nation of superb ability, that no aggressor can ever conquer our nation again and our nation is able not only to attain independence but also to build a rich and strong, advanced democratic Korea.

But the US imperialists calculate that they can enslave our nation again because the Korean nation had been a colonial slave fettered to Japanese imperialism for a long time in the past. We must clearly show them what an absurd delusion this is.

The Korean people of today are not the Korean people of the old, feudal era of Li dynasty. The Korean people are a people who waged a tireless, unyielding struggle against foreign aggressors even under Japanese imperialist despotism and, especially after liberation, have become masters of the country and have unshakable faith in the path they are to follow. Moreover, through the victorious democratic reforms and successful economic construction in north Korea, the Korean people have come to possess solid assets for winning the independence and sovereignty of the country and acquired the national sense of dignity that they can solve all their problems for themselves splendidly and a firm confidence in victory. There is no force on earth which can destroy such a nation.

Such national sense of dignity and power is highly precious for the liberation struggle of the people. A nation without it may be ruined, but a nation that has national pride and confidence in victory is invincible.

How is it that we suffered from Japanese imperialist aggression and failed to repulse it by ourselves? It is, first of all, that we lacked a national sense of dignity and power before and our people were weak in awakening and in united strength.

In a little more than two years following liberation, however, the Korean people were awakened and tempered, their strength grew incomparably and our national sense of dignity and power rose higher than ever before. The pride and self-respect of our nation which had been repressed and trampled down under the long Japanese imperialist colonial rule, began to revive and unfurled their wings and soared higher with each passing day in the struggle to create a new life after liberation. This is the most precious thing, which cannot be got for money nor can it be exchanged for any other things. This is a sure guarantee for our nation to grow stronger and our country to prosper and develop further in the future.

Our nation can never again be reduced to a humiliating status as before. Our nation has already got out of that status completely and is waging an indomitable struggle for the independence, sovereignty and prosperity of the country. We are powerful and confident enough to repulse any aggressors and safeguard the honor of the country by the united strength of the whole nation should they turn upon our Korea in an attempt to swallow it up again.

Today ours is a nation that is conscious of its ability and mission, a stout nation now which no force can bring to its knees and override. Particularly, the north Korean people have become masters of the country who handle everything by themselves according to their own decisions, the masters of a new, free and happy life. In north Korea the people have not only become masters of the major industries and the land but also are rapidly developing the economy of the country by managing them ably, and everyone is devoting all his talents and passions to the building of a rich and strong, advanced independent state.

But the situation in south Korea is totally different. The rulers of dependencies who even fail to act as masters of their own countries but work for foreigners have been brought into south Korea by the US imperialists, and are now clamoring that they are going to make our Korea "independent". They are none other than the so-called "UN Temporary Commission on Korea". What on earth are they going to do in Korea, those fellows who are unable to run the affairs of their own countries properly and held in bondage to others, while driving their own peoples into a wretched plight?

Today the Korean question can be solved only by the Koreans, and no one but the Korean people has the competence and right to solve it. It is much less possible for such a gang as the "UN Temporary Commission on Korea" to solve the Korean question. It is neither United States nor India or Syria, but only the Korean people themselves that can solve the Korean question. It is precisely the Korean people who should solve the Korean question by themselves, and it is only we who are fully capable of solving it.

Originally, the "UN Temporary Commission on Korea" did not come to Korea to solve the Korean question. It has come to Korea simply in the capacity of a minion of the US imperialists who want to colonize Korea. In other words, it has come to help rig up a separate south Korean government designed to further consolidate and perpetuate, in another form, the rule by the US government-general maintained by Hodge now in south Korea.

What is the difference between the Japanese imperialist governor-general and the present governor-general Hodge? The difference, if any, is only that the people's livelihood has become more difficult and suppression is more harsh than under the Japanese governor-general. Indeed, all sorts of evils have increased astoundingly. The number of prisons has increased, the patriots and democrats are persecuted more harshly and savagely than in the years under Japanese imperialism. Forcible deliveries of farm produce have been augmented; in the days of Japanese imperialism there were police, at most, to be present at the places of forcible deliveries of farm produce, but now even terrorists accompany the police to force the deliveries. More factories are closed, unemployment has increased, and the number of children denied schooling opportunities and of students expelled from schools has grown. Traitors to the nation and quislings have increased and so have the profiteers.

So, the people are shivering from fear, hunger and cold, and suffering from lack of rights and poverty. Not content with this, the US imperialists have even brought in the "UN Temporary Commission on Korea" with the help of the UN for the purpose of carrying out their colonial enslavement policy more rigorously because the military government alone is not strong enough to do that.

However, the south Korean people, not to speak of the people in north Korea, are not taken in by such a thing, and are filled with the resolve to fight against it to the very end. Only the handful of reactionary elements like Syngman Rhee, who are afraid of the judgment of the people, support and welcome the "UN Temporary Commission on Korea" under the shameless slogan against the withdrawal of foreign troops. This only calls forth the indignation of the entire Korean people.

The statement of General Shtikov, representative of the USSR, who suggested that the Soviet and US troops withdraw from Korea simultaneously to open up the way for the Korean nation to decide its destiny by itself, constitutes a just and reasonable proposal which indicates the shortest cut to the independence and sovereignty of the Korean nation today. And why is the reactionary clique dead set against it? The handful of reactionaries are opposed to the withdrawal of foreign troops so as to prolong their days by hanging on the US imperialists, because the moment the US army, their master and patron, pulls out, the game will be up for them. In the meantime, they welcome the "UN Temporary Commission on Korea", a tool of US imperialist aggression in Korea, to serve US imperialism as its lackeys by selling out south Korea at least for dollars and subordinating it to US imperialism for good.

But all the maneuvers of the US imperialists and the "UN

Temporary Commission on Korea'', their tool, all the plots of the domestic reactionaries will fall through in the end. For the Korean people, who have already demonstrated their national superiority and advance along the road of independence and sovereignty with firm confidence, are not fooled by such things but are waging a resolute struggle in a body against the enemy.

Today the liberated people of north Korea are enjoying a happy and worthy life, and our livelihood is becoming more affluent every day. But we cannot forget even for a moment the cruel reality that half of our land of 3000 *ri* is seized by the US imperialists and that our fellow countrymen and brothers, who are of the same ancestral blood as we are, groan under oppression and suffer from hunger. Under these circumstances it is natural that the north Korean people should feel deep sympathy for the bloody struggle of the south Korean brothers and extend them most enthusiastic encouragement.

We are confident that in the year now beginning, too, the south Korean people will valiantly fight to smash the aggressive machinations of US imperialism and achieve their long-cherished aspirations.

For the complete independence and sovereignty and reunification of the country, the north Korean people should further reinforce the democratic base and score greater successes in economic construction.

What, then, are the specific tasks that should be carried out in north Korea this year? I have already mentioned them in my New Year's message, but I should like to stress them again for you.

First of all, it is important to increase production further and raise the people's standard of living higher still. It is true that our national economy has been rehabilitated rapidly and the people's livelihood improved markedly till now. But we cannot, and must not, rest content with it on any account.

What we have done is but the start in the light of the boundless prosperity and development and the abundant, civilized life that are to be achieved in the future in our people's country where the people have taken power and hold the levers of control in the economy. As you all know, the democratic reforms have been brought to a victorious conclusion in north Korea, but this has only provided us with favorable conditions for the future development of our society into one better and nicer to live in. And a big success has been achieved in economic construction in 1947, but this, too, is no more than the first step in the development of the national economy and improvement of the people's life in our country. Some say, "Now that the 20-Point Platform has all been translated into reality in north Korea, it is unnecessary, isn't it?" This is an erroneous view. True, each article of the platform has been adopted as a law and is being materialized in actual life, but practices running counter to it have not yet been wiped out altogether. We should further consolidate and develop the successes achieved in the implementation of this platform and wage an unyielding struggle to carry it into effect on a nation-wide scale.

In a word, the victories we have already scored do not signify the completion of social reform and construction, though they are tremendous. They only mean that yet broader vistas have been opened up before us in democratic construction. We should continue to advance with full confidence towards a still brighter future along the road of unlimited development and further develop all our work in terms of quality.

For example, the agrarian reform has already been carried out triumphantly in north Korea. But this does not mean that the agricultural question has all been solved in our country. Our agriculture should be developed further still, and the problems arising in assuring it should be solved in good time. From now on we should improve the methods of farming, increase the number of draught oxen, improve and supply farm implements in larger quantities and undertake irrigation projects on a wider scale. At every opportunity that offers, I emphasize that irrigation projects should be pushed forward energetically so as not to let the rivers flow into the sea uselessly, but to draw their water into the paddyfields, and this is a really urgent task. Our country has rich water resources and an abundance of electric power, and we have also become able to manufacture motors by our own hands. Under these circumstances, if only we make the effort, we will be able to extensively carry out the work of converting dry fields into paddies yielding three times more harvest.

The same applies to the nationalization of industries. The

law was promulgated and the major industrial establishments monopolized by the Japanese imperialists have come into the hands of the people, but it does not mean the complete solution of the industrial questions. We should increase production rapidly by rehabilitating the dilapidated factories, building new ones and skillfully managing and operating our industries which have come into the people's possession. Only then will the building of a new life by our people be promoted further, our country built into a wealthy and powerful, independent and sovereign democratic state and the entire people lead a happier and more abundant life.

Today the life of the north Korean people is being improved remarkably, indeed. This is beyond all comparison either with the life of the Korean working people in the days of Japanese imperialism or with the miserable life of the south Korean people today. We cannot rest content with this, however. Our people who have become masters of the country can and should enjoy a more affluent and civilized life. It is our aim to liberate the people and make all of them enjoy a happy and comfortable life, and only when this is attained, it could be said that the revolution has triumphed completely.

And we will earn the support of the people only when we make them well-off. The people always support a government that guarantees freedom and happiness for them and practically sees to the improvement of their life. Only when our democracy secures welfare for the people in reality, will it be proved to be fundamentally different from the "democracy" in the capitalist countries and the entire Korean people will say, "Our democracy is really good!" and will be rallied closely under the banner of our democracy.

We should not talk about democracy only in words, but should embody genuine democracy in deeds. We may say that this is the very point which distinguishes us from the reactionaries. The reactionary clique in south Korea can give nothing to the people, but, on the contrary, they only rob them, while paying lip service to democracy very noisily.

What has the reactionary clique done in a little over two years since liberation during which time we have carried out great undertakings for the people and the country? What else have they done except that they have sold out the country for dollars and made the people tremble with fear, cold and hunger by suppressing, slaughtering and exploiting them? That is why the south Korean people, far from being hoodwinked by them, are more indignant and hate them, and are rising against them.

What we do, however, is quite contrary to what they do. We have brought freedom and happiness to the people not in words but in deeds, and are steadily improving their life. We are zealously carrying out practical work, and are speeding up construction and production. Practice is precisely the best method of publicity and the best politics with us. With us, the most valuable thing is practice, and it is precisely through practice that we will win the people over to our side and gain victory in the revolution.

This year, too, we should increase production, improve the people's livelihood markedly and further strengthen our democratic base through practical struggle.

Our greatest aim is to build the whole of Korea into a rich and strong, independent and sovereign democratic state. And to realize it, the economic basis should be further consolidated and the people's livelihood be stabilized and improved by rapidly developing the national economy in north Korea. The day when our country achieves complete independence and sovereignty can be hastened, only if the south Korean people are shown more clearly how nice life is in north Korea where democracy has triumphed and only if the might of the democratic base is strengthened decisively.

Then, along what lines should we rehabilitate and develop the national economy in order to consolidate the economic basis and improve the people's livelihood in a short space of time?

Some people lay stress exclusively on heavy industry and take up the wrong position that heavy-industrialism should be followed right away. It is important, of course, to rehabilitate and develop heavy industry. Only when heavy industry is developed can the foundations be built for an independent national industry and the material conditions be also created for improvement of the people's standard of living.

But the present conditions do not permit us to expand heavy industry in a big way at once or devote our efforts only to it. For the time being we should follow the course of turning out and supplying raw and other materials needed for development of the national economy by rehabilitating and readjusting the existing heavy industry plants. And we should build light industry, which has no foundation whatever, to keep an adequate balance with heavy industry, and energetically push ahead with the development of agriculture. Only by so doing can our people's life be stabilized and improved rapidly and the zeal and creative initiative of the masses of the people be raised higher in economic construction.

As is to be seen from this, it is wrong to neglect the rehabilitation of heavy industry and consolidation of the economic basis of the country, but it would also be wrong not to build light industry for the improvement of the people's life, placing stress on heavy industry alone.

To improve the people's living standard, production should be increased speedily as a whole, daily necessities turned out in large quantities and prices reduced systematically. The struggle for increased production should be intensified everywhere—in towns, farm villages, mines and fishing villages. Only when production is boosted and products of good quality are turned out in large quantities, can we use them to further expand production and improve the working people's life and export part of them to foreign countries to buy goods we badly need. In all branches, every factory and every working man should over-fulfill their production assignments and increase production further still.

First of all, economic plans should be worked out correctly. Without a correct plan nothing can be done properly, much less can the industries which have come into the people's ownership be developed. Each branch and each enterprise should draw up correct and feasible plans on the basis of carefully investigated and studied data.

A defect of the functionaries here is that they are weak in planning their work and do not know how to prepare the economic plans well. Planlessness is glaringly revealed in the work of the consumers' cooperative in particular. There are no small number of functionaries who know little of the actual conditions in their respective domain and are not versed in their work. Such being the case, they can neither work out a plan properly nor push ahead with their work in a long-sighted way.

In olden times, too, people said that a day's plan should be formed in the morning and a year's plan in the spring. The spring mentioned here means the beginning of the year, of course. Half a month has now passed since we rang in the New Year, and yet this year's plan has not been drawn up correctly. I think this is a serious matter. The plan for 1948 should be worked out correctly on the basis of carefully examining the lessons drawn from, and the merits and shortcomings of work revealed in, the carrying out of the plan for 1947, and even each person, not to speak of each institution and enterprise, should work regularly according to concrete plans.

The economic plans should be interrelated, and should be realistic plans based on a careful calculation of all conditions made from a national standpoint. At the same time, the plans should always be progressive and enterprising. A passive plan confined to maintaining the status quo is of no use to us, it hinders our onward movement.

Take Kanggye County for example. First of all, you have no end of timber resources here, and yet why do you not make a plan to increase the output of timber and use it to turn out larger quantities of various wood products? You may produce, say, vessels and furniture, or writing tables, desks, chairs and blackboards to be used in offices or schools. If you produce such things in large quantities and sell them at reasonable prices, it will be nice because the people's demands will be met; the gains of the enterprises will increase and the workers will get more incomes, and how nice this would be! Nevertheless, the County People's Committee does not give guidance to the state enterprises to make them turn out such products in large quantities nor does it encourage the individual entrepreneurs to do so. Such simple consumer goods may be produced either by the consumers' cooperatives or by individuals who may run a suitable form of enterprise by pooling efforts and funds. It is high time that the individual traders and entrepreneurs conducted trade or ran enterprises by honest means, instead of only trying to engage in speculations.

And why do you not make up a plan to further develop stockbreeding and sericulture in this nice area? You can raise as many hogs and sheep and silkworms as you please, to say nothing of cattle. If you do so, it will be nice because more draught animals will be available; it will be nice because a large quantity of highly nutritive non-staple food can be supplied; it will be nice because more raw materials for daily necessities including hide can be furnished; and it will be nice because plenty of raw materials for silk much needed for the people's life can be obtained. Why not do such a nice thing?

This year each farm household, too, should do farming and sidelines according to clear-cut plans as to what kinds of crops should be planted and how to plant them, what kinds and how much of grains be produced, how many domestic animals be raised and how to raise them, and how many more *pil* of cotton cloth be woven. Each village, too, should draw up detailed plans as to how much more land should be reclaimed into dry field, how the irrigation projects should be undertaken, when and how much fertilizer be procured through barter, how seeds be obtained through mutual help and how draught animals be utilized.

It is necessry for all the *ri, myon* and county people's committees, political parties, social organizations and other institutions to shape proper working plans and push ahead with all their work methodically. If all the institutions, enterprises, and individuals from bottom to top draw up correct plans in this manner and over-fulfill them by displaying a high degree of patriotic zeal and creative initiative, we will certainly achieve a fresh victory.

There is nothing impossible or unrealizable for us. If we work with full confidence and with energy in this way, the results will be still more remarkable. Let the reactionary clique make noise as they please. Some day stock will be taken of who has done what. Then, the world will be startled once again at the great achievements of our people and the serious crimes of the enemy.

The important task we have to carry out this year is to practice economy while increasing production. No matter how much we may increase production, it will be no use if we keep wasting on the other hand. Particularly, it is of great national importance to practice economy and lead a frugal life in the light of the situation in our country where everything is not yet sufficient. We should thoroughly establish the spirit of practicing economy and leading a frugal life everywhere, from the state institutions down to each family.

It is necessary not only to take good care of and protect state property and wage a resolute struggle against all needless ex-

penditures and wasteful practices, but also to eliminate wastage for useless purposes in private life. From now on, the institutions or organizations should refrain from having banquets
frequently, and an end should be put once and for all to the
practice of giving feasts on every possible pretext or committing excessive extravagances particularly on mournful or
joyous occasions in private homes.

You should also learn how to use state funds effectively. We
started construction not long ago, and it can be said that really
large-scale construction work will be undertaken from now.
Nevertheless, there are still not a few instances of squandering
money of the state and the people on useless things in many
places. A monument or monumental tower of one kind or
another is built with hundreds of thousands of *won*, and then a
carousing "ceremony" is held under the name of inaugural
ceremony or others. This sort of evil practice should be eliminated as soon as possible, and a system should be established
under which all funds are used effectively and economically in
the interests of the state and the people.

Some Koreans still have a habit of pretending to know what
they do not know and to have what they do not have, and this
is a big vice with them. Even homespun cotton clothes and
straw sandals are not bad in the present conditions. Yet, even
primary school children think they cannot go to school without
Western clothes and rubber shoes on. And there are many public houses everywhere and it is desirable to reduce them to a
degree.

We have very ample room for increasing production and improving the working people's livelihood at a faster pace by
practicing economy. We should use sparingly even a penny
and a small amount of materials and turn all that are saved to
the building of a rich and powerful country. This is our sacred
duty, and this is precisely the idea of national construction.
Only when the entire people are armed with this idea and enlist
all reserves and potentialities in the cause of national construction is it possible to further consolidate the democratic base of
north Korea and realize as soon as possible the complete independence and sovereignty and reunification on democratic
lines of the country, the long-cherished desire of our nation.

While carrying on economic construction successfully in
north Korea, we should fight to realize democracy such as in

north Korea on an all-Korea scale by giving an active encouragement to the south Korean people. Only by unfolding a heroic struggle in firm unity can the entire people in north and south Korea beat the US imperialists and the domestic reactionaries and win ultimate victory.

We are now engaged in a work which is of great significance in achieving this cause, and that is precisely the framing of a Provisional Constitution of Korea. All should rise to see to it that the Constitution, which reflects the new, democratic life attained by the north Korean people, be made the Constitution of the entire Korean people and that the building of an independent democratic country where the people are genuine masters be finally achieved.

Victory surely belongs to our people. Today we are provided with every condition for victory. We have the united democratic forces and the genuine people's power. We have a great national pride, burning patriotism and firm faith in victory. We have accumulated a wealth of experience in carrying out the democratic reforms and economic construction and have already trained no small number of cadres. Besides, we have the powerful support and selfless aid of the great Soviet Union. No one can bring such a people to their knees, and neither the US imperialists nor the "UN Temporary Commission on Korea", their tool, nor the domestic reactionaries will ever be able to block the way of the Korean people, no matter how desperately they may attempt to. The day will certainly come when the aggressors are driven out of Korea, the reactionary traitorous clique is brought to judgment before the people and Korea is reunified and attains independence and sovereignty.

Let us all unite our strength and march forward vigorously for a fresh victory!

THE POLITICAL PROGRAM OF THE GOVERNMENT OF THE DEMOCRATIC PEOPLE'S REPUBLIC OF KOREA (Excerpt)

Political Program Announced at the First Session of the Supreme People's Assembly of the Democratic People's Republic of Korea, *September 10, 1948*

Fourth, the Government of the Republic, with a view to building Korea into a rich, strong, independent and democratic state, will rid our economy of its colonial dependence, oppose the economic enslavement policy of the foreign imperialists, and build an independent national economy capable of steadily improving the well-being of the Korean people and assuring independence and prosperity for our country.

The Government will work out a unified national economic plan so as to make a rational use of all the resources of the country in the interests of the people and will actively develop the national economy and culture according to that plan.

For the successful carrying out of this task, the Government will take the following measures:

(1) The metallurgical industry, machine-building industry, chemical industry, shipbuilding industry, light industry, fishing industry, etc., will be actively developed in order to abolish the colonial distortion of industry, lay the basis of an

independent national economy and meet in full the country's needs for manufactured goods, and the railway, motor and shipping transport services will be developed to satisfactorily ensure transportation.

The Government of the Republic will see that the factories now in operation work to full capacity, rehabilitate all the factories not yet restored and build a number of new factories.

With the object of rapidly expanding the production of consumer goods for the people, the Government will actively develop the textile, leather, shoemaking and other light industrial branches, and, especially, will give generous assistance to the cooperative enterprises and encourage the creative initiative of the private enterprises in this field.

(2) While consolidating the results of the agrarian reform carried out in north Korea, the Government of the Republic will on this basis vigorously develop farm production and stock-breeding.

In developing agriculture the Government will encourage in every way the creative initiative of the peasants, render them every possible state assistance such as supplying an adequate amount of fertilizer and farm implements and taking measures for the improvement of the methods of farming, and will give active guidance to their farming.

The arable land and the sown area will be extended to increase grain output. Especially for the purpose of extending the paddies and increasing rice yields, the Government will vigorously carry on irrigation projects with state funds and, on the other hand, will encourage and help the farmers in their voluntary irrigation works.

The Government will enlarge the area sown to cotton and develop sericulture in order to meet the demands of the people for textiles, and will also develop forestry to satisfy the requirements of the national economy for timber.

(3) To supply the people with sufficient necessaries of life, the Government will pursue a policy of ensuring commodity circulation smoothly between town and country and of reducing prices systematically.

The state and the consumers' cooperative trade will be developed rapidly by setting up state and consumers' cooperative stores widely in towns and farm villages, and private trade, too, will be encouraged to supply the people with necessaries.

The Government will actively expand exports by tapping the resources of the country to the full and steadily increasing production and, at the same time, import machinery, equipment and other goods essential for the economic development of the country and the people's life.

ON ELIMINATING DOGMATISM AND FORMALISM AND ESTABLISHING JUCHE IN IDEOLOGICAL WORK

Speech to Party Propaganda and Agitation Workers, *December 28, 1955*

Today I want to address a few remarks to you on the short-comings in our Party's ideological work and on how to eliminate them in the future.

As you learned at yesterday's session, there have been serious ideological errors on the literary front. It is obvious, then, that our propaganda work also cannot have been faultless.

It is to be regretted that it suffers in many respects from dogmatism and formalism.

The principal shortcomings in ideological work are the failure to delve deeply into all matters and the lack of Juche. It may not be correct to say Juche is lacking, but, in fact, it has not yet been firmly estalished. This is a serious matter. We must thoroughly rectify this shortcoming. Unless this problem is solved, we cannot hope for good results in ideological work.

Why does our ideological work suffer from dogmatism and formalism? Why do our propaganda and agitation workers only embellish the facade and fail to go deeply into matters, and why do they merely copy and memorize things foreign, instead of working creatively? This offers us food for serious reflection.

What is Juche in our Party's ideological work? What are we doing? We are not engaged in any other country's revolution, but solely in the Korean revolution. Devotion to the Korean revolution is Juche in the ideological work of our Party. Therefore, all ideological work must be subordinated to the interests of the Korean revolution. When we study the history of the Communist Party of the Soviet Union, the history of the Chinese revolution, or the universal truth of Marxism-Leninism, it is entirely for the purpose of correctly carrying out our own revolution.

By saying that the ideological work of our Party is lacking in Juche, I do not mean, of course, that we have not made the revolution and that our revolutionary work was undertaken by others. Nonetheless, Juche has not been firmly established in ideological work, and this leads to dogmatic and formalistic errors and does much harm to our revolutionary cause.

To make revolution in Korea we must know Korean history and geography as well as the customs of the Korean people. Only then is it possible to educate our people in a way that suits them and to inspire in them an ardent love for their native place and their motherland.

It is of paramount importance to study and widely publicize among the working people the history of our country and of our people's struggle.

This is not the first time we have raised this question. As far back as the autumn of 1945, that is, immediately after liberation, we emphasized the need to study the history of our nation's struggle and to inherit its fine traditions. Only when we educate our people in the history of their own struggle and its traditions, can we stimulate their national pride and rouse the broad masses to revolutionary struggle.

Yet, many of our functionaries are ignorant of our country's history and so do not strive to discover, inherit and carry forward its fine traditions. Unless this is corrected, it will lead, in the long run, to the negation of Korean history.

The mistakes made recently by Pak Chang Ok and his kind are due to their negation of the history of the Korean literary movement. They closed their eyes to the struggle waged by the fine writers of the KAPF—Koreen (Coreen) Artiste Proletarienne Federation—and to the splendid works of progressive scholars and writers. We urged them to make a profound study of excellent cultural heritages and give them wide publicity, but they did not do so.

Today, ten years after liberation, we possess all the conditions for collecting material on our literary legacy and putting it to full use. Nevertheless, our propaganda workers remain wholly indifferent to this.

At the Fifth Plenary Meeting of the Party Central Committee it was decided to publicize energetically the history of our people's struggle and our precious cultural heritages, but workers in the field of propaganda failed to do so. They did so much as forbid the newspapers to carry articles on the anti-Japanese struggle of the Korean people.

The Kwangju Student Incident, for example, was a mass struggle in which tens of thousands of Korean students and other young people rose against Japanese imperialism. It played a big part in inspiring broad sections of Korean youth with the anti-Japanese spirit. Propaganda workers should have publicized this movement widely, as a matter of course, and educated our students and other young people in the brave fighting spirit displayed by their forerunners. While they have failed to do this, Syngman Rhee has been making use of this movement in his propaganda. This has created the false impression that the Communists disregard national traditions. What a dangerous thing! If we go on working in this way, it will be impossible for us to win over the south Korean youth.

Up to now, such publicity and education work has been dropped and laid aside, though no one has ever given instructions to this effect. Newspapers do not write about it, nor is any meeting held to commemorate it. Events like the Kwangju Student Incident ought to be taken up by the Democratic Youth League. This incident is an excellent example of the struggle waged by our students and other young people against imperialism.

The same must be said of the June Tenth Independence Movement. This was another mass struggle in which the Korean people rose up against Japanese imperialism. It is true that the struggle was greatly hampered by the factionalists who had wormed their way into it. Considering that even after liberation, the Pak Hon Yong-Li Sung Yop spy clique crept into our ranks and wrought mischief, it goes without saying that in those days the factionalists were able to carry on subversive activities more easily. But, even so, was the struggle itself wrong? No. Although it ended in failure because of a few bad elements who had wormed their way into the leadership of the organization, we cannot deny its revolutionary character. We should learn a lesson from the failure.

No publicity has been given either to the March First Movement. If you work in this way, you cannot expect to lead progressive people with a national conscience along the right path. The lack of Communist Party leadership was the principal cause of the failure of the March First Movement. But who can deny that it was a nationwide resistance movement against Japanese imperialism? We ought to explain the historic significance of this movement to the people and use its lessons to educate them.

Many revolutionary movements in our country ended in failure because of the scoundrels who managed to get themselves into the leadership, but no one can deny the people's participation in those struggles. The masses of the people always fought courageously. Pak Chang Ok may have taken upon himself to deny this, but no true Marxist-Leninist dare deny the people's exploits in these struggles.

When I asked Pak Chang Ok and his followers why they rejected the KAPF, they answered that they did so because some renegades were involved in it. Did they mean to say then that the KAPF, which had as its very core prominent proletarian writers, was an organization of no importance? We must highly value the fighting achievements of the KAPF.

What assets do we have for carrying on the revolution if the history of our people's struggle is denied? If we cast aside all these things, it would mean that our people did nothing. There are many things to be proud of in our country's peasant movements of the past. In recent years, however, no articles dealing with them have appeared in our newspapers.

In schools, too, there is a tendency to neglect courses on Korean history. During the war, the curriculum of the Central Party School allotted 160 hours a year to the study of world history, but very few hours to Korean history. This is how things were done in the Party school, and so it is quite natural that our functionaries are ignorant of their own country's history.

In our propaganda and agitation work, there are numerous examples where only things foreign are extolled while our own are slighted.

Once I visited a People's Army rest home, where there was a picture of the Siberian steppe on the wall. Russians probably like that landscape. But we Korean people prefer the beautiful scenery of our own country. There are beautiful mountains such as Kumgang-san and Myohyang-san in our country. There are clear streams, the blue sea with its rolling waves and fields with their ripening crops. If we are to inspire in our People's Armymen a love for their native place and their country, we must display many pictures of our landscapes.

One day this summer when I dropped in at a local democratic hall of culture, I saw diagrams of the Soviet Union's Five-Year Plan on show there, but not a single diagram illustrating our own Three-Year Plan. Moreover, there were pictures of huge factories in foreign countries, but not a single one of the factories we are rehabilitating or building. They do not even put up any diagrams and pictures showing our economic construction, let alone study the history of our country.

I noticed in a primary school that all the portraits on the wall were of foreigners, such as Mayakovsky and Pushkin, but there were none of Koreans. If children are educated in this way, how can they be expected to have national pride?

Here is something ridiculous. Foreign ways are aped even in attaching a table of contents to a booklet. Thus, it is put at the back. We should learn, as a matter of course, from the good experience of other countries' socialist construction, but why on earth is there a need to put the table of contents at the back of a booklet in foreign style? This does not suit the taste of Koreans. As a matter of course, we should put it at the front of the book, shouldn't we?

In compiling schoolbooks, too, material is not taken from our literary works but from foreign ones. All this is due to the lack of Juche.

The lack of Juche in propaganda work has done much harm to Party work.

For the same reason, many comrades do not respect our

revolutionaries. At present more than 100 comrades who took part in revolutionary struggle in the past are attending the Central Party School, but until recently they were buried in obscurity.

We sent many revolutionaries to the Ministry of the Interior, but many of them were dismissed on the ground that they were incompetent. At the Central Party School, I once met a comrade who had taken part in revolutionary activities. He had been left in his post as chief of a county internal security station for eight years. This attitude towards revolutionaries is entirely wrong.

Today our functionaries have become so insolent that they show no respect for their seniors. They have been allowed to fall into such a habit, in spite of the fact that Communists naturally have a higher moral sense than others and hold their revolutionary seniors in high esteem.

In our People's Army, a vigorous struggle has been waged to uphold revolutionary traditions and, as a result, most of the people who once took part in revolutionary activities have become either regimental or divisional commanders.

If we had not organized the People's Army with old revolutionary cadres as its core, what would have been the outcome of the last war? It would have been impossible for us to defeat the enemy and win a great victory under such difficult conditions.

During our retreat, certain foreigners predicted that most of our army units, trapped by enemy encirclement, would not be able to get back. But we were firmly convinced that all of them would manage to come back. In fact, all of them except those who were killed returned. The foreigners were greatly impressed by this and said there were few armies like ours in the world. How did this come about? The explanation is that our army cadres were comrades who had taken part in guerrilla warfare or in local revolutionary movements in the past. That is precisely why our army is strong.

Ten years have passed since our Party was founded. Therefore, Party members should naturally be taught the history of our Party. If our functionaries are not taught the revolutionary history of our country, they will be unable to carry our fine revolutionary traditions forward, nor will they be able to know which direction to take in the struggle, or show enthusiasm and initiative in their revolutionary activities.

We should study our own things in earnest and get to know them well. Otherwise, we shall be unable to solve new problems creatively in keeping with our actual conditions, problems that crop up one after another in practice.

As a matter of fact, the form of our government should also be suited to the specific conditions in our country. Does our people's power take exactly the same form as that in other socialist countries? No. They are alike in that they are based on Marxist-Leninist principles, but the forms they take are different. There is no doubt, too, that our platform is in keeping with the realities of our country. Our 20-Point Platform is the development of the Program of the Association for the Restoration of the Fatherland. As you all know, this association existed before liberation.

Our functionaries often commit errors because they do not clearly understand these matters.

Some people even think it strange that our agricultural cooperative movement is progressing rapidly. There is nothing strange about this. In the past, the Korean peasantry's economic base was very weak. Under Japanese imperialist rule, the peasant movement grew and the revolutionary spirit of the peasantry ran very high. What is more, the peasants were tempered politically through the building of democracy after liberation and during the bitter years of war. So, it is natural that the agricultural cooperative movement should be making rapid progress in our country today.

Pak Yong Bin, on returning from the Soviet Union, said that as the Soviet Union was following the line of easing international tension, we should also drop our slogan against US imperialism. Such an assertion has nothing to do with revolutionary initiative. It would dull our people's revolutionary vigilance. The US imperialists scorched our land, massacred our innocent people, and are still occupying the southern half of our country. They are our sworn enemy, aren't they?

It is utterly ridiculous to think that our people's struggle against the US imperialists conflicts with the efforts of the Soviet people to ease international tension. Our people's condemnation of and struggle against the US imperialists' policy of aggression against Korea are not in contradiction with, but conducive to the struggle of the peoples of the world to lessen international tension and defend peace. At the same time, the struggle to ease tension on the part of the peace-loving people the world over, including the Soviet people, creates more favorable conditions for the anti-imperialist struggle of our people.

Pak Chang Ok was ideologically linked to the reactionary bourgeois writer Li Tae Jun because he did not study the history of our country and our realities. Besides the remnants of bourgeois ideology in his mind, he was conceited enough to think he knew everything, without even studying the realities of our country. Consequently things went wrong. The harm he did to our ideological work is very serious.

After liberation, he and his ilk said that since Li Gwang Su was a talented man, it would be better to give him prominence. But I pointed out it would be wrong to do so. Li Gwang Su wrote a novel, *A Revolutionary's Wife*, in which he insulted revolutionaries let out of prison. He used to rave that the Korean people and the Japanese imperialists came from "one and the same ancestry and the same roots". Therefore, I told them that it was unthinkable and absolutely impermissible to give prominence to such a man.

Some comrades working in the Propaganda Department of the Party tried to copy mechanically from the Soviet Union in all their work. This was also because they had no intention of studying our realities and lacked the true Marxist-Leninist approach to educating the people in our own merits and revolutionary traditions. Many comrades swallow Marxism-Leninism raw, without digesting and assimilating it. It is self-evident, therefore, that they are unable to display revolutionary initiative.

Propaganda workers have so far failed to take proper measures to study our history and national culture systematically. Ten years have passed since liberation, yet we have failed to tackle the matter energetically. We have conducted it only in a hit-or-miss way. We had few cadres before, but now we have scholars, funds and material, and sufficient conditions for doing it. It is quite possible if only you make a good study and organize the work. Every effort should be made to ascertain, uphold and promote our national heritage. True, we should energetically learn from what is progressive internationally. But we should develop the fine things of our own while intro-

ducing advanced culture. Otherwise, our people will lose faith
in their own ability and become a spineless people who only try
to copy from others.

Hearing us say that it is necessary to establish Juche, some
comrades might take it in a simple way and get the wrong idea
that we need not learn from foreign countries. That would be
quite wrong. We must learn from the positive experience of
socialist countries.

The important thing is to know what we are learning for.
Our aim is to turn the advanced experience of the Soviet Union
and other socialist countries to good account in our Korean
revolution.

During the war, Ho Ga I, Kim Jae Uk and Pak Il U once
quarrelled stupidly among themselves over how to do political
work in the army. Those from the Soviet Union insisted upon
the Soviet method and those from China stuck to the Chinese
method. So they quarrelled, some advocating the Soviet fashion and others the Chinese way. That was sheer nonsense.

It does not matter whether you use the right hand or the
left, whether you use a spoon or chopsticks at the table. No
matter how you eat, it is all the same insofar as food is put into
your mouth, isn't it? Why need one be fastidious about "fashion" in wartime? We do political work to strengthen our People's Army and win battles, and any method will do so long as
our aim is achieved. Yet Ho Ga I and Pak Il U squabbled about
such a trifle. This only weakens discipline within the Party. At
that time, the Party center maintained that we should learn
the good things from both the Soviet Union and China and, on
this basis, work out a method of political work suitable to our
actual conditions.

It is important in our work to grasp revolutionary truth,
Marxist-Leninist truth, and apply it correctly to our actual
conditions. There should be no set rule that we must follow the
Soviet pattern. Some advocate the Soviet way and others the
Chinese, but is it not high time to work out our own?

The point is that we should not mechanically copy the forms
and methods of the Soviet Union, but should learn from its experience in struggle and from the truth of Marxism-Leninism.
So, while learning from the experience of the Soviet Union, we
must put stress not on the form but on the essence of its experience.

In learning from the experience of the Soviet Union there is a marked tendency merely to model ourselves on the external form. If *Pravda* puts a headline "A Day in Our Country", our *Rodong Sinmun* carries the same title: "A Day in Our Country". What is the point of copying this sort of thing? The same is true of clothing. When there are very graceful Korean costumes for our women, what is the point of discarding them and putting on clothes which are unbecoming? There is no need to do this. I suggest to the Women's Union functionaries that our women dress in Korean costumes as far as possible.

Merely copying the forms used by others instead of learning the truth of Marxism-Leninism does us no good, only harm.

In both revolutionary struggle and construction, we should firmly adhere to Marxist-Leninist principles, applying them in a creative way to suit the specific conditions and national characteristics of our country.

If we mechanically apply foreign experience, disregarding the history of our country and the traditions of our people and without taking account of our own realities and our people's political preparedness, we will commit dogmatic errors and do much harm to the revolutionary cause. This is not fidelity to Marxism-Leninism nor to internationalism. It runs counter to them.

Marxism-Leninism is not a dogma, it is a guide to action and a creative theory. So, it can display its indestructible vitality only when it is applied creatively to suit the specific conditions of each country. The same applies to the experience of the fraternal parties. It will prove valuable to us only when we study it, grasp its essence and properly apply it to our realities. But if we just gulp it down and spoil our work, it will not only harm our work but also lead to discrediting the valuable experience of the fraternal parties.

In connection with the question of establishing Juche, I think it necessary to touch on internationalism and patriotism.

Internationalism and patriotism are inseparably linked with each other. You must realize that the love Korean Communists bear for their country does not conflict with the internationalism of the working class but fully conforms with it. Loving Korea is just as good as loving the Soviet Union and the socialist camp and, likewise, loving the Soviet Union and the socialist camp is just as good as loving Korea. They constitute a complete whole. For the great cause of the working class knows no frontiers and our revolutionary cause is a part of the international revolutionary cause of the working class throughout the world. The supreme goal of the working class of all countries is to build a communist society. The only difference, if any, lies in the fact that some countries will do this earlier and others later.

It is wrong to stress patriotism alone and neglect internationalist solidarity. For the victory of the Korean revolution and for the great cause of the international working class, we should strengthen solidarity with the Soviet people and with the peoples of all the socialist countries. This is our sacred internationalist duty. The Soviet people, on their part, are doing all they can to strengthen solidarity not only with the countries of the socialist camp but also with the working class of the whole world, both for the building of communism in their own country and for the victory of the world revolution.

Thus, patriotism and internationalism are inseparable. He who does not love his own country cannot be loyal to internationalism, and he who is unfaithful to internationalism cannot be faithful to his own country and people. A true patriot is at once an internationalist and vice versa.

If we cast aside all that is good in our country and only copy and memorize things foreign in ideological work, we will certainly bring losses to our revolution, and thereby fail to fulfill our obligations to the international revolutionary cause properly.

In the report to the Second Party Congress, I quoted the following passage from the statement of the Commander of the Soviet army, published on the day the army entered our country: "Korean people! . . . You hold your happiness in your own hands. . . . Koreans must create their own happiness themselves." This statement is perfectly correct, and if we fail to act accordingly, we may lose broad segments of the masses.

The formalism of our propaganda workers also finds expression in exaggeration in propaganda work. For example, such bombastic expressions as "all have risen," "all have been mobilized," etc., have long been in fashion in speeches and articles.

We advised Pak Chang Ok more than once against it. Pak Chang Ok made mistakes because he could not break away from this "all" type of bombast he had created. Later, he took a fancy to the superlative of the Chinese character "great", and used this adjective everywhere. I do not know whether this practice was due to his ignorance of Chinese characters or to his erroneous ideological stand.

When propaganda work is conducted with such empty exaggeration, it will lead people to be carried away by victory and to become easy-going. This bad practice is also responsible for the false reports handed in by junior officials.

The use of an adjective may seem a simple matter, but its wrong use may spell failure in our work. In future, this practice should be completely stopped.

Now, I should like to refer to a few other immediate problems in ideological work.

The Party Central Committee has issued written material on the nature and tasks of our revolution, to help in the study of the documents of its April Plenary Meeting. So, I will not make any further comment on this.

I would just like to stress once more the prospects of our revolution. Our revolution has two prospects. One is the peaceful reunification of our country, and the other is its reunification in circumstances in which the forces of imperialism are drastically weakened by a big war.

We, of course, have been striving with all our might to realize the first prospect.

Our struggle for peaceful reunification boils down to two points—to carry out construction successfully in the northern half of the country and direct effective political work towards the southern half. If we strengthen the democratic base by promoting socialist construction in the north and rouse the people in the south to struggle for liberation through effective political work directed to the south, peaceful reunification can be realized.

Political work directed towards the south means strengthening the influence of the north on the people in the south and getting the broad masses there to support us. To this end, socialist construction in the north should be carried out successfully. The living standards of the people should be raised and the economic base strengthened in the north through successful economic construction, and the entire people should be rallied around our Party. Then, no matter how desperately

Syngman Rhee may try, he will never be able to dampen the fighting spirit of the people in the south, who are constantly inspired by socialist construction in the north.

A man who came over from the south some time ago said: "Syngman Rhee says in his propaganda that the north has a population of only 3 million and there is nothing left of Pyongyang but a heap of ashes. But I have seen here that the bridge over the Taedong-gang River has been rebuilt and Pyongyang is being built into a much more beautiful city than before. Syngman Rhee has talked nonsense." This is what will happen when we carry out construction successfully.

In 1948, when a joint conference of political parties and social organizations from north and south Korea was held, we in the north did not have much to our credit in construction. But all the Right-wing personalities of south Korea came to us, with the exception of Syngman Rhee and Kim Song Su. The joint conference was of very great significance. Many of those who came to the north at that time remained here.

This is what Kim Gu said: "I have found north Korea to my liking. I have seen many Communists both in Shanghai and in south Korea (if he met any, they must have been those of the Tuesday group or the M-L group), but north Korean Communists are different. I thought before that Communists were narrow-minded and evil people, but I have found here that you are broad-minded and generous people with whom I can cooperate fully. I am resolved to cooperate with you. I am old now and have no desire for power. If I do not go back to south Korea, Syngman Rhee will ceertainly claim I have been detained. I want to go back and make known the fine things I have seen here. So I have to go back. Do not think that I am going to collaborate with the Yankees. When I come here again later, please give me an apple orchard, for I want to live in peace in the countryside for the rest of my life." Kim Gyu Sik, too, spoke in the same vein. Afterwards, Kim Gu fought against the Yankees.

As you all know, Kim Gu was a nationalist. From the beginning he was against both imperialism and communism, and he came to us with the intention of negotiating with the Communists. In view of the fact that even Kim Gu, who once regarded communism as an inveterate enemy, changed his ideas of our endeavors to build up the country, it is quite easy to imagine what workers, peasants and public figures with a national con-science in south Korea will think once they come and see the northern half of the country.

Before liberation, merely to hear that in the Soviet Union the working class held power and was building socialism made us yearn greatly for that country where we had never been. How then can the people in the south not yearn to see the socialist construction in the north carried out by our people who are of the same stock as they?

That is why successful construction in the north is more im-portant than anything else.

Thus, when the people in the south are roused to action against US imperialism and the Syngman Rhee regime through successful socialist construction in the north and ef-fective political work directed towards the south, peaceful reunification can be brought about.

This is the internal factor which makes peaceful reunifica-tion possible.

The external factor conducive to peaceful reunification should likewise be taken into consideration. If we succeed in maintaining peace for a five to ten year period, China, with her population of more than 600 million, as well as the Soviet Union, will grow incomparably stronger and the power of the whole socialist camp will be even greater.

Parallel with the growth of the might of the socialist camp, the national-liberation movement of the peoples in the colonial and dependent countries has further intensified and many countries have won national independence. The peoples of In-dia, Indonesia, Burma and other independent states in Asia and the peoples of the Arab countries are fighting for peace and against imperialist aggression.

All this constitutes a telling blow to imperialism, especially US imperialism. As the forces of peace, democracy and social-ism grow stronger, the US imperialists will finally be com-pelled to withdraw from Korea.

Of course, the struggle for the peaceful reunification of our country is an arduous and protracted one. But when we grow stronger and the international forces of peace, democracy and socialism become more powerful, we will be able to achieve peaceful reunification. This is one prospect for the develop-ment of the revolution in Korea and for reunification.

The problem of reunification might also be solved by war, not by peaceful means. If the imperialists unleash war on a worldwide scale, we will have no alternative but to fight and then it would be quite possible for us to defeat the US imperialists in Korea by our own strength. Although it would be rather hard for us to fight against US imperialism single-handed, we should be able to defeat it relatively easily if it is compelled to disperse its forces all over the world. In that case we shall sweep the forces of US imperialism from Korea and achieve the reunification of the country. This is the other prospect for the development of the Korean revolution and for reunification.

But we do not want this prospect. We desire the first prospect, that is, reunification by peaceful means, and we are struggling to achieve it.

No matter which prospect for the country's reunification comes about, the most important thing of all is to strengthen our Party and steel the members' Party spirit.

In case negotiations start between the north and the south, then the barriers between them are torn down and we go to work among south Koreans, what will things be like if our Party is not strong? Only when our Party is strong, can it take advantage of such a favorable situation.

The proportion of our Party membership to the population is now one to ten, as we have a million members out of a population of 10 million. This is indeed not a small proportion. But, when compared with the 30 million population of Korea, one million is by no means large.

In south Korea the growth of the Party cannot help but be seriously limited because the underground movement there is carried on under extremely difficult circumstances.

After reunification, it will be difficult to carry on our work with a small number of Party members, although the number will grow in south Korea, too. What is wrong with our training a large number of Party members in the northern half from now on and assigning them to work both in the north and the south after reunification? Nothing. Yet, at the time of the Fourth Plenary Meeting of the Party Central Committee, Ho Ga I insisted that the Party close its doors in spite of the fact that it had no more than 600,000 members. The Party criticized his view at the time, and has continued to increase its membership.

The point now is to educate our one million Party members

well. Among our members there may be some who lag behind
the non-Party masses. But even so, these people must not be
expelled from the Party. They must be kept in and educated. If
they are expelled, our Party might be weakened. This is all the
more so since ours is not the only party.

It is our consistent organizational line to constantly train
the core of the cells while building up a mass-based party. By
the core we mean those Party members who know communist
truth and can follow the road of revolution without vacillating.
It is difficult to arm the one million Party members overnight
with an equal degree of communist thinking. We must follow
the line of training the core elements first and then gradually
raising the political level of all Party members.

Our line is to educate Party members with the help of core
members. So, since the Fourth Plenary Meeting, the Party has
put special emphasis on the question of training the core members of the cells. It will be all the more gratifying if their number increases from five today to ten tomorrow so that all Party
members become core elements. But even if only 50 percent of
the Party membership does so, it will be a good thing.

The merging of the Communist Party and the New Democratic Party was of great significance in turning our Party into
a mass political party. As a result of our correct organizational
line and energetic struggle to win over the broad masses of the
working people, our Party has now become a mass political
party embracing one million members. This success was by no
means easy, but was achieved through extremely hard
struggles.

We fight for democratic rights and freedoms in south Korea
—freedom of speech, the press, assembly and association—
which are prerequisites for the peaceful reunification of the
country. We aim at securing conditions for our own free activities in the southern half, while allowing political parties of
south Korea to conduct political activities freely in the northern half.

When a situation is thus created in which political struggle
in the north and the south is free, whoever wins more of the
masses will win the day. Therefore, it is of the greatest importance to strengthen our Party and the Party spirit of its
members.

In order to steel the Party spirit of our members, we should get all of them to make a constant and deep study of the documents of the Fourth and Fifth Plenary Meetings of the Party Central Committee.

Our comrades must direct more effort to the organizational and propaganda work of the Party, instead of being engrossed only in economic campaigns. Party cells must be built up well and Party members educated by the cell core. It is particularly necessary to temper the Party spirit of those members who hold leading posts—ministers, vice-ministers and bureau directors. Throughout the Party, vigorous educational measures should be taken to fortify the Party spirit.

The composition of our Party is very complex. All sorts of people have joined it—those who once belonged to the Tuesday group and the M-L group, those who joined the Toiling People's Party after liberation, and others. Many had been under the influence of the factionalists. These people are to be found both among responsible cadres in the central organs and among the members of the Party Central Committee.

Are all of these people worthless? No. Education will make them all useful. But their education must not be conducted in a short-term campaign. Prolonged, patient education and criticism are needed.

We must wage a determined struggle to arm every Party member firmly with our Party's ideology and eliminate the remnants of bourgeois ideology which persist in the minds of Party members and the working people. Our members' Party spirit should be thoroughly steeled until their shortcomings are overcome and their ideological maladies completely remedied.

We were too late in criticizing Pak Chang Ok and Ki Sok Bok. If they had been criticized at the time of the Fifth Plenary Meeting of the Party Central Committee, things would not have gotten into such a mess. Therefore, it is especially important to remold the thinking of those leading cadres who were influenced by Ho Ga I or Pak Il U and help them arm themselves firmly with the Party's ideological system. The Department of Organizational Leadership and the Propaganda and Agitation Department of the Party must take up this work.

The important thing in educating Party members is to get them, especially the cadres, to establish a correct viewpoint on the masses. Because this is lacking, bureaucracy continues to manifest itself. This is a grave shortcoming in our Party work.

In order to achieve our lofty aim of reunifying the country and building socialism and communism, we must win over the masses. We must be clear on what great losses bureaucracy will cause to the revolution.

Listening to the voice of the masses and championing their interests is an entirely different matter from basing one's work on misleading opinions heard in the street. The latter has nothing in common with the revolutionary viewpoint on the masses. By the masses we mean the basic masses we rely on— the workers and the peasants, and our allies who support and follow us. We should listen to them and defend their interests. Everyone, whether a Party worker, an administrative worker or a functionary in a social organization, must work consistently in the interests of the revolution and the masses.

How was it possible for the anti-Japanese guerrillas to hold out for such a long time? Why was it that the Japanese failed to destroy us even though they had a formidable armed force? Because the guerrillas had the correct viewpoint on the masses and the support of the masses. When guerrillas were wounded and entered a village, the peasants took care of them as though they were their own sons. They managed to get rice, which they could hardly afford for themselves, and cooked it for them. Even the peasants living inside the earth walls of the concentration villages set up by the Japanese imperialists, sent food to them outside the walls.

The masses supported and protected us in this way because we had always defended their interests and fought for them at the risk of our lives. All Party members must learn from the guerrillas' attitude towards the masses.

In the days of Japanese imperialist rule everything was imposed upon us by force—compulsory military service, compulsory labor, compulsory delivery of farm produce, etc. We are resolutely opposed to such practices.

A party divorced from the masses is like a fish out of water. With whom can the party carry out the revolution if not with the masses? A party divorced from the people not only cannot bring the revolution to victory, but will eventually find its very existence endangered.

It is solely for the purpose of protecting the interests of the masses that the party puts forward its program and seizes state power. Therefore, would it not be against the aims of the party and the revolution to encroach on the interests of the masses?

It is beyond dispute that our laws and decisions are excellent. But they will all come to nothing if, in putting them into effect, our functionaries harm the interests of the masses. You comrades must bear this in mind and intensify educational work among Party members so that they can liquidate bureaucracy and acquire a correct viewpoint on the masses. If only 50 percent of all Party members acquire this viewpoint, it will mean a great change in our Party.

At the moment quite a few Party members are not firmly equipped with the correct viewpoint. The situation is especially bad among cadres. Whether a Party member has the correct viewpoint on the masses or not also depends on his Party spirit. So, tempering Party spirit is of decisive importance in this respect, too.

Further, it is important to imbue the Party members with faith and optimism regarding the prospects of the revolution. If they lack firm faith in the final victory of our cause and optimism regarding the future of the revolution under whatever circumstances, it will be impossible to overcome the difficulties one inevitably encounters in the course of revolutionary struggle.

In order to make our Party members indomitable fighters who are always optimistic about the future of the revolution, it is necessary to intensify their Marxist-Leninist education. Without a clear understanding of the laws of social development and the inevitability of the triumph of socialism and communism, one can neither have faith in victory nor have the lofty spirit and combativeness to withstand any difficulty.

Let me give you an example of vacillation and defection in the revolutionary ranks that was caused by a lack of knowledge of the laws of social development and of a clear understanding of the trend of developments in a complex situation.

When the defeat of Japanese imperialism was in sight, some people in the guerrilla detachments lost faith and deserted. This was partly because of certain formalistic defects in our propaganda work at the time. In those days propaganda about the Soviet Union was of special importance, and it was propagandized in the guerrilla army that "A big clash is bound to occur some day between the Soviet Union and the imperialist states, because fundamental contradictions exist between them. Then, Japanese imperialism will perish and our country will attain independence." That was wrong. Though it was right to propagandize about the contradictions between the socialist state and the imperialist countries, the truth about current developments was not explained. As a result, when a non-aggression pact between the Soviet Union and Hitler Germany was signed and a treaty of neutrality was concluded between the Soviet Union and Japan in 1941, some elements in the guerrilla ranks lost hope in the future and faltered. These waverers deserted our ranks, saying that after 10 years with the guerrillas they only saw a dark future, uncertain whether they would have to spend another 10 or 20 years fighting. So we explained the revolutionary situation and the truth about the revolution fully to the guerrillas. After that, there were no more deserters.

There is no doubt that sooner or later we shall see the great revolutionary event come about. That event, as I have already said, may either occur peacefully or non-peacefully. Whatever form it takes, we must always be prepared to meet it.

In order to meet this great revolutionary event, the members' Party spirit should be steeled. They should be educated to have a correct viewpoint on the masses, faith in victory and optimism regarding the future of the revolution.

Another important thing is to struggle correctly against every anti-Party tendency. If we had not had the experience of fighting the Minsaengdan in Chientao in the past, we would not have been able correctly to lead the struggle against the counterrevolutionaries in Korea after liberation, especially during the war.

The Japanese imperialists set up a counterrevolutionary espionage organization called Minsaengdan and infiltrated its agents into the revolutionary districts of Chientao. Then they resorted to the vile trick of alienating the Koreans from the Chinese and inciting strife among the Koreans. For a time those in the revolutionary camp fell victim to the enemy's crafty scheme, going to the length of killing one another. As a result, many people were killed without any justifiable reason.

This experience proved very useful when we dealt with the case of the Pak Hon Yong clique. We adhered strictly to the principle of drawing a sharp distinction between spies and non-spies. We emphasized this many times in the Political Committee. If we were not vigilant we might play into the hands of the Yankees and ruin many persons.

Of course, the struggle must be relentless. Otherwise, some spies may escape punishment. But the struggle must always be carried on as an ideological one.

Those who were influenced by Pak Hon Yong cannot all be his ilk or spies. But his ideological influence still remains in their minds. We must fight against this.

The experience acquired in the struggle against the Pak Hon Yong clique and in the counterespionage campaigns should be made fully known to the Party members so that they may wage a rigorous struggle against espionage agents and correctly distinguish the spies from others. If you do not do this, but suspect everybody, in the end you will find yourselves suspicious of your own shadow.

In order to disintegrate our ranks from within, the enemy always plots to make people distrust one another and set them at odds. You must learn to discern clearly and combat such plots and slanders concocted by the counterrevolutionaries. Party members should be educated in such a way that they can spot spies, waverers, nepotists, parochialists and factionalists.

Such a struggle can be conducted properly only when the cadres and all members of the Party have a high political level. Without attaining a high level of Marxist-Leninist knowledge, Party members cannot properly carry out such a difficult task. In order to enable them to fight skillfully against the counterrevolutionaries, it is necessary to intensify their Marxist-Leninist education and, at the same time, acquaint them with our extensive experience in the fight against the counterrevolutionaries.

Further, propaganda and agitation should be stepped up among the broad masses. Education of the masses in socialist ideology should be the main content of our work of propaganda and agitation. The most important thing in this connection is to make the workers and peasants, especially the workers, clearly aware that power is in their hands. When they are highly conscious of this fact, the workers will act as the masters in everything—take good care of their places of work, machinery and equipment, work hard, maintain good discipline and effectively combat counterrevolutionaries.

The same is true of the peasants. If they realize that the working class is not only their ally but also their leader, and that they too hold power in their hands, they will work their land well, take good care of their implements and willingly pay the tax in kind.

Everyone will show enthusiasm when he realizes that he is the master. When we were engaged in revolutionary activities in the past, who could have got us to do so for money? We fought without sleep and forgot our hunger because we realized that by making revolution we could not only carve out our own destiny but save our country. The workers will likewise throw all their energy and zeal into their work when they are clearly aware that their labor is for their own happiness and for the prosperity of society.

Prolonged, persistent education is needed to get all the working people to become as politically conscious as this. We must patiently educate the masses and unite them more closely around our Party.

In conclusion, I should like to make a few remarks about our newspapers. Our papers still do not fully discharge their duties.

The central task of the *Rodong Sinmun*, our Party organ, is to educate the Party members through day-to-day explanation of the Party's lines and policies and their fighting tasks. The central task of the *Minju Choson* is to mobilize the masses to put state policies into effect by fully explaining the laws and regulations of the people's government and the policies of the state. The papers of the General Federation of Trade Unions, the Democratic Youth League, and other organizations should likewise be edited in accordance with their respective characteristics and tasks.

Our newspapers have no specific features which distinguish one from another. This is a big failing. Whether this is because they are all furnished with material by the Korean Central News Agency or because some of them are limited in space, I do not know.

Here, too, much formalism and dogmatism can be noted. I think it necessary for you to look into this matter seriously.

I have so far touched upon some problems arising in the ideological work of our Party. I hope you will take note of them, eliminate the shortcomings revealed and strive to raise our Party's ideological work to a higher level.

TO BRING ABOUT A GREAT REVOLUTIONARY UPSWING IN SOCIALIST CONSTRUCTION

Concluding Speech at the Plenary Meeting of the Central Committee of the Workers' Party of Korea, *December 13, 1956*

Comrades,

At this plenary meeting we discussed the national economic plan for 1957, the task for the first year of the First Five-Year Plan, and made a unanimous resolve to fulfill this plan without fail, valiantly getting over all hardships and trials ahead of us. When the meeting is over, members and alternate members of the Party Central Committee and all other comrades who are present here will return to their respective posts where they must wage dynamic struggles for the implementation of the decision of the plenary meeting and fulfill their pledge to the Party come what may.

As many comrades said in their speeches, the national economic plan we are going to fulfill next year is a very tightened plan. However, this is by no means a totally impossible plan which had been forced through against our will. It is a scientific and practical plan which we can fulfill with our ability. We have all possibilities and conditions for the successful carrying out of this plan.

The 1957 national economic plan was drawn on the basis of our Party's basic line of economic construction, a line of giving priority to the development of heavy industry while at the same time developing light industry and agriculture. As in the past, so next year, we are planning to direct great efforts to heavy industry, concentrating investments on it. This is an entirely correct measure.

I was told that in some countries there has been much debate as to whether heavy industry should be curtailed or not. However, in our country this sort of problem can never arise. Because unless heavy inudstry is developed first, it is impossible to consolidate the foundation of the national economy as a whole or raise the people's living standards. The priority development of heavy industry is an objective requirement of the socialist economic construction in our country.

Particularly the heavy industries on which we are concentrating our efforts are directly related to the people's living conditions. If we do not concentrate our efforts on the chemical industry and produce plenty of fertilizer, we cannot increase the per-*chongbo* yield in agricultural production and, accordingly, we cannot solve the food problem for the people. And only by quickly developing the chemical industry and securing large quantities of chemical fibres, can we supply our people with an adequate amount of cloth.

The same is true with the mining industry and other branches of heavy industry. Unless we exert our efforts for the mining industry and exploit more mineral ores, we cannot obtain much foreign currency, to say nothing of providing the metal industry with raw materials and, accordingly, cannot import different goods badly needed for the people's lives. So, in order to further consolidate our country's economic foundations and more quickly raise the people's living standards, we must continue to make large investments in the machine-building, electric, mining and chemical industries and other branches of heavy industry.

Needless to say, since our population increases very quickly every year, we should feed our people evenly and, especially, be deeply interested in lightening the peasants' burdens and improving their living conditions. In this situation, it is hardly likely to increase the rate of investment in heavy industries next year above that of this year. However, next year also, we should maintain the proportion of the production of means of production to the production of consumer goods, at least at the same level as this year. We consider that proportion we are maintaining now just fits our nation's present level of industrial development.

We must not in the least hesitate or vacillate in the fulfillment of next year's plan. Let me again stress that if we work well, we can fulfill next year's plan; we must fulfill it come what may. Only when we carry out next year's plan without fail even though it may be a bit hard, can we increase the state accumulation and secure reserves. And this will enable us to carry out the plan for 1958 without difficulty and readily cope with any emergency which may be caused by change in the situation. Therefore, all of you must clearly realize that the struggle for the successful implementation of next year's plan is a hard but a worthy and honorable struggle.

In the last few years we were confronted with many more hardships than now but we audaciously overcame them through a tense struggle, so that we could victoriously fulfill the Three-Year Plan. As a result, our people now have foundations and assets with which to live on their own efforts and are able to draw a tremendous long-range perspective plan such as the Five-Year Plan and buckle down to its implementation.

We are planning to increase the total industrial output value next year, the first year of the Five-Year Plan, 21 percent above that we are envisaging this year. This is 2.4 times as much as that in the prewar year of 1949. It is obvious that if we had not the solid foundations and assets prepared during the Three-Year Plan, we could not set this high goal.

Under next year's plan we also envisaged many specific measures for improving the people's living conditions. Right here at this plenary meeting, we have discussed interesting problems—on producing more consumer goods, improving the quality of goods, turning out more fertilizers for the countryside to increase grain production, and making more boats to catch more fish next year. What does this mean? It means that we have grown stronger and increased our assets, which enable us to do all these things with our own efforts.

Today we have such a great strength and solid assets solely because we have had our Party's correct line of giving priority to the development of heavy industry while at the same time developing light industry and agriculture, and, under the Party's leadership, all of our people have striven to carry out this line with credit, tightening their belts.

If we had not concentrated our efforts on the advancement of heavy industry in the Three-Year Plan period in accordance with the Party's policy, and if we had just consumed all the aids from the fraternal countries allegedly to raise the people's living standard, we could have been well-off for a year or two but we would find ourselves in a hard situation today where we could not do anything for ourselves.

If in the last few years we had not built machine-building factories, produced spinning and weaving machinery and built textile mills, sparing pennies, we could not have silk clothes however we wanted today and could not adopt a decision on producing more silk cloth at this meeting. And if we had not built up solid centers of the machine-building industry during this period, we could not eat fish however we wanted nor could we confidently send out directives on the production of a definite number of vessels such as angle-net boats and fish carriers.

However, displaying the revolutionary spirit of self-reliance, we have created the machine-building industry of our own and laid strong centers of heavy industry. As a result, at this plenary meeting, we could freely discuss and decide on all essential matters for next year and have a firm conviction that we are quite capable of executing the decision. In other words we can now resolve to do anything if it is necessary for the development of the national economy and the improvement of the people's living conditions, and can fulfill this resolve. The question is that from now on we must set a clear-cut goal of struggle and rush bravely and quickly toward this goal.

We cannot go at a slow pace; we must rush ahead several times, scores of times faster than others. However great the achievements we made in the postwar economic construction, we must never be satisfied with this. Our achievements are just initial ones, nothing but a foundation for the attainment of a still greater victory in the future.

Our country's economic foundation is still weak as a whole and the people's living standard is not high. Moreover, we have not yet been able to achieve national reunification, our people's most anxious desire. In this situation, how can we idle away time or go at a slow pace? We are never allowed to do so. We must never lead slackened, easy lives; we must wage a tense struggle every hour and every day.

Particularly, the present internal and external situation is more strained and complex than ever before. Not long ago, in the Middle East the imperialists headed by US imperialism put up the Zionists as their shock brigade and unleashed a savage war of aggression against the Arab people. In Hungary they incited their agents to a riot against the government. Of course, all these foul maneuvers ended in an ignominious fiasco. However, instead of drawing a lesson from their setbacks, the imperialists, following the two incidents, are conducting crazy anti-communist clamors without precedent.

On the one hand, the imperialists are blowing a vociferous anti-communist trumpet, maliciously slandering the socialist countries and, on the other, they are resorting to every possible means to drive a wedge between the socialist countries and subvert the socialist camp from within. At every opportunity they send spies, saboteurs and wreckers into the socialist countries and maneuver to seek for a pretext of military aggression.

In our country also, as if they were given a golden opportunity, the US imperialists and their lackeys, the Syngman Rheeites, are running mad and hurrying with preparations for aggression against the northern half of the Republic. The US imperialists have brought their Pacific Fleet near our territorial waters and the Syngman Rheeites, in keeping with this, have reportedly ordered the puppet armed forces to complete all preparations by the end of the year to take military actions for "march north".

In addition, they are trying to use for their subversive plots the remnants of the overthrown exploitative classes and anti-Party counterrevolutionary factionalists in the northern half of the Republic. Of late, the Syngman Rheeites are openly clamoring to this handful of counterrevolutionaries every day, "Rise up in a riot as in Hungary, then we will attack again." Furthermore, they are dispatching many spies into the northern half of the Republic to align them with wicked elements lurking within our ranks, in an attempt to hatch sinister designs against our Party and the Government of the Republic. The number of the spies, saboteurs and wreckers worming their way into the north with these purposes is considerably increasing these days.

Meanwhile, the class enemies and anti-Party counterrevolutionary factionalists hiding among our ranks are raising their heads in keeping with the aggressive activities of the US imperialists and Syngman Rheeites and are opposing our Party and our social system. The anti-Party counterrevolutionary factionalists have been dealt blows by our Party but they are still wriggling. These fellows are criticizing the Party's policy with regard to cadres and slandering the Party's lines and policies from various angles.

The anti-Party counterrevolutionary factionalists are aiming at undermining the deep trust of the Party members and the people for our Party's Central Committee and destroying the Party's unity and cohesion, thereby to frustrate our revolutionary cause. The analysis of their different arguments shows that in many respects they are exactly the same as those of the Syngman Rheeites.

All these maneuvers of the enemies at home and abroad are laying tremendous obstacles in the way of our Party and people and preventing our advance.

We must sharpen our vigilance against all their maneuvers. Needless to say, it is obvious that whatever maneuvers the enemies make, they will fizzle out in the long run. As long as our tested Party Central Committee leads the revolution and the Party and the masses are firmly united as one body, neither the "march north" plan of the US imperialsts and Syngman Rhee clique nor the conspiratorial maneuvers of the anti-Party counterrevolutionary factionalists will succeed. However, this never means that we are allowed to slacken our vigilance and feel at ease.

If we are drunken with our victory, soften our vigilance and fail to secure unity and solidarity of our ranks, the situation may be different. Then, the US imperialists and the Syngman Rheeites may actually attack us and our revolutionary cause may face a grave difficulty.

The most important guarantee for our victory in the revolutionary struggle and the work of construction is our Party's steel-like unity and solidarity. This is the conclusion we have drawn in the course of our long revolutionary struggle.

We must not allow any factional activity within the Party and must not allow any alien element to infiltrate into our ranks. We must never permit but mercilessly shatter in time the act aimed to split the Party, the working class and the masses. We must wage the anti-factional struggle throughout the Party more powerfully and see to it that all cadres and Party members protect the Party's unity and cohesion like the apple of the eye.

At the same time, we must make sure that all our cadres and Party members correctly establish their revolutionary mass viewpoint and do work with the masses well, so as to firmly unite them all around our Party. Especially, it is very important to strengthen ideological education of the working class and raise their class consciousness. Only by increasing their class consciousness, can they unhesitatingly defend and firmly protect their Party and government in any difficult and complicated situation and play a vanguard role among the masses of the people.

While fighting to consolidate the unity and solidarity of the revolutionary forces in our country, we must strive to defend the socialist camp and increase its might.

As I mentioned above, at present the imperialists are resorting to every maneuver to estrange the socialist countries from each other and undermine the might of the socialist camp at all costs. We must not be deceived by their crafty maneuvers for alienation. The more they intensify their maneuvers for our estrangement, the higher we must raise the banner of proletarian internationalism and defend the socialist camp more actively and protect it more firmly than ever before.

Next, we must sharpen our vigilance against our class enemies who obstruct our advance and further intensify the struggle against them.

At present our Party is carrying out the revolutionary tasks of the transitional period from capitalism to socialism and building socialism amidst a harsh class struggle. In the northern half of the Republic there still remain quite a few landlords deprived of their lands by us, capitalists deprived of their factories and the pro-Japanese elements and traitors to the nation expelled from power organs. On the other hand, the spies, saboteurs and wreckers of US imperialism and Syngman Rhee-ites are unceasingly infiltrating from south Korea. They are working hard to seize every opportunity to destroy our revolutionary gains, foil our socialist construction, overthrow our socialist system and restore the old exploitative system.

We must keep a sharp watch over every movement of our class enemies and when they maneuver against us, we must never compromise with them, but resolutely mete out judicial punishment to them. At present, because of their misconcept of our Party's united front and class policies, some of our officials just leave the wicked criminals alone or even if they have been arrested, they are hesitating to apply judicial punishment to them. This is very dangerous.

Having mercy on the class enemies is not the attitude of the revolutionaries. Clamors for "abidance by the law" and so on are part of the maneuvers of the anti-Party counterrevolutionary factionalists to weaken the function of our state's proletarian dictatorship. We must thoroughly crush these absurd maneuvers of theirs and must mercilessly fight against all attempts to compromise with the class enemies. Especially, Party officials and personnel of the People's Army, interior service, judicial and procuratorial agencies must conduct their struggle vigorously.

We must secure the steel-like unity and solidarity of the revolutionary forces and intensify the struggle against the counterrevolutionary forces and, on this basis, we must organize and mobilize the masses' revolutionary zeal for the fulfillment of next year's national economic plan and bring about a new upswing in the socialist economic construction.

The goal we are going to achieve next year is very high and we have many hardships ahead of us, so we must fight a tense battle. Members of the Party Central Committee and other comrades present here have all made a firm resolve, but if we do not rouse the masses' revolutionary enthusiasm, we cannot succeed in next year's plan nor bring about a great upswing in socialist construction.

Our victory in socialist construction depends largely on how commanding personnel organize and mobilize the masses of the people. If you conduct political and organizational work well and make sure that the working class and broad sectors of the people uphold the Party's call as one man, there will be neither hardship which we cannot get over nor fortress we cannot occupy.

On your return to your places, you must inform all your cadres, Party members, all the workers, technicians and office workers about the intentions of this plenary meeting and forcefully organize and mobilize them for their implementation. Particularly you must make sure that at a time when the internal and external enemies are carrying out their obstructionist activities more overtly than ever before, all Party members and working people have a firm conviction in victory and fight without the slightest vacillation.

It is said that at present some people who are not politically awakened are ill at ease and do not work well, saying, "At a time when Syngman Rhee is saying he's going to attack us, what's the use of continuing with the work of construction?" This is very bad. We must conduct a proper explanatory work for the workers and all the rest of the working people so that this sort of thing will never recur.

We need not be in the least afraid of Syngman Rhee's "march north" trumpet. The more the enemy blows the "march north" trumpet, the better we must build socialism and show him our mettle again. To do this we must educate our people well and unite them around the Party more firmly; and all the Party members and working people must be roused to work in a state of strained and mobilized readiness and build more and produce more in all branches of the national economy.

Our slogan is: "Let's produce more, practice economy and over-fulfill the Five-Year Plan ahead of schedule!" If we produce more and economize more, fulfill next year's plan and over-fulfill the Five-Year Plan before schedule, our country's economic foundation will be consolidated much more, the people's living standard quickly raised and, accordingly, the day of national reunification hastened.

In all branches and units of the national economy, you must uphold the slogan of increased production and economy and step up innovation movements, so as to over-fulfill the plan daily, monthly, and quarterly without fail from the very first day of the new year.

Indeed, our Party and our people have grim trials ahead. However, we must not back down from the trials; we must not stop our great advance to push ahead with socialist construction even for a moment. Under the Party's leadership, we must wage an all-Party, all-people struggle against the subversion and sabotage of the enemies at home and abroad, while at the same time, dynamically organizing and mobilizing the people's heightened revolutionary enthusiasm for socialist construction; thus we will smash to atoms all the anti-communist clamors of the imperialists, the "march north" hullabaloo of the traitorous Syngman Rheeites as well as the maneuvers of the class enemies and anti-Party counterrevolutionary factionalists lurking in our ranks. By doing this, we must again demonstrate to the whole world the indomitable, revolutionary mettle of our heroic working class and the masses rallied firmly as one man behind the Party.

FOR THE SUCCESSFUL FULLFILLMENT OF THE FIRST FIVE-YEAR PLAN

Concluding Speech Delivered at a Conference of the Workers' Party of Korea, *March 6, 1958*

Comrades,

We have discussed very important problems at this conference. We have discussed how to carry out socialist construction in the northern half of the Republic and how to further consolidate our Party, the General Staff of our revolution. The discussion of these problems is of tremendous importance.

To further strengthen our Party and successfully build socialism in the northern half, the source and main position of our revolution, means precisely to further increase the political and economic forces of our revolution.

In our country only our Party devotes its all to the struggle, in whatever adversities, for the benefit of the entire people, for the welfare and prosperity of our nation and for the reunification and independence of the country; it alone shows all the people the path of struggle. This proves that it is natural for the entire Korean people to trust their destiny to our Party and that our Party alone is capable of carrying the destiny of the

Korean people on its shoulders.

You have unanimously supported the draft First Five-Year Plan for Development of the National Economy submitted by the Party Central Committee and have firmly resolved to struggle for its fulfillment. You have also shown your strong determination to rally closely around the Party Central Committee and defend the unity of our Party like the apple of your eye by completely smashing the anti-Party groups, in order to achieve the cohesion of Party ranks in thought, will and action; you have expressed a unanimous desire to remain true to the banner of Marxism-Leninism and thus to carry our revolution through to a victorious conclusion.

I am very much gratified by the profound trust expressed by you comrades in the Party Central Committee and by your firm resolve. When our Party marches forward with such firm unity, there will be no insurmountable difficulties before us; all shades of anti-Party groups and reactionary forces opposed to the revolution will have to give way before the united force of our Party and people, and we will achieve complete victory.

I would like to speak once again about the Five-Year Plan, although you have thrashed it out in your speeches.

The Five-Year Plan, as many comrades said, is the first of its kind in our country. There could be no planned economy in our country in the past—neither during feudal reigns nor under Japanese imperialist rule. Only when the people have taken power into their own hands, only under the socialist system, is it possible to develop the national economy in a planned way.

We have already experimented with a one-year plan, a two-year plan and a three-year plan, and today we are discussing our five-year plan and carrying it out.

That we are carrying out a five-year plan is in itself striking evidence of how firm the economic basis of our country has become, how far it has developed and how much the people's democratic system has been strengthened in our country. If our economic power were weak and the people's democratic system not consolidated, it would be impossible to draw up and implement such a comparatively long-term perspective plan.

Today we are engaged in economic construction, looking ahead not one or two years, but five. A one-year plan, as you know, envisages small-scale construction over a short space of time. But a five-year plan envisages magnificent, large-scale construction over a long period. If the economic basis of our country were unstable and all the necessary preparations had not been made in every sphere of our national economy, we could neither envisage nor realize such a project. Therefore, the mere fact that today we are discussing the Five-Year Plan and have begun carrying it out is, in itself, something in which the Korean people should take great pride, and an unprecedented historic event in our country.

Another political significance of the Five-Year Plan is that it offers great prospects to all the people. In the past our people lived in destitution, not even knowing how they would make a living the next day. As a worker said in his speech a little while ago, our people's conditions were such that they had to live from hand to mouth. But today our people can clearly foresee what they will have to do at least for five years, and how much our country will have developed and how much our life will have improved at the end of that time. This affords the prospects of socialist construction and a bright future for the entire people, confirming their faith in victory. Hence, our people can surmount any difficulty with still greater courage, realizing that it precedes fresh victories and advances. Thus, the very fact that for the first time we have drawn up and are carrying out a five-year plan is of tremendous significance.

What, then, are the central tasks of the Five-Year Plan which our Party is discussing at the present conference? These tasks we have put forward are to lay the foundations of socialist industrialization in our country and basically solve the problems of food, clothing and housing for the people.

What does this mean? This means that our country will devote its attention to all aspects of the problems of economic construction and the people's living standard and solve them in a proportionate manner by combining them rationally. In other words, while stepping up all work of construction for the future development of our country and for the further consolidation of the nation's economic foundations, we plan simultaneously to solve the problems of food, clothing and housing in order to improve the people's material and cultural life.

The basic tasks of the Five-Year Plan we have advanced are based on the lawful requirements of our country's economic development and are in full accord with the interests of the whole nation for the reunification and independence of our country and its future prosperity.

The laying of foundations of socialist industrialization in our country will convert it from a backward agrarian country into an independent industrial-agricultural state.

For a long time our country was an extremely backward agrarian country under the rule of the feudal dynasties. Then for nearly 40 years it was a colonized dependent country under the colonial rule of Japanese imperialism, supplying it with raw materials. The industry we inherited with the liberation was a colonial dependent one that had been providing the imperialists with raw materials. Agriculture was also extremely backward and utterly devastated.

Our aim now is to eliminate the colonial dependence of our industry and the backwardness of our agriculture. In other words, we intend to completely liquidate colonial lopsidedness in industry and build an independent, modern socialist industry. Constructing an independent, self-supporting economy means building a country in which we can earn our own living, that is, a country which can support itself.

The creation of such an economic foundation requires both heavy and light industries with modern technological equipment. As you all know, heavy industry in the northern half had, in the past, been geared to supplying raw materials, and there was practically no light industry. Now we are going to build an independent heavy industry and a developed light industry.

As for agriculture, we are going to convert this backward rural economy of the past when we could never anticipate a stable harvest because of yearly disasters, into an advanced rural economy, which will enable the peasants to work easily, reap bumper harvests at all times free from disasters and guarantee sufficient food supplies and industrial raw materials.

That is why all the people, in response to our Party's call, are mobilizing to build this kind of hopeful, joyful and prosperous socialism.

Some people might ask: Can we reach this goal? Is it possible to build such a country? Is it not a dream? Of course, it is attainable; it is not at all a dream.

Some people scoffed at us even when we were working out

the Three-Year Plan. What did they say when they derided us? Certain cadres of the Democratic Party said: "The Communists talk sheer nonsense." They vacillated. Within our ranks there were also waverers. It is clear now that anti-Party elements were busy backbiting.

As you know, we set out on the Three-Year Plan empty-handed under extremely difficult circumstances: we literally had nothing—neither bricks, cement nor reinforcement rods. Factories had been virtually reduced to ashes. We started rehabilitation under conditions where we even found it impossible to determine the extent of destruction.

However, we surmounted all the difficulties and won a great victory. Today all the factories and enterprises are turning out more and better products than before the war. Many new factories have been built. A machine-building industry, nonexistent in our country before, has been newly created, and the colonial lopsidedness in industry has been largely eliminated. Namely, we undertook the construction of heavy industry after determining our priorities in urgency; in reconstructing factories we rebuilt them into modern ones. Those formerly engaged in the production of semi-finished goods were restored to turn out finished goods, and those which previously manufactured raw materials were rebuilt to put out semi-finished goods. Thus, every factory has been developed onto a higher level. We have created the bases of light industry although we started practically from scratch.

Then, will we be able to fulfill our plans in the future? I think we are fully capable in view of what we have already accomplished.

If we are to carry out our present plan, it is necessary to continue adhering to the line our Party has followed until now, that is, the line of laying the main emphasis on heavy industry while, at the same time, developing light industry and agriculture. This line is the one most suited to our country. The correctness of this line has been verified through practice in our country.

Our country has favorable conditions for the development of heavy industry. Though ours was a colonial industry, there was some foundation in heavy industry. Besides, our country is rich in mineral resources. If we make efforts to exploit our mineral resources and utilize them properly, we will be able to develop heavy industry further. Therefore, the development of our country's heavy industry must be given priority. Without heavy industry, it is hardly possible to develop light industry and agriculture. It goes without saying that the heavy industry we are going to build up is one which will be able to serve the development of light industry and agriculture, which will lay the foundations for our future socialist industrialization and is essential today for the solution of the problems of food, clothing and housing for the people.

Thus, the line of laying the main emphasis on heavy industry while, at the same time, developing light industry and agriculture is entirely correct. Therefore, during the Five-Year Plan, too, we must adhere to this line of laying the main emphasis on heavy industry simultaneously with the development of light industry and agriculture.

At the same time, it is important to find rational solutions to the questions of economic construction and the people's living standard both in financial policy and in investment. In other words, the balance between accumulation and consumption should be properly fixed and maintained.

We cannot follow a policy of eating up and consuming all we earn without accumulation. We must constantly increase accumulation for the future, for our country's prosperity, for its industrialization and for the sake of further consolidating the basis of socialism. Accumulation is, of course, for the people. It is different from consumption only in terms of time. In other words, consumption meets immediate needs, whereas accumulation is geared to the systematic improvement of the people's livelihood. We must increase accumulation for the future.

Yet, we should not put too much stress only on accumulation, only on the future, neglecting the present living conditions of the people. Therefore, it is of great importance to solve the problems of economic construction and the people's standard of living rationally by keeping a proper balance between accumulation and consumption as we have done up to now.

We can never accept the views of those dullards who disregard production and construction, shouting only about the people's living standard. It is also inadmissible to emphasize accumulation alone, while paying little attention to the people's living conditions.

We must fully convince the entire people of the fact that for their future well-being a high level of accumulation is necessary and that the country will become rich and strong, and the people's living conditions will improve only when economic construction goes well and production steadily develops through accumulation. This is the law of economic development, and all the people, especially our Party members, should be brought to have a clear understanding of this law.

Insistence upon eating up as much as we obtain without constructing and accumulating, without doing anything, is nothing short of the assertion of the anti-Party groups. This we cannot do. We must continue to observe the principle of regulating accumulation and consumption in a rational way.

Another important problem is to eliminate the distinctions between town and country in improving the people's living standard.

Under capitalism, the towns thrive excessively and everything converges upon them, whereas the countryside becomes more and more desolate and living standards there fall far below those in the towns.

We Communists aim to eliminate this gap between town and country. Since we have thus far made proper adjustments in the relations between town and country, the gap between them is not so great at present. This means that the living standards of the peasants and the workers are being adjusted proportionately in our country.

We must see that no large disparity is allowed to exist between urban and rural construction or between the living standards of the workers and the peasants since we develop the economy according to plan.

It is necessary to develop our national economy along this line.

Then, which branch should we emphasize in industrial development, especially in giving priority to the development of heavy industry?

First, the ferrous metal industry should be developed, so that pig iron and steel are produced in as large quantities as our country needs. We are fully able to do this. We have the Musan, Chongdong and Hasong mines. We have huge deposits of iron ore. Besides, we have the previously existing blast furnaces, electric furnaces and revolving furnaces for granulated iron. If all of them are rehabilitated, some newly built and expanded, that will do.

At present, owing to the shortage of steel, we are unable to build many houses and undertake many projects—bridges, harbors, railways, etc. Large quantities of steel are needed to set up factories, dwellings and many other facilities, to develop numerous mines and to manufacture a lot of machines. We must meet the shortage of steel. Even last year 80,000 tons of steel was imported. We can import, but why should we when we are fully capable of producing it for ourselves? We must do what we can by ourselves. We must develop the ferrous metal industry and meet our country's needs for steel. To this end, Party members, workers, engineers, assistant engineers, managers and other management personnel in this branch should make greater efforts.

Second, coal and power production should be developed. Without coal and electricity, factories, mines, railways and all other domains are unable to operate. Therefore, the power and coal industries should be continuously developed.

The development of the power industry is very important, for it strengthens the power bases. In order to develop industry, it is necessary to keep the power industry ahead of other branches. The important thing in solving the problem of electric power, as the Minister of Electricity said in his speech, is to mobilize to the maximum the latent reserves for the increased production of electric power through complete rehabilitation and readjustment of the existing power stations, and, at the same time, prevent loss of electricity by perfecting the power-transmission networks and establish a strict system of economy in the consumption of electricity. We must take these initial measures, and then begin new construction. It is wrong to undertake many new projects without fulfilling the tasks you have already been given. The first task in this sphere, therefore, is to produce more electricity by perfecting the existing equipment and to make the most of the electricity produced. Then to meet the electricity shortage, we must speed up the construction of the Tokno-gang and Kanggye Power Stations. Also, we must take the course of newly building small hydroelectric and thermal power plants and making use of all the existing ones.

It is also of great importance to develop the coal industry. At the Third Party Congress we pointed out, "You are crying for coal while sitting on a pile of coal." Now, I find the draft resolution using mild terms: "Coal resources are not properly exploited." In fact, we are crying for coal while sitting on a mountain of coal. There is no place in our country which does not have coal. As the manager of the Aoji Coal Mine said in his speech yesterday, the Aoji region alone has a deposit of at least 100 million tons. If it is mined at a rate of one million tons a year, we can go on mining for 100 years. One hundred years is a century! Then what do we have to be afraid of? However, malicious elements entrenched in this field have continued their malevolent actions and, therefore, the Party's policy has failed to reach the lower levels smoothly. Now, the coal problem must be solved without fail. The draft plan envisages 9.5 million tons, but we should surpass 10 million tons at least.

Further, one of the important problems in solving the questions of food, clothing and housing is that of fiber. We are facing great difficulties owing to the lack of fiber. The Party, therefore, has set the production of chemical fiber as an important task of the chemical industry.

The problems of food, clothing and housing are vital to man, but we are now unable to manufacture more knitted goods, fabrics and fish nets for lack of fiber. When we visit factories, we hear the workers say that they have no knitted goods. The reason why the Koreans cannot manufacture knitted goods is not the lack of know-how, but rather the shortage of yarn.

The vinalon that the chemical research institute has been studying must be put into production. It is advisable for the Party to direct great attention to this. In my opinion, the comrades working in the chemical industry should find bold and prompt solutions to the problems presented by Comrade Li Sung Gi. While thus perfecting vinalon, it is important to see that the Chongjin Spinning Mill produces more rayon yarn and staple fiber.

We will have to solve the fiber problem in our country completely by means of chemical fiber. At the present time all the technically advanced countries are taking the course of solving the fiber problem with chemical fiber. Chemical fiber acquires special significance in our country where cotton does not grow well, and even if it did, it cannot be planted extensively because of the limited amount of arable land.

Next we come to the problem of fertilizer. As was emphasized in the report, chemical fertilizer is very important for the solution of the food problem. The plan envisages the production of 630,000 tons, and this is no small figure. A certain comrade said it would be possible to turn out up to 700,000 tons, and it would be even more gratifying if work were done so well that you exceed the plan.

Not only fertilizers but also medicines for both men and domestic animals, agricultural chemicals and various other chemical products should be turned out in large quantities. Our supply of medicines and chemicals is now greatly deficient. We are short of agricultural chemicals, reagents, and medicines for men. We must meet the need for all kinds of medicines and chemicals.

In heavy industry emphasis should also be put on the mining and nonferrous metal industries. These constitute important sources of foreign currency for our country. As I have often mentioned, hoarding gold is of no use. It is now necessary to mine large quantitites of gold and rare metals and sell them to other countries, so that we build up industrial bases and carry out effective industrial construction in our country. Therefore, those branches of the mining industry which would bring us foreign currency should be further developed.

Another important question is to expand the building-materials industry, especially the production of cement. Cement is required both for the solution of the housing problem and for the productive construction aimed at expanded reproduction. The more cement, the better. With large quantities of cement we can undertake various projects. Farming, too, can be done quite easily if we have cement. There are many large mountains and ravines in our country. If we build reservoirs by damming up all these ravines, we can produce electric power, stave off flood damage, and supply water to rice paddies and dry fields in dry weather. In this way we will create the most important conditions for developing agriculture.

It is desirable to undertake such projects during the Five-Year Plan. South Hamgyong Province now suffers from flooding every year. Therefore, water conservation work should first be undertaken on the Ryonghung-gang and Namdae-chon Rivers in that province. In such places, when the stream is dammed up in the lower reaches, the embankment will often

give way, so the stream should be stemmed in the upper
reaches where it rises, instead of taking pains to build embankments in the lower reaches. Then, we can generate electricity, irrigate dry and paddy fields with that water, and prevent flood damage. Ultimately, this conservation work is good
in all its aspects, because it will enable us to irrigate fields, produce electricity, and, moreover, breed fish in well-maintained
reservoirs and provide an area for boating, too. Why then
should we not carry out the conservation work? It will be still
better if vacation hostels are set up there.

There is no end to our needs for cement. Some comrades ask
if we do not make too much cement, but that is a wrong idea. If
we now had plenty of cement, we could make concrete blocks
and wall off the sea in the tidelands on the west coast. Then we
would obtain hundreds of thousands of *chongbo* of new land.
We have to build roads and harbor facilities. Therefore,
tremendous quantities of cement are required in our country.

Emphasis should be put on those branches of heavy industry mentioned above.

As the Minister of Metal Industry said in his speech, iron
and other industries should develop those branches which can
secure raw materials in our country. This is important. Industries which depend upon foreign countries for raw
materials are not stable. Of course, fraternal countries can fill
mutual needs and cooperate with one another; but there is a
limit to this; it is impossible to rely entirely upon others. Thus,
this factor must be taken into account in developing heavy
industry.

Of paramount importance in solving all these problems is
the development of the machine-building industry. Without
developing this industry it is impossible to carry out the
technological reorganization of all branches of the national
economy. The same applies without exception to agriculture,
fisheries, chemical, power and coal industries.

To mine coal, rock drills must be produced; to undertake
high-speed tunnelling, debris-loading machines must be
manufactured. Thus, the question of mining plenty of coal
hinges upon the machine-building industry.

In order to speed up construction, we are going to introduce
the assembly-line method, which requires cranes. Machines are
also needed in building new factories and developing mines in

the future. All these should be manufactured in the machine-building industry.

In order to catch more fish, it is necessary to build boats, and, in the future, not wooden, but iron vessels. In addition, the development of agriculture calls for the production of more farm machinery. The same is true of the development of light industry. Everything depends on the machine-building industry.

For the development of all branches of the national economy, the machine-building industry is of the greatest importance. Although I have already mentioned this at the recent Conference of Activists in the Machine-building Industry, I would like to emphasize it again here: workers in the machine-building industry must be once more profoundly conscious of their great responsibility in the fulfillment of the Five-Year Plan and in the acceleration of the general development of our country's national economy. If they do their work well, everything will go well, and if not, everything will go badly.

We must continue to expand and develop the machine-building industry. And it is important to make proper use of its existing facilities. Those who are working in the machine-building industry should also muster up their courage to surmount difficulties and carry out their tasks.

As for the tasks of light industry, I mentioned them at the recent Meeting of Activists of the Ministry of Light Industry and they have been clearly pointed out in the report this time. It is important for light industry to solve the problem of fiber and expand the production of cotton and silk fabrics. In the report our target is 18 meters per head of the population, but it is necessary, in my opinion, to struggle to boost the figure to 20 meters.

Next in importance is the food-processing industry. It is the most backward branch in our country. Among the socialist countries we are most behind in regard to the food-processing industry.

We must develop it through an all-people movement. The food industry should be developed so we may process our fruit, vegetables, meat, fish, etc., tastily at low cost and supply them to the people.

It is also important to widen the variety of daily necessities.

At present articles of daily use are in very short supply. Why are they scarce? It is because in the past the Japanese did not produce daily necessities in Korea at all; they only brought Japanese goods and sold them in our country. Even paper came from Japan. Nothing was produced in Korea.

We must struggle in every way to turn out daily necessities in larger quantities. Their production must be expanded in the producers' cooperatives, local industry and light industry enterprises and in the by-product shops of heavy industry enterprises.

It is advisable for all the heavy industry factories to set up shops on a small scale to produce articles we use every day. When I went to the Soviet Union, I visited an aircraft factory. It was so big and impressive. Yet, on one side they were making airplanes and, on the other, milk cans out of the waste materials.

Our managers are so pompous that when instructed to make things of this sort, they say they cannot make so trivial things. Why are such things trivial? What is loftier than serving the people? In our heavy industry, too, we should use the waste materials of its factories to produce daily necessities.

We should produce a great deal of daily necessities in all branches such as producers' cooperatives and local and light industries. While increasing the variety of goods, quality should be improved through the introduction of a strict checkup system.

Now, I would like to touch upon construction. An important thing here is to lay the main emphasis on the construction of productive facilities while, at the same time, initiating a movement to build more dwellings that are most vital to people's life. Construction work should be undertaken in an all-people movement in towns and in the country side. As we see by the figures stipulated in the Five-Year Plan, housing with a total floor space of 10 million square meters will be built in towns. This is an enormous figure. It is equivalent to almost 300,000 flats. And if the 200,000 houses in rural areas are added, it amounts to building some 500,000 houses. This is not an easy task. If we exert every effort to speed up construction, use the assembly-line method in construction in accordance with the line laid down by the Party, and widely utilize materials locally available in the areas where the assembly-line method is not feasible, this huge task can be carried out successfully.

The houses we build must be national in form and socialist in content. What do we mean by socialist in content? It means building convenient and useful homes for the people. We must build modern homes which are attractive, neat, useful and convenient for the people.

In agriculture we must struggle to lay the main stress on grain production while simultaneously developing industrial crops, animal husbandry and fruit growing. In increasing grain production it is important to raise the utilization of land boost per-unit-area yields. What is important in increasing per-unit-area yields?

First of all, irrigation, that is, the problem of controlling water. We should undertake irrigation projects on a large scale so that dry fields, to say nothing of rice paddies, can be watered to prevent drought damage; river improvements should be carried out and many reservoirs built to avoid floods. This is one of our main tasks in agriculture today.

Second, we have the problem of fertilizer. The chemical industry has to produce a lot of chemical fertilizer and the peasants must make large quantities of compost.

Further, to ease the work of the peasants and increase the harvest yields, we must provide them with farm machinery and means of transport. We must increase the number of machine-hire stations, tractors and lorries and give priority to the production and supply of many animal-drawn farm implements, thereby making work easier for the peasants and increasing the harvest yields.

Socialist cooperativization is now nearing completion in our countryside. Therefore, the problem of strengthening the cooperative economy is assuming importance. In order to consolidate the cooperatives economically it is necessary to further increase agricultural production and raise the living standard of the cooperative members to the level of well-to-do middle peasants.

Another important problem in the rural areas is to remold the outdated ideological consciousness of the peasants into a socialist one. With the change in the form of the economy alone, we cannot say that the socialist revolution has been completed. For the consummation of the socialist revolution it is essential to transform the people's consciousness by strengthening the work of socialist education in the country-side. We should see to it that the peasants become staunch socialist fighters who hate the system of exploitation, combat all shades of reactionary ideology that seek to restore that system, and defend the socialist system and socialist gains with their lives.

Besides, the cultural revolution should be carried out in the countryside. Without this, the continuous development of our countryside is impossible. Important in the cultural revolution is the problem of introducing compulsory education, par-ticularly of having all the people acquire a secondary school education or above. What then should be done for those who are old now? We must see to it that, excepting the aged, all of those who are now between 30 and 40 acquire a primary school education and the rising generation, a secondary school or higher level. Only when these levels are attained will we be able to say that the cultural revolution has been completed in the countryside.

Attention should also be paid to sanitation work in rural areas. When man's consciousness is developed, needless to say, sanitation work will be improved. Owing to negligence in sanitation, our country still has cases of distomiasis, typhoid fever, measles and other epidemics and endemics. These various diseases must be completely wiped out and the peo-ple's health promoted.

All the people want to live prosperous, and they wish long lives because they are in a good era, and why is it impossible for our Party to solve this problem when it is doing everything else? In order to solve it, hygienic and epidemic-prevention work should be undertaken in an all-people movement.

In rural construction, we should give priority to productive construction. At the same time, we should initiate a mass movement to build modern houses, nurseries, clinics, schools, and so forth, in a cultured way.

Thus the appearance of the countryside should be radically changed during the Five-Year Plan.

Next, I would like to refer to the problem of trade. Our com-rades at present are taking a very passive attitude towards trade. In particular, the local Party organizations and people's power organs pay it very little attention. Such attitude is wrong. It should be clearly borne in mind that the development of state trade and consumers' cooperative trade constitutes one of the tasks of the socialist revolution, a task of combating intermediary exploitation.

Everyone participated enthusiastically in the organization of the agricultural cooperatives, even going without sleep, but no one pays attention to trade. This is quite incorrect. The chief aim of the socialist revolution is to abolish the system of exploitation once and for all. But nobody thinks of fighting intermediary exploitation by tradesmen.

What kind of exploitation still exists today in our countryside and towns? It is only intermediary exploitation. Merchants individually practice usury, buy farm produce cheaply from peasants and sell it at high prices to workers and office employees. This is how they are engaged in intermediary exploitation. This is the only kind of exploitation which still exists.

How are we to combat the phenomenon of exploitation which is still in existence? We must abolish the exploitative system by the method of emulation, that is, emulation which shows who is the better hand in trade, by strengthening the trade of the state and cooperative organizations. However, quite a few comrades, forgetting that this is a socialist revolution, regard trade with contempt, attach little importance to it, and do not even try to learn it. No cadre, when asked about trade, shows that he is aware of statistics on commodity circulation. The same is true of the chairmen of the provincial people's committees, to say nothing of the chairmen of the county or *ri* people's committees.

Without strengthening state and cooperative trade, we cannot combat private trade. If we do not strengthen our trade and cooperativize private trade but only verbally urge the private merchants to desist from exploitation, they will not listen to us. It is no use begging them. That would be as effective as praying to deaf ears.

Then, what is to be done? The only way is to strengthen the trade of state and cooperative organizations and transform the private tradesmen along socialist lines by displaying the same great zeal and energy as when we organized cooperatives in the countryside.

How did we organize the agricultural cooperatives? We should learn from the experience of the struggle for the cooperative economy, shouldn't we? As a woman from Yonan County said in her speech, we have waged a really difficult struggle for the victory of socialism in the countryside. As a result of this struggle, the socialist transformation of agriculture has been completed up to 95 percent, 97 to 98 percent in certain provinces!

The same is the case with trade. Here, too, a hard struggle is required. We must improve our procurement of agricultural produce, and lay out commodities more neatly for sale.

As I have always said, the seaweed undaria pinnatifida, for example, is piled up in one place at our state stores, all crumpled and covered with dust, until it is sold. But how do the private merchants handle it? Having purchased it at the same cost, they spread it out with care and pile it up in such a way that it looks clean and appetizing. Then they sell it at a price only slightly higher than at state stores, about two *won* more per *kun*. In this way they gain credit. Customers go to the private merchants rather than to state stores. What does this mean? It means that our state trade has been outdone by private trade. In spite of this, the workers in state trade are not ashamed of having been beaten out by the private merchants. They mumble: "It can't be helped, can it?" Such an attitude is not worthy of a Communist. This means that socialism has lost the battle in trade, yet the cadres do not feel responsible for it.

Some time ago we began a checkup on the trading networks in the Central District of Pyongyang. The checkup is not yet over. I myself inspected some stores. If our trade workers run stores as they are doing in the Central District of Pyongyang, they can neither compete with private trade nor properly discharge their duty of supplying consumer goods to the people.

All the products turned out at hundreds and thousands of our factories are channelled through the trading organizations. Funds amounting to tens of thousands of million *won* are placed in the hands of the trade workers. Nevertheless, how are the trading organizations carrying on their business? They have no sense of responsibility whatsoever. And no one is dealing with the education of the trade workers. One day I had a talk with Party members of a primary Party organization in a trading establishment. There were nine Party members and none of them had ever taken even a week's training course. That is why our Party's policy has not been carried out in the field of trade.

Important in socialist trade is the question of properly distributing and supplying commodities to the people. Distribution and consumption should be effected in a planned way, just as our production proceeds according to a plan.

Is our trade coping with this task? No, it is not. Selling is conducted haphazardly anywhere. So people living in remote places are not supplied with the quota of commodities to which they are entitled. This means that the trade workers have failed to carry out their duties. Under the conditions where the socialist economic system dominates supreme, trade should play the role of distributing commodities evenly, stimulating production and satisfying the needs of the population. But it fails to fully perform this role. This fact offers a big obstacle to the struggle against capitalism and to the socialist remolding of the private merchants in the period of transition from capitalism to socialism. Therefore, the entire Party today should direct its attention to trade.

We must bring about a great change in trade. This alone will make it possible finally to abolish the system of exploitation in town and country. I do not mean that we should depend on the interior service organs to settle the problem. Private trade should be abolished through competition, by improving everything—our procurement work, our organization of sales, quality of commodities, etc. Only by so doing will we be able to transform private trade along socialist lines. It is necessary, therefore, to develop the trade of state and cooperative organizations in order to wipe out the exploitative system still existing in counties and ri.

Now, the increase of transport capacity is also important in the fulfillment of the Five-Year Plan. Transport is one of the serious problems in the Five-Year Plan.

The Minister of Transport spoke about the transport service yesterday, and I support his speech. The problem of transport should be solved in such a way as to reduce the turn-round time of freight cars and, in addition, to further strengthen highway, river and maritime transport.

One of the most important problems in the Five-Year Plan is the development of science.

As the President of the Academy of Sciences pointed out in his speech, scientists should not waste their energy and time doing research on useless, fantastic subjects. Rather, they should concentrate on the problems which are vital to our national economy today and require an immediate solution. This must be their primary task. Our country does not have many scientists. It is important to solve the burning questions of the present, instead of going in for "far-reaching projects".

How important it is for our country to find an early solution to problems such as the problem of fiber! It is necessary to solve a number of problems: how to develop the nation's iron industry, using less coke or none at all; how to obtain substitutes for fuel oil in view of the absence of an oil base in our country, and an assortment of other problems which confront us.

Another matter of importance is first to introduce and popularize the scientific and technological achievements of foreign countries to suit our conditions, rather than producing inventions and making new things in our country now. In view of the fact that we Koreans are not yet well informed about achievements made by the advanced countries in the development of science and technology, it is important first to study and popularize those achievements.

Also, it is desirable that scientists, instead of just staying in their laboratories, go directly to the factories and productions sites, give practical help in the solution of urgent problems and do their research work there. Since we do not now have enough laboratory equipment and research instruments and materials, satisfactory research cannot be expected in laboratories alone.

For a successful fulfillment of the Five-Year Plan the leading functionaries should be skillful in guidance.

As shown by the experience acquired after the December 1956 Plenary Meeting of the Party Central Committee, it is important to further develop such leadership methods as keeping closer contact with the lower units, listening to the creative opinions of subordinates, discussing matters with them, giving correct solutions to the questions raised by them, and popularizing useful experience. This, in my opinion, is the most important factor in carrying out the Five-Year Plan.

Now, I would like to talk about Party work. As was keynoted in the report and unanimously expressed in your speeches, we must continue to fight resolutely against factionalism, parochialism and nepotism in defense of the unity of the Party.

Factionalism, parochialism and nepotism are entirely alien to Communism. We must oppose them more staunchly. In essence, parochialism and nepotism are both factionalism, the only difference being that one is larger and the other smaller, but they are, in fact, all factionalism.

Factionalism has its origin in capitalist ideology. It comes from nowhere else. Therefore, it is in no way compatible with communism which is opposed to capitalism. It is hostile to our ideology and has nothing in common with it.

The factional elements, however, contend that progress can be made only when factionalism exists. They think that factions such as the M-L group, the Tuesday group, etc., contributed in some important way to our country's revolutionary work in the past. In actual fact, far from carrying on the revolutionary cause, they wrought havoc with the revolution. If they ever waged a revolutionary struggle, why was the Communist Party destroyed in the 1920's? Who delights in seeing the Party's ruin? Who gloats over it if not the capitalists?

If the M-L group and Tuesday group had not indulged in factional feuds and had not destroyed the Party, the Korean people would have had their own revolutionary Party by the time the liberation came. Our Party would be stronger today, and our country might not be split as it is now.

The factionalists have done very great harm. All those who go around preaching the "theory" that factions benefited the communist movement and the revolutions, are opposed to our Party and to communism.

Certain factional elements speak out, "Say what you will, our M-L group is superior." And others prattle, "Why, after all, our Tuesday group is better." In my opinion, there is nothing to choose between them. No faction is better or worse than any other. All come from the same mold; they are all products of capitalist influence in the working-class movement. And all are a poison that destroys our Party and the working- class movement in Korea.

Factionalism, parochialism and nepotism all stem from selfishness. In other words, they are the products of personal lust for fame, high position and power, individual political am-

bition; they are not in the interests of our Party or the state.
This is why the factionalists are never satisfied, no matter how
high their promotions. We thought they would be content with
a high position. But give them an inch and they take a mile.

Our Party's experience in its struggle for over ten years
shows that the factionalists, regardless of their promotions,
distrust the Party and do not open their hearts to it. Ryu Chuk
Un, for example, even was suspicious of his appointment as
minister.

Once I asked Choe Chang Ik and Kim Ung, "Why are you so
suspicious?" I said to the latter, "You are Chief of Staff and
were Frontline Commander. Why do you always doubt
whether our Party trusts you?"

The Party trusted him, but he suspected the Party. What
was the reason? He was not candid with the Party because he
was egoistically obsessed with a greed for power and position.
Outwardly he supported the Party while playing treacherous
tricks behind the scenes. This is why he always tried to read
the Party's mind. He was anxious to know if we were at all of-
fended, whether a Party meeting was tense, or how his case
was discussed. A faint rustle nearby was enough to make his
eyes round with suspicion as to whether anything about him
was being called into question. Criticism of someone else even
startled him, giving him a guilty conscience. Such is the case
with all factionalists. They behave like this, because they,
prompted by self-interest, always distrust the Party and
suspect that it distrusts them.

Although the Party promotes and trusts them, their personal ambition continues to grow. We may take the example of
Choe Chang Ik. We trusted this man and promoted him, but
his ambition grew even larger. Just as these factionalists are
never satisfied and their ambition is insatiable, their suspicion
also inevitably grows.

The case of Kim Du Bong is similar. We worked with him for
ten years. But during those years he was dreaming of other
things. While uncommunicative with us, he opened his heart
only to Han Bin and Choe Chang Ik.

Despite the fact that Han Bin is a man hated by our Party
for his subversive activities against it, Kim Du Bong considered him his closest friend. If Kim Du Bong had ever been a
Communist, if he had ever been devoted to the Party, why had

he been on the most intimate terms with a man hated by the Party? This is how things were. Kim Du Bong always valued Han Bin's words more than the decisions of our Party.

The same applies to O Gi Sop. As a member of the Party Central Committee, O Gi Sop worked with us for ten years. But his mind was always preoccupied with other things, and he was not going in the same direction that we were.

Why do the factionalists and parochialists behave like this? Because they think they are the smartest men, the cocks of the walk. Kim Du Bong, too, thought himself the wisest. Thus he was entirely discontented with the Party, was finding fault with what had been proposed by the Party and tried to put forward something original himself. O Gi Sop also considered himself the cleverest of men. For some time he was a minister, and his subordinates would say: "Our Minister O Gi Sop doesn't do his job, but is absorbed in a study of policies day and night." And it was by no means in the Party's interest that he studied the policies. He did so because he distrusted the Party's lines and policies and wanted to propose something in opposition to the Party.

All this stems from individualist heroism which is characterized by disloyalty to the Party, careerism and a thirst for fame.

The factionalists always draw people around them to advance their own careers. Instead of trying to build up prestige by the quality of their work, they attract people by throwing drinking parties and making a show of their generosity at the expense of the state; when they get together, they talk secretly about all the things that are not discussed in the Party. At such gatherings they talk about all sorts of things, prefaced by, "This is strictly between us." In this way, they place personal friendship above the Party organization, putting greater faith in the former.

Kim Du Bong used to suggest something new whenever he had stayed overnight at Han Bin's house. This was always aimed at undermining our Party.

Factionalism, parochialism and nepotism all place the interests of one's own group and of oneself above those of the Party.

Our Party members must value the interests of the Party more than their own lives and make it an iron rule to sacrifice themselves for the good of the Party. We must have the lofty characteristic of giving all we can for the unity and cohesion of the Party. Otherwise there can be no Party unity.

Next, we must criticize the attitude of self-importance that causes someone to keep the activity of his branch of work from everyone else and to brag that his branch is doing the best work. No one should consider that the branch, locality or ministry (bureau) in his charge is the first rung up the ladder of a brilliant career.

We must resolutely combat the tendency to factionalism, parochialism, nepotism and departmentalism, and further intensify the struggle for the whole Party to obey the leadership of the Party center.

What should we do, then, to oppose factionalism? We should not just talk about the M-L group, the Tuesday group and the crimes of Pak Hon Yong and Choe Chang Ik. We must give our Party members a clear idea of the harm of factionalism, nepotism and parochialism, which brought ruin on our Party in the past and which today may tear it into shreds again and revive capitalism.

You should not educate Party members in such ways as simply criticizing Pak Hon Yong for having done wrong in the past and Choe Chang Ik for being wrong this time. You should give Party members a clear understanding of the essence of factionalism, nepotism and parochialism, of how the factionalists behave and wherein lie the roots of their ideology. In this way we must make sure that there is no room left for the factional elements to gain a foothold. We will thus prevent people from being inveigled into factional actions and help them to recognize anyone who might try to do so and oppose him in advance. This is of great importance.

The crime of Kim Du Bong is really serious. He spoiled many young people. The Party and the state gave Party assignments to simple and honest people to work at the Presidium of the Supreme People's Assembly. However, many of them were ruined there.

In order to prevent the recurrence of similar crimes in the future, it is very important to make all the Party membership aware of the evil effects of factionalism. This requires strengthening the Marxist-Leninist education of Party members. We have to raise their ideological and theoretical levels of

Marxism-Leninism, thus helping them to acquire foresight, learn to analyze every problem, completely do away with bourgeois ideological viewpoint and form the working-class world outlook. Only by so doing, will we be able to root out factionalism, parochialism and nepotism.

Now, I will make a few remarks about revisionism. Though revisionism in our country has not appeared in a systematic way, those who stood against our Party, carried away by the so-called "international trend," spread revisionism. Thus, in our country, too, there has appeared the revisionist trend which disrupts the communist movement, opposes Marxist-Leninist principles and capitulates to capitalism.

The imperialists and their servants, the revisionists, are now spreading revisionism in opposition to Marxism-Leninism and the communist movement. It would be silly to declare that revisionism will not find its way into our country. It has made and is making inroads into our country, too, and the anti-Party groups have already exploited it for their own ends. In his speech yesterday a comrade said that the anti-Party groups had smuggled in revisionism, and, indeed, that is what they have done.

In our country revisionism found expression in the rejection of Party leadership and the dictatorship of the proletariat. Kim Du Bong said that the Presidium of the Supreme People's Assembly stood above the Party. What does that mean? It means that the Presidium rejects the Party's leadership. So Hwi said: "The Party is not entitled to lead the trade unions. The membership of the trade unions is greater than that of the Party; they are a larger organization than the Party. Those who are working in Party organs should obey the leadership of the trade unions because they are all trade union members. The trade unions should get rid of the tutelage of the Party." Kim Ul Gyu said that the People's Army was not the army of the Party, but rather "the army of the united front." All these are ideological viewpoints which reject Party leadership.

There is a tendency today in some ministries and people's committees to dislike the Party leadership of administrative work. This attitude is also a rejection of Party leadership. It is true that the Party should refrain from improperly taking the place of administrative bodies. But the Party should lead all the work of the power organs.

We are also witnessing the wrong tendency among some people to believe in the omnipotence of technique, thinking themselves the greatest authorities in technical matters and refuse to accept the Party's leadership readily. This, too, is a very harmful propensity. What is the use of technology if it is separated from the will and leadership of the Party? The Party only needs technology of the kind that is in the service of socialist construction and helps implement the revolutionary tasks of the Party. It does not need any other technology.

Our Party is a militant organization which builds socialism and communism, leading the working class and all other sections of the working people. And ours is the only Party that leads the class struggle and the revolution in Korea. To reject our Party's leadership means precisely to deny the revolution and capitulate to capitalism. Therefore, it is necessary not only to fight against the revisionists who reject Party leadership, but also to combat relentlessly all the unhealthy elements that provide good soil for revisionism.

Some people say that our people's power is not one that exercises the dictatorship of the proletariat because it is based on a united front. This is an entirely erroneous view. Today, our people's power is a state power that belongs to the category of the dictatorship of the proletariat. In the northern half of the Republic, now in the period of transition from capitalism to socialism, the functions of the proletarian dictatorship of our people's power must be strengthened even more.

Others have an incorrect idea of the character of our state power and revolutionary tasks and so hold that it is unnecessary to promote the socialist transformation of private merchants and industrialists, because there are not many capitalist elements in towns and the countryside. This is also incorrect.

Although a great triumph has been achieved in our socialist construction, we cannot say that the exploiting classes have now been completely wiped out in the northern half. And even if they have been, ideologies antagonistic to socialism will survive for a long time.

As long as small commodity producers, private merchants and manufacturers, even in limited numbers, remain in urban and rural areas, as long as the tasks of the socialist revolution have not yet been accomplished and, moreover, there exists a regime of landlords and capitalists in the southern half, how can we neglect to consolidate the dictatorship of the proletariat? For the triumphant accomplishment of the socialist revolution in the northern half, we must further strengthen our proletarian dictatorship.

The dictatorship of the proletariat is a powerful weapon of the working class in thoroughly crushing all the counter-revolutionary elements hostile to the socialist revolution and in defending the interests of the working people and the revolution.

Our judicial organs, however, under the pretext of "protecting human rights", disturbed social order by freeing hostile elements such as Li Man Hwa, a Christian, who had turned against our Party and the revolution, and by releasing many prisoners who had perpetrated hostile acts. Our state power is a weapon for protecting the interests of the working people and the revolution; it cannot be a weapon which protects the interests of the hostile classes that oppose us. This tendency in the judiciary is a revisionist one which conflicts with the dictatorship of the proletariat.

Revisionism which has found expression in our country is aimed entirely at undermining our revolution by making our Party and revolutionary forces impotent to fight the enemy. Therefore, a resolute struggle must be waged against it.

I will not bring up other subjects because, by and large, they have already been discussed.

I would like to mention only one more thing, the question of strengthening the Party life of our Party members. Whoever is disloyal in Party life may commit errors and mistakes of one sort or the other at any time. It is therefore necessary to combat forcefully the tendency to evade Party life. At the same time, Marxist-Leninist ideological education should be further intensified. Especially, it is very important to study dialectical materialism. In this way, every Party member should be helped to have the Marxist-Leninist world outlook and become a member with a strong Party spirit.

I would like to conclude with a few remarks about the questions and suggestions that have been made.

How should we deal with Kim Du Bong, Pak Ui Wan, O Gi Sop and others of their kind? So far there is no evidence that

Kim Du Bong, Pak Ui Wan and O Gi Sop took part in the conspiracy for counterrevolutionary revolt. Kim Du Bong and Pak Ui Wan tried to overthrow the Party and oust the Party leadership. In other words, they were both involved in factional activities. O Gi Sop did not openly carry out factional activity, but was caught doing it snakily like some stray cat.

Our Party has done much to educate these people; it has educated them perseveringly for a year and a half. Nevertheless, they still do not show sincerity to make a clean breast of their misdeeds honestly before the Party and make amends for them. True, they now admit all what we have discovered and promise not to repeat them, but they have confessed to none of them voluntarily and candidly. Only when confronted with evidence, do they acknowledge them. In short, they are still two-faced, and do not open their hearts to the Party.

The struggle with these people should be guided by the following principles: those who have committed serious crimes should be strictly punished, and those who have not committed serious crimes should be examined ideologically. Their ideological examination should be conducted strictly and they should be punished leniently. In other words, what should be brought to full light is how they got involved in factional activities and what is the ideological basis. Then punishment should be leniently applied. Thus, they should be given the opportunity to correct their mistakes. In our struggle against the factionalists half measures will not do; facts and root causes must be unearthed and assurances given. All of their factional crimes should be laid bare for everyone to see, and then the factionalists should be completely disarmed. Yet it will be good to punish them leniently. It is advisable to deal with them on these principles.

As for Kim Du Bong, Pak Ui Wan and O Gi Sop, our opinion is that, according to the "socialist principle of distribution", they should be given as much as they have "earned". It is advisable to deal with them on this principle. What have they earned and what do they fairly deserve? This you comrades should decide here.

The most important thing in the struggle against factionalism is to defend the Party Central Committee in order to safeguard Party unity. Without the Central Committee there can be no Party. Therefore, the principle of democratic centralism, a principle which calls on the individual to obey the Party organization and on all Party organizations to obey the Central Committee, should be observed. This is the Leninist organizational principle. Only by observing it can we increase our Party's fighting capacity. Without it our Party cannot become a strong party.

ON IMPROVING THE WORK METHODS OF THE COUNTY PARTY ORGANIZATION IN ACCORDANCE WITH THE NEW CIRCUMSTANCES (Excerpt)

Speech Delivered at a Plenary Meeting of the Kangso County Party Committee, *February 18, 1960*

. . .

Since our revolution is developing every day, our thinking, too, makes progress and so does the Party policy. The Party center studies the continuously developing realities of our country and frames new policies to suit them.

Our Party's policy is an application of Marxism-Leninism to our country's realities. One can neither write, nor guide work without studying our Party's policies, no matter how many Marxist-Leninist books he may have read.

The instructors should study the Party policy systematically and know a new policy in good time whenever it is set forth by the Party. A good knowledge of the Party policy is essential to broadening one's mental vision, to finding the right way of looking at things, and carrying on one's work with conviction and daring.

The instructors of the Party Central Committee are on a higher level than the comrades at the county Party committees not because they have been chosen from among those who

were county Party committee chairmen. Among them are comrades who were county Party committee chairmen before, but
there are many who were not. The instructors of the Party Central Committee are on a higher level than the functionaries of
the county Party committees because they are well aware of
the intentions of the Party center.

The Party center sums up the experience of all the activities
of our Party, but the county Party committees have only the
experience of work within the county limits. True, it is natural
for the functionaries of the county Party committees to have a
broader view of things than the *ri* cadres who are in charge of
the work of the *ri*, since the county Party committees sum up
the experience of work on the county level. But if we do not
discuss and study the Party policy every day, we shall become
ignorant of even the experience of the county level, to say
nothing of the experience of the struggle of the entire Party,
and shall eventually find our perspectives too narrow to lead
the cadres of the *ri*.

At present the Party center pays great attention to the
education of the instructors. The Party leadership promptly
acquaints the instructors with the Party policy.

Before, persons such as Pak Chang Ok ensconced in the Party leadership used to tell only what they copied from foreign
newspapers and magazines without making the Party policy
known, and so education of the instructors was unsatisfactory.
Even in writing an article, they used difficult terms and mar-
shalled many propositions of various kinds. To the uninitiated
eye, such an article appears to be impressive, but, in fact, it is
hollow and empty. It amounts to making noises merely with
empty words without the least knowledge of the substance of
Marxism, and is tantamount to licking only the rind of a
watermelon without so much as tasting its meat to find out
whether it is sweet or bitter. What good is it to play with
words using difficult terms without knowing our Party's
policy when all our work is associated with our revolution?
Those who do not know Party policy and the substance of their
own work, have no view to call their own, after all, and so they
dogmatically copy from others, thereby prejudicing the work.
In a word, they are persons who lack Juche.

What we call Juche means doing everything in accordance
with the actual conditions of our country and creatively apply-

ing the general principles of Marxism-Leninism and the experience of other countries to suit our realities.

It is the duty of the Korean Communists to carry out the Korean revolution well in conformity to the actual conditions of our country, and that is our way of making a contribution to the world communist movement. Our task is to build socialism in our country and develop its politics, economy and culture for the welfare and prosperity of our people. And how can he who is ignorant of his society, his people, the history and the revolutionary and cultural traditions of his own country, carry out the revolution in a way congenial to his country? And how can he who slights his own things and only praises others' develop his own things?

Once some artists offered to throw away our national musical instruments, saying that they were uncivilized and undeveloped and that it was even impossible to use the musical notation for them. We severely criticized such a view. The Party's policy on literature and art was not carried out properly because a person such as Pak Chang Ok who praised only foreign things was entrenched in the Propaganda Department. Our national musical instruments perfectly suit the sentiments of our people. So why should we discard them? And it is also untenable to assert that the national musical instruments of Korea cannot be fitted to musical notation. The trouble lies in the wrong ideological viewpoint of making light of our national art.

How can a person who is said to be engaged in the Korean revolution do his own thinking as master of his own revolution if he does not proceed from the actual realities of Korea, and belittles his own things and only copies from others? If one acquires the habit of only copying from others, he will eventually find himself totally devoid of his own thought and will also lose the ability of developing new ideas. Suppose a lazy pupil does not write a composition himself, but always has somebody else write one for him because he dislikes composition; the result will be that he will always be unable to write a composition. The same is true of our revolutionary work. As long as one relies on others and only copies from them without establishing Juche in his work, he can display no creative initiative.

Since the question of Juche was put forward, a change has taken place in the people's way of thinking. Everybody is now doing his work in accordance with the actual conditions he finds himself in, and so tremendous creative initiative which was formerly unimaginable is now displayed.

We should educate the cadres and members of the Party in such a way as to enable them to display creative initiative. They should have a good knowledge of the Party policy and be able to advance their work by thinking independently when carrying out their assigned tasks. A *ri* Party committee chairman should be able to carry on his job independently in accordance with the Party policy even when he is given no direct guidance and assistance from the county Party committee.

THE PEOPLE'S ARMY— A COMMUNIST SCHOOL
(Excerpt)

Talk with Soldiers of the 109th Army Unit of the Korean People's Army, *August 25, 1960*

4. On Opposing Dogmatism and Revisionism

In political work, we must first eliminate dogmatism and formalism.

Before, foreign publications were copied mechanically when preparing documents or lecture programs for lower echelons. This practice has now ceased, but the old style and method of work are still lingering.

If a formal report is made and a resolution read out at a meeting, whether or not Party members understand the report, this is also a manifestation of dogmatism and formalism. We must put an end to this formalistic work method which is refined outwardly but has no substance.

Till the March 1958 Plenary Meeting of the Party Central Committee, Choe Jong Hak, then in charge of the General Political Bureau of the Korean People's Army, had had foreign publications uncritically copied in preparing the materials which the lower units were forced to use. He made a mess of the army's political work. Because he had neglected political work, the factionalists had been able to wriggle into the army. Otherwise, they would not have done so.

Pak Chang Ok and Pak Yong Bin, who had been on the Party Central Committee during the war, were so ignorant that they also gutted foreign papers and forced the lower units to accept their plagiarisms. They worked in such a manner that they mechanically repeated what foreigners said.

Westerners use knives when eating bread but we scoop rice with spoons. Foreign customs and things do not always suit the taste of us Koreans. We should assimilate what is excellent and progressive out of things foreign but not what is inexpedient to our actual conditions.

Our guardhouse system was a mechanical imitation of foreign things. The anti-Japanese guerrillas had fought well for 15 years, none of them ever being detained. We can dispense with the guardhouse; when they are properly educated, the soldiers will voluntarily observe discipline.

The Irkutsk group used to make demagogic attacks on any opponents to dogmatism or to their views, claiming that they were against the Soviet Union. This made it impossible to fight against Choe Jong Hak's misdeeds.

Our opposition to dogmatism does not undermine our solidarity with the Soviet Union. Lenin and Stalin, both Soviets, also advocated opposition to dogmatism.

Thanks to our Party's struggle against dogmatism we could accelerate socialist construction. Had we clung to dogmatism we would have gotten nowhere.

Some foreigners have often criticized our work though not acquainted with our situation. When we were organizing cooperatives they claimed that it was too premature. However, because we formed the cooperatives at the time we have been able to live on. After the war, we had nothing on hand. The war destroyed everything we had had. There were only a few cattle in the countryside. Such being the situation, how could we subsist without organizing cooperatives?

The fraternal parties now praise the Workers' Party of Korea as being second to none in socialist construction. This is also because we did not slide into dogmatism.

We must firmly oppose revisionism, as well as dogmatism.

Revisionists refashion Marxism-Leninism. They laud themselves as cleverer Marxists-Leninists than Marx or Lenin. Certain countries have this tendency.

Some people insist that we must peacefully coexist with the Yankees. How can we do so, without opposing US imperialism?

People of great powers may commit errors. We cannot fully agree with them or follow them blindly.

Some people asked us to withdraw our slogan "Wipe out the US aggressors!" saying that it was undesirable. Our Party Central Committee declined their claim.

In addition, they told us, "Don't shoot down intruding US aircraft but just land them." The countries which have good planes may do so, but not we. We must pursue the aircraft and shoot them down. We pay no heed to the words of the evil-minded.

It is true that we must unite with the fraternal countries. However, we need not emulate the misdeeds of individual persons in these countries.

As far back as the days of the anti-Japanese guerrilla struggle, we put up the slogan: defend and unite with the Soviet Union. Since liberation, we have continued to defend and unite with the Soviet Union and so shall we do in the future. We cannot do everything as the Soviets do because we must unite with them.

We Koreans should properly assimilate progressive things of the brother countries to suit our own taste. Only then can we hasten the construction of communism.

REPORT ON THE WORK OF THE CENTRAL COMMITTEE TO THE FOURTH CONGRESS OF THE WORKERS' PARTY OF KOREA (Excerpt)

September 11, 1961

Comrades,

More than five years have elapsed since the Third Congress of our Party. In this period great changes of historic importance have taken place in the national and international life of our people.

During the period under review our Party, leading the Korean people, achieved major victories in the socialist revolution and socialist construction in the northern half of the Republic and made great progress in the struggle for the peaceful reunification of the country. The historic revolutionary tasks of completing socialist transformation in town and countryside and building the foundations of socialism have been triumphantly carried out. Under the leadership of the Party our people, overcoming all difficulties and making the grand Chollima march, have scaled the first height of socialist construction and have made the revolutionary democratic base in the northern half of the Republic an impregnable fortress.

Inspired by the immense successes in socialist construction in North Korea and by our Party's correct policy for the peaceful reunification of the country, the broad masses of the people in South Korea have risen in a heroic struggle against US imperialism and its stooges; they have dealt a telling blow to the colonial rule of US imperialism in South Korea.

During the period under review the Party consolidated our friendship and solidarity with the fraternal peoples of the socialist camp and peace-loving peoples throughout the world. It took an active part in the struggle for peace in Asia and the Far East and greatly raised our country's international prestige.

Our Party has been strengthened and has grown into an invincible militant detachment bound by one and the same purpose around its Central Committee. The unity of the Party and the people has become unshakable.

Now we come to this Fourth Congress on the Party at a time when the whole country stands at a momentous turning point in the development of our revolution, thrilling with labor upsurge and creative enthusiasm, when all the working masses place absolute trust and hope in our Party, and when our friends unanimously support and encourage us.

This congress will open up bright new prospects in the struggle of our Party and people to conquer the high peak of socialism and hasten the peaceful reunification of the country. It will inspire all the working people of our country on to great victories.

I. Excellent Results

Comrades,

The Third Congress of our Party was convened at a time when the postwar rehabilitation of the national economy was, on the whole, nearly complete. At that time our country's economy and culture were still backward and the socialist reorganization of the relations of production was in full progress.

The prewar level of industrial and agricultural production was restored thanks to the heroic efforts of our working people in the postwar years. But our country still remained an agrarian country, and our people's life was very hard. Private farming still held an important place in the countryside, and the transformation of private trade and industry in the towns had just begun.

In this situation we had to muster all our strength to promote in every possible way the socialist revolution and the building of socialism.

Based on the requirements of the laws of socio-economic development in the northern half and the fundamental tasks of the Korean revolution, our Party had advanced the general tasks of laying the foundations of socialism in the northern half of the Republic as early as the postwar period of rehabilitation. This meant expanding and reinforcing the socialist economic sector by reorganizing small commodity and capitalist sectors on socialist lines in all branches of the national economy as well as restoring and further developing the productive forces, thereby building the solid foundations for an independent national economy and rapidly improving the people's living conditions.

The Third Party Congress approved the policy of the Party Central Committee for laying the foundations of socialism and, on this basis, defined the fundamental tasks and orientation of the Five-Year Plan.

The congress put forward the job of completing the cooperativization of agriculture and the socialist transformation of private trade and industry by vigorously carrying on the socialist revolution in urban and rural areas for the period of the Five-Year Plan.

The main task of socialist construction during the Five-Year Plan was to lay the foundations for socialist industrialization and to solve, by and large, the problems of food, clothing and housing for the people. To fulfill this task successfully, the Party consistently stuck to the basic line of economic construction, the line of giving priority to the growth of heavy industry while, at the same time, developing light industry and agriculture. This line had already been adopted immediately after the armistice, and its correctness and vitality had been fully demonstrated in practice during the postwar rehabilitation.

Without priority for the growth of heavy industry, light industry and agriculture cannot be developed nor can expanded reproduction ever be guaranteed. Heavy industry was the greatest asset of our national economy; it was the key to successfully solving all of our problems. Our Party felt that only the concentrated development of heavy industry, and the consequent speedy development of light industry and agriculture, would allow us to build the foundations for socialist industrialization and, at the same time, basically solve the problems of food, clothing and housing for the people during the period of the Five-Year Plan.

The realities of life clearly showed that our Party's lines and policies laid down at the Third Party Congress were perfectly correct. The tasks we had set forth for socialist transformation and the building of socialism were all carried out far ahead of schedule. Under the tested leadership of our Party, the working people of our country, displaying a high degree of revolutionary enthusiasm, indomitable fighting spirit and inexhaustible creative ability, surmounted all difficulties and obstacles, guaranteed a sweeping victory of the socialist revolution in towns and the countryside and brought about radical changes in the development of our economy and culture.

At this congress today we take immense pride in summing up the great victories and successes which the Party and the people, united firmly as one, have achieved through hard-fought battles.

1. Completion of Socialist Transformation

Comrades,

The socialist transformation of the old economy is a process governed by the laws of development of the socialist revolution; it is a principal task that has to be tackled in the period of transition from capitalism to socialism.

With the successful completion of the anti-imperialist, anti-feudal, democratic revolution after liberation, the northern half of our country gradually set out on its transition to socialism, and our socialist transformation also began already at that time.

Before the war, however, the necessary social, economic and material conditions were not yet fully ready, and socialist transformation was only partially carried out. Therefore, the main task was to prepare for it. In our country the socialist transformation of agriculture, handicrafts, capitalist trade and industry was all undertaken on a full scale in the postwar years, and in 1958, was completed almost simultaneously.

Fundamental to socialist transformation is the cooperativization of agriculture, and all the more so in the particular case of our country where the peasantry made up more than half the population.

In the immediate post-armistice days private farming predominated in our countryside and the socialist sector was a small part of the whole. As you all know, as long as small commodity production dominates in rural areas, the source of exploitation and poverty cannot be removed, nor can the living standard of the peasantry be radically improved. Small and scattered private farming can neither develop in a planned way nor introduce advanced techniques on a wide scale. Moreover, in most cases this type of farming cannot lead to expanded reproduction.

All the limitations of private farming in our country manifested themselves most strikingly in the postwar years, and we could not allow them to exist any longer. Owing to the war, the material foundations of agriculture were seriously damaged, the peasant economy was even more fragmented than before and a shortage of labor and draft animals was keenly felt in the countryside. Under these circumstances, further maintenance of private farming would have made it impossible to restore the ruined productive forces of agriculture rapidly and, above all, to solve the food problem for the population. There was the danger that the contradictions between socialist state industry and private farming would give rise to a disparity between industry, which was being rapidly rebuilt and developed in the postwar period, and agriculture, which was being rehabilitated very slowly. In addition, with small farming we would not have been able to rapidly improve the living conditions of our impoverished peasantry and, particularly, to solve the problem of an increased number of poor peasants produced by the war.

The only way to release the agricultural productive forces

completely from the shackles of the old relations of production and to free the peasants once and for all from exploitation and poverty is the socialist cooperativization of agriculture. The postwar situation in our country was ripe for agricultural cooperativization and permitted no further delay. The peasants themselves came to realize, through their own hardships, that they could not tolerate the old way of life any longer. That is why our Party proposed the task of agricultural cooperativization immediately after the armistice and energetically pushed it forward on the strength of the increasing enthusiasm of the peasantry.

Most important in leading the agricultural cooperative movement is strict adherence to the Leninist principle of voluntariness and promotion of the movement by giving the peasants practical examples of the advantages of a cooperative economy.

In the days right after the armistice, the poor peasants were the most active supporters of agricultural cooperativization in our countryside. Our Party started by experimentally organizing and consolidating a few agricultural cooperatives in each county, beginning with the poor peasants and Party nuclei in the countryside. In the course of this work we were able to correctly determine the specific methods and pace of cooperativization that suited the actual conditions of our country, and encouraged our cadres to accumulate experience and gain confidence in leading the cooperative movement. Besides, by demonstrating the practical advantages of a cooperative economy on the basis of our own experience, we were able to persuade and lead the broad masses of peasants, particularly the middle peasants, to join the cooperatives of their own free will.

In agricultural cooperativization the voluntary principle was applied not only to the middle peasants but to all sectors of the rural population, including the rich peasants. Taking into consideration the specific conditions of our villages where the rich peasant economy was very weak, our Party adopted the policy of gradually remolding rich peasants as the cooperative movement developed, while strictly restricting their exploitative practices. We admitted all rich peasants who accepted socialist transformation and were willing to work honestly into the cooperative economy; we applied appropriate sanctions against the tiny handful who sought to hinder the cooperative movement. During the movement's last stage, when the cooperative economy had become widespread and strong and the objects of exploitation had disappeared in the villages, the majority of rich peasants joined the cooperatives voluntarily.

Thus, in drawing various categories of the peasantry into the cooperative economy on the basis of object lessons and the voluntary principles, our Party consistently adhered to the correct class policy of relying firmly on the poor peasants, strengthening the alliance with the middle peasants and re-stricting and gradually remolding the rich peasants. We saw to it that the poor peasants played the nuclear role in all agri-cultural cooperatives. We also made sure that cooperatives were not organized exclusively with relatively well-to-do peasants and that the rich peasants were not allowed to in-fluence the cooperative work. At the same time, we took strict precautions against the tendency to weaken the alliance with the middle peasants by forcing them into the cooperative economy or encroaching upon their interests.

All these policies prevented any possible losses that might have occurred in connection with the radical changes in the countryside, developed the cooperative movement on a sound basis and ensured a steady growth in agricultural production.

Adherence to the voluntary principle in the agricultural co-operative movement in no way means that such a movement is left to the mercy of spontaneity. As is the case with the socialist system in general, a cooperative economic system in the countryside will not arise by itself or develop and become strong automatically. It will require powerful leadership and assistance on the part of the Party and the state.

In order to promote the agricultural cooperative movement our Party persistently carried out organizational and political work among the peasants and made tremendous efforts to re-inforce the newly established cooperatives politically and economically.

We strengthened the Party organizations in the villages, trained and assigned a large number of management personnel to the cooperatives and gave powerful leadership with the view towards firmly establishing a socialist system and order in the cooperatives and enhancing the socialist consciousness of their members.

Lenin said that every social system arises only with the financial assistance of a definite class, and the system which the socialist state must especially aid is the cooperative one. According to what Lenin said, we gave all-out state assistance to the cooperatives. The powerful material assistance given by the state to the peasantry, based on rapidly developing socialist industry, strengthened the young agricultural cooperatives which had been organized starting only with poor peasants; it played a decisive role both in proving their superiority over private farming and economically reinforcing the cooperatives which realized a rapid quantitative growth in a short period of time.

Only by relying on the strong leadership of the Party and the working class and on the powerful support from socialist state-run industry were we able to overcome the innumerable difficulties of the postwar years, lead millions of peasants on to the path of socialist collectivization, and guarantee a solid victory for the socialist system of cooperative economy in our countryside.

Even after the completion of agricultural cooperativization, such an economic system should not remain static. It should continually progress and strive for perfection.

Agricultural cooperatives in our country were organized on a relatively small scale. When the cooperative movement was going on, our Party saw to it that each cooperative comprised 40 to 100 peasant households. The Party did not allow organization or amalgamation of cooperatives on too large a scale. This was in full agreement with the conditions at a time when our farming techniques were still backward and when the qualifications and experience of management personnel were still inadequate.

But gradually, the comparatively small size of cooperatives became incompatible with the further growth of the productive forces of agriculture, particularly with the requirements of technical transformation in the countryside. Hence, the need to enlarge the size of agricultural cooperatives by an appropriate amalgamation. As the cooperatives were politically and economically strengthened and the level of their management personnel raised, amalgamation became a mature requirement, and the peasants themselves realized the need for it.

Therefore, towards the end of 1958 the merger of cooperatives was carried out on the principle of one for each *ri*, with the chairman of the *ri* people's committee concurrently holding the chairmanship of the cooperative management board.

The enlargement of the agricultural cooperatives made it possible to use land and other means of production more rationally and to introduce modern farm machines and advanced farming techniques extensively. It allowed us to push ahead vigorously with projects for transforming nature—irrigation, afforestation and water conservation—and improve organization of labor and develop a more diversified cooperative economy.

When the agricultural production unit and the administrative unit of the *ri* became one and when the chairman of the *ri* people's committee also assumed the chairmanship of the management board, the *ri* people's committee began to concentrate its efforts on the consolidation of the agricultural cooperative and the development of agricultural production. Consequently, the role and functions of the local people's committee in building up the economy and culture as a whole were further enhanced.

With the merger of the agricultural cooperatives, the consumers' cooperatives and credit cooperatives were placed under their management. This enabled the agricultural cooperatives to plan and manage production, commodity circulation and credit in an integrated way, and, consequently, to show greater independence and initiative in developing the cooperative economy and promoting the well-being of their members. In particular, the agricultural cooperatives' direct handling of rural commerce permitted a more smooth exchange of commodities between town and country and a consolidation of economic ties between industry and agriculture.

Our agricultural cooperatives thus became a more advanced, solid socialist sector of the economy. From all the facts and experience, we can now say that with regard to its organizational form and size, our rural cooperative economy is the most rational and advantageous socialist economic form suitable to the specific conditions of our country during the present period.

In order to effect the complete rule of socialist production relations throughout the society, we had to cooperativize private farming in the countryside as well as carry out the socialist transformation of handicrafts, capitalist trade and industry in urban areas.

The socialist transformation of handicrafts in our country was already undertaken on an experimental basis before the war.

Thanks to the assistance of the people's power after liberation, handicraftsmen, who had been ruined and impoverished during the years of Japanese imperialist rule, restored and further developed their sector of the economy and markedly improved their living conditions. Nevertheless, the handicraft economy, fragmented and technically backward, was unstable and had no prospects for development. The cooperativization of a dispersed handicraft economy was the only means of further developing its production and techniques and raising the handicraftsmen's standard of living.

In 1947, at the beginning of the transitional period, our Party laid down the policy of forming producers' cooperatives of handicraftsmen to reorganize their private economy into a socialist, cooperative one. Thus, even before the war, initial successes had been registered and some experience had been accumulated in the transformation of the handicrafts along socialist lines.

As large, state-run factories were mostly destroyed during the war, our Party devoted great attention to the expansion and development of cooperative industry alongside state-owned local industry in order to ensure a stable life for the people. After the war the Party more vigorously pushed forward the movement for cooperativizing handicrafts. The war had played havoc with the handicraft economy, further fragmentizing it. The handicraftsmen could only improve their living conditions if they united their economy and relied on the active assistance of the state. Under these circumstances they actively supported our Party's policy of cooperativization. Therefore, the handicraft cooperative movement progressed rapidly and was completed successfully within a few years after the war.

The socialist reorganization of capitalist trade and industry also proceeded with comparative ease in our country.

In the past, the prolonged colonial rule of Japanese imperialism had seriously hampered the growth of national capital in our country. Japanese imperialist capital monopolized the major branches of our national economy, and the economy of national capitalists, except for a handful of comprador capitalists, was negligible.

After liberation, nationalization of industries, transport, communications, banks, etc., formerly in the hands of Japanese imperialists and comprador capitalists, brought the socialist state sector into dominance in our national economy. Capitalist trade and industry were very weak from the beginning of the transitional period. This situation in our country provided us with favorable conditions for enlisting capitalist traders and industrialists in socialist construction and reorganizing their economy by peaceful means.

During the period of transition, our Party's policy in relation to capitalist trade and industry was to transform them gradually into the socialist economy, utilizing their positive features and controlling their negative ones.

During the postwar period, socialist transformation of capitalist trade and industry matured. The war had inflicted serious damage on capitalist trade and industry. A considerable number of entrepreneurs and traders were ruined and became factory or office workers in state-owned enterprises; most of the remaining capitalist traders and manufacturers were reduced to a status much the same as that of handicraftsmen or small merchants. Consequently, the capitalist traders and manufacturers found it impossible to restore their devastated economy without relying on the assistance of the state and the socialist economy and without pooling their means of production, funds and efforts. Moreover, as agriculture and handicrafts were being transformed on cooperative lines, they could no longer obtain raw and other materials on the private market. When the socialist economic sector overwhelmingly dominated all spheres of the national economy, a small number of entrepreneurs and merchants could not possibly maintain their private sector.

Only when they joined the socialist sector of the economy could the entrepreneurs and traders improve their condition, find a road to the future and serve the country and society better.

Taking into account our country's specific conditions, our Party advanced the policy of transforming capitalist trade and industry through various forms of cooperative economy. The entrepreneurs and merchants supported the Party's policy of cooperativization, realizing that it conformed with their interests and represented the right direction for them to take. Thus the socialist reorganization of capitalist trade and industry was completed in a short period of time.

Thanks to the correct leadership of our Party and the active assistance of the state, the socialist reorganization of handicrafts and capitalist trade and industry was successfully carried out. Adhering strictly to the voluntary principles, the Party admitted handicraftsmen and middle and small manufacturers into various producers' cooperatives according to their respective trades. Giving priority to the consolidation of the handicraftsmen's production cooperatives, entrepreneurs were gradually incorporated into the cooperative economy; here, in particular, the semi-socialist form of the cooperative economy was broadly applied. In order to transform traders along socialist lines, marketing cooperatives or production-and- marketing cooperatives were formed, and they were later reorganized into producers' cooperatives by gradually increasing the proportion of productive activities they undertook.

In transforming the private trade and industry along socialist lines, the Party closely combined the change of economic forms with the remolding of people. Joining producers' cooperatives, the entrepreneurs and merchants completely broke with their former life based on the exploitation of others; they have been changed into socialist working people who produce material wealth by their own labor. This has also speeded up their ideological transformation.

While vigorously carrying out the socialist transformation of handicrafts and capitalist trade and industry, we gave tremendous state assistance to the consolidation of the newly organized producers' cooperatives. Thanks to the advantages of the socialist cooperative economy, active state help and their members' eager participation in work, the economic foundations of the producers' cooperatives have been speedily reinforced, and their standard of living further improved. Today, the cooperative industry plays an important role in the development of the national economy. With the great pride and enthusiasm of an honorable socialist working people, members of our producers' cooperatives are taking part in the construction of socialism.

Comrades, with the completion of the socialist reorganization of agriculture, handicrafts and capitalist trade and industry, socialist relations of production are completely dominant in towns and countryside. The productive forces have been freed from the chains of the old relations of production, and exploitation of man by man has been eliminated.

In the northern half of our country we have established a social system free from exploitation and oppression—the very system our working people had aspired to for so long, the system for which many Korean Communists fought and shed their blood. This is the greatest victory our people have achieved under our party's leadership.

An important feature of our country's socialist transformation lies in the fact that it was completed in such a short time, only four or five years after the war, despite technical backwardness and the relatively low level of development of our productive forces.

Some dogmatists at one time doubted our Party's policy of socialist transformation and faltered, saying things like: "Transformation of the relations of production is impossible without socialist industrialization;" "There can be no agricultural cooperativization without up-to-date farm machinery;" or "The tempo of socialist transformation is too fast." They did not understand that the rapid progress of socialist transformation was a phenomenon governed by law that reflected specific conditions in our country during the postwar period.

Agrarian reform, nationalization of industries and other democratic reforms were carried out after liberation. Based on these changes the socialist state economy developed rapidly and overwhelmingly dominated industry and trade. Railways, communications, banking and foreign trade establishments were placed under state control from the first days of the transitional period. The socialist economic sector, thus dominant in the national economy, exercised a decisive influence on the small commodity and capitalist sectors of the economy and led them inevitably towards socialism. In particular, the rapid development of state-run industry provided a material base which could give powerful support to the socialist reorganization of agriculture, handicrafts and capitalist trade and industry.

The relationship of forces between the classes in our country also provided definitely favorable conditions for socialist transformation. In the postwar years the forces opposing this transformation in our urban and rural areas were negligible. Our peasant masses were politically awakened and firmly united around the Party through the prolonged revolutionary struggle against the Japanese imperialists and the landlords, through their struggle to create a new life after liberation and, especially, through the severe trials of the Fatherland Liberation War. The majority of entrepreneurs and merchants, together with all of the people, not only took part in the democratic revolution after liberation but also supported the policies in socialist construction established by our Party and people's power. The Party's great prestige among the popular masses, the unity of people of all walks of life around it and the masses' high political consciousness proved to be the most important guarantee for the successful implementation of socialist transformation.

With respect to socialist industrialization and modern farm machinery, it goes without saying that we cannot ensure the complete victory of socialism without further developing industry and equipping all branches of the national economy, including agriculture, with new technology. However, socialist transformation could not be held back when life itself demanded an immediate reorganization of the outdated relations of production and there were revolutionary forces prepared to carry it out. This was true even though the level of the development of the productive forces and of technology was relatively low.

Our Party's policy intended to assure the rapid advance of the productive forces and, in particular, to open up a broad avenue for the technical revolution by transforming, first of all, the relations of production along socialist lines according to the urgent needs of social development, instead of waiting for the day when industry could develop to such an extent as to carry out the technical reconstruction of the national economy. Only by transforming the relations of production could we rapidly restore and further develop the productive forces that had suffered severe damage from the war and vigorously advance the technical revolution without delay in keeping with the development of industry.

When our Party advanced the task of overall socialist transformation after the armistice, some people argued that it was "still premature", insisting that the revolution should not be given a further impulse in the northern half until north and south were reunified and the anti-imperialist, anti-feudal, democratic revolution triumphant in the whole country. They thought that the socialist revolution in the northern half would conflict with the cause of reunifying the country and would be especially detrimental to mobilizing all the patriotic, democratic forces in south Korea for the anti-imperialist and anti-feudal struggle. They, of course, were wrong.

There is no reason whatsoevever for north Korea to wait about because south Korea has not been liberated yet and the democratic revolution has not yet triumphed there. The socialist revolution and the building of socialism in the northern half of the Republic were raised not only as an irresistible demand of social development in the northern half, but also as a vital demand of the Korean revolution to politically and economically consolidate the democratic base in the northern half. The most important guarantee for the victory of the Korean revolution is to eliminate capitalist elements, totally eradicate the foothold of counterrevolution and build firm bastions of socialism in urban and rural areas in the northern half.

By mobilizing the masses of the people, our Party established and fully consolidated a socialist system in the northern half, thereby converting it into the solid base of the Korean revolution and the decisive force for accelerating the peaceful reunification of the country. Today, the growth of the socialist forces in the northern half of the Republic and the free, happy life of the people under the socialist system there exert a tremendous revolutionary influence on all patriotic forces in mendous revolutionary influence on all patriotic forces in south Korea including even the national bourgeoisie, not to speak of the workers and peasants; these factors give unlimited inspiration to the struggle of the south Korean people against the US imperialists and their henchmen.

theory to our country's specific conditions, our Party, as mentioned above, initiated the tasks of socialist transformation at the opportune moment, based on the matured requirements of our social development. It worked out correct policies for implementing the task and carried them out firmly and consistently by mobilizing the popular masses while overcoming Right and "Left" deviations of all kinds. Since the Party's policy of socialist transformation was correct, since the masses warmly accepted and took part in its implementation with great revolutionary enthusiasm, we were able to accomplish very smoothly, in a short period of time, the most complicated and difficult revolutionary task of transforming agriculture, handicrafts and capitalist trade and industry along socialist lines, and to establish the advanced, socialist system in the northern half of our country.

2. The Construction of Socialism

Comrades,

With the successful fulfillment of the postwar Three-Year Plan, our country moved from the period of rehabilitating the national economy to that of technological reconstruction. As the socialist transformation of the relations of production neared completion, socialist industrialization became a more urgent necessity in order to achieve the technological reconstruction of the national economy.

Our Party defined the period of the Five-Year Plan as the first stage of technological reconstruction. And the Party set forth the central task for industry, that of laying the base for socialist industrialization during this period, thereby to further consolidate the foundation of an independent national economy and, at the same time, prepare the material and technical conditions for equipping all branches of the national economy with modern technology. This not only called for a rapid overall development of industrial production on the basis of the priority growth of heavy industry, but also for complete elimination of the colonial one-sidedness of our industry and the decisive reconstruction of its outmoded technical equipment.

Although the assignments which the Five-Year Plan gave to industry were enormous and difficult, they were successfully carried out ahead of time. The goals under the Five-Year Plan which required a 2.6-fold increase in gross industrial output value were fulfilled in two and a half years; all projected indices for the output of major industrial products were also fulfilled or over-fulfilled in a period of four years. In the four years from 1957 to 1960, the total value of industrial output increased 3.5 times—3.6 times in the production of the means of production and 3.3 times in consumer goods. During this period the rate of average annual increase in industrial production was 36.6 per cent. Thus, in spite of the fact that more than 10 out of the 15 years since liberation were dominated by war and then rehabilitation of a destroyed economy, in 1960 industrial output was 7.6 times greater than in the pre-liberation year of 1944. All this speaks for the exceptionally high rate of growth of our industry.

Heavy industry is the basis for the development of the whole national economy. Without building up a powerful heavy industry, technological reconstruction of the national economy or consolidation of the foundation of an independent national economy is impossible.

Our Party, drawing on our rich natural resources, went as far as it could to build our heavy industry centers capable of manufacturing and supplying, chiefly on our own, the raw and other materials, fuel, power, machinery and equipment necessary for the development of our national economy. It was important in this connection, while making the most of the existing foundation of heavy industry, to technologically reconstruct and continue to expand it and, at the same time, set up several new branches of industry. Proceeding from this consideration, our Party followed the policy, in building up heavy industry, of laying emphasis on the complete rehabilitation of those enterprises which had not yet been rehabilitated; and on the perfection, reconstruction and extension of existing enterprises, in combination with the building of those branches of industry and enterprises our country did not have before. This policy enabled us, firstly, to build up a powerful heavy industry with relatively limited funds, thus creating favorable conditions for simultaneously and rapidly developing light industry and agriculture; and secondly, to dynamically push ahead the technological reconstruction of industry while ensuring a high rate of growth in production.

In the four years from 1957 to 1960 production increased 1.8 times in the electric power industry, 2.8 times in the fuel industry, 2.6 times in the ore mining industry, 3 times in the metallurgical industry, 4.5 times in the chemical industry, and

4.7 times in the machine-building industry. This year, in heavy industry we will turn out 9,700 million kwh of electricity, about 12 million tons of coal, 960,000 tons of pig iron and granulated iron, 790,000 tons of steel, more than 700,000 tons of chemical fertilizer and about 2.4 million tons of cement.

In all heavy industrial enterprises the technical equipment has been radically improved, advanced methods of production and advanced technological processes have been widely introduced and more workshops have been set up to manufacture new products. Along with this, a considerable number of new factories equipped with up-to-date technology have been built.

In the ferrous metal industry, we have overcome the limitation of producing only pig iron. This industry now turns out large quantities of different kinds of standard-sized shape steel, round steel, sheet steel, and special steel, largely satisfying the growing demand for steel materials of capital construction and the machine-building industry. We have further developed the ore mining industry and at the same time have built new smelting and processing facilities, so as to mine and process different nonferrous and rare metals which are abundant in our country and make more effective use of them for the development of the national economy.

We have also achieved tremendous successes in developing the chemical industry. Our country's chemical industry in the past produced only inorganic chemicals, chiefly nitrogenous fertilizer. Today, however, we have an organic synthetic chemical industry with a number of newly-built chemical factories, including the vinalon and vinyl chloride factories. We have thus laid a solid foundation for the extensive development of all branches of the chemical industry—plastics, synthetic fibre, synthetic rubber, to say nothing of various chemical fertilizers, agricultural chemicals, and medicines—by relying entirely on our own raw materials.

We have rehabilitated the Supung and Changjin-gang Power Stations and others that already existed on the basis of new technology and have built large new power stations, including the one on the Tokno-gang River; we have expanded coal mines and improved their technical equipment. As a result, we have further consolidated our country's fuel-power bases.

One of the greatest successes in industry during the period

under review was the establishment of the machine-building industry. Even during the war and ever since it ended, our Party has tried to develop this industry; many new machine-building factories were set up in the postwar period of rehabilitation. During the Five-Year Plan, with a view to satisfying the country's needs for machinery and equipment mainly with domestic products, we improved the equipment of the existing machine-building factories and raised their production capacity; at the same time we built new factories, thus widely expanding this industry. In 1960 the machine-building industry's share in the total value of industrial output was 21.3 per cent as against 17.3 in 1956, and our country was 90.6 per cent self-sufficient in machinery and equipment as against 46.5 per cent. In the past our country had no machine-building industry. But today it is fully capable of producing by itself not only medium and small-sized machines and equipment but also metallurgical and power-generating equipment, motor vehicles, tractor, excavators and other types of large machinery and equipment. We now have our own machine-building industry capable of promoting an overall technical revolution in our country.

Light industry was one of the most backward branches in our country. We have established strong centers of light industry by further expanding the textile industry and rapidly developing the food-processing industry and the production of daily necessities during the Five-Year Plan.

Between 1957 and 1960 the output of the textile industry went up 3.5 times, that of the food, beverages and tobacco industries 4.2 times, and goods for cultural and household use 6.8 times. In 1960 nearly 190 million meters of different kinds of fabrics were produced. This is an increase of 15 times over the 1949 level and 138 times over the 1944 level. The output of many manufactured goods and foodstuffs rose sharply, their variety increased, and their quality improved markedly.

We have constantly directed serious efforts to the development of large-scale, modern light industry factories, the backbone of the production of consumer goods for the people. During the period under review most of the existing factories were rebuilt and expanded and many new light industry factories, equipped with modern technology, were built.

Our experience shows that in the production of consumer goods it is rational to develop medium and small-sized local factories together with large ones. Light industry should in general process various kinds of raw materials available all over the country and satisfy the diversified demands of the working people in all local districts. This kind of production cannot be organized rationally only on the basis of large factories. Moreover, in our country, if we relied solely on large-scale, centrally-controlled industry, we could not rapidly increase the lagging production of consumer goods for the people or meet their growing demands at all. In addition to large-scale, centrally-controlled industry, it was necessary to develop medium and small-sized local industry extensively and utilize handicraft methods along with modern technology.

Proceeding from this consideration, the Central Committee of our Party advanced, at its June 1958 Plenary Meeting, the task of developing consumer goods production by exploiting all available resources through a movement of all the people. As an important means to this end, more than one local industry factory in each city or county would be established. The decision of the plenary meeting opened up the possibility to exploit the enormous reserves latent in local areas and effect great innovations in increasing production of consumer goods for the people. In only a few months after the June Plenary Meeting more than 1,000 local industry factories were built throughout the country by using idle local materials and manpower, with little expenditure of state funds. As a result, various consumer goods were produced in large quantities. At present our state-owned and cooperative-owned local industries account for half of the total output of consumer goods. They are playing an important role in satisfying the needs of the people.

As a result of the establishment of local industry, the initiative and activity of the provinces in economic construction have grown, and locally available raw materials are tapped and used on a wider scale. In addition, many housewives have taken jobs in local industries. Thus, per-household income of the working people has gone up and women's political and cultural level has increased rapidly.

We have also scored big successes in the development of the fishing industry, which is essential to improving the living standard of our working people. The material and technical basis of the fishing industry has been reinforced, and further progress has been made in fishing, sea plant and fish culture and seafood processing. We now catch 500,000 to 600,000 tons of fish annually, and higher-quality processed fish can be supplied to our working people.

As is evident from the above, our industry has not only grown at a very high rate but it has also undergone a radical change in the composition of its branches and its technological equipment.

We have built and developed industry not for foreign, but primarily for home markets, that is, for meeting domestic requirements for manufactured goods and consolidating the economic foundations of our country. We have put an end to the lopsidedness in our industry which formerly produced mainly raw materials and semi-finished goods and was almost entirely dependent on foreign countries for machinery, equipment and consumer goods. Our industry is not dependent today on raw materials from abroad; it relies basically on domestic natural wealth and raw materials. This proves that we have put our industry on a solid independent footing.

Of course, our country's industrial production still falls short of demand and the quality of some of our industrial products is not high. Nevertheless, electric power stations, metallurgical works, chemical factories and other large modern industrial enterprises are now being built with materials, machinery and equipment which we produce. Technological reconstruction of the national economy is moving ahead quickly by relying mainly on our own heavy industry. And the daily needs of the people are being met with domestic consumer goods.

We have turned a backward colonial industry which, to make matters worse, was severely damaged in the war, into an independent, modern industry in a short period of time, thereby laying the material and technological foundation for equipping all branches of our national economy with the latest technology and for improving the life of our people in the years to come.

During the period under review the basic task confronting agriculture was to strengthen its material and technological foundation and increase agricultural production quickly.

Although organized on the basis of an outmoded technology, the agricultural cooperatives in our country have demonstrated the immense advantages they have over private farming. But without renovating our backward agro-techniques, we can neither fully display the superiority of a cooperative economy nor further develop the productive forces of agriculture.

With cooperativization of agriculture nearly complete, our Party promptly embarked on its technological transformation. The Party defined irrigation, electrification and mechanization as the main content of the technical revolution in the country-side, and concentrated all its efforts on irrigation as its first target.

Irrigation was the first important task in the technological renovation of our agriculture. Immediately after the armistice, we built irrigation works on an extensive scale together with agricultural cooperativization. During the Five-Year Plan, with cooperativization completed, we specifically carried on a vigorous, all-people movement to promote a nature-transforming project for irrigation. From 1957 to 1960 the state invested a total of 97,500,000 *won* in irrigation and supplied the country-side with large quantities of machinery and equipment, including pumps and motors, and building materials. Large-scale irrigation and river-dike projects were carried out with state funds, while agricultural cooperatives were widely encouraged to undertake small and medium projects at their own expense, receiving technical assistance from the state. As a result, 800,000 *chongbo* of land, or seven times the area of pre-liberation days, is now under irrigation; all the rice paddies are irrigated, and a system of irrigating dry fields has recently been introduced. This means that we have basically solved the task of irrigation in our country. It means that the centuries-old dream of our peasantry, plagued by drought and floods for thousands of years, has come true.

As in irrigation, there has also been great progress in rural electrification. Together with large power plants, we have built small and medium power stations extensively in the country-side to further accelerate rural electrification. Electricity is presently supplied to 92.1 per cent of all rural *ri* and 62 per cent of all peasant households in our country. Electricity is being used more and more in rural areas not only in lighting but as

power for mechanizing various operations such as water lift-
ing, thrashing and fodder processing.

Mechanization is the most difficult task in the technological
reconstruction of our agriculture. Having a backward
machine-building industry, we were at first unable to supply
large quantities of modern farm machinery to the countryside.
Consequently, we began by trying to improve conventional
farm implements and to use animal-drawn farm machines extensively. This action played an important role in increasing
labor productivity and in stepping up agriculture production.

At the same time, the amount of modern farm machinery
has been gradually increased; particularly since 1960, when
our machine-building industry began mass production of tractors, agricultural mechanization picked up momentum and we
have already had considerable success. By 1960 the number of
farm-machine stations had nearly doubled compared with
1956, the total number of tractors (in terms of 15 hp units) in
use in the countryside had increased 4.2 times and tractor-
worked area 10 times in the same period. Rural areas now have
more than 13,000 tractors and a large number of farm
machines of different types. The level of mechanization of farm
work has risen markedly.

As a result of the cooperativization of agriculture and consolidation of its material and technical foundation,
agricultural production has grown rapidly.

Formerly our agriculture was too strongly biased in the
direction of grain production. Yet it was so backward that it
could not even satisfy the population's needs for staple foods.
Our task was to convert our countryside not only into a reliable food-supply base but also into a source of raw material
for light industry by solving the grain problem and developing
many branches of agriculture. Thus, our Party pursued the
policy of giving priority to grain production and simultaneously developing the production of industrial crops, animal
husbandry, sericulture and fruit growing.

The basic agricultural problem is grain, especially for our
country which suffered a serious food shortage. With a view to
increasing grain output, we have strengthened the material
and technical basis of agriculture while taking various
technical and economic measures such as making more efficient use of land, improving distribution of crop areas, apply-

ing more chemical fertilizers and manure and widely introducing advanced methods of farming. The utilization of land rose from 138 per cent in 1956 to 174 per cent in 1960, and the area under high-yielding crops, rice and maize, rose from 1,101,000 *chongbo* to 1,284,000 *chongbo*. During the same period the amount of chemical fertilizer used increased by 42 per cent and that of manure, much more. Besides, various advanced agrotechniques have been extensively introduced, and farming methods on the whole have further improved. As a result, grain production has significantly increased in the last few years, reaching as much as 3,803,000 tons in 1960. This was a gain of 32 per cent over 1956.

This year, on the basis of results already achieved, our Party has set the huge target of a million-ton increase in grain output over last year; it has done everything it can to fulfill this goal. Now on the eve of the autumn harvest, fields all over the countryside are yielding unprecedented bumper crops. This shows that we will undoubtedly reach our target of the million-ton increase.

We can say that we have already basically solved the food problem, one of the most difficult in the economic construction of our country.

Besides grain, the output of industrial crops such as cotton and tobacco has considerably increased and production of vegetables has gone up sharply.

Animal husbandry used to be the most backward branch of our agriculture. Our Party has created the foundation for further developing animal husbandry based primarily on livestock breeding by the cooperatives along with that by their individual members. Compared to 1956, in 1960 the number of cattle increased by 39 per cent, sheep and goats more than 100 per cent, pigs 58 per cent, and rabbits about 1700 per cent.

In fruit growing, 100,000 *chongbo* of land has been brought under cultivation. The result is that the area under fruit trees has increased 6 times and total fruit output 3.6 times.

Further progress has been made in sericulture, bee raising and various other sidelines in agriculture. In particular agricultural cooperatives in the mountainous areas are making effective use of the hills, thereby increasing their income.

The socialist agriculture of our country is now protected from the damage of flood and drought. It is rapidly doing away with outmoded technology, replacing it with the latest one, and it is becoming an advanced diversified sector of the economy.

With the rapid development of the national economy, it has become a very urgent task to meet our transport needs.

To meet these fast growing needs, we had to strengthen railway transport definitely before anything else. During the years under review, we either newly laid or double-tracked the lines linking Haeju and Hasong, Pyongsan and Chihari, and Susong and Komusan, and we electrified more than 100 kilometers of railway lines. We considerably improved the technical equipment of the railway and made more efficient use of the rolling stock. At the same time discipline and order in railway transport have been strengthened and its organization has been improved.

In 1960 the total turnover of rail freight more than doubled the 1956 figure; the cultural level and the quality of service on the railways were generally higher, both in freight and passenger traffic.

Road, sea and river transports, too, have developed rapidly. In 1957-60 the number of motor vehicles was nearly doubled; freight turnover by motor vehicles increased 4.3 times; and cargo shipping increased 4.4 times.

In the field of communications the telegraph and telephone network spread, wire broadcasting service was made available for 88 per cent of all rural *ri*, and radio broadcasting facilities were further strengthened.

Capital construction is of tremendous importance for the expansion of production and the improvement of the people's living standards. Especially in our country, which had formerly been backward and had suffered severe destruction in the war, we had to carry out a huge amount of construction during the Five-Year Plan.

Between 1957 and 1960, the state invested more than 2,000 million *won* in capital construction for the national economy and cultural construction. Compared with the period of the Three-Year Plan, this accounts for an average yearly increase of 40 per cent.

In order to successfully carry out the huge construction work it was important to build more quickly, efficiently and cheaply. This could only be done by discarding once and for all

the outdated primitive methods and basing construction work
on industrial, assembly-line methods. Industrialization of
capital construction—this has been the basic construction
policy that our Party unswervingly followed.

Overcoming all difficulties and obstacles we have
thoroughly implemented the Party's policy and brought about
a great change in capital construction. In 1960 we used
assembly-line methods in over 20 percent of industrial construction and about 60 per cent of housing construction. The
rate of mechanization in construction went up to 53 per cent in
excavation work, 50 per cent in loading and unloading, about
90 per cent in hoisting and 70 per cent in the mixing of concrete. We have expanded the production of building materials
greatly and have raised their quality. We have also made
marked improvements in our design work.

Along with this, we have carried out urban and rural construction through an all-people movement. Particularly in outlying areas locally available building materials were extensively used to build many dwellings and cultural and welfare
facilities.

As a result of the successes in capital construction,
numerous factories, enterprises and productive establishments have been restored, expanded or newly built, and
our towns and countryside have changed beyond recognition.
Pyongyang, the democratic capital, has become a modern city,
beautiful and magnificent. All the towns in our country have
been built up from ashes, taking on a new, beautiful look. Now
that the old mud huts have been torn down, our farm villages
are also becoming attractive, modern and pleasant places to
live in.

One of the major successes in construction work is that the
material and technical foundations have been strengthened,
cadres for the building industry have been trained and rich
experiences have been accumulated. In major towns and
industrial centers we have set up construction enterprises
equipped with new techniques and have established solid bases
for the building-materials industry. Our designers, construction technicians and workers have learned to design and build
excellent modern factories, enterprises and cultural
establishments by themselves. These achievements will serve
as assets to undertake larger-scale construction in the future.

Comrades, the cultural revolution is an important component of socialist construction. In the years under review we have seen tremendous achievements in improving and strengthening public education, in raising the cultural and technical level of the working people and in developing national culture and art.

In the field of education a compulsory primary school system was introduced in 1956 and a compulsory secondary school system in 1958. At present preparations are going along well for the enforcement of a compulsory nine-year technical education. Our network of different levels of schools has been enlarged extensively and enrollment has increased. In our country today 2,530,000 students, or about one-fourth of the population, are studying in more than 8,000 schools at different levels.

In order to build socialism and communism, the new generation should be brought up as cultured and harmoniously developed workers possessing general elementary knowledge and modern technology. Taking into consideration these practical needs of socialist construction, our Party reorganized the public school system in 1959 and took important measures to radically improve the work of all schools. Abolishing the previous system of senior middle schools which were divorced from real life and neglected technical training for students, we established the system of secondary and higher technical schools in its place, enabling all of our young people to acquire not only general knowledge of the fundamentals of science but also technical knowledge in a specific field. Along with this, we have improved both content and methods of education in all of our schools on the principle of combining education with production and theory with practice. This reorganization of the public education system has completely eliminated the hangovers from the old society in the field of education. It fully embodies the Marxist-Leninist theory of education, and is in complete accord with the requirements of socialist construction in our country.

The training of our nation's technical cadres was a very important problem in our country, once an underdeveloped colony. Our Party has paid a great deal of attention to the training of national cadres ever since liberation and has achieved impressive results in this area. As a result of the continuing progress made in secondary and higher technical education during the period under review, the ranks of technical cadres have grown rapidly. There are now 133,000 engineers, assistant engineers and specialists, or twice as many as in 1956, working in all spheres of the national economy. Today, all modern factories and enterprises in our country are managed and operated by our own technicians and specialists. This is one of the greatest successes achieved by our Party and people in the building of a new society.

Further acceleration of socialist construction, however, requires more technical cadres. In order to satisfy the growing need for technical personnel, our Party exerted great efforts both to increase the number of institutes of higher learning and to improve the quality of cadre training. During the Five-Year Plan the number of universities and colleges grew from 19 to 78, with an enrollment of 97,000 students, a fivefold increase. Particularly, with the aim of giving the working people the opportunity to receive higher education without interrupting their work in production, we have effected a large-scale expansion of the network of night schools and correspondence courses, and at the same time, have opened new kinds of colleges such as factory and communist colleges. Factory colleges have now been set up in over 20 major factories and enterprises and a communist college has been established in every provincial center. These colleges have enrolled a large number of workers, functionaries of local government institutions and personnel in economic organs, who both work and study. Thus, we can now train cadres not only in ordinary colleges but at production sites as well. Factories and other enterprises in our country are serving a dual function: production centers and cadre training centers.

In the one year since the factory and the communist colleges were established, our experience has proved to us that a factory is capable of managing a college; also, such colleges have many advantages. These colleges make possible the mass training of a new type of intellectual who comes from the working class, and provide the possibility of most closely combining education with production and theory with practice. In addition, a large number of core workers have acquired a higher education without being separated from production, and the development of production and technology has been accelerated.

The general rise in the cultural and technical levels of our working prople represents a major success in the cultural revolution. In order to improve the cultural and technical levels of the working people, the Party advanced the following principal slogan: All workers and peasants should acquire at least a general education at the junior middle school level and master more than one technical skill. To attain this goal we have vigorously carried on general and technical education among the workers and peasants with the production units as the base. There are now many adult primary and secondary schools in town and countryside with an enrollment of nearly one million workers and peasants. At the same time, the strengthening of technical studies and on-the-job technical training in factories and other enterprises has rapidly improved the working people's technical and skill levels.

In the period we are reviewing there were also considerable achievements in the development of science. Compared with 1956, in 1960 the number of scientific research institutes has increased 2.6 times and the number of scientific workers 2.8 times. Our Party saw to it that we directed our main efforts in science to solving the practical problems arising in socialist economic construction, particularly the pressing problems of technology for further industrial development using domestic raw materials. Following the Party's policy, our scientists and technicians have conducted their scientific research in close coordination with production and have achieved great successes—the completion of vinalon research, the solution of the problem of gasifying anthracite, semi-conductor research, and so forth. In this way they have greatly contributed to the development of our national economy.

Our literature and art have entered a period of full bloom. Our Party's consistent policy on literature and art is to develop a new national culture reflecting the life and sentiments of our people under the socialist system while, at the same time, critically carrying forward our time-honored cultural heritage and assimilating, also in a critical way, the achievements of advanced culture of foreign countries. We have resolutely fought against all manifestations of reactionary bourgeois ideology in literature and art as well as against their penetration from the outside. We have endeavored to develop revolutionary literature and art that truly serve the working people.

Acting consistently on the Party's policy on literature and art, our writers and artists have created many excellent literary and artistic works depicting the history of our people's glorious struggle and our working people's gigantic struggle in the present. Our literature and art have become the possessions of the workers and peasants, and are flourishing with added vigor among the broad masses.

Thus, literature and art have become powerful media in our country for the communist education of the working people, inspiring their struggle to build a new society.

The rapid development of industry, agriculture and all other branches of the national economy and the elimination of all types of exploitation have resulted in further improvement of the material and cultural life of the people.

In 1960 the national income was 2.1 times greater than in 1956. In our country this income belongs to all the people; it is used to expand socialist production and to enhance the working people's well-being. Important here is to properly combine accumulation and consumption and to correctly adjust these two factors in order to eliminate considerable differences in the living standards of workers and peasants.

In our country one-fourth of the national income is now earmarked for accumulation and about three-quarters goes to the working people for personal consumption.

The real wages of factory and office workers in 1960 were 2.1 times higher than in 1956. Their real wages have now reached the level necessary to provide stable living conditions.

During the same period the real earnings of the peasantry, too, showed a marked increase. The peasants' living conditions in mountainous areas have also improved, attaining a level as high as that of the peasants on the plains. The problem of poor peasants, unsolved in our country for a long time, has been completely settled. Thus, the living standards of our peasants as a whole have come up to the level of the former middle peasants or well-to-do middle peasants.

The large-scale construction of housing in rural and urban areas has also improved housing conditions for the working people. From 1957 to 1960 alone, we provided 6,220,000 square meters of new houses in towns and 5,060,000 square meters in the countryside.

Today, our working people are free from worries about food, clothing and housing, although they still do not live in abundance.

Not only has the problem of food, clothing and housing essentially been solved, but also the supply of commodities to the working people has in general improved. Compared with 1956, the turnover in retail trade in 1960 increased 3.1 times—2.5 times for foodstuffs and 3.7 times for other goods. During this period the trade network grew 1.9 times. As a result, our working people can buy the articles they need at the same prices anywhere—whether in town, village, or remote mountain regions.

The working people in our country enjoy enormous state and social benefits in addition to the income from their labor. In 1960 the state budgetary expenditures for social and cultural services were about four times as great as in 1956.

Tuition fees have been abolished in all schools. Thus, the younger generation receives free education. In addition the overwhelming majority of university, college and specialized school students even receive state stipends.

Free medical care in our country has already been made universal. Compared with 1956, the number of doctors in public health in 1960 increased two times and that of hospitals and clinics 2.9 times. Medical service for the working people has continued to improve. By 1960 the death rate of the population had dropped by half compared with the years of Japanese imperialist rule, whereas the growth rate had increased 2.7 times.

Workers and office employees have the benefits of paid holidays; hundreds of thousands of working people enjoy a good rest every year at vacation homes and sanatoria at the expense of the state. A large number of nurseries and kindergartens, where children are excellently brought up, have been set up and maintained at state and public expense. Women are thus provided with the conditions for participating in social labor. In 1960 there were 31 times as many nurseries and kindergartens as in 1956, accommodating about 700,000 children.

All this is strong witness to our Party's and the state's tremendous concern for the welfare of the working people, a veritable burgeoning of communism in our country.

Comrades, we have scored great achievements in the construction of socialism. Our country, once a backward, colonial, agrarian state, and reduced to ashes by the war, has now been transformed into a socialist industrial-agricultural state with independent economic foundations. Our working people in the past were ill-clothed, hungry, and lived in ignorance and darkness, far removed from the civilized world. Today, however, they are leading a happy life full of hopes, free from any worries and anxieties, they are mastering science and technology, and they are becoming well-educated and enlightened builders of society.

Today we can say with confidence that our country and our people have completely rid themselves of the age-old backwardness and poverty.

3. Chollima Movement

Comrades,

Our country has made tremendous achievements in socialist construction amidst its great upsurge and in the course of the advancement of the Chollima Movement.

The Chollima Movement manifests the great creative force of our people firmly united around our Party. It is an all-people movement to push the construction of socialism to the utmost.

Our country inherited a backward economy and culture from the old society; moreover it went through a fierce three-year war. With our country divided into north and south, we are building socialism in direct confrontation with the US imperialists while at the same time struggling for the peaceful reunification of the fatherland. This situation demanded of us a hard unyielding struggle. In order to eliminate our historical backwardness rapidly, in order to accelerate the reunification of the country, which is our supreme national goal, we had to move ahead much faster than other peoples.

In view of this particular necessity for the revolution's development, our Party mapped out a policy for definitely speeding up the construction of socialism in the northern half of the Republic, and, on this basis, it organized and mobilized all the working people for this heroic struggle.

The working people of our country, educated and trained by our Party, had a profound awareness of the urgent requirements of our revolution's development and of their historic mission. And they unanimously supported the Party's policy of accelerating socialist construction.

Responding eagerly to the appeal of the Party, "Rush at the speed of Chollima!" our working people fought through thick and thin to carry out the tasks proposed by the Party; they pushed themselves to the limit, vying with each other to be the foremost and bravely overcoming all obstacles and difficulties.

Thus, we made innovations and wrought amazing miracles almost every day on all fronts of socialist construction.

Our heroic working class built 300,000 to 400,000 ton-capacity blast furnaces in less than a year, laid a standard-gauge railway more than 80 kilometers long in 75 days, and erected a huge, up-to-date vinalon factory in a little over one year on a spot which had been mere waste land. Our working people produced more than 13,000 extra machine tools over and above tha state plan within a year by the let-one-machine-tool-make-machine-tools movement. Within a period of three to four months they built over 1,000 factories for local industry by utilizing idle materials and manpower in localities. And in six months they carried out tremendous projects for transforming nature aimed at irrigating 370,000 *chongbo* of rice paddies and dry fields. There are innumerable cases like these.

All these symbolize the heroic spirit and creative talent of our people who are rushing ahead at the speed of Chollima under the leadership of the Party.

Steadily advancing the Chollima Movement, we have ensured an annual industrial growth rate of at least 30 to 40 percent, boosted our backward rural economy in a short time and rebuilt from ruins cities and villages which now have a completely new appearance.

The great upsurge of socialist construction and the Chollima movement in our country are lawful phenomena that took place on the basis of the great social and economic changes made in the postwar period and of all the material and moral forces our Party and people built up in the course of their protracted, difficult struggle.

The decisive victory of the socialist revolution and the laying of the country's independent economic foundation provided the social, economic and material conditions for a great upsurge in economic and cultural construction and were objective causes of the Chollima Movement.

Objective conditions and possibilities alone, however, are not always enough to stimulate a great upsurge in socialist construction. We also need our own inner forces, that is, the Party's ability to lead the masses to a revolutionary upsurge and the firm determination of the masses to carry through the will of the Party.

Through its arduous struggles the Party has earned unquestioned prestige and trust among the masses and has rallied them firmly around itself. The steel-like unity of the Party ranks and the comprehensive establishment of the Marxist-Leninist leadership system in the Party increased its fighting capacity and decisively enhanced its prestige and influence among the masses. Thus, the will and ideas of the Party have always penetrated deeply into the masses and have become their own will and ideas.

Our people have accepted the Party's lines and policies as a matter of vital personal interest and have devoted all they have to the struggle for the revolutionary cause and for the prosperity and progress of their country. It is only natural that our people should display exceptional revolutionary zeal to bring their backward country into the ranks of the advanced ones and to improve their difficult living conditions as soon as possible. It is only natural because, deprived of power in the past, our people have seized power in their hands and defended it with their blood and because, oppressed and humiliated before, they have freed themselves from all exploitation and oppression.

Relying firmly on the high political enthusiasm and inexhaustible creative power of the working people, our Party has launched bold projects on all fronts of socialist construction and has vigorously carried them out.

In formulating its policy for each period of our revolution's development, our Party not only analyzed the present and immediate future but always scientifically foresaw the long-range prospects of the country's development; it showed the masses the right way to go and a clear goal in their struggle. Once a policy had been formulated, our Party never flinched for a moment in front of any complex and difficult circumstances, and with untiring tenacity it carried its lines and policies to their ultimate conclusions.

Dynamically prompting the masses to ever higher revolutionary zeal, our Party would settle one problem and immediately go on to another, and feed the flames of continual advance and uninterrupted innovation in all areas of socialist construction. At the same time, the Party correctly grasped the central link in every stage of socialist construction and concentrated on it, thereby completely solving one problem after another and gaining full control of the whole chain of socialist construction.

The scientific foresight that went into each of our Party's policy decisions, its fidelity to Marxist-Leninist principles and the unexcelled revolutionary sweep in implementing a policy always gave the working people complete confidence in their work and helped them advance without the slightest vacillation along the road indicated by the Party towards the triumph of the great cause of socialism.

The wise leadership of the Party, its strong unity with the people, their singular resolve to advance rapidly and their revolutionary enthusiasm—these underlie the great upsurge in socialist construction and the Chollima Movement and constitute the decisive guarantee for all our victories.

Comrades, as Marxism-Leninism teaches us, the masses of the people create history. Socialism and communism can be built only by the conscious, creative labor of millions of working people. Therefore, in the construction of socialism it is crucial to stimulate the creative power of the masses to the utmost and bring their enthusiasm, initiative and abilities into full play. The might of the Chollima Movement in our country lies in the very fact that it is a mass movement that gives full scope to the revolutionary zeal and creative talent of our people.

As is true of all mass movements for change, the Chollima Movement has started and developed in the course of struggle against the old, in the course of breaking through difficulties and obstacles. When socialist construction entered the period of upsurge in our country, the main obstacles to rousing the revolutionary zeal and creative activity of the working people were passivism, conservatism and the mystification of technology. Passivism and conservatism in socialist construction expressed themselves in distrust of the strength of heroic working class and the inexhaustible creative power and talent of our people. The passivists and conservatives tried to suppress the masses'creativity by clinging to old rated capacities and standards and by presenting science and technology as mysteries. Intimidated by difficulties and fearful of innovation, they attempted to inhibit the great onward movement of the masses. Without shattering passivism, conservatism and mystification of technology, we could not have brought about the great upsurge in socialist construction nor could we have developed the Chollima Movement.

Our Party has waged a powerful ideological struggle among the cadres and working people against passivism and conservatism. Tirelessly it has worked to arm them with the revolutionary spirit of thinking boldly, acting boldly and making continual advance and uninterrupted innovation. The Party has always believed in the masses' great creative power and has actively supported their daring suggestions and initiatives, giving them as much help as possible to put them into practice. Boundlessly inspired by the correct leadership of the Party, our working people have smashed passivism and conservatism, courageously surmounted all kinds of difficulties and realized many achievements in work totally inconceivable in the past.

In promoting a high degree of labor enthusiasm and creative activity for socialist construction among the masses of the people, it is vital to continuously raise their political and ideological consciousness, properly combining this with the principle of material incentive.

A real upswing in the labor of the masses and real mass heroism in socialist construction will be possible only when the broad sections of the working people are armed firmly with the spirit of faithful service to the Party and the revolution and with the spirit of devotion to the struggle for the country and the people. Unless we consistently raise the political awareness and the level of consciousness of the masses, real communist attitudes towards work cannot be cultivated among them.

Under socialism, the political and moral stimulus to labor should always be backed by material incentive. Distribution according to the quality and quantity of work performed is an objective law in socialist society. It is a powerful way of opposing those who do not work and try to live on the work of others and of giving a material impulse to the working people's enthusiasm for production.

Our Party has consistently followed the policy of giving priority to political work in all activities and strengthening communist education among the working people so that they may display voluntary enthusiasm and devotion in work, and of properly pursuing the socialist principle of distribution to stimulate material interest.

The correctness of this Party policy has been clearly manifested in the unprecedented labor upsurge of our working people. Today they are working with all their energy and talent for the benefit of the state and society, for their own happiness. The excellent communist traits of loving work and regarding it as the highest honor, helping each other, working collectively and enjoying a happy life together are rapidly being fostered among our working people.

The enthusiasm for work and creative initiative of the masses can only be really effective when combined with science and technology. Mass enthusiasm alone, without scientific development and technological progress, neither takes us very far nor encourages continued innovation.

For the rapid development of science and technology, the active participation of the broad masses of working people is necessary, and creative cooperation between the workers and peasants and the scientists and technicians should be strengthened. We have thoroughly discredited the incorrect view that only specially qualified people can develop science and technology. We have evolved a mass movement among the working people to acquire new technical know-how and have inspired them to make constant technical renovations. In our development of technology we have strongly opposed the tendency to underestimate the creative proposals and initiatives of the workers and peasants while, at the same time, strictly guarding against the tendency to ignore the significance of science and the role of scientists. We have always tried to combine labor and science and to promote close cooperation between the workers and peasants and the scientists and technicians. As the working masses are becoming familiar with science and technology and as cooperation between the workers and peasants and the scientists and technicians has been strengthened, science and technology have developed even faster in our country, and a collective movement for technological renovation has been launched widely in all spheres of the national economy.

As a result, all the wisdom, talent, enthusiasm and creative power of our people, which had been suppressed, denigrated and buried before, have blossomed in the Chollima Movement and have accomplished uninterrupted innovations in the construction of our economy and culture.

The major political and economic importance of the Chollima Movement lies first of all in the fact that it has assured a high rate of socialist construction.

A high rate of economic growth is a law of socialist society and presupposes the planned and proportionate development of the national economy. If we violate the principles of planning and balancing in economic development, a tremendous amount of materials, funds and labor will be wasted and general economic development will eventually slow down, although certain branches may temporarily attain a high rate of development.

We achieved a high rate of socialist construction in our country on the basis of a planned and proportionate development of the national economy. That is why we could steadily maintain the continuous high rate of growth and accelerate socialist construction in all areas even more throughout the Five-Year Plan period, to say nothing of the postwar rehabilitation period.

However high the rate of economic development may be, there will never be unevenness as long as it is strictly based on realistic possibilities. Of course, it is extremely difficult to keep things balanced while moving ahead very quickly. But the rate of development should not be reduced in order to maintain an equilibrium. Planning and balancing are not ends in themselves; they are a means to achieve a high rate of development. Thus, it is essential that we develop all branches simultaneously at a rapid rate by relying on the advantages of the socialist system, the creative power of the masses, and making the maximum use of the latent reserves and potentialities of our national economy. In our work of socialist construction we have always calculated material conditions and possibilities accurately and trusted in the revolutionary zeal and creative power of our people who have been tempered in hard struggle. On this basis we have consistently drawn up ambitious and dynamic plans and mobilized the masses to fulfill them.

At the same time, our Party properly connected and adequately coordinated the development of all branches of the national economy, thereby boosting those falling behind before it was too late and preventing possible imbalances. Our Party made the year 1960 a period of adjustment. This was the most reasonable and judicious way to secure the right balancing in the national economy and maintain a high rate of development. In 1960 we eased the strain some branches had begun to feel in the course of the rapid development of the national economy, bolstered certain lagging branches, and further raised our people's material and cultural standards. Thus in all branches we fulfilled or over-fulfilled the assignments of the Five-Year Plan, consolidated our successes, and made full preparations for the successful completion of a new perspective plan. This has enabled us to maintain and stimulate the upsurge in socialist construction. It has allowed us to continue with the Chollima advance on a higher level.

Comrades,

In the Chollima Movement our Party found a definite guarantee for the successful building of socialism in our country. It has firmly taken the reins of this movement in hand and continuously developed it in scope and depth.

The Chollima Movement gained momentum after the socialist transformation of productive relations was complete and during the all-Party struggle against the survivals of all outdated ideas such as passivism, conservatism and mysticism. It was given special impetus during the intensification of communist education among the masses and the radical transformation of Party work into active, creative work with people.

Regarding as the primary task in Party work the education and remolding of all the people and their firm unity around itself, our Party strengthened its work with people in every way. Above all, it carried out intensive communist education among the masses, which was combined with the education in the revolutionary traditions. Since the masses accepted the Party policy of education and remolding of all people, the transformation of men has been taken over by the masses themselves, and has been linked more closely with their productive activities.

The main feature of the Chollima Workteam Movement,

which is now widespread among our working people, lies in integrating the drive for collective innovation in production with the education and remolding of the working people.

The Chollima Workteam Movement, as an intensified and developed form of the Chollima Movement, has become a powerful impetus to the development of the national economy and an ideal method of mass economic management by the working people, as well as an excellent means of mass education for remolding everyone into the new type of communist man. Our Chollima riders are not only innovators in production; they are also capable management personnel, expert organizers and real communist educators.

In our country the Chollima Workteam Movement is presently going on in all fields of industry, agriculture, transport, construction, science, education, culture, public health, and so on, and the ranks of the Chollima riders, the heroes of our age, are growing from day to day. As of the end of August this year, over 2 million working people had joined the movement; 4,958 workteams and workshops, comprising 125,028 people, had received the title of Chollima; and 55 workteams with 1,459 people had been honored with the title of Double Chollima.

Thus, the Chollima Movement has become a great revolutionary movement of the working millions of our country, sweeping away everything antiquated from all spheres of the economy, culture, ideology and morality, and constantly making innovations and accelerating socialist construction at an unprecedented rate. The movement has become our Party's general line in the construction of socialism.

The essence of this line is to unite all the working people more firmly around the Party by educating and remolding them in communist ideology, and to build socialism more solidly and quickly by allowing their revolutionary enthusiasm and creative talent full expression. The indestructible vitality of this line lies in the fact that the masses of people initiated it, that the Party advanced this line by reflecting the will of the masses and generalizing their practical experience in struggle, and that the masses therefore accepted it wholeheartedly.

On the strength of this line our Party has won great victories in socialist construction. By continuing to follow it, the Party will achieve even greater victories in the future.

4. Consolidation of the State and Social System

Comrades,

As a result of the great socio-economic changes which have taken place in our country, the people's power has been further strengthened and our state and social system has been consolidated as never before.

Our people's power, a mighty weapon of the socialist revolution and the construction of socialism, has fulfilled its functions well and demonstrated its indestructible vitality. Today, the basis of our state is the socialist economic system which is completely dominant in town and countryside. Our state relies on the foundation of an independent national economy. The people's power has its own firm economic basis and can make more efficient use of all the country's resources for the welfare of the people and the national prosperity.

The class structure of our society has also undergone a fundamental change.

The working class has strongly maintained its position as the leading force in our society. During the period under review, working-class ranks have grown rapidly, their organization and political consciousness have been strengthened and their technical and cultural levels have been raised even more.

In our country today factory and office workers make up 52 per cent of the total population. Our working class, having taken power into its hands, has displayed an untiring fighting spirit and revolutionary stamina in leading all the working people and even non-working people along the road to socialism. It has thus honorably carried out its historical mission to abolish forever all systems of exploitation. Showing inexhaustible creative power and talent, our working class has made miraculous achievements in socialist construction, and it is now advancing at the head of the Chollima Movement of the entire people.

The peasants now participate in the collective socialist economy and have freed themselves once and for all from centuries of exploitation and poverty. Not only has the peasants' position in the society amd in the economy changed, but their ideological consciousness has altered considerably and their cultural level is rising rapidly. Today our peasantry, a reliable ally of the working class, has become a powerful force in socialist construction and has displayed a high degree of patriotic enthusiasm in all spheres of political, economic and cultural life.

Our intellectuals have also changed radically. Thanks to the patient education by our Party and through struggles of revolution and construction, intellectuals from the old society have turned into socialist intellectuals. At the same time, a large army of new intellectuals from the working people has been trained. Today our intellectuals serve the Party and the cause of the working class faithfully and play a major role in socialist construction.

In our country now there are neither exploiting nor exploited classes. Participating in the socialist economic system, all our people have established comradely relationships with each other; they work together in close cooperation for their common interests and prosperity. The worker-peasant alliance has been further solidified on the basis of socialism, the political and moral unity of the entire people has become as strong as steel on the basis of that alliance.

Thus, our people's power has established a firmer political foundation than ever before.

So that the people's power can function successfully, we must steadily strengthen the state organs at various levels and constantly improve the work of the state. During the period under review we took a series of important measures designed to reorganize the work of these organs in accordance with the new changing reality and to enhance their role and functions in socialist construction.

With the complete triumph of socialist relations of production and after all branches of the national economy had been brought under the state planning system, the most important tasks were to increase the functions of the state organs, in particular the local people's committees with regard to the management of the economy, and to raise their level of planning. In the past, the people's committees dealt mainly with the private economy, and at most their role was to control and adjust its development. The socialist economy, however, cannot be guided in this way. The new situation required that the people's committees guide local industry and the rural economy in a planned manner, and that they directly organize and administer the supply services to the working people, educational and cultural work and city administration. With a view to the people's committees successfully performing these economic-organizational and cultural-educational functions, we reorganized the work of the people's committees, changing the former system of guiding the private economy into one of guiding the socialist economy. Moreover, we further reinforced the planning commissions of the local people's committees.

In addition, because industry was expanded on a gigantic scale and local industry, in particular, had made great progress, the old system of industrial management became incompatible with reality. In order to bring the state organs' guidance of industry closer to the local level and to guarantee concrete and flexible guidance, it was necessary to relieve the central ministries and bureaus of a large part of their responsibilities and definitely strengthen the local organs of industrial management. Hence, our Party saw to it that quite a few industrial enterprises, formerly controlled directly by the central ministries and bureaus, were transferred to the provinces and that provincial economic commissions were set up to administer local industry and construction. Along with this, we merged some central ministries and bureaus, greatly simplifying their apparatus, and sent a large number of management and technical personnel to work in the local areas. The reorganization of the industrial management system has led to the strengthening of centralized, unified guidance in industrial management and, at the same time, to the enhancement of the role of the provinces and the further promotion of democracy. This reorganization enabled ministries and bureaus to concentrate their efforts on the control over industrial enterprises of national importance by freeing those central organs from cumbersome paper work on the one hand, and on the other, it enabled them to contribute to a more rapid development of local industry by reinforcing the local bodies of industrial management. The establishment of provincial economic commissions has widened the independence and initiative of the provinces and made possible the more effective exploitation of local sources of raw materials and all the reserves latent in the outlying areas.

It is important in consolidating state organs to raise the

guidance level of the functionaries and improve their style of work.

In order to put an end to a situation in which the level of guidance of our functionaries lagged behind economic development, we have both intensified cadre formation and education and strengthened guidance and assistance to lower organs by higher ones. At the same time we have constantly waged a vigorous struggle to eliminate bureaucracy and establish the popular method of work in state institutions at all levels. Today, in all state organs, we have essentially corrected bureaucratic and armchair work methods where functionaries simply sit at their desks, collect complicated statistics and issue various orders. In its place we are instituting the work method of going down to lower level organizations, factories and enterprises to see how things are on the spot and to give real assistance to the lower organ functionaries. In addition, our functionaries in state and economic organs are acquiring a genuinely popular work style: they go among the masses and work with them, at which time they bring them the Party lines and policies and solve all problems by discussing them directly with the masses and stimulating their enthusiasm and initiative.

As a result, the role and functions of the state organs at all levels in building socialism have been further raised, the government organs have begun to influence the people deeply, and broad sections of working people are taking an active part in state affairs.

Comrades, the Democratic People's Republic of Korea is the genuine homeland of all the Korean people and enjoys their unreserved support and love. Ours is an authentic people's state, which guarantees not only political freedom and rights for the people, but also a happy material and cultural life. Our state is most democratic and stable; it was founded by the people; it is led by the working class; it relies on the united, combined strength of all the people based on the worker-peasant alliance; and it enlists the vast majority of our popular masses in the affairs of the state.

Our people see their future freedom and happiness in the prosperity and development of the Republic and they have an unshakable faith in its invincibility. Our working people have complete confidence that they can build a paradise of socialism and communism on the soil of their homeland, and they devote all their energy and talent to the struggle for their country's eternal prosperity. Our people are staunchly determined to crush any imperialist invasion decisively, to safeguard the independence and honor of their country and to reunify their divided land, by further strengthening the political, economic and military power of the Republic.

The prosperity and development of our Republic exert a powerful revolutionary influence on the south Korean people who suffer under the cruel oppression and exploitation of the US imperialists and their henchmen. The striking contrast between the situation in north and south Korea has led the South Korean people to realize even more clearly that they can only enjoy real freedom and happiness when they are completely freed from the yoke of foreign imperialism and when the people take power into their own hands. The people in south Korea see their bright future reflected in the prosperity and development of our Republic; and they are gaining infinite energy and courage from its growing might. Regarding our Republic as the mighty stronghold for the country's reunification, they fight ever more stubbornly against the US imperialists and their lackeys.

The Democratic People's Republic of Korea is exercising a tremendous influence upon all Korean citizens abroad. Since they were people without a country of their own, a great number of Koreans in the past were subjected to national discrimination and all sorts of humiliation in foreign countries and they suffered from a complete lack of rights and abject poverty. Today, however, as citizens of a proud independent state, they can claim their rights as well as return to the bosom of the homeland to live happily. Already tens of thousands of our countrymen in Japan have returned to the Republic and settled down, free from any inconvenience or worry, and still more of them are coming home.

All these facts demonstrate that the Democratic People's Republic of Korea, the glorious home of all the Korean people, has become the banner of their freedom and happiness and that its influence continues to grow.

For nearly half a century the Korean people were dispossessed of their country. Today our people have a mighty country of their own—a country in a period of unprecedented prosperity. Our people are immensely proud of their fatherland, the Democratic People's Republic of Korea, and consider it a high honor to be its citizens.

No force can break the strength of the Korean people or block their march forward now that they have rallied under the banner of the Republic.

II. Far-Reaching Prospects
1. Basic Tasks of the Seven-Year Plan

Comrades,
Broad new horizons are opening for our people who have already achieved outstanding successes in building a new society. With a victorious feeling of immense pride, with greater hope for the future, all of our working people have set out to fulfill the Seven-Year Plan for the Development of the National Economy. These seven years will mark a decisive period in the socialist construction of our country.

The fundamental tasks of the Seven-Year Plan are to carry out a comprehensive technological reconstruction and the cultural revolution, and to make radical improvements in the people's living conditions by relying on the triumphant socialist system. We must carry out socialist industrialization, equip all branches of the national economy with modern technology, and decisively raise the material and cultural standards of the whole population. Thus, we will attain the high peak of socialism.

In a brief time, our people, under the leadership of our Party, have brought about historic changes in their society and economy and have built a socialist system free from exploitation and oppression. But these accomplishments are not enough to achieve the complete victory of socialism. We must lay a firm material and technological foundation for socialism by thoroughly industrializing the country and making the technical revolution.

The technical revolution—this is a momentous revolutionary task which will relieve our people, free of exploitation, from hard work, enable them to produce more material wealth while working easily and ensure them a richer and more cultured life. The technical revolution will solve the most crucial question for the ultimate victory of a new social system in our country—a country which inherited backward productive forces from the past.

With the fulfillment of the Five-Year Plan, our country took a big step towards building an independent industry and technologically reconstructing the national economy. But this means that we have merely laid the basis for industrialization and taken only the initial steps towards the technical revolution. Hence, the prime tasks of the Seven-Year Plan are to realize socialist industrialization and implement an all-round technical revolution in all spheres of the national economy. We must continue to develop industry rapidly and equip all branches of the national economy, including agriculture, with modern technology, thus converting our country into a socialist industrial country with modern industries and advanced agriculture.

All-round technological reconstruction of the national economy calls for more scientific and technical cadres and for high cultural and technical standards on the part of the working people. The technical and cultural revolutions are closely related, and without the latter we can scarcely expect to implement the former successfully. Although significant results have been achieved in eliminating the country's cultural backwardness, in this field as well, revolution must be continually pushed ahead. We must greatly expand the ranks of scientific and technical cadres; we must see to it that all the working people gain knowledge and skill in operating modern machinery efficiently; and we must educate the coming generation so that they will be well-rounded, capable builders of communism.

The object of socialist construction is, after all, to ensure a plentiful and cultured life for all the people. Our Party removed the social source of exploitation and poverty and developed the productive forces, thereby solving the most basic problem in our people's material life. Now, our task is to raise their general standard of living to a level high enough for a socialist society. During the first half of the Seven-Year Plan we should direct our efforts to improving the working people's welfare. During the second half we should continue to pay serious attention to this so that in six or seven years all the people can be well-off in all respects.

Socialist construction in the northern half of the Republic is the determining factor for the nationwide victory of the Korean revolution. The fulfillment of the Seven-Year Plan for the Development of the National Economy will further develop the revolutionary base set up in the northern half into an invincible force and be decisive in promoting the peaceful reunification of the country. Completion of this plan will not only lay an adequate foundation for the prosperous material and cultural life of our people in the northern half. It will also further consolidate the base of the independent national economy enough to rehabilitate the devastated economy of South Korea and to relieve its people from famine and poverty in the future.

In order to accomplish the historic tasks of the Seven-Year Plan successfully we must continue to follow the Party's line of giving priority to the growth of heavy industry, while, at the same time, developing science and culture. In the postwar period, even on the debris, we overcame all difficulties to carry this line through, laid the foundation of the national economy, further consolidated it, and markedly improved the material and cultural life of the people. In the future as well, we must continue to abide firmly by this line. Thus, we must effect an overall technological renovation, bring about a flowering of national culture and quickly raise the people's standard of living.

For another great leap forward in socialist construction, we must maintain the high speed of our advance and move ahead even more rapidly. Our realities demand this, for the country still lags behind economically and technologically; and the situation in our country demands this, for its southern half continues to be occupied by the US imperialists. Our people are now trying to speed up socialist construction in the northern half of the Republic with renewed effort. They are filled with revolutionary will to rescue their brothers in South Korea, a living hell, as rapidly as possible.

We must consolidate the socialist system we have already won and raise the communist consciousness of the working people even higher so that all the people participate in the construction of socialism with exalted spirits and continue the grand Chollima advance. All Party members and working people must devote their full energy to master new technology, arm themselves with advanced scientific knowledge, sweep away everything obsolete and stagnant, create new norms and records everywhere, and make uninterrupted innovation and continual advance.

Therefore, it is incumbent on us to strengthen the power of the Democratic People's Republic of Korea in every possible way and forge an even stronger unity of all the people of north and south Korea around the Workers' Party of Korea and the Government of the Republic. In this way we will prepare powerful political and economic forces for building a unified, independent, wealthy and strong Korea.

2. Industry

The Seven-Year Plan envisages rapid quantitative and qualitative progress in industry.

Total value of industrial output will increase annually by an average of 18 per cent. By 1967 it will be about 3.2 times as great as in 1960, representing 3.2-fold increase in the output of the means of production and 3.1-fold in the output of consumer goods. Industrial production will then surpass the prewar level more than 20 times, and far more manufactured goods will be produced in one year than were produced in the entire period of the last Five-Year Plan. This means that our industry will continue to advance at Chollima speed and our country will be industrialized in a short period of time.

The central task confronting industry in the Seven-Year Plan period is to establish in our country an independent industrial system which is developed in a many-sided way, has its own stable base of raw materials and is fully equipped with the latest technology. This is to be done by further perfecting the structure of industrial production and reinforcing its technological foundation. Only this kind of industry will make it possible to develop and utilize the rich and varied natural resources of the country rationally, to effect the technological reconstruction of the entire national economy, and to radically improve the living conditions of our people.

Heavy industry will play the leading role in achieving industrialization and promoting the people's welfare.

The greatest efforts our Party has directed to developing heavy industry have resulted in the establishment of the machine-building industry and all the other key branches of heavy industry. But our country's heavy industry, which developed quickly in a short period of time, still lacks a number of auxiliary branches and is inadequate in many respects. We have build the skeleton of heavy industry, so to speak, but have not yet put enough flesh on it.

Hence, the first important task before us is to fill the gaps in heavy industry, put flesh on its skeleton, and then expand its bases. To this end, we must continue to reequip and expand existing heavy industry factories and equip them with new technology. At the same time we must build new, large-scale enterprises to produce and supply all branches of the national economy with the machinery, equipment, raw and other materials they need. During the Seven-Year Plan we must rapidly develop the machine-building, chemical, fuel and power and iron and steel industries; we must rebuild and better equip heavy industry as a whole. Thus we should markedly increase the country's economic strength and enable our heavy industry to serve the development of light industry and agriculture more effectively.

In order to ensure the rapid development of the national economy, the first necessity is to expand and consolidate our fuel and power bases. In particular, the electric power industry should be developed ahead of other branches in order to accelerate the electrification of the country, which is of great significance in technological progress.

Our Party's policy for developing the power industry is to continue to build large hydroelectric power stations by extensively tapping our country's rich waterpower resources and, simultaneously, to promote the construction of thermoelectric power stations. Not only can we build a thermoelectric power station in less time and at lower costs than a hydroelectric power station; it will also allow us to guarantee a regular supply of electricity during the dry season and to use power for many purposes. Only by combining the construction of water and thermal power stations in a rational way can we considerably increase our generating capacity in a short period of time, eliminate the bias of our power industry to hydraulic power, and thus qualitatively consolidate the electric power bases.

During the period of the Seven-Year Plan, we should build

many new thermoelectric power stations as well as large hydroelectric ones to increase power generating capacity by over 2,000,000 kw and bring the total generating capacity to 3,300,000 to 3,500,000 kw.

An urgent problem in expanding our power bases is to produce our own generating equipment. This is, of course, a difficult job; but we should try to domestically manufacture and supply, little by little, complete sets of equipment for water and thermal power stations including large-sized generators.

As for the fuel industry, in order to increase coal output rapidly, we should concentrate investment on coal mines which have large deposits and favorable mining conditions and should step up capital construction so that the gangways of every coal mine are almost completely lined with concrete. All the collieries should raise the level of mechanization in every possible way and carry on a vigorous movement for technical renovation beginning with the extensive application of the hydraulic coal-cutting method. Thus, we should increase annual coal output to 23,000,000 to 25,000,000 tons by the end of the Seven-Year Plan.

The metal industry, particularly ferrous metallurgy, is of tremendous significance in speeding up the technological reconstruction of the national economy and reinforcing the foundation of the country's independent economy. Unless we produce and supply a large quantity of iron materials, it will be impossible to manufacture lots of machinery and equipment and carry out large-scale construction.

We should reequip and expand existing iron and steel works and make better use of different metallurgical facilities. We should begin extensive construction to develop the Kim Chaek Iron Works so that within the next ten years it will be a steel producing center with an annual capacity of 3,000,000 tons. The first stage of the project must be to create an annual output capacity of 1,800,000 tons during the Seven-Year Plan. In addition, a new steel plant should be built to process the ore dust abundant on the west coast.

Thus, towards the end of the Seven-Year Plan the annual output of pig and granulated iron should reach 2,200,000 to 2,500,000 tons, steel—2,200,000 to 2,500,000 tons, and rolled steel—1,600,000 to 1,800,000 tons. At the same time we should direct our efforts to expanding the variety of steel materials and, in particular, to developing the production of alloy steel.

In nonferrous metallurgy we will expand the production capacity of the existing smelteries and will build rolling mills for nonferrous metals so that domestic products meet the demands for various nonferrous rolled goods.

We should pay great attention to the production of light metals. First of all, we should process nephelite in a comprehensive way and thus produce our own aluminum for industrial use.

To meet the growing demands of the metal industry for various ores, we should expand existing mines, improve their technological equipment and develop more new mines during the Seven-Year Plan.

At the same time, we should step up geological prospecting in every way. We should produce and supply this field with more equipment and materials and set up enough laboratories and assaying centers, while at the same time placing more emphasis on training specialists in this field.

One of the most important tasks under the Seven-Year Plan is the large-scale development of the chemical industry.

The development of the chemical industry will not only accelerate technical progress in the national economy but also play an important role in ensuring the varied and more effective use of domestic natural resources. From those resources available in our country the chemical industry obtains substitutes for those not available. It also provides us with different kinds of synthetic materials, with properties far superior to those of natural materials, for production and construction. We must meet our raw material needs by chemical synthesis, particularly because in our country whose arable land is limited agriculture cannot supply light industry with sufficient raw materials. That is why our Party attaches great importance to the development of the chemical industry— among others, the organic synthetic industry—and to chemicalization for the national economy.

To begin with, we must increase production of artificial fiber considerably and build a large vinalon factory and a vichlon factory, thus completely solving the problem of raw materials for textile fibres. We should quickly increase the production of synthetic resins, including vinyl chloride, and build a new base of the chemical industry so that it can mass-produce synthetic rubber.

In order to supply the countryside with larger quantities of various chemical fertilizers and to increase the production of agricultural chemicals such as insecticides and weed killers, and urea, we should expand and strengthen the bases of the chemical industry concerned.

Thus, towards the end of the Seven-Year Plan, the annual output of artificial and synthetic fibers should reach 80,000 to 100,000 tons, synthetic resins—60,000 to 70,000 tons, and synthetic rubber—15,000 to 20,000 tons. The output of chemical fertilizers should increase to 1,500,000 to 1,700,000 tons. Along with this we should build an oil refinery that will, in its first stage, process 1,000,000 tons of crude oil in the Aoji region. We will then meet the demands for chemicals in industry and agriculture and will make a major stride forward in chemicalization for the national economy.

The acid and alkali industries, the foundation of the chemical industry, should be developed and the pharmaceutical industry should be expanded so that we can meet our requirements for medicines and veterinary drugs with goods produced at home.

The whole Seven-Year Plan period is one of overall technical revolution in all branches of the national economy. If we fail to develop the machine-building industry quickly and thus manufacture and supply enough modern machinery and equipment, we will not be able to take even a single step ahead. The solution of all problems of technological renovation, such as mechanization and automation of production process, electrification and chemicalization, depends, after all, on the development of the machine-building industry.

We must satisfy the demand for mining machinery, metallurgical and chemical equipment, electrical machinery and other equipment for heavy industry, various types of light industry equipment, construction machinery and transport equipment. In particular we should produce large quantities of tractors and other farm machinery, ships and other kinds of fishing equipment to mechanize our backward agriculture and fisheries. This requires expanding the existing machine-building plants, reinforcing their technological equipment, and creating new bases for the machine-building industry.

Our machine-designing capability should be significantly increased so that more various new types of machinery and equipment including heavy machinery and precision machines are devised and manufactured. In particular, we should rapidly step up the production of various kinds of meters, electron tubes and weak-current apparatus for the technological progress and automation of the national economy.

Careful attention should be paid to technological renovation in the machine-building industry—active application of advanced casting methods in the production of materials, extensive introduction of stamping methods along with cutting, and the application of assembly-line or serial production methods in processing and assembling machines.

We must also introduce extensive specialization and cooperation in production by relying on the foundations of the machine-building industry we have already created. We must eliminate labor and iron wastage and raise the quality of produced machinery considerably by specializing in the production of casting forgings and spare parts.

The building-materials industry must be developed systematically to ensure the success of the large-scale construction works envisaged in the Seven-Year Plan.

We should expand cement factories and build new ones so that cement output can reach 4,000,000 to 4,500,000 tons in 1967. We should also take measures to work stone and weathered granite, and make wide use of local materials in construction.

To achieve maximum economy in iron and timber we must construct new building-materials factories that utilize wood-shaving and wood-fiber boards, synthetic resins and the like. We should build or expand sanitary ware factories, tarred paper mills, and plants turning out various kinds of fittings.

In order to raise the level of industrialization in construction we should continuously expand the production of structural components and start making them both large and light.

One of the important tasks before industry is to satisfy the increasing demands of the working people for consumer goods. Our country's light industry is as a whole still unsatisfactory. During the years of the Seven-Year Plan, we should bring about a radical development of light industry on the basis of the priority growth of heavy industry.

In the production of consumer goods, our Party will continue to pursue a policy of simultaneously carrying forward the centrally-controlled industry which is technologically rather complex and to be developed on a large scale and local industry to be developed on a medium or small scale with the use of locally available raw materials. Many new large light industries must be built and existing enterprises rebuilt or expanded. In particular, measures should be taken to replace gradually the handicraft techniques still used in local industry with modern technology.

The most important problem in light industry is to extend the variety of products and radically improve their quality. We should exploit all our resources and possibilities and produce a wide variety of higher-quality consumer goods necessary in the daily life of the working people. We should catch up with the advanced countries soon in the quality of light industry products.

Considering the fact that cotton cultivation is extremely limited in our country, we should concentrate efforts in the textile industry on producing fabrics from vinalon, staple fiber, artificial silk and other chemical fibers, and linen. The output of silk and woolen fabrics should also increase rapidly. Doing these things we should raise the annual capacity for textile production to 300 million meters in the first half of the Seven-Year Plan and to 400 to 500 million meters by 1967. The entire population will then be supplied with various kinds of cloth in sufficient quantities and the clothing problem will be satisfactorily solved.

In order to produce and supply enough kraft paper and cardboard, to say nothing of the paper necessary in the people's daily life, we should extensively develop the paper industry. We should build big paper mills in areas where pulp wood is abundant, and at the same time set up and put into operation many medium and small ones which will make use of different kinds of locally available raw materials.

We must also develop the rubber industry to satisfy the demands of the national economy and the people for rubber products and rapidly expand the production of daily necessities made from synthetic resins. As regards footwear, the production of shoes from real and simulated leather should be gradually increased to replace rubber shoes. We should produce all kinds of household goods, including electrical appliances for daily use, and supply enough of the different kinds of furniture the working people need in their homes.

We should continue to develop the food industry rapidly in order to meet our working people's needs and to lessen the burden of women in the home. Maize processing factories should be expanded on a large scale. We should build or expand factories and processing plants, to provide soy and bean pastes, edible oils and bean curd, meat and fish. Their production capacity should be increased markedly.

Our country borders on the sea on three sides; thus, the proper exploitation of marine resources is very important in improving the people's living standards. We should continue to direct great efforts and more funds to this field to bring a marked increase in our catch. By the final year of the Seven-Year Plan, products from the sea should reach 1,000,000 to 1,200,000 tons.

It is necessary to mechanize all our existing boats and build many big fishing vessels to create conditions for deep-sea fishing in addition to inshore fishing. Fishing boats should be fully equipped with communications gear, shoal detectors, and up-to-date fishing tackle for scientific fishing.

We should recondition our existing ports and put them in good order. New fishing ports should be built and the fishing grounds continuously expanded. We should improve facilities for processing marine products and effect technological renovation in this area.

In order to develop fresh water fish-breeding and sea plant and fish culture in shallow seas, nurseries should be set up in all areas; and we should also adequately supply them with the necessary materials.

The organization and economy of fishing cooperatives should be further strengthened. To ensure a sufficient supply of necessary materials, we should expand factories producing fishing materials and improve their supply system.

To improve the supply of seafood to the population, refrigeration plants should be established in cities, the number of refrigerator cars should be increased and refrigerators should also be installed in ocean freighters.

In this way, we will continue to develop heavy and light industry at a high rate during the period of the Seven-Year Plan. We will thus provide different kinds of materials, machinery, equipment and consumer goods necessary for the overall technological reconstruction of the national economy and for a radical improvement in the people's standard of living. Our industry will become modern, developed and diversified, and this will further reinforce the foundations of the independent economy of our country.

3. Agriculture

The central task confronting agriculture in the period of the Seven-Year Plan is farm mechanization and a further increase in farm production by accelerating technological reconstruction.

At present it is of the utmost importance in the technical revolution of our country to replace outdated agro-technology with up-to-date machine technology. With the completion of socialist cooperativization, mechanization of agriculture is indispensable to further developing productive forces in agriculture and consolidating the cooperative economy. Only when agriculture is equipped with modern machinery will it keep pace steadily with rapidly developing industry and will it be possible to ease the peasants' work and make their life full.

We should throw all our efforts into speeding up the mechanization of agriculture. Farm machine stations should be increased so that every county may have its own, and the number of tractors, lorries and different farm machines should be significantly increased. The number of tractors in terms of 15 hp units should be raised from the present 13,000 to more than 80,000 by 1967.

What is important in agricultural mechanization is the rational distribution of large, medium, and small tractors and lorries according to geographical conditions and their use in coordination with various farm machines. Only in this way can we carry out the all-round mechanization of the whole countryside—from plains to remote mountain areas—and mechanize all major farm work such as ploughing, sowing, furrowing and weeding, harvesting and threshing as well as livestock breeding and transport.

At the same time we should make further successes in irrigation. Because of our country's climatic conditions, we get the stablest and highest yields from the cultivation of rice. The area of paddyfields should be expanded to 700,000 *chongbo*, and that of irrigated dry fields should also increase during the Seven-Year Plan. In areas along the east coast we should continue our work in afforestation and water conservation, to prevent flood damage, such as river improvement, reservoir and river-dike projects.

Our Party will continue to follow the policy of giving preference to grain production and simultaneously developing the cultivation of industrial crops, stockbreeding, fruit growing and sericulture.

The solution of the grain problem is one of the most fundamental tasks in socialist construction. Without a decisive increase in grain production it is impossible to supply enough food to the people and further develop other branches of agriculture. We should direct our main efforts to grain production and, on this basis, develop a diversified agriculture.

In our country with its limited amount of farm land, we must reclaim more new land by transforming nature; we must conserve existing land, and improve and utilize it more effectively. The systematic expansion of land under cultivation constitutes an important guarantee for rapid increase in grain production and an all-round development of agriculture. Based on a far-reaching program to obtain another million *chongbo* of land within the next ten years, we must continue to vigorously push ahead with the magnificent projects for transforming nature to reclaim tidelands along the west coast, hills all over the country, and plateaus such as Pochon and Paegam. Thus, we have to ensure that during the Seven-Year Plan period 500,000 more *chongbo* of land is brought under the plough to bring the total area of cultivated land to 2,500,000 *chongbo*.

Along with this, the total sown area should be markedly expanded by an extensive introduction of the double-cropping system and by raising the utilization of our farm lands.

In our country the key to increasing grain yields lies in raising the per-unit-area yield by developing advanced methods of intensive farming.

We should take all thorough-going measures to raise crop yields—active soil improvement, deep ploughing, planting of high-yielding seeds, sufficient watering and manuring, weeding, and prevention of blight and harmful insects.

In particular we should pay close attention to the chemicalization of agriculture. Improving land fertility, stimulating crop growing, weeding and killing harmful insects—all this should be done by chemical methods. Only when chemicalization, coupled wtih mechanization, is effected in the countryside can we ease difficult and toilsome labor, farm intensively with less manpower, and decisively increase our yields.

We must take all these economic and technical measures in order to increase the total annual output of grain to the 6,000,000-ton mark by the end of the Seven-Year Plan. Such a rise will not only enable our country to solve the food problem definitively but also to lay a firm foundation for the speedy development of all branches of agriculture.

While increasing grain production, we must concentrate on cultivating cotton, flax and other fiber crops, various oil-bearing crops, tobacco, sugar beets, *insam* and hops, all on suitable soil, and raise their yields in order to provide industry with raw materials; and we should also boost our production of vegetables to supply more of them to the urban population.

One of the major tasks of agriculture during the period of the Seven-Year Plan is to make a marked advance in stockbreeding. We should continue to consolidate the foundations of stockbreeding which we have so far built up with great effort, do away with historical backwardness in stockbreeding, and further increase the output of meat and other animal products.

To increase meat and milk production rapidly during this period, we must raise the number of pigs to over three million and of cattle to one million. Grazing animals such as goats and rabbits must be raised in greater numbers, while strenuous efforts should be made to obtain milk cows from cows no longer needed for farm work because of the progress in the mechanization of agriculture. Sheep breeding should be widely introduced on the plains as well as in the mountainous areas so as to sharply increase the output of wool, and poultry farming should also continue to develop.

Our consistent policy for raising livestock is to lay the main emphasis on stockbreeding by the state and joint stockbreeding by the agricultural cooperatives, parallel to stockbreeding development as a sideline of cooperative members. Each cooperative, while steadily developing its joint stockbreeding, should supply young pedigree stock to its members, and all peasant households should take part in a wide-scale movement for raising pigs, rabbits, chickens and ducks.

The creation of reliable bases for fodder is of prime importance in stockbreeding. In order to solve this question, we should grow fodder extensively as a semi-annual crop on rice paddies and dry fields and actively push ahead with the creation of fodder fields and pastures wherever possible—at the foot of mountains, in valleys, on hillsides, and so on.

We should improve the breeding stock, steadily improve the raising and care of animals, take decisive steps to prevent death from disease by strengthening our work against epizootics, and raise animal productivity considerably.

It is of great significance in the development of the national economy to make comprehensive and effective use of the mountains which cover nearly 80 percent of our country's land area. Mountains can be utilized not only to develop lumber production and livestock farming; they are also very important for advancing fruit growing, sericulture and for meeting industrial needs for various raw materials by creating economically valuable forests.

The Seven-Year Plan envisages the extensive development of fruit growing. The area for fruit trees in our country must be increased to 300,000 to 350,000 *chongbo* by creating over 200,000 *chongbo* of orchards through the reclamation of hillsides. At the same time, the fruit-bearing area must be rapidly expanded by properly nursing young trees. In this way, we should produce 500,000 tons of fruit in 1967, so that the population will be supplied with different kinds of fruit in all seasons.

Sericulture must be further developed to produce more silk fabrics of high quality. The area of mulberry fields must be increased to 100,000 *chongbo* by adding 40,000 *chongbo* of mulberry groves on hillsides, and the per-*chongbo* yields of mulberry leaves and cocoons must be raised by improving the fertilization and care of mulberry trees. The groves for breeding tussah worms and the area with castor bean must be expanded, and advanced methods of breeding widely applied.

The work of converting forests with little value into ones with economic value, such as those that provide raw materials for fiber and oil, must also be carried on in a far-sighted and planned way. We should plant trees that grow quickly, such as poplars and white ashes, everywhere, in the fields and on the hillsides, so as to ensure raw materials for pulp in a short amount of time. We should plant paulownias, walnut, black walnut, chestnut and pine-nut trees to be used in the future as raw materials for light industry. In order to provide trees that will be used to create forests with economic value, priority must be given to saplings and an all-people movement for afforestation must be enthusiastically launched.

The Seven-Year Plan envisages full-scale development of agricultural production and, at the same time, continued large-scale rural construction.

We must readjust paddy and non-paddy fields, build roads and bridges and erect a greater number of homes, schools, hospitals and other cultural and public service establishments. In order to ensure construction on such a vast scale, the state will supply the necessary machines, equipment and materials and render technical assistance. For rural construction we also need to make an active use of local materials as well as the financial resources of agricultural cooperatives.

The rapid development of agriculture and the successful fulfillment of rural construction will completely eliminate all traces of the age-old poverty and backwardness of our countryside, turn it into a modern and cultured rural society, and radically promote the well-being of the peasants.

4. Transport and Communications

The rapid growth of the national economy requires a marked increase in freight haulage during the period of the Seven-Year Plan. It is impossible to satisfy our growing transport demands without speedy development of railway, water and motor transport.

It is important, first of all, to strengthen the material and technological basis of railway transport and to expand its traffic capacity in every possible way.

The Pyongsan-Pokgye and Chongjin-Rajin lines should be completed, and the narrow-gauge railway that still exists in South Hwanghae Province should be replaced by a standard-gauge line.

Electrification of railways clearly helps increase their

economic efficiency and modern operation. Electrification will cut fuel consumption to one-fifth, greatly save manpower in transport, and nearly double traffic capacity. The Pyongyang-Chongjin, Pyongyang-Sinuiju, Pyongyang-Kaesong, and Huichon-Koin lines should be electrified during the Seven-Year Plan so as to complete the basic electrification of the major trunk lines.

Furthermore, the production capacity of railway factories must be improved to provide the railways with sufficient electric locomotives, freight cars, passenger coaches and all other necessary machinery and materials.

Thus, by strengthening technological equipment and at the same time improving the utilization of the rolling stock, railway freight turnover should be increased to 75 million tons by 1967.

In order to ease the strain on railway transport and to ensure smoother freight haulage for the national economy, water transport should be extensively developed. Vessels should be built for sea and river transport in order to raise water transport capacity considerably. In particular, to keep up with the expansion of foreign trade, measures should be taken for long-distance ocean shipping. In addition, major ports on the east and west coasts should be put in good condition.

To raise motor transport capacity, we should vigorously push forward the repairs and building of roads and bridges; roads should be paved on a large scale in those areas where traffic is heavy, and the utilization of motor vehicles and trailers should be greatly raised.

In the communications field, we should complete the telephone networks between county and ri and increase the automatic exchange capacity in all cities. The wire broadcasting network will be expanded so that broadcasting facilities can be installed in every rural ri. At the same time we should greatly increase the output to strengthen radio broadcasting and begin television broadcasting.

5. Development of Science and Culture

All-round technological reconstruction of the national economy demands marked progress in all branches of science.

Science plays an increasingly important role in the development of productive forces, and only crossing the frontiers of science can we achieve high labor productivity and ensure a complete victory for socialism.

We must opportunely solve the urgent scientific and technological problems arising in the practical socialist construction. We must constantly assimilate the advanced scientific achievements of progressive mankind and raise all our country's science up to international levels in the near future.

The fundamental task confronting our country's science at present is to serve the technical revolution in a positive way.

We face a number of difficult, complex tasks of technological renovation: to mechanize all branches of the national economy, including agriculture; to introduce comprehensive mechanization and automation in certain sectors; to push ahead with electrification throughout the country, and so on. To fulfill these tasks successfully, we should systematically invent various kinds of machinery and equipment suitable for our country's actual conditions, design both highly-efficient automatic machines and equipment for automation, and investigate rational methods of automation.

The force of science should be harnessed to investigate the country's natural resources and study how to use them effectively. At the same time, it should work towards establishing a self-supporting industrial system based on domestic natural resources.

Above all it is very important to develop the ferrous metal industry by relying on domestic fuel sources. Instead of crying about the lack of coking coal, we must study methods of manufacturing iron with anthracite that is abundant in our country. For this purpose, we must perfect the reduced pellet process and the continuous production process of steel making with granulated iron as soon as we can.

It is also essential to speed up chemicalization of the national economy using domestic resources and save as much electric power as possible in our chemical processes. To this end, we should advance the research and widely introduce the results of the gasification of anthracite in the synthesis of ammonia and other branches of the chemical industry, in metallurgy and in other spheres of the national economy. We should also complete the tasks of producing carbide by the oxygen heat treatment and of carbonizing lignite at high temperatures. Further-more, we should continuously promote research to develop the synthetic fiber and synthetic resin industries and to industrial-ize synthetic rubber production. The raw materials for these industries are anthracite and limestone, buried in inexhausti-ble quantities all over the country.

We must open new fields of science, introduce the latest achievements of science and technology throughout the na-tional economy, and actively develop the important areas of the basic sciences.

Research work for introducing atomic energy into produc-tion should be carried out under a far-reaching program. Radioisotopes and radiation should be widely applied in various fields, including industry and agriculture. We should carry out profound studies of supersonic waves and high fre-quency electronics, efficiently apply these technologies in pro-duction and construction, and introduce the production of semi-conductor materials using domestic raw materials as well as extend the range of their application. We should devote proper attention to the development of electronics which is of great importance in the national economy. Work in basic sci-ences such as mathematics, physics, chemistry, biology, etc., should be improved decisively so as to contribute to the solu-tion of technical problems that come up in all spheres of the na-tional economy.

A number of urgent tasks which will ensure high agricultur-al yields and help to develop stockbreeding should be carried out. In order to guarantee better health and longer life for the working people, we should intensify medical research work to develop *Tonguihak*, or traditional Korean medicine, along with modern medicine and to work out a theoretical systematiza-tion of the folk cures bequeathed to us by our ancestors.

Our Party and people have already accumulated a wealth of valuable experience in the revolutionary transformation of society and economic and cultural construction. Social scien-ces should provide theoretical generalization of this experi-ence, thoroughly explain and propagate the Party's lines and policies on the basis of Marxism-Leninism, and make a com-plete study of the Party's revolutionary traditions and the na-tion's cultural heritage. At the same time, the new social and

economic problems raised in socialist construction should be
solved rapidly to help the growth of the national economy. In
particular, social scientists should make a profound study of
south Korea's current economy and culture and collectively
elaborate ways for rehabilitating and developing them in the
future.

The important thing in the cultural revolution is to increase
the general and technical knowledge of the working people.
Without this we cannot accomplish the technical revolution or
achieve the complete victory of socialism.

Our tasks in the field of education are to arm the working
masses firmly with accurate information and a correct viewpoint on nature and society and to raise their cultural and technical standards. The public educational establishments should
educate and train the children and the youth in the latest
achievements of science and culture and also in the communist
world outlook by increasing the contact between school and
practical life and combining education closely with productive
labor. In this way we should bring up the younger generation
to be a new kind of people who are loyal to the Party and the
revolution and are well-rounded in their development. Thus we
should steadily replenish the ranks of cultured and conscious
working people in our society.

Based on the successful enforcement of compulsory secondary education, compulsory nine-year technical education
should be fully introduced during the period of the Seven-Year
Plan. Going over to universal compulsory technical education
means a further development of the socialist education system. It marks an epochal change in the work of training the
younger generation to be capable builders of communism.

Today, with the technical revolution taking place throughout all branches of the national economy, the need for technical
personnel is greater than ever before. Progress will not continue unless our training of technical personnel keeps pace with
the high rate of development of the productive forces and of
the technical revolution in the country.

To meet the present and future demands of the national
economy for technical personnel, we must, during the Seven-
Year Plan, train 460,000 assistant engineers and junior specialists and strengthen higher education to train about 180,000

engineers and specialists. Especially we should concentrate our training of specialists for areas where they are badly needed, such as machine-building, electricity, chemistry, biology, transport, light industry, fisheries, farming, animal husbandry and public health.

One of our Party's consistent policies is to develop a system of various forms of higher education which permits working people to study without leaving their productive activity, in conjunction with the regular system of higher education. In particular, we should greatly increase factory colleges, whose advantages we know by experience, and train a large number of competent working-class technical cadres who are versed in both theory and practice.

By strengthening adult education and putting into operation the system of learning technology and skills in productive enterprises on a regular basis, the cultural and technical level of the working people should be radically raised and the Party's call for everyone to acquire more than one technical skill should be put into practice.

Literature and art play an important role in the communist education of the popular masses. Writers and artists are entrusted with the important responsibility of portraying the real heroes of both our revolution and the building of a new life, thereby educating people in the ideas of the Party and the working class.

The most important thing of all is to describe our reality vividly—a reality in which miracles are performed everywhere, everyone is being remolded into a new, communist type of man, and the grand Chollima advance is on—and to create typical images of the Chollima riders, the heroes of our time. Today our life glows with the indomitable will and optimistic passion of the working people for building a new society faster, and it provides countless beautiful stories which embody unlimited love for man and collectivist morality. Writers and artists should penetrate deeply into this valuable life of ours and produce fine literary and artistic works that make an active contribution to remolding the people's ideas and inspiring the masses to the revolutionary cause.

Furthermore, by creating images of the communist fighters who waged the long, difficult struggle to liberate the fatherland and win the revolution, they should continue to raise their standards in educating our generation in the lofty revolutionary spirit of these fighters.

The characteristic features of the best literary and artistic works lie in the high ideological content and artistic value which conform with the demands of the times and the people's aspirations. Such valuable works can be produced only on the basis of socialist realism, the only correct method of creative expression at the present time.

There is not the slightest room in our society for bourgeois literature and art which run counter to the revolution and hinder the advancement of the people, and we have infinite possibilities now to explore revolutionary literature and art which will serve the workers and peasants. Writers and artists should wage a resolute struggle against all the poisons spread by reactionary bourgeois literature and art, and they should devote all their talent and creative zeal to enrich our Red literature and art, making it more militant.

Literature and art can only touch people's hearts and evoke love when the socialist content is correctly bound up with the varied and ingenious forms characteristic of our nation. We should incorporate and develop the traditions of our brilliant national art so that all the beautiful and progressive contributions of our ancestors can burst into full bloom in our time.

We should energetically develop mass cultural work, search out the talent among our people, and bring this talent into full play so that the working people themselves can participate in literary and artistic activities and enjoy art as much as they want wherever they are.

We will turn our country into an advanced socialist state with modern science and a developed culture by thoroughly carrying out all the tasks that arise in the course of the cultural revolution.

6. Improvement of the People's Standard of Living

Under the socialist system, solicitude for man is the supreme principle. Under this system technology advances and production grows steadily, thus promoting the material and cultural well-being of all working people. This principle of socialism is strikingly expressed in the Seven-Year Plan for Development of the National Economy.

An important task before our Party is to radically improve the people's standard of living in the shortest possible time on the basis of a thoroughgoing technological innovation and a great upsurge in production.

The Seven-Year Plan envisages a 2.7-fold increase in the national income which will surpass the prewar level 9 times in 1967.

We will adjust accumulation and consumption so that we may correctly relate the future development of the national economy to the satisfaction of the people's immediate requirements, and combine the interests of the whole society with the personal interests of the working people. In the future as well, we will continue to allot a large proportion of the national income to popular consumption, while ensuring the steady growth of accumulation.

The real income of factory and office workers is expected to rise 1.7 times during the period of the Seven-Year Plan. During the same time the number of factory and office workers will grow 1.5 times. The number of members of factory and office workers' families who take jobs will continue to increase, and real per-family income will more than double in seven years. The peasants' real income will also increase more than two times during the same period, which will bring their general living standard up to the level of former well-to-do middle peasants.

We should achieve a more rational wage scale for the workers in all branches of the economy and an even increase in the income of peasants in different areas. At the same time we should, as we have always done, correctly adhere to the principle of raising the general living standard of factory and office workers and of the peasants proportionately.

Our Party envisages the abolition of taxes levied on the population at the earliest possible date.

At the moment the overwhelming majority of our state's revenue is obtained from accumulation in socialist state enterprises. Tax revenue from the population is negligible. We will be in a position in these very days to abolish taxes completely now that necessary funds for economic and cultural construction can come entirely from state accumulation.

By abolishing the income tax on factory and office workers and the agricultural tax in kind on the peasants, we will finally eliminate the tax system, a legacy of the old society; we will completely free the working people from the burden of all taxes, thus raising their real income still more. This can be translated into reality only by a Party of Communists who regard the promotion of the working people's well-being as the law governing their activities. This is possible only under the socialist system where the working people themselves have become the masters of the country.

In line with the rise in the working people's income, we should increase the supply of commodities and further develop public catering.

The turnover of retail trade in town and countryside is expected to grow 3.2 times during the period of the Seven-Year Plan.

A marked change is also expected in the composition of commodity circulation. Now that the problems of food, clothing and housing have been basically solved, the working people demand foodstuffs and clothes of higher quality and different kinds of articles for cultural use in greater quantities. We should solve the problem of providing sufficient cooking oil and fish in the shortest possible time and noticeably increase the supply of vegetables, meat, milk and eggs. The sale of overcoat and suit materials and various other fabrics, underwear and shoes as well as sewing machines, electrical appliances for home use, radios, refrigerators, bicycles, furniture and a wide range of daily necessities should also be sharply increased.

We should decisively modernize our commerce and improve service by expanding the trade network, further modernizing its facilities, packing and delivering commodities properly, setting up night-service shops or mobile stalls, etc.

The number of different kinds of restaurants should be increased, and the quality of public catering should improve. Food stores should prepare a great variety of supplementary foods for the convenience of the working people.

At the same time, we should provide more public service establishments, such as laundries, public baths, barber shops and hotels and furnish them in a modern way, thus giving better service to the working people.

Construction of new homes should be undertaken on a large scale to find better solutions to our working people's housing problem.

New flats for 600,000 households will be built in cities and workers' districts during the period of the Seven-Year Plan. Standard designing should be developed to build more attractive, modern and convenient homes. In big cities, central heating systems should be gradually introduced.

The Seven-Year Plan also envisages the construction of 600,000 modern houses in rural areas. To carry out this vast construction successfully, the state should organize a rural construction corps in each county which will follow a long-range program to build convenient, comfortable dwellings for the peasants. This will enable an overwhelming majority of the rural inhabitants in the next few years to move from old thatched houses into new, modern homes.

Additional benefits to the working people from state budgetary expenditures will grow on a huge scale.

Increased expenditure for social security will make it possible to pay more subsidies and pensions and enable a greater number of working people to enjoy free vacations at the state-owned holiday centers, convalescent homes, and camps.

Increased state expenditures for the development of education, culture and public health will further enhance the people's cultured life. In the last year of the Seven-Year Plan, the total enrollment in schools at all levels in our country will reach over 3,100,000, of which more than 220,000 will be students in institutions of higher education. We can easily imagine what enormous expenses the state will have to bear to give free education to so many students and even grant state stipends to the students in specialized schools and colleges. Such state expenditures, together with expenditures for other social and cultural needs, are designed solely for the welfare of our factory workers, office workers and peasants.

In our social system nothing is more precious than man. We must keep developing the public health service so as to protect man's life and promote the working people's health. Public hospitals in the cities and counties and the clinics in each *ri* should be expanded and receive more doctors so that the section medical care system, an advanced medical service, may be put into practice in the near future. At the same time we should set up more maternity homes, children's hospitals, and hospitals for tuberculosis and other specialized hospitals in various places, and build more sanatoria in the vicinity of our major hot springs and spas. In the sphere of public health the line of preventive medicine should be firmly maintained, and sanitation and anti-epidemic work should be carried out regularly and vigorously in urban and rural areas.

We should build more nursery schools and kindergartens and radically improve their work in order to take the best care of our children, the hope of the future, and make life more convenient for mothers.

Thus, we must make sure that all the working men and women work with great facility and lead a rich and cultured life.

Comrades,

The Seven-Year Plan for Development of the National Economy is the most far-reaching, long-term plan in the history of our country. It is a grandiose blueprint of economic and cultural construction for the prosperity and progress of the homeland and for the happiness of the people. This vast plan which envisages a high rate of economic development reflects the requirements of the situation in our country and fully accords with the aspirations of our people.

When the Seven-Year Plan is fulfilled, our country will have grown stronger than ever before, and our society will take on a new appearance.

Towards the end of the Seven-Year Plan we will have a developed socialist industry which will always be capable of providing all sectors of the national economy with new and more efficient machines and equipment and will be able to meet the requirements of all the people satisfactorily. We will also transform our country's nature on a large scale and equip agriculture with modern machines and technology, bringing in a big harvest every year. Our towns and countryside will be more beautifully built up, and all aspects of our people's life will become bountiful, modern and more enjoyable.

The fulfillment of the Seven-Year Plan will have a deepgoing influence upon the general situation in our country. Our revolutionary base in the northern half of the Republic will become an impregnable fortress, and the foundation of the national economy for the reunification and future prosperity of the country will gain strength. This will greatly inspire the people in South Korea to the struggle for freedom and a new life.

To realize the grand program of socialist construction presented by the Party, it is necessary to introduce continual technological renovations in all fields of the national economy, fully mobilize all our resources, and enforce a system of strict economy.

We should decisively raise labor productivity throughout the economy by promoting technical development, raising the level of technology and skills of the working people, and by constantly improving the organization of labor while cultivating a communist attitude towards work among the people.

At the same time, we must systematically cut production and construction costs by utilizing the means of labor more effectively, by economizing on electricity, coal, metals, timber and other materials in every way, and by reducing nonproductive expenditures.

All the working people should always lead an intense and simple life, combat extravagance and depravity of every kind, and actively tap all potentialities for building socialism.

To hasten the complete victory of socialism all Party members and working people should eagerly study science and technology, work against time with an ever-growing zeal, strive to increase the quantity and quality of our products and carry out construction more quickly.

There is no height which cannot be conquered if only we continue to advance the great Chollima Movement of our times and carry through the general line of the Party.

The triumphant socialist system, revealing greater advantages every day, gives a strong impetus to the development of the country's productive forces. The foundation we have already laid for an independent economy has inexhaustible potential.

All the workers, peasants and intellectuals are rallied more firmly than ever before around our Party that is leading them to happiness and glory, and they are firmly convinced that a bright future and victory will be theirs.

Our people never stop rushing forward at the speed of Chollima along the path to socialism. Just as they have successfully laid the foundations of socialism by overcoming all difficulties and trials, they will undoubtedly win another splendid victory in the new battle to execute the great far-reaching tasks laid down by the Party and to conquer the high peak of socialism.

ON IMPROVING AND STRENGTHENING ORGANIZATIONAL AND IDEOLOGICAL WORK OF THE PARTY (Excerpt)

Concluding Speech at the Third Enlarged Plenary Meeting of the Fourth Central Committee of the Workers' Party of Korea, *March 8, 1962*

3. On Strengthening the Struggle against Revisionism

Everyone knows that the Moscow Declaration adopted at the Meeting of Representatives of the Communist and Workers' Parties in 1957 pointed out that modern revisionism is the main danger to the international communist movement.

Of late, revisionism has raised its head more overtly in various fields and is having a serious disintegrating effect on the ranks of the international communist movement.

Revisionism has not been in existence for only a day or two. It has quite a long history. The entire course of the emergence and development of Marxist-Leninist ideas is a history of struggle against Right and "Left" opportunist trends of all descriptions, against revisionism and dogmatism.

Revisionism came into being after the death of Marx and Engels, that is, between the late 19th century and the early 20th century, as an opportunist trend to revise the revolutionary essence of Marxism under the cloak of Marxism.

As the struggle between working class and the capitalist class became sharper with the advent of the imperialist stage of capitalism, the monopoly capitalists, intensifying the suppression of the revolutionary labor movement, pursued the policy of bribing the upper stratum of labor and using them as their agents with the aim of splitting the labor movement and disrupting it from within. Thus, the degenerates and renegades of the revolutionary movement sold out to the imperialist bourgeoisie, revised Marxism to please the capitalists. Hence, their opportunism came to be called revisionism.

The opportunist, revisionist trends in Europe were represented by the Bernstein school in Germany, the Millerand school in France, the Fabian Society in Britain, and the legal Marxists, economists and Mensheviks in Russia. Later, the parties of almost all countries under the Second International, except in Russia, slid into the slough of revisionism.

Only the Bolshevik Party led by Lenin put up an uncompromising struggle against all kinds of opportunist trends and upheld the revolutionary banner of Marxim to the end. At the time, the revisionists attacked Lenin as a dogmatist because of his refusal to revise Marxism.

Lenin's chief enemy in his struggle for the creation of a revolutionary Marxist party was economism, a Russian variety of international revisionism. From the very first day that economism emerged in Russia, Lenin conducted a relentless struggle against this revisionist trend. He thoroughly exposed the anti-Marxist essence of economism in a booklet *A Protest by Russian Social-Democrats*.

Likewise, when the Party Program and Rules were being adopted at the Second Congress of the Russian Social-Democratic Labor Party in 1903, Lenin had to conduct a fierce struggle against the opportunists. The opportunists came out against the insertion of clauses concerning the dictatorship of the proletariat, the peasant question and the national question in the Party Program. But, by virtue of Lenin's determined fight, the Party congress succeeded in crushing the opposition of the opportunist elements and in adopting the first Marxist program of the revolutionary worker's party.

The Mensheviks, who after 1903 formed an opportunist faction within the Russian Social-Democratic Labor Party, degenerated into a group of Liquidationists who insisted upon the liquidation of the illegal party during the period of reaction following the failure of the first Russian revolution.

When the First World War broke out, the parties of many countries under the Second International denied the imperialist nature of the war, and called upon the workers of their countries to fight in "defense of their homeland." Thus, the Second International opportunists completely surrendered to the imperialist bourgeoisie and overtly turned into social-chauvinists.

Only the Bolshevik Party led by Lenin thoroughly exposed the imperialist nature of the war, opposed the workers of all countries killing one another in the interests of the imperialists, and launched the revolutionary slogan of converting the imperialist war into civil wars. Thus, under the leadership of the great Lenin, who upheld and further carried forward the banner of revolutionary Marxism, the October Socialist Revolution triumphed in Russia.

Today, the revolutionary forces throughout the world have grown incomparably strong. More than one-third of the world's population is building a new life of socialism. In Asia, Africa and Latin America, a powerful anti-imperialst national-liberation movement is under way; within the imperialist countries the working class is stepping up its struggle against the domination of monopoly capital.

In these circumstances, the imperialists are becoming more and more frantic. While intensifying the plunder and suppression of their own peoples and the peoples of weak and small countries, they are making desperate efforts to bribe the cowards in the ranks of the labor movement who are flinching from the revolution and to use them as their agents for carrying out their imperialist policies. The modern revisionists, as well as such fellows as Choe Chang Ik and Pak Chang Ok in our country, fall into this category.

The modern revisionists deny the leadership of the Marxist-Leninist party and the dictatorship of the proletariat which constitute the general principles of the socialist revolution.

They are maintaining that the aggressive nature of imperialism has changed and, therefore, socialism can get on well with imperialism; they are raving that the transition from capitalism to socialism can be realized peacefully through the parliamentary struggle.

The revisionists are making a noise about disarmament and calling for an abandonment of the anti-imperialist struggle. They say: if a war breaks out in this age of thermonuclear weapons it will certainly be a thermonuclear war, so what is the use of building communism after a ruination of the world and a destruction of all humanity?

They spread the illusion that the imperialists might voluntarily disarm themselves without any struggle on our part. But can we ever imagine that the imperialists will lay down their arms of their own accord? It is quite incompatible with the nature of imperialism for it to give up its arms of its own free will.

Just as the old revisionists asserted that the doctrine of Marx was obsolete, so the modern revisionists contend that the theories of Lenin do not fit the changed new age.

As they are afraid of the revolution and do not want it, the revisionists are revising Marxism-Leninism and overhauling the theory of class struggle which is the cornerstone of that doctrine in order to please the capitalists.

The sources of revisionism are acceptance of domestic bourgeois influence and surrender to external imperialist pressure. Both old revisionism and modern revisionism are one and the same in essence and in aims. Both deny the basic principles of Marxism and call for a renunciation of the revolutionary struggle on the pretext that times have changed.

The revisionists' most absurd act at present is that they are sowing discord in the socialist camp, while doing all they can to curry favor and develop close ties with imperialism.

If the revisionists do not want to make a revolution, they are welcome to go their own way alone. But the danger lies in the fact that they are even opposed to other people making a revolution and go to the length of imposing revisionism upon others.

In doing so, they call the revolutionary Marxists-Leninists who refuse to follow their revisionist line "dogmatists", "nationalists", or "Stalinists", rejecting them and trying to isolate them from the socialist camp. This is the modern revisionists' most absurd act and presents a serious danger to us.

Which path should we take, the path of revolutionary Marxism-Leninism or the path of revisionism under the baton of a certain person?

The Korean people's history of anti-imperialist struggle covers several decades now. If we take the anti-Japanese armed struggle as our starting point, it covers 30 years. Though we have been fighting against imperialism for over 30 years, we have not yet completed our revolution.

We have liberated only half of the country and one-third of its population. The Korean Communists, therefore, still have to continue the revolution and fulfill the tasks of driving out US imperialism and accomplishing the revolution for national liberation.

How can we quit the struggle against imperialism when half of the country and two-thirds of its population still remain under imperialist oppression? How can we join in prettifying the US imperialists when the US scoundrels are daily spilling our fellow countrymen's blood and humiliating our brothers and sisters? For us to give up the revolution and quit the anti-imperialist struggle means leaving south Korea to US imperialist aggression for ever and allowing the traitors to the nation to exploit and oppress the south Korean workers and peasants.

Let certain people renounce Marxim-Leninism and take the revisionist path, but we cannot allow ourselves to waver and compromise with imperialism. There is a revolutionary song which says: "Let cowards flinch and traitors sneer. We'll keep the Red Flag flying here." This expresses our invariable determination. We must continue with the revolution and resolutely fight against imperialism to the end.

Our task cannot be confined to the safeguarding of the revolutionary gains already attained in the northern half. We are duty bound to help our fellow countrymen in south Korea to accomplish the south Korean revolution and continue to fight until the day when socialism and communism will have been built in the whole of Korea. We can by no means rest content with the victory we have won in the northern half, nor should we relax in the least. We cannot degenerate into cowards who are afraid of shedding blood in the revolution and fear prison and the gallows.

We must not forget even for a moment that the northern half is the base of the Korean revolution. We must firmly build up a mighty political, economic and military force in this revolutionary base and, relying on this base, must bring the Korean revolution to final completion. This is the duty of the Korean Communists.

We must be prepared for the pressure that the revisionists might bring to bear upon us in many ways. No matter how they may calumniate and slander us, we will brush them aside and uphold Marxism-Leninism to the last.

We will do everything in our power to support the anti-imperialist national-liberation struggle of the oppressed peoples throughout the world and give active support to the revolutionary struggle of the working class in all countries against the domination of monopoly capital.

This line of ours is fundamentally opposed to revisionism. Because we are for the revolution and against imperialism, we have no alternative but to combat revisionism which is an agent of imperialism. The choice is between two roads: whether we firmly safeguard the banner of revolutionary Marxism-Leninism against revisionism or degenerate into revisionists and yield to imperialsm. We have no other way.

We must resolutely repudiate revisionism and continue our unyielding fight for the victory of the revolutionary cause.

Not only our Party but the Communist Parties of many Asian countries subjected to imperialist encroachment are asserting that the revolution must be continued and a resolute struggle must be waged against revisionism.

As long as imperialism exists, there will be imperialist oppression; and as long as there is imperialist oppression, the people will struggle against it and revolution will break out. Only through their struggle and revolution can the people free themselves from the yoke of imperialist oppression and exploitation. The revolution calls for the firm safeguarding of Marxism-Leninism and the struggle against revisionism.

The peoples of many countries in the world are still subjected to imperialist oppression and exploitation. Therefore, more and more people will make a revolution in the future. Whatever the revisionists may do in their attempt to paralyze the revolutionary consciousness of the masses and emasculate the revolutionary spirit of Marxism-Leninism, the revolutionary movement will continue and Marxism-Leninism will remain alive and triumph without fail. Just as the fall of capitalism and the victory of socialism are inevitable, so are the ruin of revisionism and the triumph of Marxism-Leninism.

In the whole Party, ideological work should be conducted thoroughly to oppose revisionism. While strengthening the Marxist-Leninist education of the Party members, the revisionist viewpoints and conceptions should be explained clearly to them, so that they will unerringly be able to tell right from wrong. It is very important here to make Lenin's attitude towards revisionism and how he criticized it known to the Party members. Ideological education has thus far been remiss in opposing revisionism. From now on, this work should be improved.

While waging the struggle against revisionism, we must fight against the Western way of life. Our struggle against the Western way of life is aimed at rejecting the American way of life, not everything Western. It can be said that revisionism is a first cousin to the Western way of life. When revisionism comes in, the Western way of life comes along with it and vice versa.

Now, concretely, what is the Western way of life? In music, for instance, it is represented by "jazz", and in dance, by mambo (naked dance). When we speak of a Western lunatic or a frivolous and vain fellow, we refer to those who are infected with this Western way of life. National nihilists, flunkeyists, people who hate revolution and depraved persons readily accept the Western way of life.

We should prevent the infiltration of the Western way of life by strengthening Marxist-Leninist education, by establishing the Party ideological system, by stepping up education in the revolutionary traditions and by strengthening revolutionary order and discipline among the Party members and the working people. Party ideological work to repudiate revisionism and the Western way of life should be conducted energetically among the writers, artists and scientific workers in particular. Those who despise everything their own and worship everything foreign and those who lack the spirit of self-reliance are most susceptible to the Western way of life and revisionism.

Certain persons are denouncing self-reliance as nationalism.

But how can it be nationalism? Self-reliance is the lofty revolutionary spirit of Communists. Why is it wrong to carry out revolution through one's own efforts and build socialism for oneself?

It is impossible to make a revolution by depending on other countries. Dependence will lead to mistrust of one's own strength and also prevent efforts to make the best use of the domestic resources of one's own country. Self-reliance means building socialism and accomplishing the revolution on one's own by every means. This is the only way to be loyal to internationalism and contribute to the common cause of socialism.

We are not the people who reject foreign aid. We welcome the aid of the fraternal countries. Nobody will refuse to accept an offer of aid. But what should we do when nobody offers us aid? Even if nobody gives us aid, we must carry out the revolution and build socialism.

Comrades, formerly we had to buy grain from foreign countries every year. But, from this year on we need not do so because we had a good crop last year. What a good thing it is to harvest a good crop and lighten the burdens of our brother countries! I think this is real internationalism. How are we to interpret the mental attitude of those who do not give aid and at the same time slander self-reliance by calling it nationalism?

Even among our people there are also some who question self-reliance. Such people are found from time to time among the scientific workers. Having no faith in our own strength, these people think we cannot get along without aid from others. It is not true that we cannot live without aid. We can not only live as well as we wish even without aid, but also build socialism splendidly, and must certainly do so.

In order to instill the spirit of self-reliance in the Party members and the working people, we must continue to wage a vigorous struggle to reject flunkeyism and dogmatism and establish Juche, and, at the same time, must always educate them so that they will not become degenerate, but live frugally.

As for our Party's attitude towards the problem of unity in the international communist movement, we, of course, must always work for unity with the Soviet Union, China and the other socialist countries and for strengthening the unity of the socialist camp.

But even though we work to cement unity with the fraternal countries, we can under no circumstances accept the demand to renounce the revolution and take to revisionism. We will support the fraternal countries in whatever is right but will not follow them in whatever is wrong. This is our Party's attitude towards the problem of unity in the international communist movement which has been raised in connection with the struggle against modern revisionism.

As regards revisionism, I think you will have an opportunity for a more profound study of it in the future. So, I will not speak of it any more today.

In conclusion, I once again emphasize that the whole Party, by strengthening its organizational and ideological work in accordance with the spirit of this plenary meeting, should strive to become a party which is militant and always dynamic, and to train our Party members to be indomitable revolutionary fighters capable of faithfully carrying out Party assignments under any difficult circumstances.

ON THE IMMEDIATE TASKS OF THE GOVERNMENT OF THE DEMOCRATIC PEOPLE'S REPUBLIC OF KOREA (Excerpt)

Speech Delivered at the First Session of the Third Supreme People's Assembly, *October 23, 1962*

2.

Comrades,

The historic Fourth Congress of the Workers' Party of Korea summed up the shining victories of our people in the socialist revolution and in the construction of socialism and set the impressive goals of the Seven-Year Plan.

By carrying out full-scale technical and cultural revolutions during the period of the Seven-Year Plan, we will build the solid material and technical foundations of socialism and radically raise the people's material and cultural standards.

Today, socialist construction in our country has entered a new and higher stage.

For the end of the Five-Year Plan period, our main task was to lay the foundations of socialism and to transform our backward agrarian country into an independent socialist industrial-agricultural state. To carry out this task we concentrated all efforts on completing socialist transformation in town and countryside, laying the foundations for socialist industrialization, and substantially solving the problems of food, clothing and housing for the people.

Our main task in the Seven-Year Plan period is to further accelerate socialist construction and turn our country into a socialist industrial state with a modern industry and developed agriculture. By thoroughly carrying out socialist industrialization in this period, we will equip all branches of the national economy with modern technology and reach the high level of development of the productive forces characteristic of an advanced socialist society; we should not only solve the problems of food, clothing and housing for the people more satisfactorily, but enable everyone to live a rich and cultured life.

If the period of the Five-Year Plan was the one in which the great tree of socialism took deep root and its trunk grew strong, then we can call the Seven-Year Plan a period in which the tree will grow, blossom beautifully, and bear fine fruit.

When the Seven-Year Plan is fulfilled, all spheres of the new socialist life will really be in full flower.

Our industry will develop in a diversified way and will be more fully equipped with new technology. Different kinds of machines, equipment and other means of production, as well as different high-quality consumer goods, will be produced in far greater quantities. As a result of the technological modernization of agriculture, we will achieve a decisive increase in the output of all farm produce, including grain and animal products, and free the peasants from backbreaking toil.

We will build more beautiful towns and villages and all our people will live as well as other peoples.

The construction of socialism in the northern half of the Republic is in harmony with the vital interests of the people not just in the north but in the entire nation. The fulfillment of the Seven-Year Plan will strengthen the revolutionary base in the northern half and make it invincible; it will open up a decisive phase in achieving the peaceful reunification of our country. By fulfilling the Seven-Year Plan we shall also lay more solid material foundations for quickly rehabilitating the South Korean economy and for radically improving the living conditions of the people there in the future.

Thus, our Seven-Year Plan is an impressive program for the construction of socialism in the northern half of the Republic. At the same time, it is a great national program for building a reunified, independent, rich and powerful Korea and for ensuring the future happiness of 30 million Koreans. This is why all the working people in the northern half are showing extraordinary revolutionary zeal and patriotic devotion for the fulfillment of this program and why the entire Korean people are most interested in its realization.

As was clearly outlined by our Party and the Government of the Republic, in the first half of the Seven-Year Plan we will work hard to put flesh on the skeleton of heavy industry, use it more effectively and, on this basis, speedily develop agriculture and light industry and radically improve the people's living conditions. In the second half of the plan we will put major emphasis on radically reinforcing the material and technical foundations of socialism by expanding centers of heavy industry and improving their technological equipment while continuing to better the people's living conditions.

We have already taken a big step forward towards the fulfillment of the first half of the Seven-Year Plan. Always responding faithfully to the call of the Party, our working people showed their unlimited creativity and talents in all fields of socialist construction and successfully fulfilled the national economic plan for 1961—the first year of the Seven-Year Plan —and are performing brilliant feats of labor in their struggle to reach this year's six heights.

The national economic plan for this year has the six heights as its main targets, a tremendous and difficult program envisaging a high rate of growth in industrial and agricultural production.

Over two months still remain before the end of the year, but we can say with confidence that we have already won a decisive victory in the battle to conquer the six heights.

Agriculture plays a very important part in economic construction under socialism. Only when we bring in good harvests will we have enough to eat and will everything go well in the economic life of the country. The target of five million tons of grain is the most important of this year's six heights.

We struggled under totally adverse weather conditions to

reach this height of production. This year our country was struck by a severe drought, followed by a long rainy spell that lasted more than three months and caused four big floods. In addition, we suffered damage from frost, blight, harmful insects and typhoons. Indeed, we might say this was the year in which our agriculture suffered nature's worst trials.

But our socialist agriculture has successfully overcome these difficulties. Not only has this year's grain output not fallen compared to last year's but we have reaped an unusual bumper harvest in the countryside.

The fact that we have harvested successive bumper crops in recent years and, moreover, have done so again in a year like this one, proves that our agricultural production is not affected by varying weather or other chance factors but, instead, like industrial production, it grows soundly and steadily according to the laws of the development of socialist economy.

This brilliant victory in agriculture represents a victory for our Party's agricultural policy—a victory of the Chongsan-ri spirit and Chongsan-ri method in the countryside. Above all, this clearly shows the superiority of the socialist system of cooperative economy established in our rural areas, the solid material and technical foundations of our agriculture and, in particular, the strength of the irrigation system, afforestation and water conservation facilities which have been built up by the supreme efforts of the Party, the state and the entire people. This has also been made possible because our Party, imbued with the Chongsan-ri spirit and Chongsan-ri method, has given precedence to political work and has actively conducted communist education among the peasants so that they display conscious enthusiasm and devotion in their work. Our victory in agriculture has also been possible because our Party has thoroughly put into practice the line of providing a material stimulus to arouse the enthusiasm of the peasants for production by correctly enforcing the socialist principle of distribution and introducing a bonus system for the workteams.

In the course of the fight for the height of five million tons of grain, we have strengthened the material and technical foundations of agriculture and furthered the progress of our farm technology. In the countryside our tractor stock now totals 15,000 in terms of 15 hp units and the level of agricultural mechanization has continued to rise. This year the area under irrigation has been expanded by 30,000 *chongbo* and the amount of chemical fertilizer applied is 13 percent higher than last year.

Along with grain production, all other branches of agriculture such as industrial crops, stockbreeding, sericulture and fruit growing have shown a high growth rate.

In light industry all efforts have been concentrated on this year's height of 250 million meters of fabric.

The rapid development of the textile industry for producing good quality fabrics in greater quantity is an important task to satisfactorily solve our people's clothing problem. Out to reach the textile production target set by the Party, the workers and technicians in the textile industry have already successfully surpassed the plan for the first half year and are now rapidly increasing production in the second half. There is every indication that 250 million meters of fabric will be turned out this year. This is an increase of over 30 per cent on last year's figure and means that the per capita output of fabrics will reach approximately 25 meters. The proportion of high quality fabrics has begun to rise gradually, and the rapid development of the clothing industry has alleviated women's work in the home and made it possible to supply the population with better clothes.

This year, our centers of light industry have generally been expanded and strengthened. Expansion projects have been completed in the Chongjin Chemical Fiber Mill and the Kilju Pulp Mill; the existing textile mills have been equipped with 105,000 more spindles; construction projects like the Hyesan Textile Mill, with 15,000 spindles, the Hyesan Paper Mill, with a production capacity of 20,000 tons, and other new light industry factories have been successfully carried out. Mechanization has also been vigorously pushed forward in local industry and all of its factories have been better equipped.

The intensive exploitation of our country's rich marine resources is of great importance for the improvement of the people's standard of living.

Thanks to the correct leadership of the Party, to large-scale state investment and the devoted labor of the workers in the fisheries, the material and technical foundations of the fishing industry were decisively reinforced in the postwar period. In 1961, the output of marine products reached 590,000 tons.

On the basis of these achievements, the Party and the Government set the impressive target of 800,000 tons of marine products this year and are working hard in this area. Boundlessly inspired by the the Party's policy, all our workers in the fishing industry are working heroically to complete this gigantic task and have already achieved great results. Needless to say, there is no ground for us to get complacent because the major fishing season—November and December—still lies ahead. We are, however, firmly convinced that in view of the results already achieved and with the present progress in production and the rising spirit of the workers in the fishing industry, we shall be able to fly the flag of victory, achieving our target of 800,000 tons of marine products.

The struggle to reach the height of homes for 200,000 families is a glorious one because by reaching that target, we will improve the housing conditions of the working people and, especially, transform the appearance of our countryside by clearing away the mud huts which have been in existence for thousands of years.

Our Fourth Party Congress set the huge task of building modern houses for 600,000 families in urban as well as in rural areas during the period of the Seven-Year Plan. We set about carrying out this task this year. Such an immense project for housing construction for the working people can be undertaken only in our society where power and all the wealth of the country are in the hands of the people and strong economic foundations have been laid.

So far we have carried out housing construction on a large scale. But never before have we built as many houses as we did this year, nor built dwellings in the countryside for 100,000 families in a single year. Nonetheless, our construction workers are successfully doing this difficult job with the active assistance of the entire people. Decisive results have already been achieved in the construction of rural housing, not to speak of urban housing; now we are in the final stage of housing construction for 200,000 families in the cities and the same number in the countryside.

This year heavy industry is confronted with the weighty task of reaching the heights of 1.2 million tons of steel and 15 million tons of coal; and of giving a powerful support to reach the remaining heights. On the whole, our heavy industry has substantially completed its job.

Workers and technicians in the iron and steel industry will also reach their target of 1.2 million tons of pig iron and granulated iron and will produce 1.1 million tons of steel this year. This means that steel production will fall slightly short of the target, but a 29 per cent increase in production of pig iron and granulated iron and a more than 40 percent increase in steel over last year is a big achievement for one year.

In the coal industry thorough measures were not taken against flood damage, despite the fact that the Party has stressed their importance time and again. As a result, pits were waterlogged after heavy rains and work at the coal face and transportation were greatly hindered. We thus fell short of the coal production target by a considerable margin. We now expect that coal output will rise by some 10 percent as against last year. However, if the personnel in this sector had carried out the Party's instructions promptly and correctly, they would certainly have been in a position to reach the height of 15 million tons of coal.

The electric-power, chemical and machine-building industries have all achieved good results and production has sharply increased. Our machine-building industry, in particular, has made an important contribution to speeding up the technological reconstruction of the national economy by supplying large quantities of equipment needed for the mechanization of agriculture and fishing as well as metallurgical, chemical and electric power equipment, and installations for the coal and other mines and for light industry.

Heavy industry this year has witnessed the construction of many new factories and shops such as the new medium-plate rolling shop in the Songjin Steel Plant with a production capacity of 80,000 tons, the drawn-steel pipe shop of the Kangson Steel Plant with a production capacity of 30,000 tons, the Nampo Smeltery nonferrous metal rolling shop with a capacity of 12,000 tons, the Pyongyang Electric Wire Factory with a capacity of 12,000 tons, the Pongung Caustic Soda Factory with a capacity of 50,000 tons, and the sulphuric acid shop with a capacity of 45,000 tons in the Munpyong Smeltery. At the same time technical equipment has been improved, advanced production methods and technical processes have been introduced extensively and productive capacity has been sharply raised in all heavy industry plants.

Better equipped and strengthened in this way, our heavy industry is now more effective in serving the development of light industry and agriculture and the improvement of the people's living conditions.

This year we have waged a very intense struggle in all areas of socialist construction. This has been a proud and glorious battle for boundless prosperity in our country and the happiness of our people, and in it we have won a shining victory.

Comrades,

The tremendous successes in the first two years of the Seven-Year Plan open up bright prospects for the radical improvement of the people's living conditions in three or four years. To turn these projects into reality, we must determinedly continue the struggle in 1963 and 1964.

The basic task of the national economic plan for 1963 is simultaneously to consolidate the gains made this year in scaling the six heights, and to make preparations for even higher goals. In the following years we shall also direct our efforts to the development of agriculture and light industry and, in the field of heavy industry, we will reequip and reinforce all our factories and do everything in our power to develop the mining industry. At the same time, in the light of ever-increasing aggressive machinations by the US imperialists entrenched in south Korea, and the military fascist clique, the Party and the Government will pay close attention to further fortifying our national defenses.

The radical development of the mining industry is an important task for heavy industry next year. Mining is the primary process in production and, for that reason, unless we give priority to this industry we can hardly develop the other sectors of the national economy at a normal rate.

The Party and the Government, while continuing to develop the processing industry, will concentrate investments in mining during 1963 and 1964, so as to strengthen the material and technical basis of the ore and coal mines, and see to it that the growing requirements of the national economy for various kinds of ores and coal are fully satisfied.

The great historic task we are now engaged in calls for the extensive exploitation and use of our country's abundant mineral resources. In the coal industry we must definitely reach the height of 15 million tons of coal next year and continue to increase output in the future. The ore mining industry should supply enough ore to the iron and steel industry and also increase the output of various nonferrous and rare metal ores and nonmetal minerals. It is particularly necessary to step up the extensive exploitation, refining and processing of nonferrous metal ores such as copper, lead, zinc and nickel and raw materials for alloys and to expand both variety and output of steel and alloys. Only in this way can we fully prepare for a new upsurge in the development of heavy industry.

To develop the mining industry, we should give priority to geological prospecting. The ranks of prospecting workers and the technical equipment in this field should be further reinforced so as to expand this work and do it more thoroughly.

We must also continue to make large investments in the power industry and speed up the construction of the Kanggye Power Station, the Unbong Power Station, and the Pyongyang Thermal Power Plant, all of which are already under construction, thus guaranteeing their going into operation on schedule.

Further development of the machine-building industry is an important task throughout the whole period of the Seven-Year Plan. Within the next year or two, rapid progress is expected, particularly in the manufacture of large-scale machinery, which is still lagging behind. We should expand the large-scale machinery plants we now have, operate them at full capacity, and build more new factories to be able to provide enough equipment for the power stations, coal mines, ore mines and other big plants. We should also improve the utilization of equipment to the utmost and organize production rationally in all the machine-building factories so that they may supply the national economy with more machinery and equipment.

Although the bases of our heavy industry have been much more consolidated in the last couple of years, they have not yet been fully equipped. Therefore, we should energetically continue to push ahead with the work of putting flesh on the skeleton of heavy industry.

All heavy industry plants should be better equipped, and a strict system of inspection and maintenance of the equipment should be established, and the necessary auxiliary equipment and other conditions must be fully guaranteed, thereby stabilizing production completely. Moreover, we must boldly and positively introduce the achievements of science and technology into production, stepping up the mechanization and automation of production processes by bringing into play all our potential resources, and the movement for technical innovation should be more widely developed.

In the field of technology we should pay particular attention to the manufacture of substitutes for those materials and raw materials not available in our country. We should do everything possible in the iron and steel industry to make wide use of ferro-coke and pellets and to raise the standard of iron ore so as to increase iron production while, at the same time, substantially reducing the consumption of coking coal. Measures should also be taken to introduce the extensive application of the oxygen-blast method in the process of manufacturing iron and steel and to put gasification of coal into practice.

The main task of light industry next year is to maintain production levels, consolidating this year's height of 250 million meters of fabric, and to provide all conditions for the production of 300 million meters in 1964. At the same time, we must improve the quality of daily necessities and foodstuffs and expand their variety, markedly increasing their output.

To accomplish this task we should, above all, strengthen the raw material bases for light industry and markedly increase the production capacity of light industry factories.

We must fully normalize the operation of the February 8 Vinalon Factory, the Chongjin Chemical Fiber Mill, and the Hyesan Textile Mill, and increase production in all other branches which supply raw materials to light industry. Textile mills and all other light industry factories should make rational use of floor space to install more machinery, improve their equipment, and raise the workers' technical and skill levels to boost production at a steady rate.

More than 2,000 locally run factories in our cities and counties have enormous possibilities for a rapid increase in the production of consumer goods for the people. It is planned that in 1964 local industry alone will turn out 100 million meters of fabric and 40,000 to 50,000 tons of paper, and that within each locality, the considerable local demands for daily necessities and processed food, as well as soy sauce, bean paste and vegetable oil will be met. It will be possible to realize this plan when we have developed local industry to a higher stage by carrying through the tasks laid down at the Changsong Joint Conference of Local Party and Economic Functionaries.

Dynamic acceleration of technical reconstruction is most important for the rapid development of local industry. Locally run factories must get rid of backward artisan technology, introduce mechanization and semi-automation into all production processes, and steadily improve the workers' technical knowledge and skills.

We should consolidate raw material bases for local industry so that most of the necessary raw materials can be obtained in local areas; we should pay close attention to improving factory management and promoting general production culture.

In this way all of our locally run factories will be made attractive, modern and efficient; they will be equipped with new technology, manufacture various consumer goods mainly from local raw materials and greatly benefit the state and the people.

In agriculture next year we should concentrate our efforts on increasing the rice output and thus improve the proportion of better grain in total production.

We are now supplying enough food for the entire population and even have a certain amount of grain in reserve. But we cannot rest content with this. We must supply not only enough but also better quality food to the working people and thus improve their standard of living.

Our Party and Government have initiated the huge task of increasing the rice output to more than three million tons within the next few years so that all the people in the northern half can live on rice. This is really a splendid program which gladdens everybody. It is one that we can surely fulfill.

To secure a higher output of grain, especially rice, it is necessary to continue projects for transforming nature.

The state will concentrate efforts on speeding up the construction of the large-scale Amnok-gang River irrigation network which will water about 90,000 *chongbo* of fields. In the future the state will undertake a big irrigation project along the Ryesong-gang River to bring under irrigation over 100,000 *chongbo* of rice paddies and dry fields in North and South Hwanghae Provinces. It is also necessary to use the existing irrigation facilities to greater advantage, carry on the construction of medium and small irrigation projects, and energetically push ahead with the reclamation of land from the sea along the west coast. Especially, the reclaimed land is yielding good results: more than 4,000 *chongbo* reclaimed last year have already given us an average of over three tons of rice per *chongbo* this year. There is no doubt that as the salinity of these paddyfields goes down, the output of crops will grow. This is very fine and we should continue this work.

Starting now, we should, by spring 1964, expand the area of paddyfields by over 60,000 *chongbo*, making a total of 600,000 *chongbo* under rice cultivation in 1964.

Along with irrigation, land conservation work must be done properly. Drawing on the experience of this year we should regularly and carefully conserve not only big rivers but also small ones and, where necessary, undertake improvement projects. We should continue to energetically do forest and water conservation work—to plant and tend forests properly, build all river embankments on solid foundations and dredge river beds—so that floods bigger than this year's will not cause us damage.

In agriculture, it is necessary to step up mechanization and chemicalization, continue to improve seed strains, and develop all sorts of new farming techniques. During 1963, the state will also supply the rural areas with many tractors, lorries, and other modern farm machinery of various types. Next year, 700,000 tons of chemical fertilizers will be applied, and the supply of different chemicals for agriculture and weed killers will increase considerably.

In this way when we plant rice on 600,000 *chongbo* of paddyfields, expand the double-cropping area, and steadily improve farming technique to increase the per-*chongbo* yield of all kinds of crops, we shall be able to continue harvesting more than five million tons of grain annually; of this, rice output will undoubtedly hit the three-million-ton mark.

With the food problem being fully solved, new possibilities are opening up for the rapid development of stockbreeding.

From 1964 onwards the Party and the Government plan to set aside large quantities of grain for animal fodder. Anticipating a sharp increase in the supply of fodder grain, we should start from now to build up the foundations of our stockbreeding by securing superior breeding animals and increasing their number and by improving and expanding stalls and veterinary and anti-epizootic establishments. We should not only breed pasture animals but also pigs and ducks on a large scale to bring meat production up to 200,000 tons by 1965.

We should expand the areas planted with different types of oil-bearing plants and fiber crops such as flax, hemp and ramie so as to increase their output and further develop fruit growing and sericulture.

While developing industry and agriculture, we must push ahead with housing construction for the working people. In the future, too, our construction workers must build a greater number of modern houses which are more comfortable, attractive and functional for the working people in urban and rural areas.

By successfully carrying out all these tasks, in three to four years we should be able to radically improve the living conditions of the people and consolidate the economic foundations of the country.

There will be a new, great change in the material and cultural life of our people three to four years later. By then we shall be producing three million tons of rice, 200,000 tons of meat, and 300 million meters of fabric; and new modern houses for hundreds of thousands of families will have gone up in town and country. This will enable all of our people to lead a life of plenty—to live in tile-roofed houses, eat rice and meat, and wear silk clothes. This means that within our time, the long-cherished desire of the working people of our country will be accomplished. This, indeed, will be a very happy and proud thing.

Moreover, in the near future, the compulsory nine-year technical education which we have been preparing for will be introduced universally. Its enforcement will enable us to bring up the whole younger generation as competent builders of socialism and communism, with a knowledge of advanced science and technology. With the continued rapid expansion of higher education as well as the enforcement of compulsory technical education, the total number of technicians and specialists will exceed 400,000 in two or three years. Thus, shop managers and other higher cadres in all our factories and enterprises will, without exception, be qualified engineers and specialists, or assistant engineers and junior specialists.

This bright prospect is a source of great excitement for all the working people of our country, inspiring them more powerfully in their heroic labor effort. Solidly united around the Party and the Government, our working people are now marching confidently towards new victories with greater hope and courage and with the clear prospect of a bright future. Through their heroic struggle our people, under the leadership of the Party, are sure to fulfill the Seven-Year Plan triumphantly.

In order to successfully carry out the enormous tasks confronting us in socialist construction, we must further enhance the role and function of the state bodies as a weapon in the construction of socialism and continue to improve the management and guidance of the national economy.

Our Party and Government have taken a series of important measures to reorganize the work of the state and economic bodies as well as to raise the level of leadership of their functionaries in keeping with new, changed conditions. With these measures they have achieved great successes and accumulated valuable experiences in this field.

In particular, there has been a great change in the work of the state and economic bodies in the course of generalizing the guidance experience gained in Chongsan-ri. Revolutionary methods of work have been established; leadership has been brought closer to the lower bodies and higher bodies help those below them; in addition, functionaries go deeply among the masses to educate, remold, and rally them round and solve all problems by giving full play to their enthusiasm and creativity.

In order to establish the Chongsan-ri spirit and Chongsan-ri method more thoroughly in the guidance and management of the national economy, we took new, radical measures this year to reorganize the structure of factory management and to establish the county cooperative farm management committees and the provincial rural economy committees.

Although it is not long since their establishment, the new systems of management in industry and agriculture are already fully showing their superiority.

The reorganization of the factory management structure made it possible both to manage factories under the collective leadership of Party committees and to decisively strengthen the leadership and supervision of Party bodies over industry and improve the Party's political work among the working class. The leading cadres of the factories are now freed from petty tasks and thus able to make much effort to give technical guidance to production and go deeper among the masses to do better work with them; all this is due to the establishment of a clear division of responsibilities and assignments among the different sections of the factory, the improvement of leadership and assistance by the ministries and management bureaus to factories, and the introduction of a new system in which higher units deliver equipment, materials and consumer goods to the lower.

In agriculture we have set up the county cooperative farm management committees, putting at their disposal agronomists and bringing them those state enterprises serving agriculture, such as farm machine stations, local farm implement factories, and irrigation administration offices. Thus it became possible to direct agriculture more effectively—not by the administrative method, as in the past, but by the industrial method of management—and more vigorously promote the development of the productive forces of agriculture, in particular, the rural technical revolution. In addition, by radically improving and strengthening the leadership and the material and technical assistance given by the state to the cooperative farms, we have further enhanced the leading role of state ownership over cooperative ownership. This has also strengthened the production links between town and country and between industry and agriculture and has consolidated the worker-peasant alliance, enhancing the leading role of the working class in that alliance.

Specialized bodies set up for directing agriculture in the rural areas are also having a very positive influence on the work of the local people's committees. Provincial, city, and county people's committees are now able to give great attention to commerce, construction, education, culture and public health and, consequently, to give better leadership to the work in these fields.

We can say with conviction that these management systems in industry and agriculture initiated by our Party are excellent new forms of managing a socialist economy, forms which are in full harmony with the principles of Marxism-Leninism and the actual conditions of our country.

The question now is to improve our officials' work methods and decisively promote their level of leadership on the strength of the superiority of the existing management systems. The work methods of our functionaries have not yet been completely changed to conform with the new management systems and their guidance still fails to keep pace with the high revolutionary enthusiasm of the masses. These shortcomings should be eliminated as soon as possible.

We must first strengthen political work, and in this way steadily heighten the ideological consciousness of the masses and inspire them to participate voluntarily in carrying out the revolutionary tasks. We must continue to hold firm to the principle—to give priority to political work in all fields and give a vigorous communist education to the working people in combination with education in the Party's policies and, at the same time, to correctly link this with practical and administrative work as well as with the work of ensuring the material and technical conditions.

Along with this, we should bring leadership closer to the lower units and improve its methods. The important thing in leadership is to establish more thoroughly the revolutionary work method—the method of relying on the masses—and the work system of giving real assistance to the lower units.

It is the workers and peasants who are directly engaged in production and construction. They know better than anyone else the state of affairs in their work places and can suggest more new ideas. Therefore, our leading functionaries should always go deeply among the masses where they work to consult with them, listen to their opinions, use their knowledge to find solutions to problems, and mobilize them to carry out all the tasks which the revolution faces.

The precise aim of giving guidance to the lower units is to help the workers there to correct their shortcomings and get good results in their work. When going down to the lower units, leading functionaries should not dictate to the workers nor order them about but should give them practical assistance by kindly teaching them and working with them to solve their difficult problems, so that they can do their work well.

Thus fully practicing the Chongsan-ri spirit and Changsan-ri method in all fields, we should make skillful use of the high revolutionary enthusiasm of the masses and mobilize the unused reserves and potential of our national economy to the maximum.

The unlimited creativity and talent of our working people are a decisive guarantee for the success of the great program of socialist construction.

We should expand and strengthen the Chollima Workteam Movement among the working people and educate and remold all of them in communist ideas, so as to unite them more closely around the Party and give free rein to their revolutionary zeal and creative ability. In this way we will continue to bring about innovations and rapid progress in all fields of socialist construction.

All our cadres and other working people should build up more firmly the revolutionary spirit of opposing immorality and laziness, living a modest life, never letting down their guard and valiantly surmounting every difficulty with a revolutionary spirit of self-reliance.

As Communists fighting for the revolution, we must always have a spirit of self-reliance. Otherwise, we would lose confidence in our own strength and make no serious effort to develop the internal resources of our country, thus failing to accomplish the cause of the revolution.

Of course, we shall continue to need help and support from the fraternal peoples of the socialist countries and from all the progressive people of the world; that is important to guarantee our victory. But it is not a revolutionary's attitude to just seek aid from foreign countries instead of exerting himself. With this kind of attitude, we could not accomplish the revolution. The decisive factor in the victory of our revolution lies in our own strength. We must build a new society in our country and achieve the final victory of the Korean revolution mainly through our own efforts. This conforms to the principles of proletarian internationalism, and will contribute to the development of the international revolutionary movement.

In building a socialist economy, we should also be firm in our adherence to the principle of self-reliance and move towards the building of more solid foundations for an independent national economy, promoting economic and cultural cooperation with the fraternal countries on this basis.

Building an independent national economy means building a diversified economy, equipping it with up-to-date technology and creating our own solid bases of raw materials, thereby building up an all-embracing economic system in which every branch of the economy is structurally interrelated, so as to produce domestically most of the products of heavy and light industry and the agricultural produce needed to make the country wealthy and powerful and to improve the people's living conditions.

Only by building the economy in this way can we utilize all our country's natural resources in the most rational and comprehensive way, rapidly develop the productive forces, steadily raise the living standards of the people and further increase the political and economic strength of the country. And only by building an independent national economy can we meet each other's economic needs with fraternal countries, ensure more effective mutual cooperation and division of labor with them on the principles of proletarian internationalism and of complete equality and mutual benefit, and contribute to the strengthening of the power of the entire socialist camp.

Under the leadership of our Party our people have built the foundations of an independent national economy through hard-fought battles. As a result, we have not only strengthened the economic power of the country and raised our standard of living still higher, but have also been able to promote greater mutual cooperation with the fraternal countries and to considerably lighten the burdens these countries bear for our country. This is our due repayment to the peoples of the fraternal countries for their active support and assistance, and it is our important contribution to strengthening the power of the entire socialist camp.

Under the banner of self-reliance, we shall continue to exert ourselves and mobilize our internal resources to the utmost, steadily developing our cooperation with the fraternal countries on the principles of proletarian internationalism. Thus we shall speed up the construction of socialism in our country and contribute to increasing the might of the world socialist system.

Rallied steel-strong around the Party and the Government, our people will continue the vigorous advance in the spirit of the Chollima riders—courageously surmounting any and every difficulty—and will definitely fulfill the Seven-Year Plan and reach the high peak of socialism.

ON IMPROVING INSTRUCTION AND EDUCATION AT UNIVERSITIES AND COLLEGES (Excerpt)

Concluding Speech at the Meeting of the Heads of Departments of the Central Committee of the Workers' Party of Korea, *April 18, 1963*

This time we heard the work report of the University's Party Committee; great successes have been achieved in the work of the University.

The University has trained a large number of Korean cadres, and this is a great achievement, of course. However, what is more important is that solid foundations have been laid for training technicians, specialists and scientists at our universities and colleges with their own efforts. This is a most precious asset that cannot be bartered for anything.

Especially conspicuous among the successes gained in the University's work is that the Party ideological system has been established among the faculty members and students and that Juche has been built up in instruction and education. They are now armed with our Party's ideology and the instruction and education is conducted basically in the direction as required by the Party. It is true that there still remains a certain amount of flunkeyism in the minds of some people. However, we can say that the tendencies of national nihilism are basically nonexistent; they are the tendencies to look up to others and think that only they are capable of training technicians and specialists equipped with advanced science and technology. Moreover, unlike former days, the students, as well as the teachers, are now able to immediately distinguish right from wrong when someone gives lectures contrary to the Juche idea. All this is good.

Although the University has achieved great successes in its work, it still has quite a few shortcomings. But they are the shortcomings revealed on the road of advancement, and they do not imply that the University's work has retrogressed or that they are doing a worse job than before. For example, the poor qualifications of the teachers have been keenly discussed this time. This does not mean that the qualitative composition of the university professors is worse than before; it means that their scientific and theoretical level is low in view of the requirements of the quickly developing reality. With the speedy expansion of the University, many young teachers have been appointed. However, the present scientific and theoretical level of the teaching staff as a whole is incomparably higher than right after the armistice, not to mention the early days of the University. The defects revealed in the work of the Party committee and the educational administration of the University, as well as in the supply service and accounting, are minor ones. They are caused mainly by the leadership personnel of the University who did not pay due attention to these problems because of their failure to have a clear understanding of the Party's requirements, or because they worked in a slipshod manner. They can be easily corrected. We must quickly rectify these shortcomings, put the University's work system to rights and further improve instruction and education to meet the demands of our revolution.

On Strengthening Educational Administration at Universities and Colleges

The basic task of universities and colleges is to educate the students, and educational administration is the most important of all their work.

In a nutshell, educational administration means directing and supervising educational work so that it is sure to go through pedagogical processes necessary to train revolutionary intellectuals.

Just as production needs technological processes, so education should pass definite pedagogical processes. If in a factory products do not go through adequate technological processes, there will be rejects. The same is the case with education. If universities ignore the essential pedagogical processes, they cannot develop cadres as required by the Party. Fundamentally speaking, there is no difference between production and education in that both need necessary processes. We must not conduct education in a random way, ignoring pedagogy. In most cases, however, the institutes of higher learning are now conducting educational work in a haphazard way, according to worn-out conventions and experiences, instead of basing this work on a strictly scientific system. Today one of the most urgent problems in putting educational work on the right track is to establish a scientific system of guidance so that the training of personnel at universities will definitively go through a necessary pedagogical course.

The educational administration staffs of institutes of higher learning must direct and supervise the whole course of university education—from the enrollment and selection of the students to their launching into the world after graduation—so that it meets the requirements of socialist pedagogy. The main content of educational administration is this: to prepare proper education programs consisting of curricula and teaching outlines, and to direct and supervise the teachers to prepare themselves well for teaching and conduct it satisfactorily in different forms, so that the knowledge of science and technology envisaged in the education programs is accurately imparted to the students and completely mastered by them.

The execution of the education program involves preparing for and giving instruction, mastering what is taught and examining how much it is understood.

Teaching preparation is something like technical outfitting at a factory; whether it is well done or not is one of the fundamental factors decisive to the success of education. Therefore, the university administration must first direct and supervise the teachers to make full preparations for lectures.

The administration must check their lecture plans. The plans must first be discussed through the model or demonstration lectures and perfected before being delivered to the students.

In the army the model lecture is first organized for commanders before they go down to train their men. For example, lectures are held for company commanders, where they are asked to answer theoretical problems, draw maps and make actual movements. Then they are made to prepare lecture plans to train their soldiers.

In the institutes of higher learning they must also frequently organize model and demonstration lectures for the teachers, and all the more so when teaching a new subject and lecturing on problems which have newly arisen. Some comrades assert that teachers have not enough time to do so. This is untenable. A university teacher is supposed to deliver 1,000 hours of lectures a year, so he has plenty of time to organize model and demonstration lectures. These lectures afford precious opportunities for the teachers to raise their qualities, so all the teachers including those newly appointed must attend them.

While properly preparing the teachers for instruction, the educational administration staffs must ensure appropriate guidance and supervision for them to conduct their instruction regularly.

The supervision of the teachers' instruction is indispensable. If there is no supervision, we cannot find out whether they write lecture plans for themselves or simply copy others', whether they impart necessary knowledge to the students and whether they lecture in the set time.

The educational administrations of universities and colleges should guide and supervise not only lectures but all other forms of instruction, so that they will be conducted without any deviation.

At the institute the lecture is the most important form of teaching. This is true. But we cannot achieve the objectives of education through the lecture alone. Only when you not only imbue the students with a definite knowledge but also have them master it and apply their acquired knowledge in practice, can it be said that university education has obtained its aims. Therefore, all forms of instructions scheduled in the curriculum—lectures, class discussions, experimental training and the presentation of theses—must be correctly executed.

However, in many cases class discussions and experimental training are neglected at universities and colleges. They only organize lectures, thinking that they may or may not carry out other forms of instruction. This is fundamentally wrong.

The qualifications of the cadres trained at our institutes of higher learning are low. Some functionaries graduated from the faculties of social sciences cannot even write a brief thesis or a lecture plan well and make a proper speech before the audience. The main reason is that in their school days they did not have enough opportunity to train themselves in practice and that the instructional work to help the students consolidate their acquired knowledge was not done properly. The leadership personnel in universities and colleges must eliminate their erroneous inclinations to attach importance only to lectures while neglecting all the other forms of instruction, and must make sure that every form of teaching is adequately conducted.

Another important aspect of educational administration is to correctly check and appraise how much the students have grasped what they were taught. At present, examination is the basic means employed at universities and colleges to find out their understanding, and their academic attainments are appraised only by the exam marks. We must admit that this method of appraisal is quite formalistic. To pass examinations, they learn by heart in a few days' time what they were taught in classes, so they forget it after some time. The educational administrations must make it a rule to check closely, through diverse methods, how much the students have digested what they were taught during their school days, whether they are armed with the Party's ideology, whether they have a revolutionary world outlook and whether or not they are prepared to apply in practice the theories, knowledge and techniques they acquired at universities and colleges. The students' attainments must not be appraised only by exam marks. An overall appraisal should be made on the basis of their attitudes towards the class discussion and experimental training, their theses on study subjects and their social and political activities.

It is also important to tighten discipline in university education. At present discipline is lacking in the execution of school curricula, and this is a serious defect. I was told that sometimes they do not even have a clear-cut plan to carry out the curricula and, what is more, that because the timetable is changed at random, the students do not know what subjects they are going to study the next day and cannot make proper preparations. These undisciplined practices must be thoroughly eliminated from educational administration. Just as it is a legal task to carry out the state plans at factories and enterprises, so the education programs must be implemented at the institutes without fail as a legal task. A strict discipline must be established so that the universities will scrupulously carry out the curricula approved by the ministry and decided on by the university Party committees and that no one will alter them at will.

Improving teaching methods is of great importance in achieving the objectives of education. Therefore, the university administrations must show deep concern for this matter.

In the report and debate you have dealt with the heuristic method of lecturing and other matters to improve teaching methods. This is good. The heuristic method should be applied to every subject and, especially, visual aids should be widely used for lectures. Teaching through visual stimulus is conducted well at military schools. They are using plenty of moving visual aids. For instance, tanks and communication devices are dismantled so that you can even see their inner structure. At the institutes of learning too, they must deliver vivid lectures by using various visual aids. As for machines and equipment, arrangements should be made to enable the students to see not only their exterior but their interior as well.

Along with lectures, we must see to it that they properly organize class discussions. The discussion is a major teaching form to consolidate the knowledge the students obtained at lectures and raise their academic level. We must interest the students in the discussion. It is said that the students are not interested in it now. There are two reasons for this. One is that the discussion is not so profitable because of the insufficient preparations on the part of the teachers; and the other is that the teachers are just as fastidious as if giving exams. In the discussion they should let the students express their views freely and take an active part in the debate, and they should prepare themselves well and dig into one problem after another, skillfully leading the debate. Then the discussion will be quite interesting and the students will learn a lot. They will not dislike the discussion but want it to be held more often.

They must organize supplementary lectures and scientific lectures in order to assist the students in their studies and, especially, must hold many seminars. It is a good idea to have many students make speeches in turn at the seminar. If the students prepare themselves well with the help of the teachers, it will be helpful not only to increasing their academic abilities but also making other students zealous for their studies. It must be made obligatory for all the students to participate in the seminar. In this way, through different media, we must interest the students in studies, encourage them to read a lot of books and lead them to take enterprising and serious attitudes in scientific researches.

Increasing teachers' qualificiations is another important aspect of educational administration.

Guaranteeing proper teaching as well as the high ideological content of education at universities depends mainly on the improvement of the teachers' qualifications. If they are to give heuristic lectures and properly lead the students' class discussions, the teachers must raise their scientific and theoretical level. Only then can they give good lectures. Otherwise, they cannot have their lectures easily understood.

At present our institutes of higher learning do not have many teachers who have academic degrees of doctors, masters and so on. Generally speaking, the scientific and theoretical level of the teachers in the realms of both social and natural sciences is not so high. The University, a huge collective of intellectuals, should have produced many theses elaborating on the achievements scored by our Party in the revolution and construction, but it has failed to do so. This single fact is enough to show that our university teachers' scientific and theoretical level is low.

As I stressed at the conference of scientists and technicians held sometime ago, our scientific and theoretical level is not yet high on the whole; we have no ground whatsoever to be so self-complacent. We must exert strenuous efforts to rapidly elevate our scientific and theoretical standards. Universities and colleges must take active measures to improve their teachers' scientific and theoretical qualifications.

We must not leave the work of raising the teachers' qualifications to themselves. As our experience shows, there are not
many people who study hard voluntarily. Even the cadres do
not study hard under various pretexts, if they are not strictly
supervised. We do not think all university teachers are fond of
studying. There may be some who are reluctant to study.
Therefore, we must establish a strong discipline of study
among them, instead of leaving this work to themselves.

University teachers have been allowed to stay at home to
study, absenting themselves from schools. This is wrong. We
cannot say their houses are provided with ample conditions for
studies. Moreover, we cannot check whether they study at
home or not. We must establish a strict discipline to have them
show up at schools every day; they must study at the libraries.

Some scientists and university teachers claim that they
have not enough time to study because there are too many
meetings, campaigns and business trips. They should not be
randomly mobilized for other work and should be provided
with sufficient time for study. This is true. But their claim that
they have no time to study is a mere excuse. A diligent man
studies at every spare moment. Moreover, it is not that the
scientists and university teachers have no time for study. The
question is, they do not study on the plea of having no time.

We must establish a strong habit of study among them and
quickly uplift our general scientific and theoretical level to the
advanced standards.

The university administrations should frequently organize
model and demonstration lectures and conduct seminars and
varied other activities to enhance the teachers' scientific and
theoretical level.

In addition, we must provide them with better conditions
for raising their scientific and theoretical level.

The Party Central Committee and the ministries should
show concern for this matter and take measures to publish
many more books for teachers and scientists. At present we
are unable to print many books because of the shortage of
paper. We must strive to produce more paper. And if we still
do lack it, we must even cut down the circulation of
newspapers to a certain extent, in order to publish enough
books on science and technology. We must also purchase many
such books from abroad. We should set up a translations

publishing house to translate and publish large quantities of foreign scientific and technical books. It is also necessary to put out a journal of translations on natural sciences. And we had better supply the University with printing equipment so that it may print all the books it needs.

In order to speedily acquire advanced science and technology, it is also necessary for the teachers and students to raise their proficiency in foreign languages. In the past all the institutes of higher learning and schools of different levels in common education only taught Russian. To quickly acquire advanced science and technology we must master many foreign languages. From now not only Russian but mainly English and French must be taught in the field of common education and at universities and colleges. It is also necessary to teach Spanish, German, Chinese and Japanese.

Universities must be provided with better conditions for experiments and training. We must not be stingy of experimental apparatuses and equipment for them. We cannot train fine intellectuals and develop our science and technology without spending money. Military schools have planes, tanks and different artilleries for educational purposes. So it is out of the question to equip each institute with a few machine tools. As for what universities and colleges require for educational purposes, we must be liberal and give them everything. And since we have not enough experimental apparatuses and equipment, it is a good idea for several institutes to pool their laboratories. All the apparatuses owned by the Academy of Sciences must be made available for university teachers and students.

In order to reinforce the teaching staffs of the University I think it necessary to assign capable scholars to it. We must recall some scholars from the Academy of Sciences to make up the university teachers and let them engage in their scientific researches while teaching at the University. Also, scholars in the Academy of Sciences should be made to give lectures at the University.

The central task for educational administration is to ensure the ideology of education. In a nutshell, this means establishing Juche in education.

University education is aimed at training revolutionary intellectuals of the working class needed for the completion of the Korean revolution and for the building of socialism and communism in Korea. Our education should be in accord with the interests of the Korean revolution and the Korean people and should serve the successful fulfillment of our revolution and construction. This is precisely Juche in education.

The Koreans must complete their revolution and build socialism and communism in Korea and live on Korea's nature. Even after the worldwide victory of communism the Koreans will have to live in Korea, and they cannot live in any other country.

The theory on the revolution and construction taught at the institutes should be one which is indispensable for the carrying out of our revolution and construction; and when teaching natural sciences, they must teach how to build a strong and prosperous country by making use of our nature.

The same is true of music and arts. We need arts which suit the Koreans' feelings which our people like. No matter how good the music of other countries may be, it will be useless for us if it does not suit the feelings of our people and they do not like it. Recently our artists produced an opera based on a foreign work which was adapted to Korean folk songs. This opera won great admiration from our people. However, previously, when they staged a foreign opera unadapted, it was not so popular among the working people because its music was alien to Korean sentiments. Our music and arts should serve the Koreans and suit their feelings.

Juche we are emphasizing is by no means nationalism. By establishing Juche we mean to solve all problems posed by the revolution and construction, in conformity with the require-ments of our revolution and the interests of our people. We must develop both social and natural sciences to meet our revolutionary demands and our actual conditions. Arts must also be developed to harmonize with the Korean people's feelings.

I was told that because they do not know much about our history and geography, some foreign-educated teachers in their lectures can cite examples of factions in other countries but none of ours and inform the students of foreign granite and marble but not of ours. This is wrong. The Koreans must know Korea above anything else. It may be necessary for you to know about foreign granite for your reference in comparison with ours. But, however hard we may make a study of foreign granite it will be of no use for us if we do not know about our own.

It is also incorrect to take chauvinistic attitudes and reject foreign science and technology on the plea of establishing Juche. In a historically brief period of time we have liquidated our centuries-old backwardness handed down from old society and made a great leap forward in all the political, economic and cultural realms of life, but our science and technology are still lagging behind. We must strive to introduce advanced science and technology in order to assimilate them and uplift our science and technology to the world standard as soon as possible. We never reject the introduction of advanced science and technology. What we are opposing is the nihilistic attitude of looking down upon our nation, while looking up to others, as well as the dogmatist attitude of uncritically swallowing up foreign things in disregard of the actual conditions of our country. Establishing Juche is not contradicted with the introduction of advanced science and technology. Only when we strive to introduce them and rapidly develop ours, can we thoroughly eliminate flunkeyism still persisting in the minds of our people.

More thoroughly establishing Juche in all the political, economic, cultural and military fields is a matter of pressing urgency now that we have to step up the building of socialism in the northern half of the Republic, complete the south Korean revolution and hasten the country's reunification.

Our Party's Juche idea and our people's struggle to establish Juche are exerting tremendous influence on the people in south Korea. Of late, we notice in the south Korean publications drifts of argument for an "independent economy", "Juche" and "opposing foreign forces". This vividly shows how greatly the south Korean people are influenced by the achievements scored through our dynamic struggle to build an independent economy in the north and apply Juche in all realms.

The northern half of the Republic, which is striving to build an independent economy, is daily prospering and developing, while, in south Korea which receives US "aid" running up to billions of dollars, the economy is depending on others more heavily and the people live in a dire misery. It is said that every year south Korea imports an enormous amount of flour from the US. However, the number of hunger-stricken people continues to increase. This stark reality convinces the south Korean people more and more clearly that they will never be well-off as long as they depend on others. So the south Korean intellectuals and the other sections of the people are raising their voices ever higher for independence against US "aid"; they are asking "Where has all the US aid gone?" and "How long must we live this way?"

The south Korean people are also criticizing more and more strongly Korean songs being Westernized and our spoken and written language mixed with English. Even the south Korean rulers, hard pressed by the people, have no other way but to advocate the development of national culture and arts. All this is a manifestation of the great vitality of our Party's Juche idea; it is also the result of our people's strenuous efforts to establish Juche throughout all the political, economic, cultural and military spheres. The achievements of the socialist construction in the northern half of the Republic are greatly inspiring the south Korean people. Inclinations to independence and self-reliance are constantly growing among the south Korean people. They say: "What they do in the north, we can do. We must chase out the US imperialists, oppose Japanese militarism and also build a strong and prosperous country relying on our own efforts."

When we continue with our dynamic struggle to establish Juche more firmly throughout all spheres, Koreans in Japan fight in support of our Juche stand and the progressive people the world over strongly support us, then the south Korean people's national and class consciousness will increase and US imperialism and its sycophants will be driven further into a tight corner. Precisely because of this urgent requirement of our revolution we are emphasizing the establishment of Juche.

The south Korean revolution cannot be carried through unless we educate the south Korean people in the Juche idea and wipe out the flunkeyist idea of worshipping the US, that is rooted deep in their minds. We must establish Juche more firmly in all domains and continue to develop our independent economy in order to give revolutionary impetus to the south Korean people so that they will rise up audaciously in the struggle for national liberation against flunkeyism.

University education must meet these requirements of our revolution. Universities and colleges must make sure that the

teachers fight against flunkeyism, dogmatism and revisionism and thoroughly establish Juche in their instruction and education. By establishing Juche in education we mean conducting all educational work in strict conformity to the demands of our Party's policies. School curricula and teaching outlines must be prepared in such a way that all aspects of instruction and education may suit the requirements of the Party's policies. We must edit textbooks and teaching materials based on our Party's policies. Scientific researches must also be conducted in order to satisfy the demands of our Party's policies. The teachers should wage a dynamic ideological struggle to improve the contents and methods of teaching in accordance with the Party's policies. In this way educational work will not only have a clear-cut working-class line politically and ideologically but the scientific and technical contents of teaching will also correctly meet the demands of the Party's policies.

In order to improve educational administration we must set up a proper leading system for the university's educational administration and enhance the role of the administrative officials.

We can say the university vice-chancellor for educational affairs corresponds to what the chief of staff is to the army. We must build up the staff office with the vice-chancellor as its chief and establish a unified scientific leadership system taking care of the whole process starting from making out the educational plan to its execution.

While putting the university system of educational administration to rights, we must enhance the role of the administrative officials.

The chancellor or the vice-chancellor of the university must not only give a unified leadership to the educational administration of the university as a whole but also personally organize and direct model or demonstration lectures on new important problems.

In order to ensure substantial guidance to the instruction and education at the institutes it is important to improve the functions of the heads of faculties and chairs. Those heads must always lead and supervise the teachers' preparations for lectures and their teaching and organize demonstration lectures in good time.

Those who have rich experience in teaching and academic

authority must be appointed as heads of faculties. If you think anybody can be appointed as administrative cadres, you are grossly mistaken. They should be most capable and prepared in the university, because educational administration is its main task. Just as the factory's production processes cannot be properly guided by the manager who knows little about production, so the university's educational administration cannot be correctly guided by an administrative official who has poor knowledge of pedagogy and low scientific and theoretical level. The task of the faculty head is not just to find out whether the teachers give lectures in time, how is the percentage of the students' attendance or fumble papers; he is supposed to check the teachers' lecture plans, organize demonstration lectures and always discuss with them scientific and theoretical problems. So one who is inexperienced in teaching and has no academic authority cannot work as head of faculty. For instance, if the head of the physics faculty of the University has no authority in the realm of physics, does not know how to organize demonstration lectures and is unable to clarify new scientific and theoretical problems, how can he guide the teachers' instructive work? Therefore, we must select a man well versed in pedagogy and science, as such.

From now, we must make it a rule for the heads of faculties to engage in instruction frequently. They should discard their erroneous viewpoint that they need not engage in instruction. We must set up a system under which they must devote some of their time to teaching, just as the chairmen of the cooperative farm management boards obligatorily participate in physical labor. The heads of faculties must deliver lectures to the students and, especially, many demonstration lectures.

Some people say that the faculty heads have so much office work to do that they cannot properly guide and supervise the teachers' instructive work. This is because they poke their nose into trifle affairs which are none of their business. If they organize all work well, they can work with teachers as much as they want. If they do have too much office work to do for the faculties, pick out deputy-heads from among the young teachers and let them deal with the work. The faculty heads must direct primary attention to increasing the role of the chairs, the basic unit of instruction and education, and to improving the teachers' scientific and theoretical level and the quality of instruction and education.

LET US DEVELOP OUR PEOPLE'S ARMY INTO A REVOLUTIONARY ARMY AND IMPLEMENT THE POLICY OF SELF-DEFENCE IN SAFEGUARDING THE NATION (Excerpt)

Speech at the 7th Commencement of Kim Il Sung Military University, *October 5, 1963*

Comrades,

On behalf of the Party Central Committee and the Government of the Republic I would like to warmly congratulate all of you graduates who have completed your course of study and are going to return to your respective units, the glorious revolutionary posts, in order to defend the socialist homeland.

Let me also extend my heartfelt thanks to Comrade President and the whole teaching staff who have devoted all their efforts and energies to educating and training the graduates.

And I wish greater success to the freshmen and undergraduates in their military and political training.

At this commencement I would like to make a few remarks to you—comrades being graduated, all of the students who will continue to study, and teaching staff who are exerting efforts for their education.

Our country you are defending is in a period of prosperity. It is changing literally into a mighty socialist state with firm foundations of an independent national economy.

We cannot yet say that we are leading an abundant life, but we have built a socialist paradise where there is neither exploitation nor oppression and all people are even in living standards and assured opportunities for work and study.

The more intensely and dynamically we fight, the more our homeland will prosper and the more our national economy will advance. And the people's lives will be enriched.

Accordingly, our revolutionary base will be further strengthened and our revolutionary force for national reunification will continue to grow and eventually lead the Korean revolution to victory.

Our country still remains divided into north and south. This is very unfortunate. More than half of the population is still oppressed and exploited by foreign imperialists, landlords and capitalists.

Therefore, our People's Army is confronted with two tasks.

One is that of impregnably defending the socialist motherland; and the other is the great revolutionary task of reunifying the divided territory and people and liberating the workers, peasants and other working people of the southern half from the oppression of US imperialism, landlordism and capitalism.

In order to accomplish these revolutionary tasks we must first strengthen our People's Army.

In making revolution we must have a few important revolutionary factors.

One of them is political force. If we are to make revolution we must first have a revolutionary force, that is, political force. Then we need military and economic strength. In other words, political, economic and military forces are more important for the completion of our revolution.

What is political force? It means a politically united force that strengthens our Party, firmly rallies the entire people around it and encourages them to strive for the accomplishment of its revolutionary cause. This is the most important force. Without it we cannot carry out revolution.

Revolution means an arduous struggle to destroy old institutions and build a new social system under which the majority of people can lead a full and happy life.

Inasmuch as this struggle is in the interests of many people, they must take part in it. Revolution cannot be carried out by a couple of men. Therefore, our Party has been emphasizing that political force is most important in carrying out its revolutionary tasks—building socialism in the northern half, liberating south Korea and reunifying the country.

Consolidating our Party is of the greatest importance in strengthening political force.

Our Party is the vanguard of the Korean working class; it is the vanguard of the working people; their heart and General Staff. Therefore, if we are to guide the people, we must first strengthen the Party, the nuclear force.

In order to strengthen the Party, it is necessary, first of all, for the whole Party membership to closely unite around its Central Committee. Without unity and cohesion the Party cannot be strong.

Furthermore, in order to carry out Party policies, all Party members should be capable of splendidly performing their tasks. They should also be well versed in the work of uniting the masses around the Party.

In other words, if we are to increase our political force, we must first build up the Party and firmly rally the masses around it. This alone enables us to succeed in accomplishing the revolutionary cause of building socialism in the northern half and reunifying the country.

Another important force in making revolution is economic force.

Economic force means material force. Revolution requires a certain amount of material force: we must lay firm foundations for our own national economy which can adequately feed our people and develop our country.

Only when we are economically strong, can we guarantee our political independence.

Our Party's present slogan is Juche in ideology, independence in politics and self-support in economy.

Ideologically, Juche must be thoroughly established; everyone must have the Juche ideology which serves the Korean revolution.

Politically, we must be independent. We must not depend on others or dance to others' tune; we must have political independence.

Economically, we must have an independent national economy. If we beg others for food and clothes and cannot make a rifle or a motor vehicle, we are not economically independent.

This material foundation is indispensable for increasing political and military strength and securing independence in politics and Juche in ideology. Therefore, economic independence is essential. Material force is most important.

Let me cite a few examples. Your uniforms or our clothes are still inferior to foreign ones. This is true. But we did not beg other countries for what we are wearing now. Until a few years ago we had not been able to fully solve the clothing problem on our own. We have long been weaving ordinary cloth. However, until three or four years ago we had imported cloth for your uniforms. But now, we are making even officers' uniforms, using our own cloth.

Before, we also imported rice—500,000 to 600,000 tons a year.

But five or six years ago we stopped importing rice. Of course, we are conducting cereal trade. We barter our maize for flour once in a while when we need it. This does not in the least affect our independence.

Because of our economic strength we are politically independent. We do not act as others dictate. When doing anything we do it according to our wish; we do it if it benefits us and suits our taste. So material force is most important.

You can find a familiar example in the situation of south Korea. It is not economically independent now.

The south Korean soldiers are fed on US surplus farm produce. The south Korean "National Defense Army" troops wear US-made uniforms. Their boots, rifles and cartridges are all supplied by the Yankees.

Do they have any amount of independence? None. The south Korean puppets act as ordered by the Americans: when ordered to get out they get out and when ordered to come in they come in. They have no independence whatsoever. South Korea is shackled to the American enemies because it is not economically independent.

Needless to say, the south Korean people are also awakening to this. Therefore, south Korean youths and intellectuals are strongly demanding the building of an independent national economy. The south Korean press, too, are now stressing independence and self-support every day.

However, an independent national economy cannot be materialized by mere words. It can be built only when social institutions and relations of production are brought to rights. Just writing articles in the press and shouting slogans for the construction of an independent economy will not do.

In south Korea today they advocate an independent economy, but this is a mere slogan, which is unrealizable.

Why? If they are to have an independent economy in the southern half, the factories should be nationalized; the capitalists and foreigners must be deprived of factories and enterprises for nationalization. They must also head off the influx of foreign goods and manufacture their own goods. But they have neither ability nor nerve to do so. Nor do the Americans allow them to do so. That is why they cannot have an independent economy.

In order to secure an independent development of the rural economy, they must collaborate with the northern half. This is how can the regime which protects the landlords do so? It cannot. Not only that. The price of rice should be fixed in the interests of peasants but such is not the case. Pak Jung Hi claims that he is carrying out a "physiocratic policy" but this is nothing more than a lip service. He cannot effect this policy. The "physiocratic policy" means a policy which puts main stress on agriculture. But he has no means to carry out this policy. Their independence is a mere slogan; they cannot have an independent economy. Anyhow we are glad to hear the voice for the building of an independent economy in south Korea. We welcome this. However, they must not build this economy with US and Japanese loans. Otherwise, south Korea will become a colony again. If they are to build an independent economy, they must collaborate with the northern half. This is one of our proposals for peaceful reunification. Should the south Korean authorities agree with the the north-south collaboration, we would say, "If you collaborate with us we can feed your army; you needn't ask the Americans for cloth and ammunition because we can supply them to you. But there is a condition. We can collaborate only when you fight against the Yankees and Japanese militarists and for the people." They dare not say that they can support the north Korean army. As you see, material force, economic independence is important.

I would not dwell on this problem today. I want to say

political independence can be guaranteed only by our independent economy, by material force. Because they have not this
material force in the south, they are not politically independent.

Our country has now built a solid independent economy. On
the occasion of the 15th birthday of our Republic we invited
many foreigners, particularly Asians and Africans. Delegates
from more than 20 nations were here. All of them admired the
independent national economy built in our country; they said
that our policy is fully correct.

. . .

The strength of our independent national economy constitutes a revolutionary economic force which will contribute to
national reunification. We have not prepared this economic
force for the well-being of the people in the northern half alone.
Our economic force is to support the south Korean revolution;
it is one which, after liberation of the southern half, will quickly build south Korea's towns and countryside, rapidly develop
the industries, speedily solve the unemployment problem and
offer many people the opportunity of learning.

To make revolution we must not only increase our political
and economic strength but also foster powerful military force.

What is military force? It means a full military strength
capable of protecting with armed forces the gains already
achieved and accomplishing the revolutionary task with armed
forces where necessary for further victory.

Of course, we will achieve the reunification by peaceful
means when it is possible without resorting to armed forces.
However, if the enemy tries to attack us by force of arms, we
must hit him with our armed forces. So, in making revolution
we need military force, as well as political and economic
strength.

What is our Party's policy to strengthen it?

It is a policy of self-defense. We must get ourselves ready to
defend ourselves. We must not expect others to defend us. By
self-defense, we do not mean, of course, that we will receive no
foreign aid whatsoever. If they give us aid, we will accept it,
but even if they do not, we can go by ourselves. This is our
principle.

Since I am speaking at a military university, I am not going
to dwell on economic or political problems but mainly on

military problems.

We must continue to strengthen our military force. Our Party intends to reunify the country by peaceful means as far as possible. However, when the enemy hampers the advance of our revolutionary movement by force of arms, we must certainly use our armed forces to reunify the country.

Therefore, military force is most important in defending our victories already won and advancing our revolution.

We strengthen our military force in order to defend ourselves.

. . .

We must be firmly prepared, both ideologically and militarily, for perfect self-defense, so as to protect ourselves with our own efforts, in the military sphere, just as in the economic sphere.

Then what is to be done?

First, we must develop our People's Army into a revolutionary army.

We have been emphasizing this ever since its inception. Our army must become a revolutionary army of workers and peasants.

A revolutionary army always faces a formidable enemy.

In national-liberation revolutions the workers and peasants arm themselves, first with hammers and axes, and then with rifles snatched from individual enemies and wage arduous battles to crush the strong enemy and attain final victory.

Fidel Castro also began the revolution with seven rifles, and won victory by defeating the strong enemy. Today the entire Cuban people are armed and defending their revolution under the very nose of the United States.

What is important is to safeguard the revolution to a man without discarding its banner, its spirit.

Before, we anti-Japanese guerrillas also fought the enemy with obsolete arms. During the Fatherland Liberation War our People's Army also worsted the enemy with old weapons. The Chinese People's Volunteers came to our aid but, in fact, their weapons were also obsolete.

In the triumphant Russian revolution the workers and peasants fought with poor weapons. So did they when fighting the White Army and the armed interventionists from 14 countries who had invaded Russia. In the war against the Hitlerite fascists the Soviet army had outworn arms. However, they crushed the formidable enemy.

The question is not whether an army has good weapons or not but whether it is a revolutionary army or not.

To form a revolutionary army the officers and all other soldiers must begin with building up themselves politically and ideologically.

Many problems arise here. Most important is to arm themselves with the class spirit. A revolutionary army fighting against the landlord and capitalist classes and the imperialists must arm itself with the revolutionary idea of the working class.

We must equip our officers and men with a revolutionary idea that they can defeat a formidable enemy even with outmoded weapons, with a revolutionary idea that they should not just count on powerful arms like nuclear weapons but should rely on the strength of the entire people, organize and unite them and fight together with them. We should equip them with the spirit of unity between officers and men and between army and people.

During the Fatherland Liberation War we fought a strong enemy and won a great victory. At that time our officers and men had an excellent mentality. What kind of people were they? They were all sons and daughters of workers and peasants. Their revolutionary consciousness was high; former hired hands, they had just been freed from the oppression of the landlords, capitalists and the Japanese blackguards, and given land or become the masters of factories.

They were people of a firm revolutionary determination to safeguard the system which guaranteed their happiness and the prosperous fatherland. That is why we could vanquish the tough enemy.

The same is true of the present. What is most important in bringing up our army to be a revolutionary army is that all the officers and men should assimilate the revolutionary traditions of the anti-Japanese guerrillas and thoroughly arm themselves with the class spirit. They should have a great hatred for the enemy and unite with one will and purpose and with a resolve to fight out, relying on the strength of the people and binding them around the Party.

The People's Army should be boundlessly true to the Party

and the country. We must firmly safeguard our revolutionary gains with blood and our prosperous socialist fatherland possessed of an independent national economy, our fatherland where there is no oppression and exploitation and everybody is entitled to employment and learning, where there are factories and enterprises we have built with our own efforts, and firm foundations which guarantee all the Korean people abundant lives. All the officers and men of the People's Army must arm themselves with ardent patriotism.

The People's Army must be faithful to the Party and defend it. We should protect and bear allegiance to our revolutionary Party—our Party, the vanguard of the working class and the working people, whose mission is to overthrow the landlord and capitalist classes and defend the interests of the working people, and one of the front rankers of the shock brigade in the struggle to safeguard the banner of Marxism-Leninism against revisionism in the international working-class movement.

Next they must hate the enemy. They must clearly realize that the landlord and capitalist classes and the Japanese and US imperialists are the arch-enemy of us Korean people, and they must arm themselves with deep hatred for them.

Thus our People's Army will become an ideologically and politically prepared revolutionary army filled with the conviction of victory, with the communist conviction that they can carry the revolution to the finish in the interests of the masses. It must develop into a revolutionary army inheriting the revolutionary spirit of the anti-Japanese guerrillas; at the start, they had not even a rifle, but snatched enemy weapons with which they waged a long, arduous struggle against Japanese imperialism, a strong enemy.

If we are to increase our defense power, our revolutionary military power, we must carry forward the ideology, work style and traditions of the revolutionary army. As we have experienced ourselves and as it is clear from the revolutionary histories of other countries, top priority must be given to assimilating the revolutionary traditions. Only then can we safeguard the ideology, work style and traditions of our revolutionary army. This is our greatest source of power.

Once we are politically armed this way, we can beat a strong enemy, even if we are a little behind others technically or lack some training. So, political and ideological arming is most important.

Next, we must carry through the Party's military policy of self-defense.

To do this the entire people must first arm themselves. In emergency we cannot fight only with the People's Army a few hundred thousands strong. The whole people must be armed and fight; and this we can do. It is one of our greatest advantages.

The south Korean puppet regime cannot do this. Because we trust our workers and peasants, we can arm all of them, but the south Korean puppet regime of the landlords and capitalists cannot arm the people. They fear that the people would level guns at them.

Arming all the people is one of our characteristics and an inexhaustible source of our military power. This is better than rockets.

What must we do if we are to arm the entire people? We must develop the People's Army into a cadre army.

It is impossible that all the people join in the army and undergo military training. Therefore, the People's Army must first be made a cadre army so that in case of emergency which requires the arming of the entire people, existing divisions can be expanded to corps, regiments to divisions and battalions to regiments. This is our Party's policy.

We are producing as many weapons as we can to arm the entire people. In exigency we will make sure that members of the Workers' Party and the Democratic Youth League and all the rest of the people carry guns. What will we need then? We will need cadres. In that case, whoever have served the People's Army will have to be commanders. Then it is possible to arm all of the people. This is most important.

In the future, every branch, whether it be the signal or artillery corps, must be corps of cadres. Thus, when all the people are armed, the People's Army will play a nuclear role and proficiently command them.

Next, the whole country must be fortified.

We have no nuclear bomb. However, we can stand against any enemy who has atom bombs.

Military science has probably taught you the effect of the atom bomb and how to protect you from it. If you dig into the earth you can protect yourselves from nuclear attack.

Our country has favorable terrain conditions. We have many high hills. Since we have chemical plants we can produce as much explosives as we want; and we are manufacturing hard alloys. So we can fortify the whole country in the future.

The science of tunnelling is taught here at the military university. This is very useful. In my opinion, this subject had better be included also in the curriculum of the Kang Gon and other military academies. It is necessary to teach it to all platoon leaders as well as noncommissioned officers at their training centers.

We must make tunnels everywhere. We must fortify the whole of the country—not only the frontline but also the rear, the second and third lines—and reinforce the air and maritime defenses. We must also build many underground plants.

How shall we look when we have armed the entire people and fortified the whole country? Perhaps you have seen a hedgehog. When it draws its head and curls itself up, its whole body is covered with thorny bristles. Because of this strong "armament" no animal dares to attack it. The same is true of us. Once we arm the entire people and fortify the whole country no enemy, however strong, will dare to attack us. Even the Yankees.

What we have done is no secret. The enemy also knows it. He has many spies. We do not know how many of them have been here, in addition to those caught by us. Some of them were caught here on a third or fourth trip. Those caught on a fourth sneak would have apparently carried out their missions up to a third trip. Therefore, the enemy must know what we have done. Nevertheless, I do not mean that we must open the door and reveal everything. If the enemy gets informed of the arming of all our people and the fortification of the whole nation, he will be scared and will not invade us. This is what I mean.

During the Fatherland Liberation War Eisenhower attempted a landing on our west and east coasts for a showdown but, finally, was forced to sign the Armistice Agreement. Do you know why? At the time our Party Central Committee addressed a Red Letter to its entire membership. The whole Party resolved to fight a life-and-death battle and started driving tunnels to get ourselves ready. The enemy spies reported this to the Americans. And they thought that if they took reckless action against us, they would be beaten to a jelly, far from winning. So they dared not make a further attack on us and were brought to their knees.

Cuba stands firm against the US under its very nose and why can't we? We can do the same, once the whole country is fortified.

That is why we must arm the entire people and fortify the whole country. Our military science should be subordinated to this.

Our next task is to make sure that in case of war every branch of the national economy serves military efforts.

During the Fatherland Liberation War we could not do this properly. Then we were weak, technologically poor and short of everything. Since we could not make rifles on our own we had to import them. Consequently we could not supply the front with rifles in plenty of time. Then we could not even manufacture enough hand grenades.

We must prepare all the realms of the national economy including engineering and metallurgical industries to serve war when it breaks out. We should see that every factory produces war materials, while laying up reserves to be needed for war.

Now we have a good harvest every year. But our slogan is economy. We are practicing economy and increasing our reserves. We are laying up everything in reserve—rice, salt, steels, cloth and so on. If we have plenty of these reserves and the whole economy can be geared to the war, we can defend ourselves. Then we will firmly safeguard the fatherland against the invasion of any enemy and be ever victorious in the future advancement of the Korean revolution.

In accomplishing the Korean revolution one of our main tasks is to successfully guarantee and protect socialist construction in the northern half. At the same time, we must completely liberate the southern half and build socialism there, thus realizing a society without exploitation and oppression throughout Korea. This also means the fulfillment of our internationalist duty.

In order to complete this revolutionary task we must strengthen our revolutionary army and increase our defense power. Therefore, the People's Army must become an army of cadres politically and militarily. We must also fortify all the defense positions and the whole country and must be capable of manufacturing weapons and everything necessary by our own efforts. Then we will defeat the enemy and he will not dare to commit aggression.

In accordance with this spirit the military university should continue to train many cadres.

All cadres must be reeducated. Most of them above the company commander level have war experience, and they should receive military and cultural training. We should ensure that they all graduate from the military university. Therefore, you should increase the faculties and chairs as you deem necessary. Of course, it is hardly possible that all of them graduate from this university in a short space of time. You must not make haste; you must make sure that most of the officers complete their education at the military university, step by step, over the period of ten years or so.

The graduates should also be given short trainings. For this, the training center attached to this university must be kept.

As for the faculties, the existing ones are all good. But I think some faculties of arms have a small enrollment in proportion to the total number of the students. You should expand these faculties and enroll more students.

In former days our forefathers produced many guns for themselves. So do we now. We must make weapons suited to our actual conditions, using materials available in our country. With this in view we must train many ordnance officers. Needless to say, other faculties should also train many more officers.

Therefore, you should set up necessary faculties or extend the existing ones.

Next in importance is to improve the teachers' qualities.

What is to be done for this? The teachers should, above all, firmly establish the Party's ideological system among themselves.

As a revolutionary army, we should serve the Korean revolution, and be faithful to the Party, the country and the people. Officers who are unfaithful to their Party and fatherland are of no use, however there are trained. Precisely the teachers must closely equip themselves with the Party's ideology because they have to train officers true to the Party and the country. In other words, they should be boundlessly true to the Party, the country and the people and have a strong Party spirit.

The teachers' level of professional knowledge should be appreciably high. I was told that some teachers are not college graduates. But I do not mean they should all be replaced by college graduates. Those who did not graduate from colleges must all reach the standard of college graduates by studying themselves while on the job. Not that only those with college diplomas have the college standards of knowledge. If they attain college standards, that will do, though they did not graduate from colleges.

A profound study of military science should be continued. In studying our military science and experiences to develop a military science which is suitable to our actual conditions, this university must play a central role; it must be a base where military science is studied and developed.

As you see, the teachers must intensify their Party spirit, make greater efforts to increase their general and military knowledge and work together with the students in intensive studies to contrive various projects.

Seizing the excellent opportunity afforded by your commencement today, I have spoken to you about a few points essential for the implementation of the Party policies. I am firmly confident that you will strengthen the People's Army as a revolutionary army and more firmly safeguard our socialist homeland and revolutionary gains.

ON ENHANCING THE ROLE OF SOCIAL SCIENCES TO MEET THE PRESENT DEMANDS OF OUR REVOLUTION

Talk with the Department of Science and Education of the Central Committee of the Workers' Party of Korea, *December 30, 1963*

I am going to touch on some questions arising in our revolution and construction, that must be solved by social sciences today.

It can be said that our Party has two major revolutionary tasks which it has been carrying out and must continue to carry out in the future. One is socialist revolution and construction on the northern half of the Republic and the other is the revolution in south Korea and the reunification of the country.

So far we have done a great deal of work in the course of the revolutionary struggle and in construction. We were able to score great victories and successes in revolution and construction because our Party worked out correct policies and lines and showed originality in carrying them out. Needless to say, in leading the revolution and construction our Party has been guided by the general principles of Marxism-Leninism and has taken into account quite a few problems set forth or solved in practice by the founders of Marxism-Leninism. However, our Party solved most problems in a unique manner by creatively applying the universal truth of Marxism-Leninism in conformity with the historical conditions and national characteristics of our country. We used our own brains and relied on our own efforts in solving some questions which Marx or Lenin did not raise and could not foresee in view of the conditions prevailing in their time.

As you all know, Marx lived in the era before the rise of monopoly capitalism and accordingly created the great Marxist theory on the basis of his analysis of the social relations of his time, thus tolling the knell for capitalist society. But Marx did not have the opportunity to lead the socialist revolution and socialist construction in practice. Lenin created Leninism, the Marxism of the epoch of imperialism which is governed by the law of the uneven political and economic development of the capitalist powers. Mobilizing and organizing the Russian working class, he successfully led the October Socialist Revolution. This opened up a new era in human history. However, to our regret, Lenin died soon after the victory of the October Revolution before he had the chance to lead socialist construction. Taking over Lenin's work, Stalin carried out the collectivization of agriculture and pushed ahead with socialist industrialization in the Soviet Union. But he too died before he could see the complete victory of socialism, much less lead communist construction.

In most cases, therefore, we had to use our own brains and find unique solutions to the theoretical and practical problems of the revolution and construction after the triumph of the socialist revolution in our country.

We must do the same today and all the more so in the future. In order to achieve the complete victory of socialism and gradually go over to communism, we must continue to be guided by the universal principles of Marxism-Leninism, but, on many questions, we must blaze a path for ourselves. It is important for us to work out our revolutionary strategy and tactics by generalizing and systematizing the practical experience of our revolution and construction in keeping with the laws governing social development in our country.

On the basis of the dialectical materialist method of Marxism-Leninism our social sciences must theoretically prove, explain and develop the correctness and creativeness of what we have already done and what we propose to do. Only then can we find the new orientation for further advance and continue to make progress.

Our social sciences have not yet theoretically explained and developed even a number of problems which we recognized and raised long ago, have they?

These include, for example, the importance of work with people in industrial management and the question concerning industrial methods of management in agriculture. I asked those concerned to prepare a book on industrial administration, but they did not say a word about work with people in their outline of the book. More than once I stressed that work with people must be regarded as essential, but their outline was incorrect and I had them correct it. Solving the peasant and agricultural questioms after the socialist cooperativization of agriculture is quite a new problem for any country, one extremely complex and difficult to solve. We have already introduced an excellent system of agricultural guidance which will enable us to solve the socialist rural question correctly. Yet, our scholars are still unable to demonstrate to the full the correctness and vitality of our new system.

Also, I have repeatedly mentioned some matters of principle concerning communist education and asked them to write a school textbook on communist education, but it is not ready yet.

Indeed, there are quite a lot of problems awaiting theoretical solution in all branches of social sciences, including political economy, history and linguistics.

We must give an orientation in every branch. Unless we explain things theoretically now, we can make no further progress.

Political economy is in a position to give a theoretical elucidation of the problem of eliminating the distinctions between town and country, and, in practice, its solution is possible. Furthermore, we must make a profound study of the conditions under which the difference between mental and physical labor can be eliminated and give a theoretical and practical answer to this problem.

The science of history, too, still has many questions to be gone into. That of the birth and development of capitalism in our country must be fully explained. This question should be gone into in detail and developed theoretically in accordance with the laws that govern social development. In addition to this question, the science of history must also elucidate the facts about ancient Korea, slave society and the origin of the Korean nation. We must correctly appraise the scholars of the *Silhak* school. I am told that a draft Party history has been prepared. It must be completed quickly.

In the field of linguistics it is necessary to push ahead vigorously with vocabulary improvement, which is fundamental for the development of the Korean language. In what direction should we develop our language? Seeing that the country has not yet been reunified, it should be developed by stages. We should begin with improving the vocabulary and tackle the problem of the form of our letters after reunification. In my opinion our "Korean Dictionary" contains more words of Chinese origin than of Korean. When coining new words, we should form them from Korean root words so as to develop our language. At present, however, most new words are coined by mixing Chinese characters. As for our characters, we must go into whether we should continue to use the present form or not. Our spoken language has good articulation but our written language has some shortcomings in its form.

We must also make a theoretical study of the problem of national reunification. Pedagogy, too, is faced with many problems which require theoretical and practical solution.

In order to find new theoretical answers to these different problems, it is very important to work properly with scientists and college teachers.

But we are not up to the mark in educating people in the sphere of science and education, in arming them ideologically and organizing and mobilizing them.

So far, we have confined our work chiefly to the training of scientists, getting them to study and solve the problems arising in postwar rehabilitation and construction and in building the foundations of socialism. But things are different now. We must strengthen our work with scientists, both natural and social, and creatively solve many of the new, theoretical and practical problems which crop up in the course of our revolution and construction.

In order to do this, it is very important to establish Juche in the sphere of scientific research. Only by establishing it firmly will we be able to do scientific research into the right channels, as required by the Party. In fact, all achievements in scientific research work over the past few years are due primarily to the struggle to establish Juche. The success of our research into vinalon is positive proof of this.

We must rally scientists closely around our Party and continue to push ahead dynamically with the work of arming them with our Party's Juche idea. Thus we will get all of them to imbue themselves thoroughly with this idea—we live in Korea, we are and will be guided by our Party's ideology and theory, and we will have nothing to do with flunkeyism and dogmatism.

If we slight the work of imbuing our scientists and college teachers with our Party's ideology, or fail to do it properly, scientific research itself will not go well and our younger generation will not be educated to become capable people useful to the revolution. Whether or not our students will be brought up to become true revolutionary intellectuals depends largely on the scientists and the teachers who teach them.

We must not only firmly arm the scientists and teachers with our Party's Juche idea but further temper them through organizational life.

Our country has only a few women scientists at present. We must train many more and raise their level.

With a view to carrying out the tasks which face social sciences more satisfactorily, we have separated the Academy of Social Sciences from the Academy of Sciences. We are planning a conference on the work of social sciences. I will have a talk with linguists and also meet natural and social scientists to discuss the compilation of an encyclopedia. Then I will speak about the concrete tasks confronting social sciences in greater detail.

SOME PROBLEMS RELATED TO THE DEVELOPMENT OF THE KOREAN LANGUAGE

Talk with the Linguists, *January 3, 1964*

I have long been thinking of having a talk with you about linguistic problems, but, what with one thing and another, it has not been possible until now. Today I would like to talk with you about problems related to the development of studies on our national language.

There have been controversies over linguistic problems several times in the past—and especially over the problem of reforming the letters.

Certain people urged carrying out a reform of letters right away, but we were firmly opposed to this. What were the main reasons for our objection to the proposed reform?

First, some failed to link the linguistic question with the national problem. Language is one of the most important common features which characterize a nation. Even though a people are all of the same stock and live on the same territory, they cannot be called a nation if they speak different languages.

The Korean people, who are of the same stock and have the same language, constitute a nation. Though our country is now split into north and south owing to the occupation of south Korea by the US imperialists, our nation is one. At present, Koreans in both north and south speak the same language and use the same letters.

What would happen if we reformed our letters now, as they insist? If Koreans in north and south used different letters, it would be impossible for them to read the letters they wrote to each other or to understand each other's newspapers, magazines and other publications. This would bring about the serious consequence of erasing the common national characteristics of the Korean people and, in the end, of splitting the nation. Concerned only with reforming the letters, they have lost sight of the national split. We Communists can never accept any letter reform which would divide our nation.

Second, they have not considered that an immediate letter reform would greatly hamper the development of science and culture.

Letters play a very important role in the development of science and culture. Newspapers, magazines, books on science and technology, and literary works are all dependent on the letters. Without letters, you can neither study nor develop science and culture.

Before liberation, the Japanese imperialists tried to stamp out our language and letters. Proclaiming Japanese the "national language", they prohibited the use of Korean and forced us to use Japanese. In consequence, only a limited number of linguists were engaged in the study of the Korean language at that time, and most of the other people had no opportunity to study it.

Liberation brought back our language and letters which we had all but lost. Following liberation, we established a policy aimed at the rapid development of our national culture, waged a vigorous campaign against illiteracy and gave a big push to our public education. As a result, all our people learned how to read and write their own letters. Newspapers, magazines and all the other publications being put out in our country today use our letters, and the people read and understand them.

What would happen if we should change our letters all of a sudden? All the people would become illiterate at once, and everybody would have to learn how to read all over again. Books and other publications would all have to be rewritten, using the new letters. And, until the people had learned the new letters, it would be impossible to propagate either science and technical knowledge or literature and art among the working people through the medium of publications. This would hold us back for decades in the development of science and culture.

At present, our country is behind the advanced nations in the development of science and technology. Therefore, we should popularize science and technology rapidly, using the letters already known to all our people. Why should we hold back the development of science and technology even more by reforming the letters?

Third, they have also failed to consider the international trend of the development of letters. We are Communists. In developing our spoken and written language, we should keep in mind the common trend of linguistic development of the peoples of the world.

It goes without saying that we should not discard the national characteristics of our language too hastily, simply in order to bring its development in line with the common world trend.

It will probably take a considerable length of time for the whole world to become communist. For this reason, our national ways should be preserved for the time being. It is wrong to see only what is national while ignoring the universal, but it is just as wrong to see only what is universal while losing sight of what is national.

From this point of view, their proposal of a letter reform is incomprehensible to us. We have listened to the explanations offered by its proponents several times, but they have failed to advance any scientific grounds for the change.

Our Party was absolutely right in objecting to their proposal of a letter reform.

They have failed to appreciate the effect the letter reform would produce on our social life, having no idea of its correct orientation, either. Disregarding the future of our nation and the development of science and technology, driven only by their desire for fame, they have simply invented new letters to their liking and tried to disseminate them right away.

Language in itself is related to questions of nationality and the state, and is closely linked with all aspects of a people's life. How to develop a spoken and written language is, therefore, a very important matter.

We are not against the letter reform in itself. Admittedly, our letters do have certain shortcomings, and a study must be made to reform them some day.

Our syllabics are square. A study should be made to determine whether or not we should use them as they are. Reforming them would also have advantages: it would make them easier to read and would enable us to type quickly and facilitate the technicalization of letters.

But, if the letter reform is ever to be carried out, it should be done after the north-south reunification and after our science and technology have reached world levels. Then the reform will not lead our homogeneous nation to use different letters, and it will not be so detrimental to the development of science and culture, even though it may take some time for the people to learn the new letters.

For the present, we should preserve the letters which are used by all Koreans, both in north and south, and should develop our science and culture using them.

Moreover, even if we reform our letters in the future, we should retain their national characteristics, while bringing them more into line with what is common throughout the world.

This is the principle that should guide us not only in reforming the letters but also in all other matters related to the development of our language.

It is a source of great pride and encouragement to us that our nation has a spoken and written language of its own. Because we Korean people have had our own language from remote antiquity, we could create an excellent national culture and always preserve the fine customs and traditions of our nation. And since our people have an excellent language, our national pride is high and our sense of unity, too, is great.

Now, as always, our spoken and written language serves as a powerful weapon in the development of the economy, culture, science and technology of our country, in all fields of socialist construction. If we did not have a good spoken and written language, if we did not have our long history and cultural traditions which have been shaped and handed down through the medium of the language, if our written language was not accepted by the entire people today and, accordingly, failed to help raise the ideological consciousness and the technical and cultural level of the working people rapidly, then we would not be able to advance quickly in socialist construction in the saddle of Chollima.

As a matter of fact, Korean is a very good language. Our language flows easily, with rising and falling inflections and long and short sounds; it has good intonation, as well, and sounds very beautiful to the ear. Our language is so rich that it is capable of expressing any complex thought or delicate feeling well, can stir people, make them laugh or cry.

Our language is also highly effective in educating people in communist morality, because it can express matters of courtesy with precision. Our national language is so rich in pronunciation that in it we can pronounce almost freely the sounds of any other language of the Eastern or Western countries.

We should be justly proud of our spoken and written language and should love it.

It goes without saying that the Korean language also has its shortcomings. We should eliminate these aspects of our national language and make it more accurate and beautiful.

The most important question which calls for our attention at present is that of the words borrowed from Chinese ideographs, which have flooded our language.

Above all, we should take a correct attitude towards the words adopted from Chinese ideographs. Many words of Chinese origin which our ancestors used and then discarded are now being revived, and scores of new words are being coined by introducing Chinese ideographs at random.

With the development of science and technology and the progress of society, our vocabulary must also be expanded. We must create a lot of new words.

But we should make it a point to form these new words from our own root words. There is no need to complicate our vocabulary system by having two kinds of words—home-grown ones and those borrowed from Chinese ideographs. There should be one unified vocabulary system based on our home-grown words. You should find out which root words are our own and which have come from Chinese ideographs, and make a list of them. You should also find out why words borrowed from Chinese ideographs keep finding their way into our language— perhaps we have not enough root words of our own. If it is impossible to manage with our own root words alone, that is something else again. But, if not, we should develop the Korean language with our own root words.

It would be a good idea to make new words for instance using our word *mot* (nail) in *nasamot* (screw) *taraemot* (bolt) and *namumot* (wood nail). Among the words coined recently, however, there are many that are incomprehensible to young people: *tonyuk* (pork), *chadon* (piglet). *modon* (sow), *myomok* (sapling) and *myopojon* (tree nursery), to name a few. If we used Chinese ideographs, as was done in the past, it would be another question, but, since we are not using them any more, such words should not be coined at random. You say *sangyop* (mulberry leaf), *sangjon* (mulberry field) and *sangmok* (mulberry tree), when *bbongip*, *bbongbat* and *bbongnamu* would do just as well. Those who know Chinese characters may understand the former, but the young people will not. If you write *sangjon*, the young people may confuse it with the word *sangjon* (master) which you use when you condemn the puppets for licking the boots of their Yankee masters. You use such words as *yangjam* (silk culture), *chamgyon* (silks) and *chamsa* (silk threads), when you already have such nice words as *nuechigi*, *myongju* and *myongjusil;* you say *tonsa* (pigsty) when *twaejiuri* does the trick, and *sipguse* (19-year-old) when *yolahopsal* serves the purpose. All this is wrong.

When you already have such a fine word as *tambae* (tobacco), why say *yoncho*? As for *sokgyo* (stone bridge), you might just as well say *toldari*.

Of course, there is no need to abandon even those words adopted from Chinese ideography which have already been fully assimilated into our language. Such words as *pang* (room), *hakgyo* (school). *kwahakgisul* (science and technology) and *samgakhyong* (triangle) have already become a part of our language. We need not trouble ourselves to change *hakgyo* to *paeumjip* and *samgakhyong* to *semoggol*. That would be a deviation.

Nor should the word *op* (work) be discarded. Such words as *saop* (work), *nongop* (agriculture) and *kongop* (industry) should all be used.

Words adopted from Chinese ideographs appear rather often especially in scientific treatises and political reports. Political terminology is somewhat complex. There seems to be no alternative but to use such words as *ryonhaphoe* (joint conference) and *punkwahoe* (subcommittee meeting).

But, in our use of a certain number of words adopted from Chinese ideographs, it will not do to use Chinese words as is, changing only their pronunciation. You also say *kongjakbogo* in the sense of *saopbogo* (report on the work), but *kongjakbogo* is Chinese. You ought to use *saopbogo,* which is familiar to all. The Korean edition of the Chinese magazine *Hongqi* is full of words borrowed intact from contemporary Chinese, only in the Korean way of writings. It uses *kwachacham* for *chonggojang*(railway station) and *kongingyegup* for *rodonggyegup* (working class). Such words are not Korean.

As for those words whose roots came from Chinese ideographs but which have already been completely assimilated into our language, there is no need to change them. What is wrong is the unnecessary use of new words coined from Chinese ideographs, instead of looking up and using their equivalents in our own rich language. We should keep the use of loan words from Chinese to the indispensable minimum and avoid coining new ones at random. If you coin words from Chinese ideographs and use them at random, as is being done at present, few of our words will survive in the end.

In short, when you have two words that mean the same thing, one being our own and the other borrowed from Chinese ideographs, you should choose the former whenever possible; and, if you have to use a certain number of words adopted from Chinese ideographs, you should be selective in this, using only those which have already become thoroughly assimilated into our own language; you should further enrich and develop our language using indigenous root words as much as possible, instead of coining new words from Chinese ideographs thoughtlessly.

This, I think, is a correct orientation for the development of our language.

To proceed. Words of foreign origin should also be screened. We should use words of our own whenever possible instead of using loan words.

Immediately after liberation, O Gi Sop tried to Russianize Korean, injecting such terms as *ideologiya* and *hegemoniya* randomly in an attempt to show off his learning. We criticized him for this. Now, the smarties in south Korea are spoiling our language by adulterating it with English and Japanese.

We, too, must plead guilty to using foreign words occasionally without thinking. For instance, sometimes *ekjamen* slips out instead of *sihom* (examination) or *klas* instead of *hakgup* (class). We now use *plan* as well as *kyehoek,* and *tempo* as well as *sokdo,* but it is easier for the masses to understand our Korean words *kyehoek* and *sokdo.*

Some people are still using Japanese words, saying *uwagi* (coat) when *yangbokjogori* would do, and *jubong* (trousers) instead of *yangbokbaji.* There are still a great many Japanese words being used—especially in our mining vocabulary.

In apple nomenclature, too, there are such terms as *uk* and *chuk,* which are the Japanese words *asahi* and *iwai,* given Korean pronunciation. If a species is from Japan, it should be given a Japanese name, but if it is from our own country, it should have a Korean name.

In other countries, liquors are usually named after their place of origin; for example, *champagne,* from Champagne, France, and *moutai-chiu,* from the Moutai district in Kweichow Province, China. This is a good system for us to adopt, calling the apple produced in Pukchong *pukchong* and the one produced mainly in Hwangju *hwangju.*

Naturally we cannot just abolish all the loan words in our language, for it is impossible to avoid using words of foreign origin, at least to some extent, and some new ones may even have to be introduced.

We have to use a considerable number of borrowed words especially as scientific and technical vocabulary. It is advisable not to modify such words as *turaktoru* (tractor), *sonban* (lathe), *polban* (drilling machine) and *taningban* (turning lathe). There were no such things as tractors before in our country and, therefore, we cannot help using the borrowed words. You should always consult the specialists before changing scientific and technical terminology.

As for a foreign country's proper nouns, we would do well to follow the way they are pronounced in that country instead of pronouncing them in the Japanese or Chinese way. The name of a country should be written the way it is pronounced in the country.

Moreover, when writing figures, we should follow our own number system. Rather than writing "10 *chon*" (thousand) for *man* (10,000), as Westerners do, we should make *man* the unit. However, it is common practice throughout the world to mark off a number at every third place, starting from the decimal point, and we should do the same.

We should screen the loan words that have flooded the Korean language, use them as little as possible and preserve our own words as best as we can.

As for the question of Chinese ideographs: should we continue to use them, or not? There is no need for us to use them. Even the Chinese, who invented them, are going to discard them in the future, for they are difficult to learn and hard to write. Is there any reason, then, why we should use them?

The Chinese ideographs are foreign characters, and we should use them only for a limited period of time.

The question of using Chinese ideographs must be considered together with that of our country's reunification. Nobody can prophesy exactly when our country will be reunified, but it is a foregone conclusion that the Yankees will go under and our country be reunified some day. And since Chinese ideographs are still being used by the people in south Korea, along with our own letters, we cannot abandon them entirely. If we discarded Chinese ideographs completely now, we would not be able to read the newspapers and magazines printed in south Korea. We should, therefore, continue to learn and use Chinese ideographs for the present. However, this does not mean, of course, that we should use Chinese ideographs in our newspapers. All our publications should be written in our own letters.

Now I would like to go into the question of giving form to words.

Words ought to be spaced. In our writing now each word does not have a fixed form. Therefore our writing looks like an unbroken string of syllabics. So, at a glance, it is less appealing to the eye than Chinese or European writing. As a matter of fact, the form of words will be fixed only when the syllabics are broken down and written sideways, like European words.

Since the form of our words is not fixed, their spelling is also difficult. But the question of fixing the form of words will have to be settled after the reunification of north and south. You would do well to begin a thorough study of this matter immediately.

It would seem that this question, too, can be solved, to a certain extent, if, while preserving the square syllabics used at present, we space our words and use punctuation properly. *Kanggwa mul* (river and water) should be written as *kang, mul,* while *kangmul* (river water) should be used instead of the spaced form *kang mul.* You must study how to give a definite form to each word, while retaining the square syllabics.

If the matter of spacing and closing up words is properly solved, our writing will become much easier to read. In typing, as well, the letters of one word must be written together and words must be regularly spaced.

There must also be many other problems related to the development of the study of our language. The scholars working in this field should make great efforts to advance our national linguistics.

In developing our language, we should not copy from the language of any other country—much less take the Seoul dialect, corrupted by English and Japanese, as the standard. We who are building socialism must take the central role in developing the Korean language, basing ourselves wholly on the pure native words of our country.

First of all, we must revise our vocabulary to some extent. It is important to do so at this stage. Only after this is done, should we turn to the form of the letters and spelling.

Revising our vocabulary is no easy task. It requires extensive investigation and studies, as well as strict control.

You should find out how many words are truly Korean and how many are Koreanized Chinese words. It would be advisable to investigate which of the words borrowed from Chinese ideographs we will have to continue to use, which of them we can discard, and boldly cross out from the dictionary what we can do just as well without. You can hardly criticize someone for using words that are in the dictionary, so those words adopted from Chinese ideographs which we will not continue to use should be given only in the dictionary of Chinese ideographs and excluded altogether from the Korean dictionary. There are so many words adopted from Chinese ideography in the "Korean Dictionary" compiled and issued by the Academy of Sciences that it looks like a Chinese-Korean dictionary. From now on, dictionaries should not be compiled in this way.

The ministries and other organizations should be prohibited from coining new words at random, and strict control should be exercised to ensure that all the organizations use correct Korean in their official documents and publications.

The Institute of Linguistics should be put in charge of revising our vocabulary and controlling the coining of new words. You should not confine yourselves to polishing up those words that already exist but should coin many fine words as well. To do this you should make a more profound study with redoubled efforts. In revising our vocabulary no confusion should be created; value judgments should not be made on the basis of personal preference alone, branding those words that sound harsh to your ears as "bad" and giving a clean bill of health to those that happen to strike your fancy.

The linguists should revise, further enrich and develop our words in accordance with the basic orientation given above.

Further, everyone should acquire the spirit of using our language correctly through ideological mobilization and mass campaign. Wide publicity should be given by the Party to the need to abstain from using difficult words adopted from Chinese ideographs and to replace them with words that are easily understood by the masses. In our socialist society unlike capitalist society, the Party has only to set the correct orientation for the masses to adopt it at once.

Beginning just after liberation, we have maintained that easy—not difficult— words should be used; nevertheless, there are still many people who use words that are over the heads of the masses.

Some people think that using a great many words borrowed from Chinese ideographs that are incomprehensible to others is a mark of learning, but such people are really nothing but ignoramuses. We must let them know that it is wiser and nobler to speak and write comprehensibly.

In fact, people who are versed in Marxism-Leninism can explain all the theories perfectly well without using difficult words. And those who lack a profound theoretical knowledge are more apt to copy phrases from books and mystify other people by letting loose a long-winded display of difficult words. This is also due partly to their lack of linguistic knowledge. Judging from the fact that even those who have been graduated from institutes of higher learning handle Korean poorly, it would seem that Korean is not properly taught in our schools.

The teaching of the Korean language should be further improved and intensified in all our schools, and its study should also be systematically conducted in all other organizations.

The Korean dictionary should be revised and, in addition, pertinent reference books should be published. Textbooks on our language should be revised and teachers of this subject should be trained in large numbers. All the other textbooks should also be reexamined with a view to revising our spoken and written language.

Through such measures, we must make sure that everyone speaks and writes our language correctly and clearly.

ON THE ORIENTATION OF THE COMPILATION OF AN ENCYCLOPEDIA AND MAPS

Speech Delivered to the Leading Officials in the Sphere of Science and Education, *April 22, 1964*

We have mentioned the necessity of publishing an encyclopedia at the Political Committee of the Party Central Committee and at the meeting of the heads of departments and stressed it on a few other occasions. Again today I should like to say some words on the orientation of the compilation of an encyclopedia.

If we are to correctly define the orientation of this work, we must first know clearly the objectives of the publication of an encyclopedia. The main objective is to give a wide range of general knowledge to the working people concerning politics, economy, science, culture, military affairs and all other spheres and further heighten their political and practical qualifications, so that they can render better service to the revolutionary struggle and the work of construction.

As you all know, we are confronted with three major revolutionary tasks: the first is to complete the building of socialism in the northern half of the Republic; the second, to carry out the south Korean revolution and realize the reunification of the country; the third, to push ahead with world revolution.

In order to successfully step up the revolutionary struggle and the work of construction, it is necessary to constantly raise the political consciousness and technical and practical level of the entire people who are the motive force of the revolution and are taking charge of the work of construction. As we mentioned in the *Theses on the Socialist Rural Question in Our Country,* in order to splendidly build socialism in the northern half of the Republic today, the technical, cultural and ideological revolutions must be accelerated vigorously. The accomplishment of these revolutionary tasks urgently requires a further enhancement of the working people's general political and practical levels, because socialism and communism can be built only through the purposeful struggle and creative labor of millions of the working masses who are politically awakened and well versed in their work. To complete the south Korean revolution and reunify the country or carry out world revolution—to accomplish all our revolutionary tasks—the purposeful struggle of the entire people is indispensable. Without this we cannot win victory. Ignorance brings no success to any work. The more all the working people's political consciousness and technical and practical ability are increased, the more successfully our revolutionary struggle and work of construction will progress. That is why they say knowledge is power.

The basic method to increase the working people's knowledge is to impart to them general as well as special technological knowledge through textbooks at schools of various levels and different training centers.

In our country compulsory secondary education system has long been enforced. As a result, many people have developed into cadres who have the knowledge of middle school graduate standard and above. And our people's general cultural level has also been raised markedly. We have a large army of technicians and specialists several hundred thousand strong. The qualifications of our civil service personnel working at state institutions and the management personnel of factories and enterprises have also improved. Sixty to seventy per cent of them have the knowledge of the middle school graduate standard and above. The level of public security personnel and soldiers of the People's Army is also high.

However, we are not satisfied with this. If we want to achieve the complete victory of socialism and gradually go over to communism, all the working people's knowledge must be raised to that of engineers or specialists. At the present stage of building socialism, the entire people must possess the knowledge of the middle school graduate standard and above. Therefore, not only those who have a high standard of knowledge but also those who have not acquired the knowledge of the middle school graduate must always study to enrich their general and scientific knowledge.

Then, is it possible to send all our working people to school in order to increase their knowledge? It is impossible because we have to build factories and produce goods. Under these circumstances we must make an encyclopedia so that all our working people can study by themselves at every spare moment. Moreover, textbooks alone are not enough to raise their technological and cultural standards. The textbooks only give us an infinitesimal part of the knowledge which we must acquire. Only when they study by themselves with the help of an encyclopedia, can they ceaselessly supplement the knowledge acquired from the textbooks.

In our country the compulsory secondary education had been enforced and the working people's general educational attainments are appreciably high. So, if we provide them with an encyclopedia, it will help them study by themselves as much as they want and will greatly contribute to raising their level of knowledge.

At present, however, we have only foreign encyclopedias but not our own. The foreign encyclopedias do not give us much help. I have seen the Japanese and Soviet encyclopedias. Both of them are entitled "international encyclopedia". But they are compiled with main emphasis on the matters of their own. Both the Japanese and Soviet encyclopedias are devoted to their respective countries. All foreign encyclopedias are edited to meet the demands of their respective countries, so that they have few entries concerning our country and scarce material we need. Moreover, when you consult foreign encyclopedias, you take much time in translating them. Even those who are proficient in foreign languages, may find it easier to read Korean books. Therefore, we cannot enrich our knowledge with foreign encyclopedias. We must compile our own encyclopedia without fail.

Then, in which direction should we compile the encyclopedia? It must be compiled in conformity with our above-mentioned objectives. Namely, it must be so edited as to help all our working people, the motive force of our revolution, acquire political, technological and cultural knowledge through routine self-studies as well as through educational institutions—the knowledge needed to complete the building of socialism in the northern half of the Republic and achieve the victory of the south Korean revolution and the cause of national reunification, strengthen our solidarity with international revolutionary forces and win the final victory of our revolution and, further, propel world revolution.

If we are to compile a good encyclopedia in this general direction so as to meet the requirements of our revolution, we must first adhere to the principle of Juche.

Our encyclopedia must necessarily be compiled from the standpoint of Juche, guaranteeing the interests of our country, the interests of the Korean revolution.

Therefore, we must first compile it in conformity with requirements of socialist construction in the northern half of the Republic.

In order to build socialism in our country with success, we must know well about our Party's history, inherit our revolutionary traditions, develop our national culture and build an independent national economy with our rich resources and techniques. On this basis we must accept foreign things which are acceptable, through necessary political, economic and cultural contacts and interchanges with foreign countries. However, even in this case we must never fall into flunkeyism and dogmatism or take nihilistic attitudes towards our nation.

Therefore, we must base our encyclopedia on our own things; it should be so compiled as to meet our requirements, giving information mainly on our things, while giving some on foreign things. In other words, all information—on fauna, flora, minerals, aquatic products, politics, economy, history, culture, customs, etc.—must basically be ours. A certain degree of foreign information should also be given if it is helpful to the building of socialism in our country.

In making our encyclopedia we must never tolerate any attempt to translate a foreign one and insert our materials in it, instead of basing it on our own information. In its recommendation the Science and Education Department proposed to translate a foreign encyclopedia and include our materials in it. We should not do so. Of course, translating a foreign encyclopedia and copying it may be easy but if we do so, we might commit dogmatist deviations and cannot make an encyclopedia we really need. Though it may be a bit hard, we must make an encyclopedia based on our own materials.

Next, we must compile the encyclopedia in keeping with our tasks of carrying out the south Korean revolution and reunifying the country. The south Korean revolution is a part of the Korean revolution as a whole and the reunification of the country is the greatest national task confronting us now. We must not only vigorously push ahead the building of socialism in the northern half of the Republic but also support the south Korean people and complete the south Korean revolution and achieve the country's reunification. Moreover, we must build socialism and communism throughout Korea. Therefore, the encyclopedia must be compiled for the whole of Korea.

In doing anything we can never exclude the southern half of the Republic. When giving the people information on our country we must not exclude the southern half of the Republic. We must make sure that they know about history, geography, culture and all other spheres of Korea as a whole. Therefore, the encyclopedia should include information not only on the northern half of the Republic but also on everything concerning the southern half.

Further, the encyclopedia should be made in conformity with our duty to strengthen the international solidarity of our revolution.

With whom should we unite to achieve our revolution and, further, hasten world revolution? We must first strengthen our class alliance with the international communist movement, especially, the countries in the socialist camp, its center. Next, we must unite with the anti-imperialist, anti-US, revolutionary forces in Asia, Africa, and Latin America. Therefore, when we include international material in the encyclopedia we have to lay more emphasis on the one concerning the socialist countries rather than the capitalist countries. Geographically, we must not lay main stress on Europe but on Asia, Africa and

Latin America, of which we must attach greater importance to Asian countries, our neighbors. Especially, our encyclopedia must include plenty of information on Southeast Asian countries such as Viet Nam, Cambodia, Laos, Burma and other countries which were colonies before. Foreign encyclopedias have little information on these countries. The Japanese encyclopedia imitates the British or French counterpart, so that it gives centrality to Europe, offering very inadequate information on the former colonies. We must not make our encyclopedia this way. To strengthen our revolution's international solidarity in the future, we will have to have intimate relations with many Southeast Asian countries, former colonies, in the political, economic, cultural and other spheres. So, we had better include a lot of material on these countries in our encyclopedia. Of course, this may be somewhat laborious because we have little material on these countries, but we must collect much information in every way.

As we see, in compiling the encyclopedia we must maintain the principle of Juche and give information mainly on our country to meet the requirements of our revolution. As for materials on foreign countries, we should adopt in the main those which are useful to us and which are directly related to cementing our revolution's international solidarity.

It is also important to adhere to the principle of allegiance to the Party and the working class.

What does it mean to adhere to the principle of allegiance to the Party and the working class in compiling the encyclopedia? It means to analyse and appraise in a Marxist-Leninist way all matters and phenomena of nature and society to be entered into the encyclopedia. Namely, fauna, flora, the movements of the universe and heavenly bodies and other natural phenomena must be correctly analysed and appraised from the dialectical materialist point of view, and social phenomena such as politics, economy, history, culture and art from the viewpoint of historical materialism and the Marxist political economy.

The encyclopedias put out in capitalist countries do not correctly analyse and appraise all matters in a scientific way but in a metaphysical way. The Marxist-Leninist viewpoint differs fundamentally from the idealist, metaphysical viewpoint. We are Communists. Accordingly, we must observe all natural and social matters and phenomena with a firm Marxist-Leninist world outlook. So we must not mechanically copy the encyclopedias prepared by bourgeois scholars in government pay.

You had better edit the encyclopedia in this direction. From this, it must be clear how to compile the encyclopedia.

You must know the Party's requirements for the encyclopedia are high; you must not try to compile it in an easy way. According to the plan submitted by the Science and Education Department you intend to compile the encyclopedia in 1964 and publish all the volumes in two or three years. However, it is impossible to make it so easily. You will need years to collect all data concerning our country. Your plan seems to show that you have set a wrong direction for the compilation of the encyclopedia and miscalculated the work force.

In order to compile a good encyclopedia you must make adequate preparations.

To begin with, you must prepare dictionaries for different realms. First, you had better make various dictionaries such as on politics, economics, physics, chemistry and botany. This may pose a problem of terminology but it will not be a big problem. You may make it clear in the preface of each such dictionary that the terminology may be changed according as our language is revised.

At the same time, you must make a general encyclopedia in three volumes. You had better name it a "general encyclopedia" rather than a "little encyclopedia".

The "general encyclopedia" should deal mainly with information on our country, imparting a general, rough knowledge of fauna, flora, physics, chemistry, mechanics, meteorology and various other realms. It must also include all necessary information on our history, our revolutionary traditions in particular, our culture, customs, geography and philosophy. As regards foreign information, the details had better be given in comparison with ours.

The "general encyclopedia" must be compiled in terms now in use. However, as far as the entries in the complete encyclopedia are concerned, they must be compiled after the terminology is somewhat revised.

It is a good idea to make each of the three volumes of the "general encyclopedia" as thick as the "Central Year Book" or the "Korean Dictionary". This will appreciably enrich the contents. I consider the book can be prepared in two or three years.

We must make a good "general encyclopedia" so that it can fully inform our cadres of most things. As it is designed for our people, the price must be moderate so as to make it available for as many people as possible to broaden their knowledge.

It is not a bad idea to make descriptions of localities in order to compile the encyclopedia. But the question is what to do with factories. Such descriptions will be of no value, if no information is given on the factories. Yet, if we write on the big factories carelessly, military secrets might be divulged. Therefore, it is good to name the factories after the mountains, rivers or heroes without specifying the districts concerned.

Also, as for the localities, you may write about their history and nature but not about their military aspects. Military affairs must not be made public until the country is reunified, so a military affairs subcommittee had better not be set up for the compilation of the encyclopedia. Of course, under entries such as "General Li Sun Sin" military affairs in his days may be mentioned because they have nothing to do with our present-day strategy and tactics. This may be done by the history subcommittee.

In order to compile a good encyclopedia you must devote a lot of time to collecting material on our country. While preparing the specialized dictionaries and the "general encyclopedia" you must gather lots of such material. If you first complete these dictionaries and the comprehensive "general encyclopedia" which contains abundant general information, you may use them as the basis for carrying out the work of determining the entries and the outline of the encyclopedia.

Therefore, after finishing with the specialized dictionaries and the "general encyclopedia", you must base yourselves on them and buckle down to edit the encyclopedia. Then you can do your work easily. If you are to use the dictionaries and "general encyclopedia", you would be able to start preparing the encyclopedia after 1967.

On the completion of the dictionaries and "general encyclopedia" we must make a large encyclopedia in 20 to 30 volumes. It is a good idea to involve many scholars and technicians in this work.

To guarantee the smooth compilation of the encyclopedia, we will see that the Political Committee and the Cabinet adopt a decision respectively with regard to this matter.

Now, let me say a few words about publication of maps.

Now we have no good, handy map. We have neither pocketable map nor atlas our students and cadres can carry in briefcases. All our Korean and world maps are poorly made. Thus, when people want to find a place on the maps, they cannot do so instantly. Yet, we cannot allow them to see military maps, nor can we ask them to carry wall maps with them. Today, world revolution is surging up and many complex problems are arising in various parts on the five continents. They must be feeling very much frustrated because they have no reliable world map.

We need not only official maps but also maps for general use as well. You must make atlases as well as large maps. We should publish many maps for general and mass usage.

As they are not provided with the maps for general usage, our officials do not know common things which they are supposed to know. Some time ago I talked with school teachers and I found that they did not even know what they have in our country. After all, this is because we have not given them maps and various other materials. We must make lots of educational maps and maps for general use and help broaden our functionaries' knowledge.

First, you must make good maps of our country. They must be prepared on both provincial and county basis. The county holds a very important place in our country, and therefore we must make the maps on the county basis. Rivers, forests, roads, factories, mines, enterprises, other industrial establishments as well as historic spots in the county must be clearly marked. It is desirable to show everything needed for general knowledge, except those connected with military secrets. This will help educate our people to love their native places and country.

The maps must also contain all materials on the southern half. The changes in the south Korean administrative units must be marked as they are and the sub-counties shown in the maps.

We must make good world maps as well. They must give fuller and more detailed information on Asia.

As regards the geographical designations of the world map you must use the original ones. However, as for the place name which is not original but which has long been fixed, you had better give it in brackets so that people may understand it. Especially, when using the originals, the geographical designations such as the names of countries and towns must be given as their peoples call them.

In addition, you must be scrupulous in the indication of borderlines on the world map. Many countries are still in dispute over the borderlines, each making territorial claims, so a complex problem might arise in connection with the demarcation. Therefore, it is a good idea to make this point clear in the preface of the atlas. If the border is indistinct you must say so; and where necessary, you must explain that the map has been prepared on the basis of factual data or that it is based on the map of a certain country. Anyhow, as far as the borderline is concerned, you must make sure that no complicated problem arises, by making clear whether it is confirmed or unconfirmed. Of course, when you prepare small maps for general use, the marking of the borderline will not be so difficult.

ON THE TASKS
OF THE LEAGUE OF
SOCIALIST WORKING
YOUTH (Excerpt)

Speech Delivered at the Fifth Congress of the Democratic Youth League, *May 15, 1964*

I.

Comrades,

Youth are the advanced fighters for social progress and the new generation that represents the future of society. Exuberant vitality and fervent energy, courage, fearlessness and persistency constitute their characteristic features. The youth are responsive to what is new, have a strong enterprise, and love justice and truth, for which they fight through thick and thin. Because of these splendid qualities, young people can assume a very important role in the social revolution and in the building of a new society.

However, whether or not the youth can really play a fundamental role in social progress depends on the kind of leadership they receive, their education and training. Only when they are led and educated properly, can all their fine qualities come to the fore. Only then, can they contribute greatly to society and the people and develop into reliable workers representing the future of their country and nation.

In our country it is precisely the Workers' Party of Korea that leads the youth movement, educates young people in progressive ideas and indicates to them the correct road of struggle.

The Workers' Party is the leading force of our people and the General Staff of the Korean revolution. Our Party is a glorious party which has sprung from the deep roots of the anti-Japanese armed struggle. It is an invincible party which has been tried and tested in the course of great revolutionary struggle. By creatively applying Marxism-Leninism to Korean realities, our Party always charts a correct line of struggle for the popular masses and confidently leads them to victory.

Neither freedom and happiness for our people, nor development of the youth movement, nor a brighter future for our youth is thinkable without the leadership of our Party.

Our Korean youth should always be loyal to the leadership of the Workers' Party, wherever and under whatever circumstances they may be working. Party loyalty must be basic to the activities of the youth organizations and all young people of our country.

Party loyalty implies defending and safeguarding the Party, rallying firmly around it and fighting through thick and thin to put all its lines and policies into practice.

The LSWY should establish the Party's ideological system more thoroughly in all of its organizations, from the Central Committee to the primary organizations, and among all young people, and rally them more closely around the Party. Our youth should resolutely defend the lines and policies of the Party, persistently endeavor for the execution of its policies and devote all their youthful energies and talents to carrying them through to the end.

Our youth are the Workers' Party's reserve and the future masters of our country. The further advancement of our revolution and future of our country rest with them. When the youth grow into the Party's Red fighters, fully qualified politically and ideologically, our revolutionary cause will continue to advance vigorously and our country will become more prosperous.

The political and ideological education of the youth acquires greater importance today especially in view of the historical epoch in which our younger generation is living and of the momentous mission to be entrusted to them.

Our youth are living in the most glorious age in our country's history, an age that began with the bloody struggle of the anti-Japanese guerrillas and was brought into bloom by our Party and people through their heroic struggle. You are living in an age in which our society is being remolded along revolutionary lines and the centuries-old backwardness and poverty of the country being abolished to make a leap forward along the road of progress and civilization, an age of great struggle for the complete liberation of our nation and the building of a unified, independent and prosperous country.

Our youth are young revolutionary fighters and young builders born in this great age and creating a new and glorious history of the country. Our younger generation is entrusted with the sacred task of carrying forward the brilliant revolutionary traditions and achievements of the struggles born of the Korean communist movement from the time of the anti-Japanese armed struggle to present socialist construction, and of ensuring the complete victory of socialism and communism in Korea. The youth can fulfill this lofty historic mission devolving on them only when they are politically and ideologically well prepared.

Therefore, the most central task of the LSWY should be the political and ideological education of the youth.

Above all, the youth should be armed firmly with the ever-victorious Marxist-Leninist theory as well as our Party's ideology and purpose.

Marxism-Leninism is the theory of scientific communism and the guiding ideology of our Party. Only with a knowledge of Marxism-Leninism can a correct judgment of the ever-changing national and international situation be formed and the correct path be found to the victory of the revolution, and the struggle be unwaveringly sustained with firm confidence in the socialist and communist future, however complex and difficult the circumstances. Our youth should make tireless efforts to learn the great theory of Marxism-Leninism and acquire the communist world outlook.

Marxism has been developed and enriched in the struggle against all varieties of reactionary bourgeois ideology and opportunism. The struggle between Marxism-Leninism and various ideological trends antagonistic to it is the expression of the class struggle in modern society—a struggle that will continue as long as the class struggle exists. Therefore, the struggle for Marxist-Leninist knowledge is not a mere theoretical pursuit but a sharp ideological struggle.

In the international communist movement today, revisionism has appeared and is frantically attacking Marxism-Leninism. The modern revisionists, like all revisionists in the past, are trying to castrate the revolutionary essence of Marxism-Leninism and replace it with Right opportunism. Complying with the demands of the imperialists, they themselves have not only given up revolution, but are out to prevent others from making revolution. Placing their hopes especially on those youths who lack Marxist-Leninist culture and revolutionary tempering, the modern revisionists attempt to spread the poison of opportunism among them and disarm and corrupt them ideologically.

The Youth League should further strengthen the ideological struggle to bar the revisionist trend from infiltrating the ranks of the youth movement in our country. The vigorous pursuit of Marxist-Leninist education for youth must embrace the anti-revisionist struggle, in order to enable our youth to discern clearly for themselves what true Marxism-Leninism is and what revisionism, in order that they will firmly oppose revisionism and defend the purity of Marxism-Leninism.

To master Marxism-Leninism means to grasp the essence of this theory and know how to apply it in revolutionary practice. We should learn the ideology and methodology of Marxism-Leninism so that we can apply Marxism-Leninism in our revolutionary practice. We should make a profound study of this theory in combination with the realities of our country, the strategy and tactics of our revolution and our day-to-day work, and turn it into our powerful ideological and theoretical weapon for revolutionary struggle and constructive work.

A struggle against dogmatism must be waged in the study of Marxist-Leninist theory and the experience of the international communist movement.

The dogmatist tries to swallow the experience of other countries whole and copy it mechanically. He neither studies the national characteristics and historical conditions of his own country nor endeavors to apply Marxism-Leninism creatively in conformity to the actual conditions of his own country. If one slides into dogmatism and loses his independence, he will, eventually, tend to rely only on others, losing faith in his own strength, and blindly imitate what others do, failing to distinguish right from wrong.

Our youth should oppose dogmatism and establish Juche more thoroughly in raising their ideological and theoretical levels as well as in practical work. The study of our country's past and present and the history of the struggle of our people should be strengthened among the youth, and their sense of national independence and their national pride should be further stimulated.

The basic task of Korean youth is to complete the Korean revolution and build socialism and communism in Korea. To fulfill this task, our youth must study profoundly the universal truth of Marxism-Leninism and, along with it, the lines and policies of our Party which are its creative application to Korean realities.

Only through the study of our Party's lines and policies can the correct strategy and tactics of the Korean revolution be grasped and the correct path be found in all our work. A thorough knowledge of the Party's lines and policies is essential for thinking and acting in pursuance of Party objectives, for acquiring confidence and developing a fighting spirit and enthusiasm in the struggle to carry out the Party's policies.

Our youth should constantly study the lines and policies of the Party to grasp the essence of its policies and deeply realize their correctness and vitality. Thus we should see to it that the Party's lines and policies become the ideas and the firm conviction of the youth themselves and serve as the guide to all their activities.

What is particularly important in the ideological education of the new generation is class education and education in the revolutionary traditions.

Today a fierce class struggle is being waged on a world-wide scale between the international working class and the reactionary forces of imperialism. The class struggle continues in socialist society, too. In particular, our country is divided into the north and the south, and we are struggling for the completion of the national-liberation revolution while building socialism, in direct confrontation with US imperialism, the chieftain of world reaction.

We must not become complacent on the ground that the socialist system has already triumphed, that the exploiting classes have been abolished and our standard of living has improved in the northern half of the Republic. Rather we must further strengthen class education and education in the revolutionary traditions among the entire working people, particularly among the rising generation.

The young people should know how ruthlessly the imperialists, landlords and capitalists oppressed and exploited their parents in the past, and they should not forget that even now the people in south Korea are undergoing indescribable suffering under the reactionary rule of the US imperialists and their stooges. The youth should be fully cognizant of the aggressive and predatory acts committed everywhere in the world by the imperialists headed by the US imperialists, of the plight of the peoples who have not yet been liberated.

Our youth should at all times deeply study the glorious revolutionary traditions built up by the anti-Japanese guerrillas and their struggle achievements and learn from their lofty revolutionary spirit. The more their conditions of life are improved, the more deeply our youth should bear in mind that our socialist system and new, happy life are precious gains won by the arduous struggle and enormous sacrifices of their revolutionary forerunners.

Thus, the entire youth should fully realize the aggressive nature of imperialism and the exploiting nature of the landlord and capitalist classes, hate them more fiercely and fight more staunchly against imperialism and the exploiting system. All our youth should fortify themselves firmly with ardent ideas of socialist patriotism and with the spirit of proletarian internationalism.

It is important to educate the youth in the revolutionary spirit of self-reliance and an indomitable fighting spirit.

We must be prepared to defend the revolutionary gains and achieve the complete reunification and independence of the country by our own efforts, and to build socialism and communism in our country with our own labor and internal resources. The youth should bring into fuller play their spirit of self-reliance to seek out what is in short supply, produce what is wanting, and courageously surmount all difficulties. The revolutionary attitude towards work and the revolutionary mode of life should be established more thoroughly among the young people.

It is a characteristic of the youth to cherish great ambition and ideals and fight passionately for them. The youth should be educated in the spirit of loving the future and always be inspired to fight on gallantly with burning aspiration for the socialist and communist tomorrow and with a firm confidence in victory. Each place they work, each place they study and each place they live should glow with the passion of youth, be permeated with revolutionary optimism and marked by a bright and lively atmosphere.

All youth should thus become communist fighters who are infinitely loyal to the Party and the revolution and creditably fulfill the revolutionary tasks set by the Party.

ON CREATING REVOLUTIONARY LITERATURE AND ART

Speech to Workers in the Field of Literature and Art, *November 7, 1964*

Big progress has been made of late in the field of film and drama art. Especially, great achievements have been gained in the film art. There are quite a few good films among those produced last year. *Red Flower, Spinner* and *Zinnia* are all excellent.

It was a big shortcoming that we had no film depicting the life of the working class and their struggle for production. But recently, films of this kind have been coming out in great numbers. This is a very good thing. *Defenders of Height 1211* and *Women of Namgang Village* produced by the February 8 Film Studio, too, can be considered good pieces. A few days ago, I saw the film *A People's Teacher,* and I think its content is very good. The documentary film *Long Live the Banner of the Republic* is also very well handled.

Such achievements made by the film art should be ascribed first of all to the improvement in the quality of script-writing.

While good results have been scored in the field of literature and art, there is one serious shortcoming. That is, the literary and art works deal very little with the life and struggle of the people in the southern half.

Our Party has always emphasized that the liberation of 20 million compatriots in the southern half is not only a job for the people in the south themselves but also a revolutionary task for the people of the northern half as well.

As I said at the Eighth Plenary Meeting of the Fourth Party Central Committee, to liberate the people of the southern half from US imperialist oppression and reunify the country, we should do our work well in three ways.

First, the revolutionary forces of the southern half should be strengthened. Since the revolution there is above all the work of the southern people themselves, they should be aroused to rise up in order to win the revolution. We should awaken them so that they will rise and settle their problems. However good the plan for reunification we may draw up here in north Korea, reunification cannot be achieved as long as the people in the southern half do not get moving.

Second, to complete the south Korean revolution and reunify the fatherland, the revolutionary base should be fortified in all political, economic, cultural and military fields by carrying out socialist construction in the northern half successfully.

Third, we should unite with the international revolutionary forces and thoroughly isolate US imperialism, and struggles should be waged against US imperialism everywhere in the world. To unite with the international revolutionary forces means to unite with the working class of the world, to unite with the socialist camp and to cement solidarity with the national-liberation movements of various countries. We have made great efforts in this direction.

We should thus strengthen both the revolutionary forces of north and south Korea and the international revolutionary forces in order to accomplish the south Korean revolution and attain the reunification of the country. But, however the north Korean revolutionary forces and the international revolutionary forces may be strengthened, the revolution cannot be carried out in south Korea without strengthening the south Korean revolutionary forces. Hence, it is important to reinforce the revolutionary forces of the southern half.

For the strengthening of the revolutionary forces of the

southern half, we should first of all persistently carry on political and propaganda-educational work among the people of the northern half so as to stimulate their concern for the life and struggle of the south Korean people and make them regard the south Korean revolution as a vital revolutionary task of their own. We must bear in mind that such political and propaganda-educational work for the people of the northern half is closely linked with the political work for the south which is aimed at awakening the south Korean people.

The more the north Korean people are resolved to save the south Korean brothers, the more our forces will be reinforced to fight for the liberation of the south Korean people and the more the south Korean people will be inspired. Further, such political and propaganda-educational work among the north Korean people is also in the interest of the south Korean people.

If we do not educate the people of the northern half in the revolutionary spirit, they will rest content with the results of construction already made, thus losing the fighting spirit of continued advance and forgetting the revolutionary task of liberating the southern half. That is why the Eighth Plenary Meeting of the Fourth Party Central Committee decided to take all possible means not only to intensify political activities in south Korea but also to conduct the work properly with those coming from the southern half and step up the revolutionary education among the people of the northern half.

The literary and art workers engaged in such fields as literature, cinema, drama, music and dance have a very great role to play in educating people in a revolutionary spirit. Our literature and art should serve not only socialist construction in the northern half, but the struggle of the whole Korean people for the south Korean revolution and the reunification of the fatherland. But our literature and art still fail to meet the demands of our revolution. We should have good literary works or films for the education of the south Korean revolutionaries, but we have very few.

The present situation in south Korea is very good. The intellectuals there are working very well. They demand an independent reunification free from foreign interference. They do not fight directly against the Yankees because they are still afraid of them. We should persist in our efforts to encourage the south Korean people to fight, holding aloft the slogan of anti-US struggle.

You should exert yourselves to create literary and art works that teach the south Koreans the methods of revolutionary struggle, boost their revolutionary zeal and raise their class consciousness. Literature and art which sing the praises of socialism are necessary, of course. They are not only necessary, but better works and in large numbers. But what we lack very much and need urgently now are works of literature and art that will educate the people and revolutionaries of the southern half, that will educate the people of the northern half in the revolutionary spirit.

With a view to contributing to the education of the people with our revolutionary traditions, you have produced quite a few works of literature and art which depict the anti-Japanese guerrilla struggle. This is certainly necessary since the anti-Japanese guerrilla struggle is the root of our revolutionary movement. You should increase the output of such works in the future. But in my opinion it is too narrow to limit the scope of education of our revolutionary traditions to the anti-Japanese guerrilla struggle. The time has now come to widen the scope of education in these traditions. Revolutionary struggles have been going on for 20 years since liberation. Why should the 15 years of anti-Japanese guerrilla struggle alone represent our revolutionary struggle? The struggles for the establishment of the people's power, for the agrarian reform, for the nationalization of industries and for the building of the Party, the Fatherland Liberation War against the Yankee aggression—all these were arduous revolutionary struggles.

More people took part in the three-year-long Fatherland Liberation War than in the anti-Japanese guerrilla struggle. The Fatherland Liberation War was literally an all-people's war in which all classes and strata of our society took part. The workers, peasants and intellectuals all fought valiantly, not fearing sacrifice. Men of literature and art should create works which portray such struggles. Not long ago, the February 8 Film Studio produced the films *Song of the Transport Fighters* and *Women of Namgang Village*. You should produce more of such pieces. Why should only the transport fighters or the women of Namgang village be chosen as heroic fighters?

The Fatherland Liberation War produced a great many people's heroes. Many people had gone as far as the River Rakdong-gang and came back to the heart of our Party, back to the revolutionary ranks by trekking over the mountains and crossing the rivers in the teeth of all hardships. This arduous retreat was, so to speak, a Long March. Why shouldn't we be proud of those who had gone as far as the River Rakdong-gang and came back, as revolutionaries? There is every reason to consider them revolutionaries. They certainly deserve to feel proud of their participation in the great revolutionary struggle.

You should, of course, keep on writing about the revolutionary struggles before liberation, but you should write more about the innumerable heroic feats and inspiring events that took place during the post-liberation revolutionary struggles. Only by so doing can you imbue the growing revolutionary fighters with a sense of honor, encourage them to fresh exploits and train more revolutionaries.

As I have already said time and again, if we want to have our country fully reunified, the people in the southern half should wage a revolutionary struggle and drive the Yankees out. Of course, it is not an easy task to force them out. However, if the revolutionaries in the southern half conduct the work of Party building well and organize the struggle of the south Korean people properly, the American scoundrels can be forced out and their puppets smashed definitely. Then the reunification of the country can be materialized in a peaceful way. Our policy of peaceful reunification is to achieve reunification precisely in that way. It can also be achieved in a different way, through war. If the American scoundrels unleash a war against us, we will have to drive the aggressors out by force of arms. In that case, they will meet with the armed counteroffensive of the entire Korean people in the north and south. Why shouldn't we arm the people of the southern half when the Yankees attack us by force of arms?

No matter in what way Korea be reunified, it is most important to educate the north and south Korean people constantly in the revolutionary spirit. Writers and artists should depict in their works of literature and art not only the experience of the revolutionary struggles of bygone days and the struggles for the revolution and construction in the northern half, but also the struggle of the people and revolutionaries of the southern half.

The southern half has many excellent experiences and heroic deeds in struggle to draw on. Why can't you describe them? Take the October Popular Resistance, for example. It does not matter who guided it. Though Pak Hon Yong ruined that struggle, the history of the valiant struggle of the people cannot be blotted out. You can also write about the cause of the failure of this heroic struggle of the people. And what glorious and gallant struggles the April 19 Popular Uprising and the June Third Demonstration Struggle were! You should write stories, produce films and compose songs about such struggles. You should write forceful works that can inspire the south Korean youth and students to fight the Yankees to the death after they read them. In our country there are so many heroic deeds performed by numerous revolutionaries in their struggle. You should create many works of literature and art, including films and novels, on the basis of such materials.

Recently I have heard of a certain comrade fighting in south Korea. The story of the tremendous struggle he has waged would fill a large volume. Even though he lost contact with the revolutionary organization, he continued to fight up until now without a day's letup. The deed of this comrade is really worthy of high praise not only in respect to the duration of his struggle but in its import. If you write a story based on such themes, it will become a fine textbook for the revolutionization of south Korean youths and students. Needless to say, it will also be good educational material for our young folks in the northern half.

You should write not only about the post-liberation struggle of the south Korean people, but also about their struggle in the pre-liberation days. The Kwangju Student Incident, for instance, can offer a nice plot. At one time Pak Chang Ok tried to ban even the commemoration of this event and also that of the March First Movement. As historical subjects, you can choose similar events from the history of the anti-Japanese, anti-US struggles of the people.

You should give as much educational material as you can to the revolutionaries and patriots of the southern half. It is all the more necessary to give the comrades fighting in the southern half plenty of literary and art works depicting their struggle in the southern half, their joys and sorrows, and their life rather than those about socialist construction in the northern half. We have done very little in this respect. As to the films, for instance, *A People's Teacher* is a good story, but the hero's splendid career comes to an end with his devoted participation in socialist construction. The question of the revolution in the southern half and the question of the country's reunification are not treated. However excellent in itself, this kind of film does not meet the needs of the revolutionaries in the southern half or answer their questions.

It is the foremost revolutionary task of our Party to reunify the country. That is explicitly provided for in the Party Rules. Our literature and art can never swerve from this revolutionary task of the Party.

At present, many good comrades are imprisoned in south Korea. We must imbue those comrades behind bars with confidence. They are waiting for the south Korean people to rise up in struggle and open the prison gates. They watch how the situation is changing, every day and every hour. We should give them hope and let them know that those who shed blood and fall in their fight in south Korea will leave their mark on the glorious history of our revolution. Only then will they fight bravely and unflinchingly in prison or on the scaffold, and a huge army of revolutionaries will follow them unceasingly into the scene of struggle.

How can we face the comrades of the southern half, if we do not produce revolutionary works of literature and art to encourage the revolutionaries in the southern half, although we have excellent paper mills, fine publishing houses and a detachment of hundreds of, thousands of writers and artists?

Our writers could write masterpieces with those already dead or still living, as models. You should not write a biography about a living person. That cannot impress people very much. Suppose you decide to write. You could produce a masterpiece using as models those comrades who fought on their missions given by the Revolutionary Army before liberation. The struggle of those comrades of the Poeple's Revolutionary Army in the pre-liberation days, their indefatigable battle in prison, arrested by the enemy during underground activities in the homeland while on revolutionary missions; the impressive reunion of long-separated comrades following

liberation and their subsequent devoted struggle for the
building of the party and for the founding of the power and the
armed forces, their amazing activities in the Fatherland
Liberation War, their arduous retreating operations after advancing as far as the River Rakdong-gang, breaking through
enemy encirclement, and their struggle for the postwar
rehabilitation and construction—these great historic events
could be your plot to portray the typical image of the heroes
growing up in the midst of the struggles along with the
development of the Korean revolution. There is your masterpiece! Only with such writings, will you be able to make people
realize that revolution is something full of ups and downs,
educate them in the spirit of revolutionary romanticism and
give hope and courage to our comrades in prison.

To cite an instance, you can write a fine work with Comrade
Kim Chaek as a model, I think. His struggle in Manchuria, his
prison-life in Seoul, his return to the organization after his
prison term to resume his struggle, his second jail-life in Kirin,
his guerrilla warfare thereafter—what an arduous and glorious
revolutionary life all this shows! When Comrade Kim Chaek
left the Sodaemun Prison, he had no money for the trip, so he
went to Comrade Ho Hon, who had volunteered to defend him
in court, and got 1 *won* and 20 or 60 *chon* in the currency of
that time, and came back to Chientao. Even now I am moved
to tears whenever I recall the scene of his reunion with his son
in Pyongyang after liberation. At that time he said to me:
"This boy hesitated to come in because he is barefooted. So I
told him, 'The General won't think ill of you for your bare feet.
Do you think the General would be pleased if you came to him
as a well-off dandy in Western clothes? I rather like you bare-
foot. Let's get in.' So, I persuaded him, and brought him in."
Why doesn't such an impressive anecdote move the hearts of
writers and artists?

You should demonstrate through your works that the life of
a revolutionary is arduous but one can live that way once he is
resolved. Especially, we should educate our young folks in the
spirit of revolutionary optimism.

When we visited the People's Army units on the occasion of
February 8 last year, we were bitterly sorry that young people
now did not know the hardships of life and did not know how
their parents and elders had suffered before. Our young

soldiers do not know well what straw sandals are, what farm rent is and what a farm hand is. A young man twenty-five years old now would have greeted the liberation at the age of six, and he has no clear idea of what the old society was like. If he has any idea of it, that is by and large but a scintilla of knowledge that he got from books. You should not forget that if we do not properly educate the new generation, our youth may lose the revolutionary spirit and become useless people who want to live in idleness.

We cannot carry out the revolution with the youth who understand nothing of landlords and capitalists. At present, most of the company commanders of our army have combat experience, but platoon leaders have no experience in battle. The makeup of cadres in our army has already changed to such an extent. Nevertheless, the cadres upwards of company, battalion and regimental commanders have tasted the bitterness of life and have battle experience. We should achieve the country's reunification before our cadres get too old. Anyway, we should not leave the task of reunifying the country to posterity.

All kinds of art are necessary for the education of our working people and young folks, but stress should be laid on novels and films. Above all, we should produce a lot of good films.

Now, I would like to say a few words about producing revolutionary songs.

At the time of guerrilla struggle, when we composed a revolutionary song, even the puppet Manchukuo Army soldiers sang it, to say nothing of the peasants. We did not know much about setting songs to music, and when we were busy we wrote only the words and sang it to old tunes. But still the people liked singing such songs. If you comrades compose a good song, men of the "ROK army" in south Korea will sing it, and so will the south Korean students.

The workers in the field of music should further develop our national music to suit the sentiments and aspirations of the socialist builders.

Almost all the songs which have come out during the last few years are good ones. How excellent the songs such as *O Blizzard, Blizzard* and *To a Decisive Battle* are! These songs are beautiful and yet august enough to arouse people to the revolutionary struggle. Songs like *Pochonbo, The Land of*

Glory; Amnok-gang River, Two Thousand ri; and *At the Well Side* for women's chorus are rich in Korean melody and suit the feelings of our people. *Bumper Year on Chongsan-ri Plain* seems to be the best of all pieces produced recently. This song, which is Korean through and through in its melody, fully reflects the spirit of the day. The militant spirit of our working people rushing ahead in the saddle of Chollima and their optimistic emotions full of confidence in victory are well expressed in the song. Our modern music must continue to follow this path.

As a whole our music is developing now in a sound and correct way. If it continues to advance in that direction, I think it would be quite acceptable. However, we should make still greater efforts to develop even further our own national music in conformity with the realities of the day.

Our music must be Korean in essence and it should suit the feelings of our people.

Our people do not like the pure European music which is alien to their sentiments.

Though our light music smacks considerably of old-fashioned crooning, people like it because it is Korean in essence. It is not fortuitous that Comrade Kim Jong Dok's songs enjoy popularity. His songs are somewhat crooned, but they are rich in Korean melody, cheerful and optimistic.

There are quite a few croon-type tunes among the songs made by our people at the time of Japanese imperialist rule. Of course, decadent crooning tunes are bad. But we can continue to sing those croon-type songs which are not degenerate but are somewhat cheerful, inheriting the forms of Korean folk songs. Because, under the vicious Japanese imperialist colonial rule of almost half a century, our people made and sang many songs deploring the corrupt society of the time, not a few of them being croon-type songs. The songs which the healthy-minded masses are fond of singing are certainly good ones. Songs which have inherited the forms of folk songs and which the masses like should be developed even though they smack of old-fashioned crooning.

As regards our national music, you had better develop mainly folk songs. Our folk songs should be compatible with the emotions of today's youth. *Ulsan Ballad* and *Moranbong* have really pleasant melodies. You should compose songs like these in large numbers. It is better to sing folk-style songs in chorus than solo.

Our classical operas, too, should have their roots in folk songs. *A New Song Flows out of the Village across the River*, which is based on folk songs of the western provinces, appeals to me very much. It seems to be advisable to develop the national music after this pattern.

Pansori lacks interest since it is too old-fashioned. The ballads of the southern provinces are what *ryangban* would chant over wine cups in those days when they used to wear horse-hair hats and get about on the donkey's back. These songs are not fit for our times. The youth nowadays do not like them. When listening to the radio, young people switch it off if *pansori* comes on. *Pansori* does not inspire the people nor arouse them to struggle. It is utterly ridiculous to imagine soldiers rushing into battle inspired by *pansori*. It is unthinkable that songs, which the aristocrats of old days used to sing while drinking, could suit the emotions of our youth who are building socialism.

Of course, I do not mean to say that you should not sing *pansori* at all. It is not bad to know that in former days there were also songs of this sort. So it would be a good thing to retain one *pansori* singer out of a hundred. We should preserve *pansori* but there is no need to encourage it.

Some comrades assert that the ballads of the southern provinces should be the basis of the national music. That is wrong. The ballads of the southern provinces are the songs of *ryangban* of the old days and, in addition, they are sung with croaky sounds unpleasant to the ear. It is entirely opposed to natural vocalization. *A New Song Flows out of the Village across the River* and *Popsongpo Boatmen's Song* are all free from croaky sounds and are really pleasant to listen to.

Koreans generally have beautiful voices, and it is really terrible to hear a good-looking girl make hoarse sounds. You may be able to stand the hoarse noise of a man or Chun Hyang's old mother, but it simply makes you really sick to hear Chun Hyang utter such tones. One of the main reasons why our classical operas, including the *Tale of Chun Hyang*, are not popular among the people is that they are being hoarsely chanted in the ballad form of the southern provinces.

Contrary to the opinion of some, it is wrong to consider this husky noise a vocalization suitable for our national melody. It is not natural but artificial. Young people nowadays neither sing in this hoarse style nor do they like it. There is no need to argue about the traditional or modern vocalization. If you produce a natural and yet beautiful tone to conform with the national melody and feelings, that is good. You should choose vocalizations which permit natural, mellow and beautiful tones. The husky noise should decidedly be eliminated from our vocalism.

Some comrades insist that the State Art Theater and the National Art Theater should not go in the same direction and that the latter should preserve the husky-style songs. If it really does, it will have to be called National Classical Art Theater instead of National Art Theater, and only those who make husky sounds should be gathered there. The National Art Theater should go forward, it cannot remain behind.

To modernize our national music, we should also consider the problem of further developing the instruments.

A shortcoming of our national instruments is that they produce croaky sounds. It seems that since the croaky voice was used in *chang*, the instruments were made to suit it. Some comrades are against improving the national instruments, but there is a need to do so. With the unimproved Korean traditional instruments, we can neither modernize the national music nor fully express the sentiments of the people of our age.

After all, national instruments are appropriate for folk songs. It is excellent to have *Moranbong* performed with national instruments.

You should not jump to the conclusion that the Korean instruments are not suitable for marches, just because they are fit for folk songs. You can inspire the people adequately even with national instruments.

Some comrades say that Korean music cannot be performed with European instruments, but that is quite incorrect. *Bumper Year on Chongsan-ri Plain* is Korean in essence. But it sounds excellent when performed with European instruments. For this piece, which gives you a fresh, keyed-up feeling, European instruments are just right. When you combine the European instruments with the national ones like *saenap* and *ggwaeng-gwari*, it is even better. I think it is a good step to take.

It is also not at all bad to accompany Korean songs with light music. It is fine to play the Korean music on the violin or piano. At present there are few Korean tunes written for piano; consequently you take it as a matter of course to start with the European numbers when you come to study the piano. It is all right to learn European music, but you should learn Korean music first.

You should not play only European strains with European instruments. If you do not play Korean music, European instruments will be rejected by the people in the end.

We should make use of European instruments for the development of our national music. You should not subordinate Korean music to European instruments, but European instruments to Korean music.

You should compose lots of good music with Korean roots that can be performed with European instruments. The secret is in the composition. You should turn out plenty of music rich in Korean idiosyncrasy and prepare schools for European instruments.

Our music should express the sentiment of the day, regardless of whether it is for European or for national instruments. The sentiment of the people changes with the times. Songs in the *sijo* style chanted by learned men of the old days in the drawing room, do not suit the reality of today. We must develop our music to harmonize with the feelings of our working people who are building socialism.

We should not carry over the same ancient tunes that are out of keeping with the sentiments of our people today. Development of national music has nothing to do with restorationism.

You should not worship the classics too much on the grounds that things Korean must be treasured and promoted in music. Do you think young people of today would like it if you put horse-hair hats on their heads?

Since songs of the old days are all, by and large, based on Chinese poetry, they are difficult to chant and unintelligible for the young folks of today. There is no need to retain them as they are. We ought to rewrite the Chinese verses into simpler language and modernize them. However assiduously you may copy the old, it is of no use if the masses do not like it. We should not strive to imitate the old material as it is, but direct our energies to remolding and developing the valuable heritage our people have created over many centuries, in conformity with the sentiments of the people of our age.

The national music department of the Conservatory should be reinforced so as to train more students specializing in folk songs and national instruments. We should, in this way, endeavor to modernize our national music and develop it in keeping with our times.

Music, like all other art, should serve the masses of the people. We should develop our music basing it on our national melodies. After all, this makes for the creation of a music which the masses of the people can understand and enjoy. As far as we are concerned, there is no place for the so-called music for music's sake which only some experts can understand, or for the degenerate music which is to the liking of the exploiting classes. We should reject all the decadent bourgeois music which dulls the revolutionary consciousness of the popular masses. We should categorically reject music that makes crazy noises out of the abyss of sentimentality and sorrow, or leads man's mind to obscenity.

We should never allow the penetration of "jazz" in the future as in the past. It depraves and emasculates the youth and dulls their revolutionary consciousness. "Jazz" is an ideological weapon of the imperialists to degenerate revolutionary peoples. How can we accept the venom they direct at us, and by so doing destroy our own positions, when we have to fight US imperialism to the end? We should thoroughly reject "jazz."

Our music should always be revolutionary as well as national.

I suggest that literary and art works about socialist reconstruction and the revolutionary struggle be represented in our creative endeavors at a ratio of five to five. And as for those dealing with the revolutionary struggle, I think it would be right to make those of north Korea and south Korea about four to one.

A few words about the question of our writers and artists going to the countryside. Actors and actresses should not coop themselves up in Pyongyang all the time but should also perform in rural areas. The arrangements should not be made as if there were separate categories of performers for Pyongyang and for the countryside.

Writers and artists will become bureaucrats or aristocrats far removed from the people after all, if they just stay in Pyongyang. Then, the writers and artists will lose contact with the reality of our country, backslide and seek comforts. Actors can develop in the mainstream of life only when they go out to the countryside. If they go out to the countryside, they can see the thatch-roofed houses still left over and the peasants engaged in hard work. In this course, they will naturally stop thinking about the easy life, live simply and have the will to fight. All artists must, without exception, go and see the countryside.

If the writers and artists do not mix with the masses, become one with them and learn from them perseveringly, they will become aristocrats and bureaucrats, and be unable to make any contribution to our revolutionary work. Our writers and artists should become revolutionary writers and artists who faithfully serve the workers and peasants, who always get in touch with the workers and peasants, unite with them and know how to find the source of their inexhaustible creative talents.

REPLY TO THE LETTER OF THE PRESIDENT OF THE KOREAN AFFAIRS INSTITUTE IN WASHINGTON

January 8, 1965

I have received your letter. It gives me great pleasure to learn that you are deeply concerned about the question of reunifying the country.

As you know, our nation has been a victim of territorial partition and national division already for 20 years.

Although a new generation has grown up, there has not even been established contact and travel between north and south Korea, to say nothing of the reunification of the country, the long-cherished aspiration of the nation, and the artificial barrier of national partition remains unchanged.

As the days go by, the gap between the north and the south is growing wider in all spheres of political, economic and cultural life, and even the national characteristics common to our people, a homogenous nation formed through a long history, are gradually becoming differentiated.

The division of the nation rules out the possibility of coordinated mobilization and use of the national wealth and the strength of the people for the development of the country; it brings unbearable sufferings to all Korean people.

The division of Korea into north and south brings immeasurable miseries and misfortunes, particularly to the people's living in south Korea.

The prosperity of the whole nation cannot be expected and the people in south Korea cannot be rescued from their wretched plight unless the division of our country is terminated and reunification is achieved.

It is natural that in south Korea today, the broad masses of the people are crying out that they cannot live unless the country is reunified, and many public figures with national conscience are fighting courageously for the reunification of the country.

Reunification of the country is an urgent national task which cannot be postponed any longer.

It is high time, we believe, for all Koreans without exception, who are patriotic and concerned about the future of the nation, to do their utmost to reunify the country.

The whole world knows that our Government, expressing the universal desire and will of the entire Korean people, has made persevering efforts to achieve the reunification of the country.

We consider that the solution of the reunification question must not be obstructed by the interests of any party, grouping or privileged circle at the expense of the national interests, and that reunification must in any case be accomplished in a democratic way, in accordance with the general will of the entire Korean people, and not by one side forcing its will on the other side. We do not allow anyone to impose his will upon us and we, on our part, do not intend to force our will on others. We have always maintained that the authorities, political parties, social organizations and individual personalities of north and south Korea should sit down together and negotiate sincerely and openheartedly to solve the question of reunification.

I make it clear once again that, just as we have done up to now, so in the future as well, our Government will exert every effort to achieve the reunification of the country in conformity with the desire of the people and the national interests, and that it is ready to accept anyone's opinion, if it is helpful towards the solution of the reunification question.

In your letter you set forth views that have many points in common with a number of proposals we have already made time and again for the settlement of the question of reunifying the country.

As we have always maintained, the reunification of the country must be carried out in accord with the principles of independence and democracy, and in a peaceful way, without the interference of any outside forces.

We consider that any attempt to reunify the country by relying on outside forces is nothing but an illusion and is designed to leave the whole of Korea in the hands of the imperialist aggressors.

The question of Korean reunification is an internal affair of the Korean people which admits no interference from outside forces. The Korean question must be settled by the Koreans themselves. Foreigners are not in a position to solve the internal affairs of our nation.

Ours is a resourceful and civilized nation, fully capable of solving its national problem by itself.

The basic obstacle to the country's reunification is the US imperialists who are occupying south Korea militarily, interfering in our domestic affairs, carrying out a policy of dividing our nation, and pursuing an aggressive policy against the whole of Korea.

The US imperialists have brought south Korea completely under their colonial domination in all political, economic, military and cultural fields and brought utter ruin to the life of its people.

Withdrawal of all foreign troops from south Korea is the prerequisite to the solution of the question of reunification.

In north Korea there are absolutely no foreign troops. The Chinese People's Volunteers withdrew completely from north Korea on their own initiative as early as 1958.

However, the US army in the guise of the United Nations is stationed in south Korea.

The United States has no ground or excuse whatsoever to station its army in south Korea.

There can be no independence or sovereignty as long as a foreign army of aggression is stationed on one's territory.

Any people who have the least spark of national conscience

ought to demand the withdrawal of the US troops and work to expel them from our territory.

We must stir up the indignation of the entire nation against the US imperialist aggressors and mobilize all the patriotic forces in the struggle to drive the US army out of south Korea.

Your proposal that all foreign troops should be withdrawn in order to solve the question of Korean reunification is a just one.

It is our consistent view that the question of Korean reunification should be solved through the establishment of a unified central government embracing representatives of people of all classes and strata, through free north-south general elections to be held in a democratic way, without interference by any outside forces, after the withdrawal of all foreign troops from south Korea.

Such general elections should be held in a completely free and democratic atmosphere, without any conditions that might hamper or repress, even slightly, the expression of the will of the people. Free, democratic elections are inconceivable as long as the democratic rights of the people are being violated and patriotic movements suppressed.

To hold free north-south general elections, there should first be full guarantees of complete freedom of political activity for all the political parties, social organizations and individual personalities, as well as freedom of speech, the press, assembly, association and demonstration, throughout north and south Korea. All the political prisoners who have been arrested and imprisoned for having demanded democratic liberties and the country's independent reunification should be set free unconditionally.

All citizens should have equal rights to elect and to be elected at any place throughout Korea, regardless of party affiliation, political views, property status, education, religious faith or sex.

Only through such genuinely democratic elections based on the principles of universal, equal and direct suffrage by secret ballot, can a unified independent and democratic government be established which represents the interests of the workers, peasants, youth and students, intellectuals, servicemen, traders, entrepreneurs and others from all classes and strata.

This proposal of ours is most fair and reasonable, acceptable to everyone.

However, the successive rulers of south Korea have doggedly opposed our just proposal, and have clamored for the so-called "elections under UN supervision."

The Korean people know only too well what "elections under UN supervision" are. It is no secret that the election of Syngman Rhee, traitor to the Korean people, was rigged up more than once, that Chang Myon's assumption to power was fabricated and the seizure of power by Pak Jung Hi was legalized, all through "elections under UN supervision," imposed on south Korea from 1948 to this date.

"Elections under UN supervision" are no more than a screen for covering the insidious aggressive plot of the US imperialists to extend to north Korea the colonial system which they forced upon the people in south Korea.

In Korea the United Nations has been used as an aggressive tool of the United States.

The United Nations has no competence whatsoever to involve itself in the Korean question.

The Korean people do not want anyone meddling in the solution of the question of their country's reunification. We must in any case achieve the reunification of the country by ourselves.

As the south Korean rulers, at the instigation of US imperialism, persisted in opposing the establishment of a unified government of Korea through free, democratic elections, we could not merely sit with folded arms waiting for the day of reunification and could not but seek ways of gradual approach to complete reunification by taking steps conducive to the reunification of the country.

You must know that we have long since been proposing the establishment of a Confederation of north and south Korea as a transitional step for settling the urgent and immediate problems of the nation even before the attainment of complete reunification of the country and facilitating reunification.

The Confederation we have proposed envisages the formation of a Supreme National Committee composed of equal numbers of representatatives appointed by the two governments, mainly with the object of coordinating the economic and cultural development of north and south Korea in a unified way and of promoting mutual cooperation and exchange between the two sides in the common interests of the nation, while retaining the existing political systems in north and south Korea and maintaining the independent activities of the two governments.

The reunification commission you have suggested can be regarded as analogous to the Supreme National Committee we have mentioned. In our opinion, it would also be a good idea to work out measures for restoring the national bonds between the north and the south and for carrying out the reunification of the country independently, not necessarily through the form of a Confederation, but by setting up some other kind of joint organ to be composed of representatives from north and south Korea.

We have maintained time and again that if the south Korean authorities cannot accept the Confederation, then the nation's tribulations caused by the division should at least be softened by effecting north-south economic and cultural exchange, leaving aside political questions for the time being.

The economic exchange between the north and the south would organically combine industrial north Korea with agrarian south Korea and facilitate the unified, independent development of the national economy, and would open the way for reviving south Korea's ruined economy and stabilizing the living conditions of its people who are in dire straits.

We have already built a developed industry and agriculture and laid firm economic foundations for an independent state in north Korea. This is the economic asset which would permit our nation to live independently after the country is reunified in the future.

When we were rebuilding, with tightened belts, the economy that had been ravaged beyond description by the US imperialist aggressors, we were always mindful of the interests and future development of the whole nation. We have not for a moment forgotten our compatriots in south Korea; we consider it our sacred national duty to help the suffering people in south Korea.

Along with the carrying out of economic exchange, cultural ties in all spheres of science, culture, arts, sports, etc., should be restored, and travel of people between north and south should be effected.

The south Korean authorities, following the dictates of US

imperialism, are opposed to free north-south general elections, opposed to a Confederation of north and south Korea and opposed even to economic and cultural exchange and travel of people between north and south.

Under these circumstances, we insist that at least the exchange of letters should be materialized as a minimum step for forging ties between the north and south. This reflects the pressing demand of the people for ending the extremely abnormal situation in which parents, wives and children, relatives and friends who are separated in the north and south cannot even write to each other.

It is of prime importance in achieving the reunification of the country to eliminate the tension created between the north and the south.

In this connection, it might be recalled, we have time and again proposed to the south Korean authorities that, after US troops are completely withdrawn from south Korea, north and south Korean authorities conclude a peace agreement pledging not to resort to armed attack against each other, and that the armed forces of both north and south Korea be reduced to 100,000 or less.

The oversized armed forces of south Korea, numbering more than 600,000 men, are an unbearably heavy military expenditure for the south Korean people and severely menace peace in Korea.

The withdrawal of all foreign troops from south Korea, the conclusion of a peace agreement between the north and the south and the reduction of the armed forces on both sides will mark a giant step forward on the road to the county's reunification.

We regard as a welcome idea your proposal that the north and south Korean armies be cut to the level of constabulary units for the maintenance of internal security and order.

We are ready to take any other steps that may be helpful to the solution of the reunification question. We are willing to abrogate the military pacts we have concluded with foreign countries on the condition that the US army is withdrawn from south Korea and the south Korean authorities abolish all the military pacts and agreements they have signed with foreign countries. We made this clear previously, when we were concluding pacts with other countries.

Ours is an independent people's power established freely in accordance with the general will of the people. We have never relied on outside forces; we maintain complete independence in all spheres—political, economic, military and cultural.

Our domestic and foreign policies are completely independent, brooking no interference from any foreign country. Our Government, whenever it deems it necessary for the interests of the country and the nation, can take appropriate actions on its own initiative.

We have devoted all our sincere efforts to the reunification of our country.

Even after the present rulers of south Korea staged a military coup and seized power, we repeatedly advanced a number of proposals of national salvation aimed at removing the national calamity and accelerating the reunification of the country, in the sincere hope that they would return to a national position.

However, following the aggressive and the divisive policy of the US imperialists and disregarding the ardent desire of the nation, they have refused to listen to our sincere advice; on the contrary, they continue to perpetuate the partition of the nation.

The responsibility for the failure up to now to achieve the reunification of our country rests with the US imperialists who have occupied south Korea by force of arms and have been pursuing a policy of splitting our nation, and with such traitors as Pak Jung Hi, the reactionary bureaucrats, the political quacks and imposters who, hand in glove with the US imperialists, are bartering away the interests of the nation.

They serve the foreign aggressive forces, opposing the independent and peaceful reunification of the country and categorically rejecting the unity of the national forces; they defend only their own personal interests and those of some privileged circles that are in league with outside forces; they can never represent the south Korean people.

They defend, and ask for the permanent stationing of, the US aggressive army which has occupied south Korea and has been obstructing the reunification of our country and perpetrating all and every kind of brutish atrocity such as plundering, oppressing, insulting and killing people in south Korea.

Those traitors, turning down our offer to receive millions of unemployed south Koreans into north Korea and give them jobs, are selling out our compatriots to European and American countries as if they were commodities.

Moreover, they are even ushering in the Japanese militarists to reduce south Korea to a colony of both US and Japanese imperialism.

Manipulated by the United States, the traitors of south Korea, dead set against contact and cooperation within one and the same nation, are hurrying through the criminal "ROK-Japan talks" for collusion with the Japanese militarists.

Those taking the lead in conspiring with Japanese imperialism are the same stooges who served it faithfully in the past, too. Refusing to repent of their past crimes, they have now again become the cat's paw of US imperialism and their old master, Japanese militarism.

To achieve the reunification of the country, we should pool the strength of the entire Korean people in north and south and fight against the foreign imperialist aggressive forces and their allies—the traitors, reactionary bureaucrats, political quacks and imposters who are hindering reunification.

How can we promote national unity and achieve the reunification of the country without fighting against those who, far from desiring reunification, categorically reject any contact or exchange between the north and south?

Needless to say, it would be a different matter if even now they were to repent of their mistakes and take the road of struggle for the withdrawal of the US army and for the independent reunification of the country.

If a man defends the interests of the nation and desires the country's reunification, we will join hands and go together with him at any time, regardless of his political views and ideology and of his past record.

If all the patriotic forces of north and south Korea unite, we will definitely open the road to contact and negotiation between the north and the south, realize mutual cooperation and exchange, force the US army to withdraw, and achieve the reunification of the country.

Without unity and struggle we can neither drive out the US aggressor army nor achieve national reunification.

The point is that the south Korean people of all walks of life—workers, peasants, youth and students, intellectuals, armymen, traders, entrepreneurs, etc.—should firmly unite and wage a more resolute national-salvation struggle against US imperialism and its stooges, for the independent and peaceful reunification of the country.

We should under no circumstances tolerate any form of interference in the domestic affairs of our nation; we must thoroughly oppose "protection" or "supervision" by anyone and must carve out our own destiny by ourselves.

When we achieve the reunification of our country on the principle of the self-determination of nations and when the whole nation fights in unity, we will be able to increase the might of the country and build a rich and powerful, independent sovereign state, without needing "guarantees" from any outside forces.

Our country will surely be reunified through the nationwide struggle of the entire Korean people.

In conclusion, I express the hope that you will make positive efforts to accelerate the independent reunification of the country.

ON TEMPERING THE PARTY SPIRIT OF FOREIGN TRADE WORKERS AND ADHERING TO INDEPENDENCE IN FOREIGN TRADE (Excerpt)

Concluding Speech at the General Membership Meeting of the Foreign Trade Ministry's Party Organization, *January 28, 1965*

The report and speeches made at today's meeting are all correct. I intended to express my view after hearing you out, but I must attend to another matter, so I will speak now.

We have learned what was discussed at the meetings of the cells under the Ministry's Party Committee over the past few days. This meeting is a very useful and necessary one for the progress of our work. It seems to me that it is a bit belated to hold such a meeting only today.

Had we held this kind of meeting once or twice a year, so many shortcomings would not have accumulated and those who are criticized would not feel so much pain.

Leaving mistakes to go unchecked when they are minor and then criticizing them when they have grown serious is tantamount to trying to wash off at a time all the dirt which has been accumulated over a long time. When a little dirty, you can wash yourself clean by using soap, but when you have got a thick layer of dirt, you cannot remove it without applying a knife. And applying a knife will probably cause you some pain.

Vice-ministers have been severely criticized, but they had better have their old dirt rubbed off clean even if they may feel a bit painful, rather than to keep it on them. You must eliminate your dirt even if you have to apply a knife if it cannot be washed off by using soap. Only then can you live as clean persons again. If one leaves one's dirt intact because of pain, one may go bad. This is why the criticism at this meeting is indispensable to save our cadres and put the work on the right track.

Our experience gained this time should serve us as a lesson, and we must make sure in the future that a meeting of the ministry's Party organization does not become a meeting of a technical or administrative-businesslike nature, but becomes one which educates people through an ideological struggle in an atmosphere of strong criticism.

The minister and vice-ministers who have been criticized at the meeting are not originally people who have many defects. All the vice-ministers, not to mention the minister who is a member of the Political Committee of the Party Central Committee, have a good family background. To see the family status of vice-ministers, all of them are of worker origin. They are new cadres our Party has brought up after liberation. As regards other comrades who have been criticized today, they are also of good origin and worked well before. The Party trusted them and sent them to the ministry.

As you see, originally they were all good people. However, they have developed many shortcomings because they lived as they pleased for a long time without receiving criticism and control from the masses, neglectful of Party life.

Once appointed ministers or vice-ministers, some people put on airs as if they became high-ranking government officials of the old society; they neither respect the Party organizations and Party resolutions nor conscientiously participate in Party life; they ignore the masses and act in a bureaucratic way. This is the trouble.

So far we have been ignorant of the fact that ministers and vice-ministers, placing themselves above the Party organizations, do not attend the cell meetings and act as they please. We have learned this time that such a practice is manifested in no small measure not only in the Ministry of Foreign Trade but also in other ministries. Many ministers and vice-ministers from other ministries are also present at this meeting. It is advisable that they all draw a lesson from this meeting.

People of bourgeois or petty-bourgeois origin are not the only ones who have bourgeois ideology. Cadres of working-class origin may also have a lot of survivals of obsolete ideologies. Even cadres with a good family background may take a wrong path and degenerate if they are not educated. The Party organization should always exercise control over the life of Party members and cadres and educate them perseveringly lest any one of them should go astray.

The most important thing in the education of cadres is collective education through organizational life. Individual education is also necessary: the minister educating the vice-ministers and the latter the department chiefs. However, the main thing is that the Party cells conduct their meetings effectively and that the Party organizations strengthen collective criticism.

The Party is an organization with a strong discipline. Party members participate in the revolutionary struggle through the Party organization; they should constantly temper themselves through organizational life. That the Party members and cadres keep out of organizational life virtually means that they have severed themselves from the Party organization. All the Party members should unconditionally obey Party discipline and deem faithful participation in organizational life their most sacred duty, a law of their life and an honor.

A Party member who hates organizational life and regards Party control as a nuisance has already contracted a serious disease. If he is not cured of this disease in time, he may eventually become a good-for-nothing disqualified even for citizenship, let alone Party membership.

For a Party member to get out of Party control is as dangerous as a baby getting out of its mother's bosom. If in a family the father and mother do not control and educate their children well, the latter will go astray.

When one regularly takes part in Party organizational life, he can learn from other comrades' criticism his shortcomings which he has been so far unconscious of. And even when he is not criticized himself, he can get pricked by the criticism offered to others and repent of his mistakes. Then he can rectify his shortcomings in good time and always remain faithful to the Party. Therefore, the Party members should willingly and actively participate in Party organizational life and the Party organization should exercise strict control lest its members should evade organizational life.

If the organizational life of the Party members and cadres is to be strengthened, it is important to create an atmosphere of criticism within the Party. The Tenth Plenary Meeting of the Fourth Party Central Committee served as an important turning point in bringing inner-Party democracy into play and intensifying criticism among the Party members.

We have failed in the past to properly train cadres through criticism. So, cadres are very much ashamed and afraid of being criticized, and the Party members, on their part, shun criticizing cadres. If this tendency grows, cadres will inevitably go out of Party life.

Only when cadres are tempered through criticism will they realize the strength of the masses, become more humble and always rely on the Party organization and the masses in their work.

Criticism must be conducted regularly. There cannot be a perfect and flawless person. Any Party member may commit errors while he is working. We should not overlook even a minor shortcoming but criticize and rectify it in good time. Criticism offered when a person has just taken a wrong path can put the work on the right track and save the man himself. If we leave a man uncriticized for a long time and cry down or sack him when the work has gone amiss altogether, it will be of no use to the Party.

Criticism should always be made in a comradely way. The purpose of our criticism is to establish a sound way of life within the Party, strengthen unity between comrades and improve our work. Therefore, those who criticize should not do so for the sake of disparaging others, but should proceed from a whole-hearted sympathy for their shortcomings and from the principled stand of defending the Party's interests.

When a mother scolds her son or daughter, she feels great pain. However, she unhesitatingly scolds them for their misdemeanor because she loves them. Our Party members, too, should not overlook but criticize in time the faults of their comrades if they truly love them. Only such comradely criticism can move a man and bring back to the right track the comrade who is going the wrong way.

Those comrades who are criticized should accept the criticism with a good grace and an open mind, even if it is a bit painful, and courageously rectify their own shortcomings. They should never be dispirited for having been criticized or think of taking revenge for the criticism. They should seriously examine the causes of their errors and tirelessly strive to eliminate them.

Mere acceptance of criticism does not yet mean that one's errors have already been corrected. Those comrades who have been criticized today should conscientiously lead Party life and discipline themselves and successfully carry out their revolutionary tasks, thus remedying their errors in actual deed.

At this meeting the minister and vice-ministers have been chiefly criticized, but this does not imply that criticism is necessary only for cadres. It is true that the minister and vice-ministers have revealed many shortcomings because they did not faithfully participate in Party life in the past. But strengthening Party life and tempering Party spirit is essential for everybody. In future it is necessary to create an atmosphere of criticism among all the Party members at the ministry and intensify the work of tempering Party spirit.

Tempering Party spirit is more essential for the personnel engaged in foreign trade.

Foreign trade plays a very important role in accelerating our socialist construction and developing friendship and cooperation with other countries.

The Ministry of Foreign Trade is an organ which is in charge of foreign economic activities for the state. Our foreign trade not only constitutes an important means of effecting economic cooperation with other countries, but also greatly contributes to developing political relations between states. Friendly relations between states usually begin with trade and gradually develop to build up political relations. In this sense we can say that foreign trade is the first process in the development of our foreign relations.

Foreign trade is not only a very important undertaking of a state but also a difficult and complex work. The Ministry of Foreign Trade has dealings with Western capitalist countries, to say nothing of the socialist countries and the neutral states

of Asia and Africa. Functionaries of this ministry visit
capitalist countries which are swept by degeneration, and
often have dealings with people of revisionist countries. If our
foreign trade personnel have a weak Party spirit and have a
low level of communist self-discipline, they may be influenced
by the dissipated capitalist way of life and become capitalist-
minded and infected by revisionism before they know it, in the
course of meeting capitalists and revisionists often.

This can be likened to a man catching cold while keeping
contact with an influenza case. When one comes in contact
with a patient, he is unceasingly infected with viruses,
although they are invisible. A person who always hardens his
body and has a great power of resistance to diseases, may not
fall ill even if he comes into contact with a patient. However, a
weak and resistless man can easily be attacked by a disease.

A person who fails to ceaselessly temper his Party spirit and
is not firmly armed with the Party's policies and Marxist-
Leninist world outlook, may instantly catch a capitalist cold
when he comes in contact with capitalists and a revisionist
cold when contacting revisionists. That is why you should constantly steel your Party spirit by regularly and actively participating in Party life and making a tireless study of the Party's policies and Marxism-Leninism as people cultivate their
resisting power against diseases by means of cold-water rub-
bing every morning and a great deal of physical exercise.

The Party spirit of foreign trade officials must be manifested, above all, in firmly adhering to independence and the
spirit of Juche in external economic activities.

In their external economic activities the foreign trade personnel should stick to Party policy and thoroughly safeguard
the interests of our people and our revolution. A person who
does not defend the political and economic interests of his
country is not eligible as a foreign trade official.

The functionaries engaged in foreign trade should ardently
love their country and people and clearly grasp all the
demands our revolution and socialist construction put forward
before foreign trade, and devotedly strive to meet them.

They are grossly mistaken if they think that it will suffice
for them to know only foreign things. They should first know
well the realities of the country and the Party's policies. They
should be versed not only in the Party's policy on foreign trade

but also in all its internal and external policies. Only then can they conduct economic diplomacy on the stand of Juche. It is a failing of our foreign trade officials today that they are ignorant of their country's realities and are not sensitive to the Party's requirements.

A person who is keen only to know foreign things and is ignorant of his own things will lose Juche in work and fall into flunkeyism towards great powers and dogmatism. If one lacks Juche, one will lose faith in his own strength and cannot fight in defense of his own country's interests.

During the past Fatherland Liberation War we felt all the more keenly the necessity of establishing Juche.

After liberation we gave much publicity to the Soviet Union, but mentioned little of our own struggle—the struggle of the Korean people themselves.

If we had informed our Party members and working people of the history of our struggle and educated them in the fighting spirit of our revolutionaries from the first, our people would have fought better during the temporary retreat and many people would not have lost their lives. But we had failed to educate our people in this manner, and so, when the Yanks came, many people hoped for others to help them, instead of trying to fight the enemy for themselves. They were discouraged, saying, "With no help from foreign troops, how can we fight against the formidable Yanks?"

We drew a lesson from this bitter experience and began to rectify our Party ideological work. At that time our ideological work was lacking in Juche and many functionaries were committing errors of flunkeyism and dogmatism.

I examined the curricula of schools and found that while hundreds of hours were allotted to the study of world history, very few hours were devoted to the devoted to the history of our country. Only when we give the students many lessons in the history of our nation and, in particular, the history of our revolutionary struggle, will they be able to inherit our revolutionary traditions and bravely fight against the enemy. However, our schools did not give much instruction in the history of our people's patriotic struggles such as the March First Uprising and the Kwangju Student Incident, and very carelessly treated the anti-Japanese guerrilla struggle.

When singing, our artists preferred European songs in most

cases, and when painting, our painters did the landscapes of Europe or Siberia. And everywhere we went we only saw portraits of Europeans hung on the walls.

One day during the war I visited an army vacation hostel, where I saw a picture of the Siberian landscape hanging in a room, which depicted a bear crawling about a snow-covered forest. So I asked the soldiers why they hung the landscape of Siberia when our country had so many celebrated mountains of rare beauty such as Mts. Kumgang-san and Myohyang-san, as well as beautiful, time-honored scenic spots. If the armymen are shown only foreign landscapes all the time, they cannot be cultivated in patriotism—love for their native places and their homeland.

Soon after we returned from the retreat, I visited a middle school. There were many portraits hung in classrooms, of which only one was Korean—mine. So I asked the teachers why we should only hang portraits of Europeans and praise them when our country had produced a large number of famous generals, excellent scholars and talented artists. I also stressed that schools should teach not only European songs but many Korean songs.

During the war our Party set the workers in the field of art the task of widely introducing national instruments into use and developing national music and national dance. At first, however, the Party's policy was not implemented well owing to the maneuvers of the anti-Party factionalists who had wormed their way into this field. Some people rejected our national instruments, alleging that the Korean instruments were not like musical instruments because they lacked two parts.

With a view to eliminating such defects revealed in ideological work, our Party started a resolute struggle in 1955 to reject flunkeyism towards great powers and dogmatism and establish Juche. Because it established Juche in ideological work, our Party has always been able to hold fast to its correct revolutionary lines and achieve great successes in the revolution and construction, frustrating the pressure and all sorts of intrigues on the part of the great-power chauvinists.

In the past, the flunkeyists and dogmatists caused heavy losses to the state in foreign trade too.

Let me cite an example from the ordnance industry. Certain fellows entrenched in this field ostensibly worked for our country, but, in fact, they served the interests of foreigners. They claimed that rifle stocks cannot be made without Russian white birch, and imported white birch spending a large sum of foreign currency. When they saw foreigners making boxes with chunks of wood in order not to throw them away, they did so much as cut good wood into pieces to make boxes of them.

We should wage a resolute struggle against the phenomenon that people in foreign trade lose independence and blindly obey the demands of foreigners, thus causing losses to the state.

In the future when the state ceases to exist and the whole world turns into a communist society, there will be no problem. However, as long as there exist frontiers and ownership is divided, clear distinctions should be made even between socialist countries. It would be naive to think that somebody will give us anything gratis.

A person who does not defend the interests of his own country in external activities, is no better than one who betrays his country and people. The functionaries of the Foreign Trade Ministry should not make the least compromise or show the slightest vacillation in defending the interests of the Party and the state.

It is a great danger that flunkeyists and dogmatists who lack Party and class spirit and are not armed with Juche should slip into the ranks of foreign trade workers. We should tirelessly strive to build up the Ministry of Foreign Trade and educate foreign trade officials to become revolutionary fighters infinitely loyal to the Party and the state.

ON IMPROVING HIGHER EDUCATION
(Excerpt)

Speech at the General Membership Meeting of the Party Organization of the Ministry of Higher Education, *February 23, 1965*

---

2. On Firmly Establishing Juche in Education and Scientific Researches

Our country has long historical roots of flunkeyism and dogmatism. As you all know, our country is hemmed in by big powers. China and Russia belong to the world's largest countries and Japan is larger than our country.

All of these countries once tried to have influence on our country. Korea's rotten feudal ruling classes despicably succumbed to the big powers and curried favor with them; they tried to prop up their rule, relying on the foreign countries. Some wanted to worship Ching and others tried to usher in the forces of Russia or Japan. Our ruling aristocrats behaved in such a sycophantic way that the country could not but ruin.

The thirty-six years of Japanese imperialist colonial rule in-

creased the flunkeyism of our people. Under the Japanese rule
quite a few people lost their national spirit and worshipped the
Japanese marauders; and they spoke in Japanese and changed
their family names in a Japanese way, just as the Japanese
asked them to do.

After the defeat of Japanese imperialism there began to
emerge among our people the tendency to worship another
country blindly. Some people, in utter disregard of the specific
conditions in their own country, proposed to do everything on
the pattern of the foreign country.

They slighted our people's history of struggle and revolutionary traditions, and even opposed our national culture and
fine manners and customs handed down by our ancestors.
They even proposed to copy foreign ways of building houses
and eating.

Immediately after liberation I heard O Gi Sop's speech at a
gathering. He cracked one foreign word after another such as
"ideology", "proletariat" and "hegemony" which the audience
could not understand. So I thought to myself that if everybody
did just like O Gi Sop there might be the danger of the Korean
language being eradicated in the future.

Of course, his speech contained nothing worthwhile to hear.
One who has learned a few foreign words by heart and brags in
front of the people cannot have a clear idea about the Korean
revolution. This sort of people are all flunkeys and dogmatists.

In the grim days of the Fatherland Liberation War, we more
keenly felt the harmful effects of flunkeyism and dogmatism.
The dogmatists attempted to apply mechanically in our
country the military theory and tactics developed in a foreign
country.

For example, in the country which has many vast plains,
direct-firing guns are effective, but in our country where there
are a lot of mountains, we must use howitzers. However, the
dogmatists saw to it that many direct-firing guns were used in
our country because a foreign country did so. This caused us
great losses.

The aftereffects of our dogmatism in the ideological work
were also glaringly manifested during the war. Before the war,
some people only talked about the war accomplishments made
by a foreign army but said little about our people's revolutionary struggles. Thus our people could not be equipped with

our anti-Japanese guerrillas' lofty revolutionary spirit and rich experience in struggle. As a result, our people were neither prepared nor determined to fight with their own efforts in complicated circumstances. As the People's Army retreated and the enemy came in, many people lost confidence in victory and were dispirited and even those willing to fight did not know how to fight and hid themselves here and there, so that they were captured and killed by the enemy in cold blood.

It is quite possible for any army to make a strategic retreat for some time during war. General Ulji Mundok, too, retreated temporarily before crushing the huge army from Sui and Russia's Kutuzov even handed Moscow to the enemy before retreating and then made a comeback and repelled Napoleon.

Therefore, we had no ground to lose our confidence in victory merely because the People's Army retreated for the time being. If we had educated the people in our revolutionary traditions before the war, they would have fought well without any vacillation behind enemy lines. They would have endured those 40 days easily if they had gone about the mountains, each carrying at least a *mal* of rice and an axe with him.

We drew a lesson from this bitter experience and conducted a forceful struggle to oppose flunkeyism and dogmatism and establish Juche.

Upholding the Party's policy to establish Juche, our intellectuals worked hard and achieved many successes.

First let me cite the successes made in the sphere of social sciences.

In former days, our people did not know their own country's history and just studied a foreign country's history. One day during the war I examined the Party School's teaching schedule, and I found out that hundreds of hours had been allotted for the lectures on world history and a foreign country's history, but only a few dozens of hours on Korean history. Therefore, I told them those who were going to make the Korean revolution must first learn their own people's history and there was no reason for them to learn a foreign history in such a detail. If they were specializing in history, the matter would be different, but it would be of no use for our Party workers to learn by heart the names of a foreign country's emperors such as "Alexanders" and "Peters".

As the Juche idea was disseminated widely, our scholars

began to study their country's history and their people's traditions of struggle, and endeavored to theoretically summarize our country's revolution and construction. Thus we recovered our history and revolutionary traditions thrown into oblivion, and deeply realized the correctness of our Party's policies. This greatly helped to foster the national pride and socialist patriotism among our people and to arm them with our Party's revolutionary idea.

There has been a great change in natural sciences and technology.

When I visited the Unryul Mine last, I also had talks with comrades on the geological prospecting team; they told me their field of work had also been greatly affected by flunkeyism and dogmatism.

The place where the Unryul Mine is located now had long been called Cholsan-ri (or the Village of Iron Mount) and our ancestors had exploited iron ore there in the days of Li dynasty. In the light of this historical fact, the comrades on the geological prospecting team should have sought for iron ore there. However, until a few years ago, they had had no intention of doing so, because they had fully believed foreigners who told them there was no iron ore in such a low place. In fact, our comrades had not known how much knowledge and experience they had in geological prospecting. But they regarded as entirely correct what the foreigners said, just because they were from an advanced country.

Later, as Juche was established among our geological prospectors, they could find plenty of iron in this low-land area. The iron deposit found so far at the Unryul Mine is estimated at as much as 100 million tons. It is said that continued prospecting will tap several hundred million tons more. Then the Unryul Mine will be as huge a mine as the Musan Mine, the largest of its kind in our country.

Because it is located on the downstream of the Taedong-gang River near the Hwanghae Iron Works, the Unryul Mine is endowed with an advantage of shipping the iron ore quickly by water at low expense. Tapping massive amounts of iron ore at this place is our great achievement.

So I asked the personnel on the geological prospecting team why they had taken the trouble of going about rugged mountains though they had such an excellent deposit near by. They answered that they had been idiots because they had had not their own senses.

Similar cases were found in other spheres. In former days our technicians thought our country had a small deposit of copper; this was based on Japanese data. The Japanese said that the Kapsan Mine had a poor prospect of development because its copper deposit was small. However, our technicians made a thoroughgoing geological survey at the Kapsan Mine and not long ago they hit a huge deposit of copper.

At present workers of the Kapsan Mine are in high spirits. They have resolved to produce 1,200 tons more of copper this year than the quota assigned them under the national plan.

In another place our geological prospectors have found a new immense vein of copper. From this we can see how foolish it is to blindly believe in the Japanese data which claimed that our country had little copper.

Having established Juche and displayed the spirit of self-reliance, our geological prospecting personnel found nickel, too. Without nickel it is impossible to make special steel and stainless steel. Once we asked a foreign country for stainless steel in order to run the Hungnam Fertilizer Factory. And we had a hard time of it because they asked us to pay for it in gold.

Our geological prospectors, aware of this difficult situation, made strenuous efforts and finally tapped the nickel deposit in our country.

This establishment of Juche among our personnel made it possible to tap iron, copper and nickel. We can say these precious ores are the wonderful gifts given by the Juche idea.

As the Juche idea was inculcated into the minds of our workers and technicians, innovations were made also in the machine-building, metal and chemical industries.

Our workers and technicians boldly buckled down to the solution of technological problems with their own efforts and succeeded in turning out different kinds of complex modern machines and equipment. In a short span of time our people built many machinery plants and have been able to produce with their own efforts large quantities of trucks, tractors and other machines and equipment needed for the nation's technical revolution.

In addition, our scientists and technicians have opened up excellent prospects for industrial development by using limestone and anthracite abundant in our country.

The scientists and technicians in the chemical industry solved the problem of gasifying anthracite and those in the metallurgical industry contrived the method of continuous steel-making from granulated iron. This is a major success that opened up a perspective of developing the steel industry with anthracite abundant in our country.

Our scientists have opened many new planes also in agronomy, biology and medical science and are achieving brilliant results.

Our literature and arts also got over flunkeyism and dogmatism, with the result that a large number of excellent works have been created which suit our people's taste and mentality.

In former days our artists used to draw not their country's beautiful landscape but foreign mountains and rivers which are alien to our people. As I once witnessed and criticized during the war, only drawings of foreign landscapes were hung even in the rooms of a sanatorium of the People's Army.

Our artists did not sing our own folk songs but sang foreign songs which were not to our people's liking. And they discarded our national musical instruments, saying that they were primitive.

If we had gone on like this, we would have lost completely the priceless heritage of the resplendent national culture accumulated by our ancestors through thousands of years. However, our Party established Juche in literature and arts so that they have flowered and developed quickly on a national foundation and served to make our working people's lives and work merry and pulsating.

Through this struggle against flunkeyism and dogmatism and for the establishment of Juche, tremendous successes have been achieved in science and technology and in literature and arts.

As you criticized, it is true that the course of the struggle to build up Juche witnessed some deviations. We somewhat neglected studying foreign languages and there were shortcomings in assimilating foreign experience. However, we need not regret in the least the establishment of Juche just because there were these trifling deviations. The successes gained as a result of the establishment of Juche dwarf the losses caused by the deviations.

Of course, deviations must be rectified. This is not a difficult job. However, had we continued to practice flunkeyism and dogmatism without establishing Juche, we would have suffered irreparable losses in our revolution and construction. What is still dangerous to us is the failure to thoroughly establish Juche, not the deviation in the course of establishing Juche.

We must, therefore, carry on the struggle to build up Juche.

Flunkeyism and dogmatism have been eliminated from the minds of our people to a large extent. This is true. But they have not yet been eradicated completely. The roots of flunkeyism which grew through a long period of history will not be pulled out so quickly.

Nor can we say that the conditions for the emergence of flunkeyism and dogmatism have been thoroughly stamped out in our country.

As in the past so at the present, our neighboring countries are all large and they have advanced science and technology. So if we are not careful, flunkeyism towards these countries might breed among us.

We should maintain Juche in our relation with socialist countries, not to mention it with regard to the militarist country of Japan.

Needless to say, every Communist must oppose great-nation chauvinism and it must not be expressed in the relationship between socialist countries. However, it will take a long time for all the socialist countries to be completely free from the survivals of outworn ideas. As experience shows there may be quite a lot of people affected by great-nation chauvinism in the socialist countries, too.

Among the anti-Party sectarians who had raised their heads in our country before, there were those who aligned themselves with the aggressive forces of imperialism but there were also some who had been manipulated by great-nation chauvinists.

The Tuesday group headed by Pak Hon Yong had been active as the agents of US imperialism with the support of an American espionage agency. On the other hand, the M-L group headed by Choe Chang Ik and the Irkutsk group had challenged our Party in alliance with great-nation chauvinists. These are not things of the remote past.

Until imperialism disappears on a worldwide scale and the triumph of communism eliminates the difference between yours and mine, there must be a line of demarcation even between socialist countries and the struggle must be continued against great-nation chauvinism and flunkeyism.

The establishment of Juche aims in the last analysis at carrying out the revolution well in one's own country with national pride and confidence. Conducting the revolutions well in their own countries is the fundamental duty of the Communists in each country to world revolution. Korean Communists can contribute to world revolution only when they first make the Korean revolution well.

The establishment of Juche does not mean nationalism; it does not run counter to proletarian internationalism. Genuine internationalism presupposes patriotism. He who does not love his own country and is not interested in his country's revolution cannot be faithful to world revolution.

Great-nation chauvinism is the national egoism of great powers and flunkeyism is the expression of national nihilism on the part of small nations. This is entirely alien to both proletarian internationalism and socialist patriotism. Therefore, true patriots and internationalists must resolutely oppose great-nation chauvinism and flunkeyism and firmly maintain their Juche position.

If one is to establish Juche, one must first know one's own country well. We must carry out revolution in Korea and build a communist paradise on Korean soil.

Even after the worldwide victory of communism, we will live on Korean soil where our people have lived through generations. Why should we live in a strange country, leaving this beautiful garden of golden tapestry?

If we are to make revolution in Korea and live in Korea, we must know the history and culture of the Korean people, know the land and seas of Korea and know its climate and natural resources.

Only when we know our country well, can we do everything to suit our specific conditions and love our country and people and have pride and confidence in carrying out revolution in our country.

Our teachers, however, do not yet know their country well, and are little interested in their country's revolution. So they will not be able to educate our rising generation to be true patriots and revolutionaries.

In waging the struggle to establish Juche in their work, our educators must first strive to know their country and revolution well.

The most essential means of eliminating flunkeyism and dogmatism and establishing Juche is to develop one's country in all the political, economic and cultural aspects of life. When our country has a better government, more advanced science and technology and higher living standards, then flunkeyism will disappear automatically. Therefore, while making conscious efforts to establish Juche, our intellectuals must make innovations in the branches of science and technology they are specializing.

In order to powerfully accelerate the technical and cultural revolutions and step up our socialist construction, we need many scientists and technicians. We must reinforce our geological prospecting personnel and must assign many more excellent technicians to the machine-building, electric and chemical industries, agriculture and all other spheres of the national economy. Our educators must radically improve the quality of their education so as to train many competent scientists and technicians.

Those who are engaged in social sciences must patiently carry on their studies on our country's history and our Party's revolutionary traditions. Also, they must make a profound study of major theoretical and practical problems solved by our Party through the creative application of Marxism-Leninism to our country's reality and must give a thorough theoretical explanation on the process of the law-governed development of our revolution and construction.

In the field of natural sciences and technology, it is necessary to conduct more vigorous researches in order to develop industry with domestic raw materials by exploiting our country's natural resources. Only if we make efforts, can we make ourselves well-off, using our own natural resources. We need not just envy other countries' resources.

To guarantee economic independence, we must build an industry largely based on our own raw materials. We must guarantee at least 70 per cent of the raw materials for industry at home and must import only certain materials which are not produced in our country.

For this purpose, our scientists and technicians must make a more active study of the sources of domestic raw materials and must seek for the raw materials which we are lacking and endeavor to make as many substitutes as possible for those which we have not.

We are opposed to flunkeyism and dogmatism, but this does not mean that we should isolate our country as Regent Taewongun did. If we boast of our things as best and do not learn from others open-mindedly, we cannot develop. If we are to quickly develop our science and technology, we must positively draw on foreign achievements in science and technology. We must oppose closed-doorism in scientific and technological advancement.

We still have a lot of things to learn from other countries.

We are lagging behind advanced countries in the machine engineering, electronics, semi-conductor technology and other branches. In the research of atomic energy, we have not yet been able to solve our many problems. Our country has plenty of nuclear materials but is still unable to treat them through an industrial method.

Nor have we solved many scientific and technological problems supposed to be settled in the Seven-Year Plan period. We have not yet solved the problem of producing ferromanganese nor the problem of producing aluminum from nepheline.

The chemical industry must direct its main efforts to producing synthetic fibers or resins by using carbide abundant in our country, but it must also study how to produce chemical products with imported crude petroleum. Of course, our scientists and technicians all know about it but if we are to build an oil refinery right now, even tomorrow, to produce chemicals, there may be many knotty problems to be untied technologically.

In addition, our scientists and technicians have a lot of things they must learn and study.

As regards the problems which we are unable to solve, we must not hesitate to learn the solutions from foreign countries if we can. Capitalism or revisionism will not come in with the foreign technology we will introduce. We need not be afraid of learning from capitalist countries, not to mention socialist countries.

Learning foreign science and technology will not breed flunkeyism in us. Only if we quickly develop our country's science and technology even by learning from others, will it rid ourselves of flunkeyism.

The question is with what attitudes we are going to learn foreign things. We learn from other countries not to worship others and shackle ourselves to them but to catch up with advanced countries and increase our nation's independence.

We have already established Juche in science and laid solid foundations of an independent economy. Now, we should bring in advanced foreign technology so as to complement some shortcomings of our industry and promote the nation's technological progress.

We do not mean that we must absorb foreign techniques without reservation. If we ignore our excellent techniques and bring in others', it will be ridiculous. We must always learn what we can hardly solve by ourselves, and apply them to suit our country's specific situation. If we do not assimilate foreign science and technology to suit our reality, it will be of no use and rather exert a negative influence.

For example, if we draw in foreign architectural techniques and build useless houses which are not in accord with the Korean way of life, then it would be worse than not learning technology. This is as much as importing pianos and only playing Western music which our people do not understand.

The piano is a modern musical instrument. We Koreans must also have pianos in order to develop our music. However, we must not just play Western music with them but must play Korean music which fits our people's taste and feeling. Only then can this modern musical instrument serve to make our people's life pleasant.

The case is true with other techniques. We must properly assimilate advanced foreign technology so that it will suit our people's life and serve our revolution and construction.

3. On Improving the Training of Cadres

To improve educational work, it is important, first of all, to raise our teachers' qualifications. Otherwise, we cannot improve the quality of teaching nor can we train excellent technicians and experts we need. If their level is low, we cannot better the quality of our industrial products, either.

At present, quite a few people say that our teachers' level is low and the technicians we have trained are not sufficiently capable. We must have a clear understanding of this point.

Our cadres' qualifications are somewhat low for some unavoidable reasons. Before liberation we had a very backward industry and few technicians of our own. Our industry rapidly developed as a large-scale modern industry in a few years after the war. So we had to train large numbers of technicians and experts in a short period of time. If we had not quickly built up the ranks of our own cadres we would have been unable to rebuild the destroyed factories and enterprises and lay the foundations of an independent national economy.

Of course, it was important to raise our technicians' qualifications. But still more urgent was to quickly train a definite number of technicians and experts and expand the ranks of our own cadres in a big way.

If our engineers had had another year to study at colleges, their qualifications would have somewhat improved. This is obvious. But our situation demanded us to send the students to the actual workplaces even a year earlier and in larger numbers. That is why we set up many colleges, although we had not enough competent teaching staff, and decided to shorten the period of training by a year.

As one factory was built after another, those who had to run the factories were not allowed just to read books at colleges. So, when the furnace of Hwanghae Iron Works started its operation, we even assigned students there half a year ahead of their graduation.

It is true that this could have lowered our college graduates' qualifications to a certain degree.

However, we must consider as a tremendous success the building up of such a huge army of Korean cadres in a short period of time. All the enterprises across the nation are being run by the technicians and experts trained by us. There is no factory which is run by foreigners. The furnaces are operated by the graduates of Kim Chaek Polytechnical Institute and the fertilizer factories by the graduates of the Hamhung College of Chemical Industry.

Moreover, all our state and economic agencies are administered by our cadres. Our planning work is not yet free from different defects, but other countries have similar defects. Our planning had better be undertaken by our own cadres than by foreign advisors who do not understand our specific conditions.

They say our technicians' qualifications are low but, in fact, they are not so low. Our technicians constructed the Vinalon Factory with their own efforts, rebuilt furnaces and set up large power stations and, recently, they have built a factory where coal is gasified. The factories we built and the machines we made are all working normally and they are highly efficient in production.

Our engineers graduated from colleges a year earlier but since they have had more training at the actual places of production, they have many merits.

They need not regret their incomplete education at colleges. They must continue to study. If our engineers apply their experience in production and construction and study patiently, they will develop to be excellent technicians.

And it was quite correct for us to train our own cadres with our own efforts. We may send our men abroad to train them to be technicians. However, there are limitations on this matter. We cannot have so many cadres of our own trained in foreign countries. In addition, if we have many people educated abroad, it will be difficult to establish Juche in our economic construction.

Our cadres were trained by ourselves in a difficult situation; so they are fully acquainted with the nation's situation, have a high national pride and are faithful to the Party and the people. Furthermore, because we have many cadres developed by us in our country, we could easily assimilate those who had studied abroad. We should have a great pride in this huge army of excellent cadres of our own.

We should, of course, develop many technical cadres of our own in the future, too. However, the number of technicians we have at present is by no means small. If the technicians already trained are rationally allocated and made to work at the right place, we will not feel a great shortage of technicians.

Recently I visited the State Construction Commission. I found there were many civil engineers and economic experts on the directorate of building operation but there was none who was versed in furnaces or machines and equipment. In order to enhance its role in factory construction, this directorate should have not only civil engineers but also many of those who know about industrial technology. We must be meticulously comcerned in the rational allocation of technicians.

Of course, we should continue to increase the number of our technicians and experts, but a major question now is that of uplifting our intellectuals' qualifications to a higher level. At present our cadres' scientific and technological qualifications fail to meet the demands of the fast developing technical and cultural revolutions.

Now that our general technical level is high, those who have ordinary technological knowledge can hardly be called technicians. If they are to lead the technical and cultural revolutions today, our technicians must radically raise their qualifications.

To raise their qualifications, our teachers, scientists and technicians must study hard.

One of the greatest defects our cadres have is that they do not study. If they do not study, they cannot but be idlers. Those who neglect studying and loaf around because they have a bit of knowledge, are worse than those who have had no schooling. We must fight resolutely against the negligence of study so as to build up a serious habit of study among our teachers, scientists and technicians.

Our Party is now demanding a system of working eight hours, studying eight hours and resting eight hours to be established even for the workers. The intellectuals should study harder than the workers.

Studying is not for moneymaking but for the better execution of the revolution. If you buckle down with this spirit, you can squeeze in time to study and increase the efficiency of your study.

In order to build up the atmosphere of study among the teachers, the leadership cadres of the Ministry of Higher Education must set an example first. The minister or vice-ministers had better go and deliver lectures at colleges. We have often stressed that not only the leadership cadres of the ministry but also the workers of the Party Central Committee should give lectures at colleges.

This is also an excellent method of making the cadres study. They cannot make pointless utterances to the students. If they are to give lectures, they will read books and brood over many problems.

The scholars of the Academy of Sciences must also deliver lectures at colleges. This will be greatly helpful to raising their qualifications.

Demonstration lectures should be held regularly for the teachers. If they are conducted properly, we can compel the teachers to study and improve the quality of their teaching. Those who are opposed to demonstration lectures seem to consider that we need not supervise college teachers, but they are wrong. Supervision is necessary for everyone. Only when they are under control, will they increase their sense of responsibility and only when many of them meet at such lectures, will they learn from each other and have uniform views.

We must also hold academic seminars extensively among the teachers. This is a good method to create the atmosphere of study and deepen their knowledge.

Next, the officials of the Ministry of Higher Education and college teachers must raise their political and ideological level. For this, it is necessary first to intensify their study of the Party policies.

Only when we know the Party policies, can we solve all problems correctly. Every problem must be solved not by any individual's subjective views or wisdom but from the standard of the Party policy. As long as the cadres are ignorant of the Party policies, they cannot direct any work.

Our colleges are training technicians and experts who must give direct leadership to work in all spheres of socialist construction. Therefore, the college students must know the Party policies and the college teachers who educate them and the officials of the Ministry of Higer Education who direct colleges must know the Party's policies better than anybody else.

Educational workers must be well versed not only in our educational policy but also in all the internal and external policies of the Party. Then they can train cadres the way the Party requires and equip them with the Party's ideology.

At present, however, when they receive the Party's decisions, educational workers read in most cases only those which directly concern their work and do not try to grasp the Party's general intentions. Those who are responsible for training the cadres required by the Party must not neglect studying the

Party policies this way.

From now, Party departments should arrange gatherings of educational workers and inform them in time of the problems of socialist construction and of international relations discussed by the Party.

Some comrades may consider that if this sort of gathering is held frequently it will obstruct teaching. But, in fact, this will be of great help to teaching. If you do not know the Party policy and just give lectures divorced from reality, without any orientation, it will be of no good.

In former days when we were engaged in revolutionary activities, we would often sit through the night and skip meals in order to discuss the policy of struggle. This is also applicable to the educational work. Educational workers must attend the gatherings where the Party policy is informed or studied, even if their sleeping hours are curtailed. Thus all of them will be throughly versed in the Party's policies.

Next, we must build up the colleges better and raise the students' qualifications.

Our country has now more than 90 institutes of higher learning. Besides numerous regular universities and colleges at the capital and provinces, there are factory colleges at large factories and plants. In addition, provincial seats and large factories and enterprises have communist colleges and their branches. The Party's policy of opening so many colleges for the speedy development of higher education was correct.

And yet, in the course of implementing this policy, there appeared a few shortcomings. Because the colleges enrolled a large number of students, there were some among them who were not qualified. Accordingly, some quitted schooling halfway and among the graduates there are quite a few people who cannot perform their duties as the nation's cadres. This is a great loss to the state.

The rapid expansion of the colleges hindered the qualitative build-up of the ranks of teachers and there were bottlenecks in providing the students with conditions for studying.

Besides, we have a difficult situation now which prevents us from enrolling as many students as before. The factories and enterprises are not willing to send to regular colleges good comrades who play a nuclear role in production, though they send them to the factory colleges. As a result, the regular colleges have a poor reservoir of good students.

In addition, providing so many students with stipends is causing a heavy burden on the state. Also, we cannot but take into account a strain on manpower in our endeavors to fulfill the Seven-Year Plan. Our situation demands us to enlist as many people as possible in production. We cannot keep increasing the enrollment of the regular college students as before.

Therefore, the Party has recently taken measures for reducing the enrollment of regular colleges, while expanding the system of studying while on the job. To enroll good people and educate them in a responsible manner even by reducing the enrollment to a certain degree is better than to admit many beyond our capacity and educate and graduate them randomly. And this is in accord with the practical requirements of the development of our national economy.

In order to improve the educational work at the colleges they must be equipped with experimental apparatuses and necessary books.

Only when we have ample experimental apparatuses and books, can we raise the qualifications of the teachers and students. In spite of our great efforts, the state has failed to secure ample experimental apparatuses needed by the colleges and scientific research institutions.

It seems to me that the State Planning Commission knew the importance of the experimental apparatuses but did not import them because they had not enough foreign currency. We are feeling a strain on foreign currency. That is true. However, if we are to develop our science and technology, we must not begrudge money on importing the experimental apparatuses. Even if they costs us some foreign currency, we must be bold enough to import indispensable apparatuses for the Academy of Sciences and colleges. First of all, Kim Il Sung University and Kim Chaek Polytechnical Institute should be provided with good apparatuses.

However, we must fight resolutely against the wrong tendency to ask the state for the things which can be made easily at our scientific institutions or colleges.

The slogan of self-reliance must first be carried into practice by the Ministry of Higher Education and colleges. Only then can the technicians and experts graduated from colleges run factories and enterprises in the spirit of self-reliance.

At present in some factories and enterprises there are quite a few officials who lack the spirit of self-reliance.

A few days ago I visited the Pyongyang Knitted Wear Factory. For the purpose of providing our working people with knitted wear, we imported this factory; we paid a large amount of gold for it. However, this factory is a cripple, still unable to stand on its own feet.

I asked the cadres of this factory if they had any request. They asked me to secure foreign raw materials because they could not use the rayon yarn produced in our country; they even asked me to get them foreign needles, too.

Producing knitted goods with expensive foreign raw materials does not pay. If the management of this factory had the spirit of self-reliance, they would rack their brains to use domestic raw materials by all means. Moreover, they would not try to import even the needles which can be produced in our country.

They also asked me for a dye shop and a boiler room. But as for dyeing, they can do it at the adjacent Pyongyang Textile Mill and they can make use of the boilers of the nearby institutions or enterprises. But these people do not think of the country's situation and just want the state to help them in everything. It seems to me that they regard the Premier as a person who carries a huge bag and gives anything they want. So I earnestly advised them not merely to put up the slogan of self-reliance but to translate it into practice.

The technicians trained at our colleges do not try to solve knotty problems at factories with their own efforts but only ask to import anything they want in this way. Because the educational workers failed to educate them in the spirit of self-reliance.

Colleges should endeavor to make experimental apparatuses and installations for themselves and the teachers must set an example here. Since necessary supplies are lacking, it will be no easy job to make good experimental apparatuses. But you should not regard it as something mysterious. You should boldly endeavor to make those which you can make for yourselves and import only those you cannot make.

Also, we should set up a system under which the experimental apparatuses and books are used jointly. The colleges can use all the experimental apparatuses and books at the Academy of Sciences and factories. Because our country is not so wide, this is quite possible.

The Ministry of Higher Education should be the first to start making an inventory of the books and machines and apparatuses in our country. Because this work has not been done, none of us knows what sorts of experimental apparatuses and books our country has.

If we take an inventory of all the books and experimental apparatuses in our country and make a joint use of them, we will find no great difficulty in education and researches.

Next, you have to endeavor to keep colleges tidy. The state has not provided colleges with satisfactory conditions. This is the truth. But you must tidy up your schools with the existing conditions.

Most of our students have experience in military service or labor. And our teachers have undergone many trials. So once they are put in motion properly, they will keep their colleges neat and tidy.

Only when the students are accustomed to run the economy industriously while at school, can they take good care of the nation's economy after they are in the world.

College education is the last process of school education. Therefore, the college graduates must be all-round cadres who are not only armed politico-ideologically and equipped with scientific and technological knowledge but know how to manage the economy meticulously.

In factories you often find some college graduates who do not know how to keep their factories tidy, nor their hostels nor their own bodies. This is also because colleges have not given them adequate education.

Educational workers must always make sure that, making full use of all conditions provided by the state and displaying creativity, they keep everything clean and tidy inside college premises and hostels and out.

In order to improve higher education, the ministry's leadership to colleges must be intensified.

In giving leadership to colleges, bureaucracy and formalism must be eliminated once and for all. Ministry personnel must not merely find fault or give scoldings at colleges. Just as the Party Central Committee has done recently at factories and enterprises, the leading officials must give substantial help to the work of colleges, working under the leadership of the college Party committees. They must go deep among the teachers and students and seriously discuss with them how to improve college training, how to guarantee the students better conditions for study and help them to untie their knotty problems in time.

From now, the leading officials of the Ministry of Higher Education should take with them many experts for guidance to the colleges. When it is beyond the power of the functionaries under the ministry, it is necessary to enlist in this work competent experts from the Academy of Sciences and other institutions. Only by doing this, can they delve deep into the work of colleges.

The minister or vice-ministers cannot know everything. If they are to give specific guidance to college work, they must have talks with the teachers and students, attend Party cell meetings, listen to lectures and inspect experimental rooms. To do this, experts on social and natural sciences and those who have much experience in education must join their efforts.

In this way, the Ministry of Higher Education must intensify the political life at colleges and firmly unite all the teachers and students around the Party and must improve educational work and build up the colleges well. This will make it possible to develop valuable persons with strong Party and class spirits, rich knowledge and high cultural development.

At the general membership meeting of the Party organization of the ministry, many good views have been forwarded on the improvement of higher educatiom. After this meeting you must quickly correct your defects and carry through the Party's educational policy so as to bring about a new change in the work of higher education.

ON SOCIALIST CONSTRUCTION IN THE DEMOCRATIC PEOPLE'S REPUBLIC OF KOREA AND THE SOUTH KOREAN REVOLUTION (Excerpt)

Lecture at the ''Ali Archam'' Academy of Social Sciences of Indonesia, *April 14, 1965*

4. On the Questions of Firmly Establishing Juche and Implementing the Mass Line

All our victories and successes in the socialist revolution and the building of socialism are attributable to our Party's Marxist-Leninist leadership and to the heroic struggle of our people for the implementatiom of the Party's lines and policies.

Thoroughgoing establishment of Juche was most important for our Party to give correct leadership to the Korean people in their revolutionary struggle and constructive work.

To establish Juche means holding fast to the principle of solving for oneself all problems of the revolution and construction in conformity with the actual condition of one's country, and mainly by one's own efforts. This is a realistic and creative stand which opposes dogmatism and applies the universal truth of Marxism-Leninism and the experience of the international revolutionary movement to one's country in conformity with its historical conditions and national peculiarities. This represents an independent stand of discarding the spirit of relying on others, of displaying the spirit of self-reliance and solving one's own affairs on one's own responsibility under all circumstances.

The Korean Communists are making a revolution in Korea. The Korean revolution is the basic duty of the Korean Communists. It is obvious that we cannot make the Korean revolution when we are ignorant of, and removed from, the reality of Korea. Marxism-Leninism, too, can become a powerful weapon of our revolution only if it is applied to our country's reality.

Masters of the Korean revolution are our Party and our people; the decisive factor in the victory of the Korean revolution, too, is our own strength. It is self-evident that we cannot make a revolution by relying on others, and that others cannot make the Korean revolution for us. International support and encouragement are important to the revolution, to be sure, but, above all, work and struggle by ourselves, the masters, are essential for the advancement of the revolution and its victorious conclusion.

In the world, there are countries large and small and parties with a long or short history of struggle. Nevertheless, all parties are fully independent and equal and, on this basis, cooperate closely with each other. Each party carries on its revolutionary struggle under the specific circumstances and conditions of its own country; by so doing it enriches the experience of the international revolutionary movement and contributes to its further development. The idea of Juche conforms to this principle of the communist movement, and stems directly from it.

The problem of establishing Juche has acquired special importance for the Korean Communists in view of the circumstances and conditions of our country and the complexity and arduousness of our revolution.

While resolutely fighting in defense of the purity of Marxism-Leninism against revisionism, our Party has made every effort to establish Juche in opposition to dogmatism and flunkeyism towards great powers. Juche in ideology, independence in politics, self-sustenance in the economy and self-defence in national defense—this is the stand our Party has consistently adhered to.

Holding fast to the principles of Marxism-Leninism, our Party studies and analyses the realities of Korea and, on this basis, determines its policies independently. Unrestrained by any existing formulas or propositions, we boldly put into practice whatever conforms to the principles of Marxism-Leninism and the realities of our country.

We respect the experiences of other countries, but always take a critical attitude towards them. So we accept any experience that is beneficial to us, but reject any that is unnecessary and harmful. Even when introducing a good experience from another country, we do so by remodelling and modifying it to suit the actual conditions of our country.

Our Party has always maintained an independent stand in its approach to the international communist movement and, likewise, in its struggle against modern revisionism in particular. We are resolutely fighting against modern revisionism, and this fight is invariably conducted on the basis of our own judgment and conviction and in conformity with our actual conditions. We consider that only by keeping firmly to such a stand can we correctly wage the struggle against revisionism and make substantial contributions to the defense of the purity of Marxism-Leninism and the strengthening of the unity of the international communist movement.

If one fails to establish Juche in the ideological and political domains, one will be unable to display any creative initiative because his faculty of independent thinking will be paralyzed, and in the end one will even be unable to tell right from wrong and will blindly follow what others do. Anyone who has lost his identity and independence in this way may fall into revisionism, dogmatism and every description of Right and "Left" opportunism and may eventually bring the revolution and construction to naught.

In our country, there was also a time when some of the cadres had been infected with dogmatism and flunkeyism towards great powers, and they did quite a bit of harm to our work. The dogmatists disregarded our realities without studying them and sought to swallow the experience of others whole and copy it mechanically. This sort of person, who simply looked up to others and got accustomed only to copy from them, slid down in the end into national nihilism, where everything that is his own is disparaged and everything foreign is lauded. This tendency was manifested most seriously on the ideological front. The dogmatists, instead of studying, explaining and giving publicity to our Party's policies, merely echoed other people like parrots. They even went so far as to deny our people's history of struggle and revolutionary traditions, and tried to paralyze the creativity of our scholars in scientific research work, to teach the students what they had copied in toto from others in education too, discarding everything national and disseminating only foreign tendencies in literature and art.

In our country the harm done by dogmatism was revealed most glaringly during the war, and became all the more intolerable in the postwar period as the socialist revolution and the building of socialism progressed rapidly. Moreover, it gradually dawned on us in this period that the revisionist trend infiltrates through the medium of dogmatism.

In 1955, therefore, our Party set forth the definite policy of establishing Juche, and has been persistently waging an energetic ideological struggle to carry it through ever since. The year 1955 marked a turning point in our Party's consistent struggle against dogmatism. It was also at that time in fact, that we started our struggle against modern revisionism that had emerged within the socialist camp. Our struggle against dogmatism was thus linked up with the struggle against modern revisionism.

It was of paramount importance in establishing Juche to strengthen the study of Marxism-Leninism among the cadres and Party members and, at the same time, to equip them firmly with their Party's ideas, its lines and policies. We have energetically conducted ideological work among the cadres and Party members so that all of them may think in terms of the Party's intentions, make a deep study of Party policies, work in accordance with them and devotedly strive for their implementation. Our experience shows that when the Party ranks are firmly united ideologically and organizationally, dogmatism can be overcome, the infiltration of revisionism can be prevented and all work can be done creditably in line with the Party's intentions.

At the same time, we decisively intensified, among all the Party members and working people, the study of our country's past and present and our people's revolutionary and cultural traditions. We saw to it that in all sectors of the ideological front including science, education, literature and art, things of our own country are given priority, national traditions are honored, fine national heritages are carried forward, and the advanced culture of other countries is also introduced, not in its entirety, but through assimilation to convert it into ours.

These measures have greatly boosted the national pride of our people and their awareness of independence, and led them to reject the tendency of mechanically imitating other people's ways, and to endeavor to do everything in conformity to the actual conditions of our country. As a result of the establishment of Juche, science and technology have progressed with great rapidity, qualitative changes have taken place in education and in the training of cadres, and a new, socialist national culture, congenial to the life and sentiments of our people, has blossomed and developed.

While establishing Juche in the ideological and political spheres, our Party has, in the economic sphere, held fast to the principle of self-reliance and the line of building an independent national economy.

If one lacks the spirit of self-reliance, one will eventually lose faith in one's own strength and make little effort to mobilize one's national resources and, accordingly, one cannot carry out the revolutionary cause. We are engaged in the revolutionary struggle and constructive work with a determination to carry out the Korean revolution by our own efforts and build socialism and communism in our country by our own labor and with our national resources.

Needless to say, we fully recognize the importance of international support and encouragement and consider foreign aid a necessity. But we reject the erroneous ideological viewpoint and attitude of slackening our own revolutionary struggle while only awaiting an advantageous international opportunity to offer itself, or of making no effort ourselves while simply turning to other countries for aid. Both in the revolutionary struggle and in constructive work, self-reliance should be given priority, while support and encouragement from outside are regarded as secondary. Only when one wages a struggle in this spirit can he expedite the revolution and construction of his country to the maximum and also contribute to the development of the international revolutionary movement.

In the period of postwar rehabilitation our country received economic and technical aid from fraternal countries amounting to some 500 million rubles (550 million dollars), and this, of course, was of great help to our rehabilitation and construction. But in those days, too, it was our principle to enlist the forces of our people and our national resources to the fullest; at the same time we also endeavored to make effective use of the aid from the fraternal countries. In fact, it was our own forces that played the decisive role in the postwar rehabilitation and construction. There is no need to make further mention of the achievements scored in the economic construction of our country in subsequent years.

We have thus laid the solid foundations of an independent national economy on the principle of self-reliance.

Economic independence is an indispensable requisite for the building of a rich and strong and civilized independent state. Without building an independent national economy, it is impossible to guarantee the firm political independence of a country, develop the productive forces and improve the people's standard of living.

Socialism means complete abolition of national inequality along with class exploitation, and requires an all-round development of the economy, science and technology. It is therefore natural that the economy of socialism should be an independent economy developed in a comprehensive way.

We by no means oppose economic cooperation between states or advocate building socialism in isolation. What we do reject is the great-power chauvinist tendency to check the independent and comprehensive development of the economy of other countries and, furthermore, to subordinate their economy to one's own on the pretext of "economic cooperation" and "international division of labor". We consider that mutual cooperation should be based on the building of an independent national economy in each country, and that this alone makes possible the steady expansion and development of economic cooperation between states on the principles of complete equality and mutual benefit.

Today our country is developing its economy by relying

mainly on its own technology, its own resources and on the efforts of its own cadres and people; it is meeting the domestic needs for heavy and light industrial goods and agricultural produce mainly with its national products.

As for our country's economic relations with foreign countries, they are those of filling each other's needs and assisting each other on the principles of complete equality and mutual benefit, and these relations are materialized through foreign trade and in various other ways.

Having laid the solid foundations of an independent national economy, we have come to possess our own economic basis for increasing the wealth and power of the country and markedly raising the people's living standard, and have developed the capacity to expand and promote economic cooperation with other countries. Our economic independence also constitutes the reliable material basis for guaranteeing the country's political independence and strengthening its defense capabilities.

Along with the establishment of Juche, the implementation of the mass line has been one of the most important questions in our Party's leadership of the revolution and constructive work.

Considering that the decisive guarantee for the acceleration of the socialist revolution and the building of socialism consists of enlisting all the creative energies of the masses of the people and offering full scope for their enthusiasm, creative initiative and talents, our Party has consistently held to the revolutionary mass line in all its activities.

Our Party has been able to achieve great successes in the socialist revolution and the building of socialism by relying on the great revolutionary zeal and inexhaustible creative powers of our people who, taking their destiny in their own hands, are out to build a new life. The Party, always placing faith in the popular masses, consulted them and enlisted their forces and wisdom in overcoming any difficulties and ordeals it encountered.

We have also successfully carried out many huge and difficult construction projects by launching mass campaigns. The let-one-machine-tool-make-machine-tools movement, the building of local industry factories, grand nature-remaking projects for irrigation, and the rehabilitation and construction of towns and villages that had been reduced to ashes—all this was carried out through mass campaigns, through all-people drives.

In our country, science and technology are also developing rapidly in a mass movement through creative cooperation between the scientists and technicians on the one hand and the workers and peasants on the other; literature and art are also flourishing resplendently with every passing day through the combination of the activities of professional writers and artists with the literary and art activities of the broad masses.

The method of relying on the masses and rousing the broad masses to activity is a revolutionary and positive method, and is a method that makes it possible to mobilize all the potentialities and possibilities to the fullest in the revolution and construction.

The Marxist-Leninist party must implement the mass line at all times, both before and after seizing power, both in the revolutionary struggle and in constructive work. And the danger of going back on the mass line increases once the party seizes power. Upon its foundation after liberation, our Party assumed the leadership of the government, and many of our functionaries had had little experience in the revolutionary struggle and mass work in the past. It was therefore a particularly important matter for us to improve the functionaries' method and style of work to carry through the mass line.

Our Party has waged a vigorous ideological struggle to eliminate bureaucracy and establish the revolutionary mass viewpoint among the functionaries. The Party has made tireless efforts to get all the functionaries to acquire the revolutionary work method of going deep among the masses, consulting them, deriving strength and wisdom from them and mobilizing them to solve the tasks ahead.

The method of work which is called Chongsan-ri method in our country, is precisely the embodiment and development of our Party's mass line in conformity with the new realities of socialist construction. The Chongsan-ri method consists fundamentally in the fact that the upper bodies help the lower ones, superiors help their inferiors, political work is given priority and the masses are roused to carry out the revolutionary tasks.

Through the popularization of the Chongsan-ri method, we

have decisively improved the functionaries' method and style of work and brought about a big turn in the work of the Party, state and economic bodies.

To give priority to political work is the most important thing in bringing out the revolutionary zeal and creative energy of the masses of the people.

The Communists always fight in defense of the people's interests and for their happiness. To this end, the broad masses of the people should be awakened and mobilized. One of the intrinsic advantages of socialism is that under this system the working people, freed from exploitation and oppression, display voluntary enthusiasm and creative initiative in their work for the country and society and for their own welfare.

To conduct political work well among the masses and thereby induce them to voluntarily perform the revolutionary tasks is, therefore, a powerful method of work stemming from the inherent character of the Communists and from the very nature of the socialist system.

It is fundamentally wrong to cling only to economic and technological work while neglecting political work, and to lay stress on material incentives only, without raising the political and ideological consciousness of the working people.

Our Party has firmly adhered to the principle of giving priority to political work in all matters.

In carrying out any revolutionary task, we began by thoroughly explaining and bringing home to all the Party members and the masses the Party's policy with regard to the task and made sure that they held mass discussions about ways and means of executing the Party's policy and strove to carry it through with a high degree of political consciousness and enthusiasm. To raise the class awakening of the working people and their level of political and ideological consciousness, we have also energetically carried on communist education among them in combination with education in the Party's policies and our revolutionary traditions.

Political work is precisely work with people, and it is basic to Party work. Lacking the Party's leadership, the masses cannot be mobilized, nor can socialism and communism be built. Only on the basis of increasing the leading role of the Party and constantly strengthening Party work in all spheres, have we been able to successfully carry out the principle of giving priority to political work.

Thus, by energetically carrying on political work, work with people, which is the basis of Party work, we have been able to bring our working people to display a high degree of revolutionary enthusiasm and creative energy and to inspire them to mass heroism and mass enthusiasm for labor.

To raise the Party's leading role and give decided priority to political work, combining this properly with economic and technological work, and to steadily raise the working people's political awakening and level of consciousness, combining this properly with material incentives, is the basic method our Party employs in mobilizing the masses for socialist construction.

To educate and remold the masses of all walks of life and unite them solidly around the Party was a very important question in carrying out our Party's mass line.

The political unity and solidarity of the people in the northern half of the Republic is not only the decisive guarantee for building a new life in the northern half, but is also one of the basic factors in reunifying the country and achieving the victory of the Korean revolution.

Our Party has consistently and tirelessly worked to rally the people of all walks of life in the northern half closely around it and to convert our revolutionary base into a stronger political force.

The protracted colonial rule of Japanese imperialism, the partition of the country and, particularly, the enemy's alienation maneuverings during the war, have rendered the social and political composition of the population of our country very complex. However, we cannot make a revolution with flawless people alone, casting away all those whose social status and social and political life are checkered.

Therefore, our Party, closely combining the class line with the mass line, has followed the policy of winning over to the side of revolution everybody save the handful of malicious elements. Under conditions where the socialist system had already triumphed and the Party's force had grown decisively and its authority and prestige had become unshakably established among the masses, we considered it possible to educate and remold all people, except the confirmed reactionaries with a hostile class origin.

Thus, we boldly trusted and embraced even those whose

social status and records of social and political life were checkered, and ensured them conditions for working in peace, provided they now supported our Party and showed enthusiasm in their work.

Life has fully confirmed the correctness of this policy of our Party. By carrying through the policy we have been able, and are successfully continuing, to educate and remold the broad masses from all walks of life. Although the composition of our population is complex and we are facing the enemy at close range, our Party has today firmly united the masses of the people around it, and a cheerful, uplifted atmosphere prevails in our society.

The all-people Chollima Movement which has been under way with unabated vigor in our country is the most brilliant embodiment of our Party's mass line.

The Chollima Movement represents a mass drive which organically fuses collective innovations in economic and cultural construction with the work of educating and remolding the working people. Through the Chollima Movement all the wisdom, enthusiasm and creative energy of our people are brought into full play, innovations are wrought in all spheres of economy, culture, thought and morality, and the building of socialism in our country is greatly accelerated.

The Chollima Movement is the general line of our Party in socialist construction. The essence of this line is to unite all the working people more firmly around the Party by remolding them through education in communist ideas and to give ample scope to their revolutionary zeal and creative talents so as to build socialism better and faster.

We will continue to expand the Chollima Movement and develop it in depth, and thus further expedite the building of socialism in the northern half of our country.

CONCLUDING SPEECH AT THE 11TH PLENARY MEETING OF THE FOURTH CENTRAL COMMITTEE OF THE WORKERS' PARTY OF KOREA, JULY 1, 1965 (Excerpt)

2. On Improving Higher Education and Scientific Research Work

One of the most important tasks for higher education and scientific research work is to revolutionize intellectuals. We already proposed this task when we were guiding the General Membership Meeting of the Party Organization of the Ministry of Higher Education. However, I would like to reemphasize this, because it may be misinterpreted and, if it is carried out incorrectly, it will bring about an undesirable effect, though it is an excellent undertaking in itself.

Some of our comrades still do not have a correct understanding of the question of intellectuals and fail to work well with them, with old ones in particular.

Now in our country there is little difference between new and

old intellectuals. If the southern half of the country is liberated
in the future, there may arise the question of intellectuals who
had schooling in the old society, but, in the northern half of the
Republic, this question has been basically solved through the
revolutionary struggle.

For 20 years since liberation our old intellectuals have
engaged in the revolutionary struggle and faithfully served
our Party and people. Our Party consistently maintains the
policy of trusting and drawing them into its fold and patiently
educating them. Today they are splendidly performing their
role in our revolutionary cause, together with a large army of
new intellectuals whom we have brought up after liberation.

At present some comrades consider that only those who
engaged in the guerrilla warfare or in the underground activities in the homeland before are revolutionaries and that those
who worked after liberation are not revolutionaries. This is a
very narrow-minded view.

The revolutionary struggle has been going on for 20 years
after liberation. Why should only those who have fought since
before liberation be revolutionaries?

Of course, there is a difference between the former guerrillas
or underground revolutionaries and those who started the
struggle only after liberation. This is the difference in the duration of revolutionary struggle. The former have 30-40 years'
history of struggle, while the latter 20 years'. They are only
different from each other in the term of struggle but all of them
are revolutionaries, no doubt. Of course, we should respect the
former as revolutionary forerunners, as veteran revolutionaries. At the same time, we must regard the latter as
revolutionaries and see to it that they are legitimately proud of
being as such.

This year we are celebrating the 20th anniversary of the
founding of our Party. The revolutionary struggle our Party
has waged for the last 20 years is no less arduous than the
guerrilla warfare or the underground activities of the past.

Now, take the struggle to found our Party for example. This
was a very arduous one. We founded a Marxist-Leninist party
through a harsh struggle against the factionalists and Right
and "Left" opportunists of all hues.

We also smashed the enemy's subversion and sabotage and
set up a people's power led by the working class.

The struggles for land reform, the nationalization of industries and other democratic reforms as well as the struggle for the emancipation of women were also hard revolutionary struggles.

The Fatherland Liberation War against US imperialism and the Syngman Rheeites was as hard as the anti-Japanese guerrilla struggle. This war was a liberation war participated in by the entire people. Our intellectuals joined the workers and peasants in the gallant battle dedicating their lives.

Many of our intellectuals went as far down as the Rakdonggang River on propaganda teams. They broke through the enemy's encirclement and came back into the Party's embrace, surmounting all sorts of hardships and ordeals.

Our writers and artists also rendered splendid service for the victory of war. The writers wrote many militant works which helped to rouse the people to patriotism and firmly convinced them of victory; and the artists went to the fields of battle under the hail of shells and encouraged the soldiers with their songs and dances. Who can say this was not a revolutionary struggle?

The Fatherland Liberation War clearly distinguished friend from foe within our ranks. Those who supported the revolution bravely fought without vacillation along the road indicated by the Party, whereas those who opposed the revolution went over to the enemy side. During the retreat, because of the mistake on the part of some of our officials, certain intellectuals allegedly with problematic political backgrounds were left behind, but even they followed the revolutionary ranks.

As you see, ours are the revolutionary intellectuals tested and trained in the midst of the severe trials of war.

After the war they devotedly strove to defend the Party and implement its policies. We, all of us, rebuilt our economy on the debris of war and worked hard to build an independent national economy. In response to the Party's call, all of us built our economy and culture, those with physical strength contributing their physical strength and those with talents their talents.

Our intellectuals also took an active part in the struggle to establish Juche against dogmatism and flunkeyism in the realms of ideology and culture. As a matter of fact, in a sense, the ideological revolution is harder than directly fighting the enemy, arms in hands.

Our postwar struggle against factionalism was also a hard one. Internally, the anti-Party, counterrevolutionary factionalists defied our Party with the backing of great-power chauvinists and, externally, the Yankees instigated Syngman Rhee to threaten to march north again. In those grim days our intellectuals resolutely fought the factionalists to defend our Party.

As you see, for 20 years, our intellectuals have entrusted their destiny to our Party and fought together with the workers and peasants for the triumph of the revolution under the banner of the Party, sharing sweets and bitters with them; and they devoted all their wisdom and talents to the construction of a new country.

Why, then, are we proposing the task of revolutionizing them today? Not that we do not yet trust them. If any comrades regard their revolutionization as digging into their past records again or examining their class origins, they are grossly mistaken.

Of course, among our intellectuals there are some who led somewhat plentiful lives and others who had to work at Japanese imperialist institutions against their will or served the capitalists in order to earn their living because they had been deprived of their country and had not had their own government in the past.

However, they came over to the side of the people after liberation and have been invariably engaged in revolutionary activity for the benefit of the country and the people. There is a saying that ten years changes the looks of mountains and rivers. And their ideology cannot but be developed now that they have carried out the revolutionary struggle for 20 long years. Even if some intellectuals committed some errors before, they were written off by the achievements they made after liberation, we should say.

Today quite a few old intellectuals are working as ministers and a great many of them are playing a very important role in the economic, scientific, cultural and educational spheres—in all branches of the national economy. Therefore, it is out of the question now to examine their class origins and dig into their past records. We must never distrust them; we must not regard the Party's task of their revolutionization as digging into their past records again.

What, then, is the revolutionization of intellectuals? It means thoroughly eradicating the residue of old petty-bourgeois ideas still remaining in their minds, equipping them with the revolutionary ideology of the working class, communist ideology, and thereby more firmly preparing them to be true intellectuals of the working class, to be ardent revolutionary fighters who faithfully serve the people.

The revolutionization of intellectuals comes to the fore as an inevitable task at the stage of socialist revolution. This is a major component of the struggle for the working-classization and revolutionization of all society.

We must educate and remold our intellectuals with communist spirit and thoroughly revolutionize them so that they will enhance their role in socialist construction and go to a communist society together with the working class.

To build a communist society we must occupy two fortresses. One is the material and technical fortress; occupying this fortress means establishing the unitary communist ownership of the means of production and raising the productive forces to such a high level that each works according to his ability and receives his share according to his needs.

To build a communist society we must also capture the ideological fortress. Unless everyone is thoroughly reeducated in communist ideology, the material and technical fortress of communism cannot be occupied and, accordingly, it is impossible to build a complete communist society.

Laying the material and technical foundations of communism is a very difficult task, but remolding people into a new communist type of men is still more difficult and arduous.

It is a hard task requiring protracted and persevering efforts to completely eradicate the survivals of old ideas of all hues such as egoism and individualism remaining in the minds of the people, and to educate and transform them into a new communist type of men developed in an all-round way.

Old ideas are surviving in everyone to some degree or other. They are still remaining not only in intellectuals but also in workers and peasants. True, the intellectuals have more remnants of outworn ideas. They retain many survivals of old ideas and they are more apt to be affected by unsound ideologies than anyone else. That is why their revolutionization has been raised today as a matter of urgency.

Old intellectuals had schooling in the old society and were greatly influenced by bourgeois ideas. Some of them were relatively well-off before, because they owned a few *chongbo* of orchard or land. Of course, they have also been considerably remolded through the revolutionary struggle with us after liberation, but, as their lives become more and more affluent along with the advancement of our society now, their old habits may revive and they may be infected with obsolete ideas which run counter to communist ideology. This is also because of the fact that intellectuals are engaged in mental labor. Since they are entirely engaged in mental labor, separated from productive activities, they have less opportunity of training themselves than other working people and lack revolutionary spirit.

It is very hard to control brain work because in most cases it is conducted individually and the daily result is not conspicuous. This is one of the major conditions that give rise to liberalism and individualism among intellectuals; from this stems their undesirable tendency to dislike strict discipline and supervision by others. Take scientific research workers for example. There is no way of knowing exactly how many pages of books they read and how much research work they perform during working hours. Therefore, if the intellectuals do not voluntarily observe revolutionary discipline, they may be indolent and lax.

At present our scientists claim that they study some subjects day and night, but they have failed to achieve any substantial success, because they are not fully revolutionized and lack staunch revolutionary will to carry out their assigned tasks to the last.

Therefore, if we are inconsistent in our endeavor to revolutionize our intellectuals, they may be captivated by the remnants of all sorts of outdated ideas—egoism, liberalism, fame-seeking, careerism and what not—and be affected by dogmatism and revisionism.

We know that in the past many intellectuals became laggards and dropped off the revolutionary ranks because they lacked ideological tempering. Some people joined us in the work of building the Party immediately after liberation, fought with us against American bandits, and in the harsh postwar days they worked together with us. However, since they neglected persevering, unceasing ideological training, they gradually became arrogant and, in the long run, went so far as to criticize the Party's policies.

The ex-chief engineer of the General Bureau of Mining was from the working class and was a new intellectual brought up by us, but he could not work at his post because he became ideologically backward. Once he visited the Holdong Mine, and made a show of himself; he perfumed a room tidied up by the miners, saying that it smelt bad. He gave a ride to a girl who had nothing to do with his work while asking the manager of the mine to come on foot to the destination 15 *ri* away and scolded him for his being late.

Quite a few writers and artists also became indolent and licentious because of the lack of ideological education. Only until recently some people received manuscript fees amounting to thousands of *won;* they deposited the money in banks and held drinking parties almost every day. They did not work and led licentious, dissipated lives, drinking wine day in, day out. They were so degenerate as to declare that beef did not taste good because it smelt of fodder.

As you see, anyone who neglects regular ideological education cannot but be rotten and, then, he will eventually have to drop out of the revolutionary ranks. He who drops out of the revolution halfway is called a fellow traveller. Figuratively speaking, the fellow traveller of the revolution is one who drops out of our ranks at Yangdok or on the Masik-ryong Pass, instead of going all the way to Wonsan, our destination. If we do not revolutionize our intellectuals and do not unceasingly temper their ideology, they may be fellow travellers who drop out of the path of revolutionary struggle to reach communism.

We must intensify communist education among our intellectuals and thoroughly revolutionize them, so that we will make them not the fellow travellers of the revolution but revolutionaries who will fight together with us to the end.

The most important method to revolutionize our intellectuals is to strengthen their Party organizational life.

We can say that Party organizational life is a furnace for training the Party spirit of the Party membership. Only when they faithfully participate in this life, can they opportunely correct their shortcomings in and out of their work and constantly enhance their Party and class spirits. If anyone deviates from Party organizational life he may be indolent, commit errors and go in the wrong direction ideologically.

Intellectuals must participate in Party organizational life more faithfully than anyone else. Otherwise, they cannot eliminate the weak points inherent in them or eradicate the remnants of old ideas in their minds.

In order to faithfully lead Party organizational life you must intensify criticism and self-criticism.

Some of our intellectuals still have the tendency to fear to be criticized and hate to criticize others. When criticized a little, some comrades tremble for fear that a terrible stigma should be placed on them. You need not fear criticism so. Why should we fix any stigma on them today, which we have never done for 20 years since liberation?

Criticism and self-criticism is the best weapon to educate Party members and cadres and revolutionize intellectuals. Our intellectuals should know how to criticize themselves, frankly admitting their errors and shortcomings to the Party organizations; they should be bold enough to point out others' errors and offer them criticisms.

Next in importance for the revolutionization of intellectuals is to intensify their education in Marxism-Leninism. They must acquire Marxism-Leninism not only as a knowledge; they must study it also for their ideological training. Only then can the theory of Marxism-Leninism be a guide to action, a weapon in practice.

Particularly, our intellectuals must firmly arm themselves with our Party's policy, which is the creative application of Marxism-Leninism in the reality of Korea. Without knowing the Party's policy, they can neither establish Juche in scientific research work nor get rid of dogmatism and flunkeyism; they cannot conduct scientific research work to meet the demands of reality, because, without knowing it, it is impossible to understand the Party's intentions. Moreover, in the present complex situation, if the scientists as well as our cadres are ignorant of the Party's policy and dance after others' pipe, they may fall in any wind.

Only when our intellectuals firmly equip themselves with the Party's policy and act solely on the Party's instructions, will they achieve successes in their scientific research work by steadily adhering to the Juche position, and contribute splendidly to the state and the people. Firmly grasping the Party's policy and fighting tenaciously to defend and carry it through to the end is precisely the real way to serve the Party and the people, the way to revolutionize themselves.

The Party's policy is not the intention of a couple of persons; it is not mapped out by any one individual. It reflects the will of the whole Party members and is decided on by themselves. They are duty bound to carry out the Party's policy without reservation.

In revolutionizing themselves it is also important for intellectuals to always get in contact with reality and go among the masses of people. They must keep close touch with the workers and peasants; they must not only impart knowledge and technique to them, but also learn from them and always spot new problems in practical production activity. Only then can intellectuals temper their ideology and receive help in their own work.

The work of revolutionizing intellectuals cannot be carried out through a a couple of days of rush campaign. This can be done successfully only through tireless ideological tempering and education, principled ideological struggle.

The Party organizations must make sure that the revolutionization of intellectuals is their own work and must steadily conduct organizational and educational work to suit their characteristic features.

What is important next in higher education and scientific research work is to overcome flunkeyism and thoroughly establish Juche.

As you know, geographically speaking, our country is situated among the Soviet Union, China and Japan. These adjacent countries are all big countries, with larger territories and populations than ours. The Soviet Union is a great socialist power, Japan a developed capitalist state, and China a highly promising country, for she has a large territory and population. Therefore, unless our country joins advanced nations by quickly developing its science and technology, flunkeyism towards these neighboring countries will remain in our people's minds.

In the final analysis, flunkeyism has persisted in our country for a long period of time because our science and technology failed to develop and we were not rich and strong. During the Koguryo dynasty there was no flunkeyism in our country because it was powerful. However, as our national power gradually declined because of the corrupt rule of the feudal bureaucrats, flunkeyism emerged, and it was especially rampant towards the end of the Li dynasty. It has thus hindered our country's development for a long time.

From old times, our country is known as a golden garden for its beautiful mountains and clear rivers; it has rich natural resources though the territory is small. Ours is an industrious people with refined sentiments, outstanding talent and sturdy will. They have a long history and cultural traditions. Why should such a wise people as we blindly admire and worship others?

Flunkeyism must be rooted out in our generation. But we cannot completely eliminate flunkeyism by opposing it only in word. We can root it out only when we catch up with advanced nations in all spheres of economy and culture and, especially, develop our science and technology to a great extent.

For the rapid advancement of science and technology we must thoroughly establish Juche in scientific research work.

If we swallow up or uncritically assimilate foreign scientific and technological achievements, they will be of no use for us. We must introduce those needed for our economic construction and cultural development and reject those which do not suit our specific conditions. Our scientists must study subjects demanded by our country's reality and endeavor to create things needed by our people. They must concentrate especially on developing industry by using our natural resources.

Even after the worldwide victory of communism, the Koreans will live in Korea. Why should we leave the golden garden of three thousand *ri* and live in an alien land? We must exploit our inexhaustible natural resources and build a wonderful paradise in this land where our people will live through all generations.

In this world today there are many people who are glad to see our country's development but there are quite a few people who do not like it. We must know that the imperialists are ceaselessly maneuvering to blockade our country.

Therefore, also in order to counter the imperialists' blockade policy, we must continue to adhere to the principle of building our industry always relying on our own natural resources. When at least 70 per cent of the demand of raw materials is met domestically, we will be able to develop the country's economy on a secure foundation and support ourselves in case of imperialist blockade.

If our scientists buckle down to their studies, we can develop our industry as much as we want by using domestic raw materials and enjoy decent lives.

The gasification of anthracite and the oxygenation of carbide into which our scientists are now conducting research are of great significance in the development of our chemical industry. Once these methods are completed and introduced into production we will develop this industry more quickly, using anthracite and limestone which are inexhaustible in our country.

The research into the process of continuous steel making from granulated iron is nearly finished. This is gratifying, indeed. Once we complete this and apply the result, we will produce as much steel as we need, using our fuel.

You must more vigorously conduct the research work to make various chemical products by processing crude oil.

In order to intensify research work, the scientists must raise their scientific and theoretical qualifications. Today their scientific and theoretical level is still below the international standard and fails to meet the demands of the rapidly developing reality.

Of course, it is true that our country's science and technology have been developing rapidly. The number of scientists and scientific research institutions has greatly increased. Today we have tens of thousands of scientists and more than 140 research institutions. It is a tremendous success that in a short period after liberation we have trained so many scientists and set up such a great number of research institutions, we should say.

Some comrades now worry about the large number of institutions. This is wrong. Right after liberation we had not a single research institution, which caused our great anxiety. But today we have so many scientific research institutions. This is a good thing; there is no ground at all to worry about it. An important task confronting us today is to improve our guidance to the existing scientific research institutions, enhance their role and radically raise the qualifications of our scientists.

The Party has long proposed to build up the habit of study as a task for the whole Party. However, this habit is not fully built up among our scientists.

They must study harder than anybody else to raise their scientific and theoretical level. The Party organizations must make sure that they fully establish the habit of study and seriously study science.

The Party Central Committee is now studying how to make our cadres and scientists study harder. The basic method is to conduct political work well so that they may consciously endeavor to study, and we are also considering the problem of enforcing an examination system.

In order to better the qualities of our scientists, we must fully provide them with necessary conditions for studies and research work. At present our institutes of higher learning and scientific research institutions are equipped with some experimental apparatuses and books, but we cannot say they are sufficient. In order to raise the scientists' qualifications they must be adequately provided with experimental apparatuses and books.

The State Planning Commission is aware that more experimental apparatuses and books should be supplied to scientific research institutions, but it seems to me that they have failed to import them because of foreign currency problems. Of course, it is true that we are feeling some shortage of foreign currency. However, we must spend some money on experimental apparatuses and books badly needed for research work; we will obtain more foreign currency in the future.

Meanwhile, we must fight the scientists' erroneous tendency to rely on the state only.

At present they are asking the state for what they can make by themselves and do not strive to use effectively the research equipment and materials and experimental apparatuses which we have in our country. Our scientists must display the revolutionary spirit of self-reliance and always try to solve problems themselves, which they can solve.

The People's Army and the public security organs have lots of equipment and materials which can be used for scientific research work. They are not top-secret affairs. It is unnecessary to hide them for no reason. They must be shown and used jointly.

Concerning higher education, I have emphasized it on many occasions, so I will just touch briefly on the question of textbooks for the students.

As you know, the general theories of basic subjects such as chemistry, physics and mathematics are the same as other countries'. I think there will be no problem in writing textbooks on these subjects.

However, the textbooks on specialized subjects for senior students should be written to suit our country's specific situation. If they only learn general theories on the specialized subjects, they will not properly carry out their tasks at the places of assignment after their graduation. Therefore, as far as the senior students are concerned, textbooks must be so prepared as to impart to them both general theories and plenty of practical information on our country. For instance, the textbooks for chemistry students should contain detailed information on vinalon and viscose which have a great bearing on our chemical industry.

Furthermore, textbooks must be revised constantly in keeping with the advancing reality, so that our student may always study with textbooks suited to our actual conditions.

ON CORRECTLY PRESERVING THE NATIONAL CHARACTERISTICS OF THE KOREAN LANGUAGE

Talk with the Linguists, *May 14, 1966*

Today I would like to tell you briefly the need to further develop our national language. I remarked on this problem before, but I am going to stress it again.

As I often said, our country is situated among China, Japan and the Soviet Union, which are large and considerably developed in science and technology. This formerly gave rise to flunkeyism towards these countries among our people and in the course of political contacts and economic and cultural exchanges with these countries large numbers of their words found their way into our country.

During the feudal Li dynasty flunkeyism towards China prevailed and a wide range of its vocabulary was imported. As a result, even now our people use a large vocabulary borrowed from Chinese ideographs. One day I visited a salt field and found most of the terms used there of Chinese origin. Beside scientific and technical terms, our day-to-day language has also numerous Chinese-style expressions. Typical examples are that at present our functionaries say *saop-sigan* or *kongjak-sigan* rather than *il-hanun-sigan* to express "work hours" and *ochim* rather than *natjam* to express "midday nap".

Once I visited Canton, China, and saw a play. I noticed an analogy between the actors' pronunciations of Chinese characters and those of our people. So we can say that many of the Chinese ideographic sounds we pronounce came from the Canton region of China.

Following the seizure of our country by the Japanese imperialist in the past, our language was also adulterated largely by Japanese words. That is why our present-day vocabulary contains a considerable number of Japanese-style words that must be corrected. Many species of apples are also called in a Japanese way. The apple our people now call *kukgwang* was named by the Japanese. Probably the apple did not come from Japan. Still, as you see, it has a Japanese name. Not only *kukgwang*. The names of apples such as *uk* and *chuk* were also given by the Japanese.

The same is true of the appellations of rice species. Now people use the names given by the Japanese, such as *ryuku No. 132* and *chungsaengunbangju*.

Even our children who did not live under Japanese imperialism say *uwagi*, *ocha* and *obong* instead of *yangbok-chogori*, *cha* and *chaban* to designate a coat, tea and a tray.

After liberation Russian words came in to adulterate our language, which we checked.

And now, words not pure Korean but Chinese-style used by the Korean inhabitants in the Chientao district of China are infiltrating; the medley language used by the south Korean people after liberation, an adulteration of Korean with English, Japanese and words of Chinese origin, is infiltrating; Japanese-style Korean current among the Koreans in Japan is also coming in with the repatriates from Japan.

Now the Koreans living in Yenpien or northern Chientao of China say *hwachacham* and *kongin-kyegup* instead of *chonggojang* and *rodong-kyegup* to denote the railway station and the working class, and they coin Chinese-type Korean words which are beyond us. There are about one million Koreans in Chientao, and the incoming of their vocabulary does not present a big problem.

The infiltration of Japanese words into our language through the returnees is not a serious matter either.

The question lies in the language current in south Korea. Newspapers now published in south Korea, for instance, use not only words adopted from English and Japanese but also words of Chinese origin at random which even the Chinese themselves do not use. In fact the situation is such that if the words of Chinese, Japanese and English origins were eliminated from the vocabulary prevalent in south Korea, there would remain nothing of our own language except such grammatical particles as -ul and -rul. Language is a major index that characterizes a nation, and now the speech in south Korea has been bastardized by Western, Japanese and Chinese vocabulary to such a degree that it does not sound like our mother tongue and that the national characteristics of our language are gradually disappearing. This is really a dangerous phenomenon. If this is left unchecked, our national language will be threatened with the danger of extinction.

Once I had a talk with a cadre of the Japan Communist Party. He said that at present the Japanese language was also becoming mixed up with foreign languages. In Japan, he said, sciences are making progress, but they have little to be boasted of as Japan's own; they are characteristically American. And sciences themselves are capitalized on as a moneymaking means by businessmen. In other words, he said, today's Japanese sciences are not true sciences.

Thus, the Japanese copy entirely after American ways in the development of sciences, with the result that English terms flood in to adulterate Japanese, I was told.

A true patriot is communist. Communists alone truly love their mother tongue and endeavor to develop it.

We, the Communists, must preserve the national characteristics of our language and develop them further. No Korean with national conscience, even if not a Communist, will be happy to see the national characteristics of our language die away. Except the landlords, comprador capitalists and reactionary bureaucrats, the masses of the people in south Korea, the overwhelming majority of the population, are patriot-minded people who love our nation and our fatherland. So I believe they all hope for the development of our national language.

We should replace the words adopted from Chinese ideo-

graphs and loan words with our legitimate ones and develop
our language systematically.

When our native word and a word borrowed from Chinese
ideographs mean one and the same thing, we must adopt the
former and discard the latter, crossing this off from the dictionary. For example, such Chinese ideographic words as *sangjon* (mulberry field), *sokyo* (stone bridge) must give way to our
native words, namely, *bbongbat* and *toldari*. Even those words
coming from Chinese ideographs which are relatively in wide
use among the people must be written off from the dictionary,
if we have equivalent words of our own to replace them. For instance, the word *habok* (summer clothes) is in comparatively
wide use, but we must eliminate it from the dictionary since we
can say *yorumot*. If we eliminate even such words, we may
hear complaints that we are going too far. But otherwise we
will not be able gradually to reduce the number of words borrowed from Chinese ideographs nor will we be able to develop
our legitimate words. If in the future the people should continue to use any of the words eliminated from the dictionary,
we could then rehabilitate them.

We must also look up fine words in our dialects and use
them. Once in the days of our anti-Japanese guerrilla struggle,
Comrade An Gil said that the cultural standard in Hamgyong
Province was generally lower than that in Seoul but that the
province had a richer Korean vocabulary. He asked if it was
not nice to say *pulsulgi* rather than *kicha* (steam locomotive).
So I jokingly retorted that Hamgyong Province had loanwords
such as *bijiggae* and *koruman* for match and pocket.

The word *pulsulgi* is really fine. Of course, now we need not
replace *kicha* with *pulsulgi*. But if we make a careful survey of
our dialects, we shall be able to find excellent words of our own
which can be accepted even now.

We must try hard to search for our native words and call the
names of places by our own words. It sounds more tasteful to
call them in our own words than by Chinese ideographs pronounced in Korean fashion. For example, if we substitute the
Chinese ideographs *chogam* (red rock) for *pulgunbawi*, it
sounds very awkward, far from better. At present, quite a few
places are called in two ways—one in Chinese style and the
other in our own. For example, *toldari-gol* (stone-bridge
village) is also called by the Chinese ideographic name of
sokyo-dong. We must investigate all the purely Korean names

of places so that Chinese ideographic names are dropped as far as possible. We have already told the Academy of Social Sciences to investigate the names of places, but we do not know how the work is proceeding. Probably, it will be beyond the power of the academy to tackle the task all alone. So it would be a good idea for the Cabinet to adopt a decision or issue an order to assure the work. When the purely Korean names of places are all found out, they will have to be put into use. Now, all that is needed would be to revise the map accordingly. Administrative districts can also be renamed by a Cabinet decision.

We must not only dig up and put back into use our native words but also coin new words from them.

True, new words sound a bit awkward at first. But with frequent use they will become familiar. Let me take the example of the appellation *choegoinminhoeui* (the Supreme People's Assembly), though it is a Chinese ideographic name. At first when we put forward this name, some people objected, saying that the term *parliament* was used in other countries and so it was improper to call the permanent establishment by name of *hoeui* (assembly). But we ignored the objection and put the name into use. At first people thought it awkward to pronounce the name. But constant use has made it familiar now, hasn't it? When necessary we can thus coin other words, too.

In my opinion, it would be good to rename *kukwang, uk chuk* and other apples after the names of the places where they are grown. After studying where a species of apple is produced in the largest quantity and which is of the best quality, you may rename it *pukchong, songhwa, nampo* or *ryonggang*.

We must also change the names of rice species after our own linguistic style.

Some comrades now say that because the present names of apples, rice and the like have become familiar to us, it will be difficult to change them. But we must change them boldly without hesitation. If we should leave even these Japanese names as they are, how could we explain to our posterity? Under the present circumstances when Japanese-style Chinese ideographic words are used as they are in south Korea, if we remain inactive, our language will really die out. We must boldly revamp the Japanese-styled Chinese ideographic words.

Formerly our ancestors were infected with flunkeyism towards great powers, so that they even used Chinese ideographic names to call people. It is advisable that from now on our legitimate words be used as far as possible in naming babies.

Foreign terms coming in through scientific and cultural exchanges with other countries should be immediately given equivalents in our language. It is the rule that any country will follow in the wake of those countries which are ahead in science and technology. This gives rise to the inflow of words from advanced countries and, accordingly, the appearance of loanwords. But it will do well to give our own denotations to foreign terms when they are first introduced. When the Soviet breeds of pig *big white breed* and *northern Siberian breed* were introduced into our country and we got a new hybrid by crossing them with our *native Chunghwa breed*, we named it *Pyongyang-jong.* How nice it sounds! It will also do well to change other foreign words into our own.

In doing this, we must not give too much amplified forms to technical terms. As for the new terms, the National Language Standardizing Commission should exercise good control over them.

You must not treat all the words borrowed from Chinese ideographs and loanwords indiscriminately just because they should be revised. Even Chinese ideographic words should be left as they are, if they have been firmly accepted by the people and established completely as Korean words. For example, such words as *hakgyo* (school) and *pang* (room) could be excluded from the category of Chinese ideographic words and, therefore, they need not be revised. Take the word *pobchik* (law) now in wide use. We have no suitable word to replace it right now. The same is true of the word *kaengdo* (level or shaft). Social and natural sciences have many such words, and it is a problem to revise them.

Besides, serious thought should be given to Chinese ideographic words and our legitimate words when they are synonymous but have different nuances. For instance, the Chinese ideographic word *chiha* (underground) is synonymous with the purely Korean word *ddangsok*, and the word *simjang* (heart) with *yomtong*, but their nuances are different. So we have no choice but to leave all of them alone. It would not do to replace the word *chiha-tujaeng* (underground struggle) with *ddangsok-tujaeng* or the sentence *Pyongyang-un naui simjang* (Pyongyang is dear to my heart) with *Pyongyang-un naui yomtong.* If all such words of Chinese origin are abolished, there will arise a chaos in our lingual life. Therefore, even when a legitimate word and a word of Chinese origin are synonymous, they must be treated differently as the case may be.

Military terms can be revised. Following liberation we refashioned a few of them. The command *charyot* (attention!) is a word we initiated. The formerly-used command *kichok* was a word of Japanese origin. The Independence Army in northeast China also used it. So did Hong Bom Do, and Li Bom Sok, too, used it in training the cadets in a military academy. So we replaced *kichok* with *charyot*. As a matter of course, a word of command must have stress on its last syllable. After liberation we thought of revising all the words of command coming down from the last years of the Li dynasty and the years of Japanese imperialist rule. But we somehow could not manage to do so. At present many words borrowed from Chinese ideographs have currency in the army.

Pangdokmyon (gas mask) has also come from Chinese ideographs and so have *u* (excellent) and *ryang* (good) which are used when giving marks. It is preferable that military terms except those which are internationally common, be expressed in our own words. The same is the case with military technological terms.

In refashioning our vocabulary we must sometimes reckon with the context of word combination. Take the word *ilgi* (weather) for example. When we just want to say *ilgi*, we can dispense with it since it can be replaced with word *nalssi*, but when we take into account the word combination *ilgi-yebo* (weather forecast) and the like, the word *ilgi* must be preserved.

For the development of our language, we must lay the groundwork well. We should preserve and develop the national characteristics of our language with Pyongyang as the center and the speech of Pyongyang as the standard, because Pyongyang is the capital city and the cradleland of the revolution where there is the General Staff of our revolution and where its strategies and tactics are worked out for all fields of politics, economy, culture and military. And the term "standard language" must be replaced with another. The term "standard language" may give rise to misunderstanding as if the Seoul dialect were the standard. So there is no need to use it. It is proper that the language we, the builders of socialism, have developed on the basis of the speech of Pyongyang, the revolutionary capital city, be given a name other than the "standard language".

Though the term "cultured language" is not perfectly suitable, it nevertheless will do well to use it.

Further. In order to make our words well polished, debates through newspapers should be encouraged. Language, too, needs to go through the appraisal of the masses. Technical terms and the like should also be printed in newspapers twice or thrice a week; some 15 newly proposed words should be carried in papers at a time, so that the masses can write critical essays and submit questions about them. The new proposals should be published in both central and local papers. Opposite views on them should also be fully made known. In the debates through papers, it is essential to make all the submitted view known to the public so that the wisdom of many people can be enlisted. We must have many debates through newspapers not only to polish our language well but also to give a wide currency to the revised words among the masses. Thus, it is advisable to put the terminologies to the mass criticism, pool good opinions and finally decide on standard words for use.

Pooling the masses' wisdom can produce good results in refining our language. Those words which are difficult to refashion like the terms of social and technical sciences should be revised after a wide debate.

The task of revising our vocabulary should not be done hastily, but should be tackled one by one over a long period of time. You can never change all the words in question into our legitimate words suddenly in a day or two. If the words handed down over scores or hundreds of years are all changed in a day, people will not accept them and, moreover, those who have changed them will also hardly remember all of them and, accordingly, will be unable to use them all. Since this work has a bearing on the daily lingual life of all the people, it will absolutely not do to handle the work in a rush from a subjective desire. You should not try to revise a large number of Chinese ideographic words or loanwords at a time, but do so in a gradual way by the finish-one-by-one-method.

To begin with, we should correct our words of daily use. Some 5,000 to 6,000 words are now said to be used in the schools of common education. It is advisable to revise and popularize that amount of words first, while preparing the next batch of words to be put into currency after the former have all been spread. Your draft plan envisages revising and putting to public use 20 thousand words at a time. The number is too great. You will do well to fix the number of words used daily by the people, say, 5,000 or 10,000, and remold them first. You must follow the method of gradual proceeding just as a silkworm eats away a mulberry leaf. Otherwise, there can be a great confusion. So we should begin with revising words of everyday use.

And as I have mentioned above, the military terms should be revised at any rate, but it is a little premature now. Their revision should be carried out some day when the circumstances allow it. Even when they are revised, they should not be included in the dictionary but should be handled separately.

A suitable number of words should recoined according to plan, and then it must be seen to that all the people use them without fail. This necessitates careful recoining and putting intelligible words into currency. If you fail to do so and publish difficult words, people will not accept them but may rather use the original ones. Therefore, this work should be tackled with great care.

In order to popularize our legitimate words among our people, a dictionary should be compiled. If a dictionary of some 7,000 to 8,000 words or 10,000 words is compiled and put out for use as a standard, people will dispense with the trouble of going to scholars for consultation. But such a dictionary should be printed in a limited number.

You have suggested to publish a glossary of technical terms, but these terms have not yet been confirmed, so you should not publish it for sale at bookstores but work out its draft and distribute its copies only to civil service institutions. Thus, the Party and state organs should be made to use the draft as a standard for some time, so that technical terms are spread by degrees from these organs down to lower units. Technical terms are not coined at the lower units but in the center, in the Cabinet and ministries, which are spread down to the lower units. Therefore, the draft glossary of technical terms should be used first at civil service organizations for five to six years, or some ten years, during which time the terms should be constantly polished and put into wide currency.

Further, in order quickly to give currency to our legitimate words among the masses, they should be introduced first in the educational field, elementary schools in particular, and also in the newspapers and the radios in good time.

At present the old people are accustomed to using Chinese ideographic words, so they liberally use them in daily speech. Take the Chinese ideographic words *ilsang-yongo* (vocabulary of everyday use) for example. Accustomed to them, the old folks prefer these to the legitimate Korean words *nul-ssunun-mal*. In spelling too, they are accustomed to the old system and so make misspellings.

Therefore, in order to popularize our legitimate words smoothly we should begin with schools. In school the teaching of the revised Korean words should begin with the first-grade pupils of the primary school. Thus, our legitimate words should all be revived and taught to the children so that the boys and girls will correct the mistakes in the speech of the grown-ups. When old folks say *ochim* for midday nap, children should be able to promptly correct them to say *nat-jam*. As for the old people, they should be aware that they had been accustomed to the Chinese ideographic words because they had been wrongly taught in the past, and should bend efforts to learn our legitimate vocabulary and make the best use of new words. Thus, we should develop our own vocabulary by discarding the old words and accepting the new ones.

In order swiftly to popularize our legitimate words, the draft standard vocabulary should be introduced in the school textbooks; as the draft vocabulary agreed upon expands, the words used in the textbooks should be changed once in several years. Copies of the draft may also be given to institutions of higher learning for their use as a standard. Such copies should also be supplied to newspapers and radios. Then within a few years loanwords and Chinese ideographic words will be eliminated to some degree which the feudal rulers addicted to flunkeyism towards great powers had brought in in the past.

In the past flunkeyism prevailed among our people, which had considerably affected not only our linguistics but also other branches.

In Pyongyang before, there had been a "Kija mausoleum", which, in the final analysis, was a product of flunkeyism. We eliminated it and erected a pavilion on the spot, so now there is no one who comes to see "Kija". Of the similar legends the wrong ones produced under the influence of flunkeyism should all be removed.

Even now some people are lingering on flunkeyism. Certain scientists are little concerned with researches into our own natural resources to develop our industry, but are thinking of waiting on other countries. We should reject flunkeyism and establish Juche in the field of economic construction, so that we go along the way of building an independent economy with our own resources.

In the linguistics, too, Juche should be established so that our language develops systematically and that our people feel national pride and self-respect in speaking and writing it.

Until the whole world turns communist the peoples will live divided into nations, and Koreans will live in Korea and continue to speak Korean. Therefore, we should make every effort to preserve and develop our language well.

As you know, our language modulates clearly and its sounds are beautiful. In our pronunciation you can easily get to speak any foreign language. Some think that those who use loanwords and words borrowed from Chinese ideographs are learned and dignified men. Such a view should be dropped.

We should lead everyone to think that those who use Chinese ideographic words and loanwords are lacking in national pride, and that those who speak their own language well are learned men with a high national pride. Thus, everyone must be brought to acquire a clear viewpoint that he is intelligent only when he prefers the legitimate vocabulary of his own country—saying *yolahopsal* (19 years old) rather than *sipguse*. Only then will it be possible to preserve and develop our language and provide our posterity with a good foundation so as not to lose it.

Particularly the scholars who translate ancient books should clearly know that those who make good use of our legitimate words are cultured men.

In their translations of ancient books many Chinese ideographic words are left as they are. Of course, they are written in our letters, but their style is purely Chinese. Because words of Chinese origin are left as they are, people do not fully understand the translations of ancient books. Our country has a

large number of ancient books. They have all been translated
in Chinese style, so that we shall have to retranslate them in
our legitimate vocabulary. That is why young people are loath
to read them. Because they do not read ancient books, they are
ignorant of the national customs and etiquette. We must solve
this question by all means.

We should modernize ancient stories and novels so that people of our times can undertand them. If we do not modernize
the old books but try to make people understand them through
teaching them Chinese ideographs, that will involve difficulty.
I once gave advice to retranslate the *Tale of Chun Hyang* in an
easy style, with the result that it has now become a little
easier. All other books too should be simplified. Not only ancient stories and novels but also legendaries and historical
stories should be modernized so that they may be intelligible to
our contemporaries. While on the subject of the ancient
writings, I am going to mention one thing more. In adapting
ancient works for the screen or the stage, they should not be
vulgarized. The screen version of the novel *Tale of Ryangban* is
too much vulgarized and therefore is uninteresting. Originally,
this work was dedicated to the class struggle of those days,
but vulgarism reduced it to a mere comedy for the chilbren.

Ancient books must be translated by those who are well
versed in Chinese characters. It will do well to open a Korean
classics course in Kim Il Sung University and admit scores of
clever students to teach Chinese characters, and literature,
too. If four years of school term is short, it may be extended to
six years.

While we restrict the use of words borrowed from Chinese
ideography as far as possible, we must initiate the students in
necessary Chinese characters and teach them how to read and
write them. Quite a few of them appear in south Korean publications and old documents. If we are to enable people to read
them it is necessary to teach them a certain number of Chinese
ideographs.

Even though we teach students Chinese characters, none of
these characters should be allowed to appear in school textbooks in any form. When we are going to disuse Chinese
characters, why should we enter them in school textbooks? If
textbooks contain them, they will look like south Korean ones.
If we cannot dispense with them, just as the Japanese who

need to use them together with their own letters, that will be another matter. But, if not so, there is no need to use Chinese ideographs in school textbooks.

While reviving and spreading our own words, we should make an extensive study to develop our letters.

Our present letters are square shaped, which cause some inexpediency in writing. Being mostly syllabic, they are easy to pronounce. But the form of words is not fixed. It is therefore a little difficult to read them, and the slightest slip in writing is a taboo. And our letters are disadvantageous for printing. They are also difficult to type.

If we are to make a writing easy to read, words should be given a fixed form so that they are appealing to the eye. True, Chinese characters have a defect, but they have a merit in that each of them has a meaning and appeals to the eye. But I do not mean to propose reforming our letters on the pattern of Chinese characters. We should reform our letters entirely in our own fashion. It will not do to try to introduce the Latin alphabet on the pretext of making our letters easy to read. It cannot fully convey all our sounds. In my opinion, it is good to break up our letters and put our alphabet sideways as much as possible so that our words are easy to type and to understand. Our forefathers, too, took great pains to reform our letters. In the *Collection of Chu Si Gyong's Posthumous Works* I saw an example of breaking up our letters to put our alphabet sideways. I think that is not bad either. It seems advisable to give more touch and polish to it. Then, after refashioning the letters, both the original forms of the letters and the new ones should be made known, so that people know the new letters while they do not cast off the original ones.

I do not mean, however, to put the reformed letters into use right now. Our people is a homogeneous nation. Therefore, we must not change our letters before the reunification of the country.

In the past a certain fellow, thirsty for fame, insisted on an immediate letter reform. What will happen if we change our letters when the north and the south are not yet reunified? When our people belonging to one nation write each other, they will be unable to understand and our nation will eventually be split. Further, a letter reform will greatly hamper the development of science and culture. A sudden change in the letters will render the literate people illiterate all at once. That was the reason why we opposed a sudden reform of letters.

Our science and culture have now made great progress. We are going to immediately put compulsory technical education into effect. This will further uplift the universal technical and cultural standards of our working people. However high their technical and cultural standards may rise, our letters should never be reformed before the country's reunification.

But this does not mean that researches on the letter reform should be dropped. A plan of the letter reform should be prepared and matured from now and perfected before reunification. When the reformed letters turn out fine, it will do well to teach them little by little at school. Preparations should thus be made that when the people's technical and cultural standards rise higher and the country is reunified, our square syllabics now in use should be abolished and the new, reformed ones put into use immediately. It will not be so long before reunification. It is therefore necessary to make preparations now for a letter reform.

While studying the letter reform plan, our linguists must strive to make even our present square syllabics easy to read. Originally, our square syllabics are easier to read when placed vertically than arranged sideways. But a good research could make them rather easy to read even when put sideways.

To make our writings read easily it is important to properly fix the spacing of words. Too many spacings as are now done make it difficult to read. Poor spacings will make even a good reader, not to mention a poor one, falter at reading. Poorly spaces articles in newspapers, for example, are hard to read. Let me take the word *inryu-munhwa* (human culture) for instance. If we write *inryu* and then *mun* with a space between them, followed by *hwa* on the next line, people will read them *inryu, mun, hwa*. This is a question. If a report is written in this manner, everyone will have a hard time reading it.

We should improve the spacing in the future so that the reading power of people may be increased. As I said more than once before, in the matter of word spacing we should proceed in the direction of closing up words to some degree. The word *sahoe-juui-konsol* (building of socialism), for example, should be closed up. If we space them like *sahoejuui konsol*, the reading efficiency will be low. Proper spacing is of great importance in enabling people to read our writings fast and readily get their meanings. Therefore, it is necessary to correctly define the rules of spacing, teach them well to the people and correctly space words in publications. Typists should also be correctly taught how to space words, otherwise they will have their own way in typing and space words differently each. If Chinese characters are used in typing together with our own letters, that will be another matter. But so far as this is not the case, words should be typed according to the rules, spaced properly so as to be easy to read.

As for spacing, the rules to be adopted newly seem somewhat better than the ones now in force. Indeed, the new rules, too, may have some defects. But while applying them as they are, we should eliminate the defects and bring them to perfection.

It would do well to publish the draft "Rules for the Korean Language" prepared by our linguists. There are two opinions as to fixing the number of Korean alphabetic letters—either 24 or 40. Before a letter reform is introduced, I prefer 40 as are now in use.

In order to refine our language and develop it further, more linguists must be trained. In the curricula of the normal and teacher training colleges more hours should be allotted to the Korean language and the students should be provided with opportunities for an extensive study of our language. Once I saw in the Kang Gon Military Academy that they were helping the cadets in their studies with necessary written materials put up on the walls of the classrooms. In the normal and teacher training colleges, too, it will be necessary to put up on the walls written materials on the Korean language.

The Party expects much of you. You must creditably measure up to the Party's expectations by making strenuous efforts to preserve our own vocabulary and improve our letters.

THE PRESENT SITUATION AND THE TASKS OF OUR PARTY
(Excerpt)

Report to the Conference of the Workers' Party of Korea, *October 5, 1966*

Comrades,

The Korean revolution is a link in the whole chain of world revolution and the revolutionary struggle of the Korean people is closely related to the struggle of the peoples of the whole world for peace and democracy, for national independence and socialism.

The international situation of our revolution is very complex today. The imperialists headed by US imperialism are trying more and more desperately to suppress the growing revolutionary movement of the peoples and are aggravating the international situation to the extreme. Many complicated problems have arisen within the socialist camp and the international communist movement, and there is no unity among the Communist and Workers' Parties. This inevitably creates certain obstacles to the development of the world revolutionary movement and affects the revolution and construction in our country.

We must correctly analyze, properly understand and rightly appraise the present situation and the state of affairs within the international communist movement. We must map out the Party's policies for internal and external activities in conformity with the prevailing situation, and implement them thoroughly. Moreover, we must fully arm all the Party members and the working people ideologically so that they will fight on resolutely for the victory of the revolution, rallied firmly around the Party under whatever circumstances.

During this conference we will fully discuss all these questions so as to successfully accelerate the revolution and construction in our country and contribute to the advancement of the international communist movement and the world revolutionary movement as a whole.

1. On the International Situation and Some Problems Arising in the International Communist Movement

Comrades,

In the international arena today, a fierce struggle is going on between socialism and imperialism, between the forces of revolution and the forces of counterrevolution. The socialist forces, the national-liberation movement, the working-class movement and the democratic movement continue to grow on a worldwide scale.

The fierce flames of the liberation struggle are raging particularly in Asia, Africa and Latin America. Imperialism is meeting the strong resistance of the peoples and suffering the hardest blows in those areas. The people who have risen in the struggle are winning fresh victories in their revolutionary cause of smashing the old world of imperialism and colonialism and creating a new world.

The growth of the revolutionary forces of the world headed by socialism and the collapse of the colonial system have markedly weakened the forces of imperialism. The internal contradictions of imperialism have become more acute and the discord among the imperialist powers has been aggravated. The imperialists are suffering telling blows from within and without being driven still further to dead ends.

The revolutionary movement must inevitably experience some vicissitudes in the course of its development, but the general situation continues to develop in favor of socialism and the revolutionary forces and to the disadvantage of imperialism and the reactionary forces. The victory of socialism and the downfall of imperialism are the main trends of our times that no force can check.

But imperialism will not retire from the arena of history of its own will. The aggressive nature of imperialism cannot change and the imperialism still remains a dangerous force. The imperialists are desperately trying to escape their doom through aggression and war.

The aggressive maneuverings of the imperialists led by US imperialism have become more open in recent years. The US imperialists are perpetrating acts of aggression against the socialist countries and the independent national states, brutally suppressing the national-liberation movements of the Asian, African and Latin-American peoples and disturbing peace in all parts of the world.

Today, the US imperialists are directing the spearhead of aggression to Asia. The US imperialists, introducing more armed forces into South Viet Nam in flagrant violation of the 1954 Geneva Agreements, are carrying out the scorched-earth operations to "burn all, kill all and destroy all". They have already extended their bombing of the Democratic Republic of Viet Nam to the Hanoi and Haiphong areas. This shows that the US imperialist policy of "escalating the war" in Viet Nam has entered a new, serious phase. The US imperialists are now running amuck to spread the flames of war to vast areas of Asia.

The US aggressors, occupying the southern half of our country, are making frantic war preparations; they are also occupying Taiwan, a territory of the People's Republic of China, and incessantly committing provocations against People's China.

The US imperialists have revived Japanese militarism to use it as the "shock brigade" of their Asian aggression. They have aligned the forces of Japanese militarism with the south Korean puppets and are scheming to rig up a "Northeast Asia military pact" based on this alignment.

The basic strategy of the US imperialists in their Asian aggression is to blockade and attack the Asian socialist countries, stem the rapid growth of the revolutionary forces and prop up their colonial rule in Asia by concentrating more and more US military forces in this region and mobilizing the forces of Japanese militarism and their satellite countries and puppets. This machination on the part of the US aggressors seriously aggravates the situation in all parts of Asia and gravely endangers world peace at large.

The intensified aggressive acts of the imperialists led by the US imperialists are no sign of their mightiness; on the contrary, they indicate that they are in a more difficult situation. The desperate moves made by the US imperialists in Asia, Africa and Latin America also prove that in these areas the forces of socialism are growing, the revolutionary anti-imperialist movement is going on fiercely and the imperialists' foothold is shaken to its very foundation.

No amount of manoeuvre on the part of the imperialists can check the growing liberation struggle of the peoples or halt the triumphant onward march of socialism. The imperialists will definitely be kicked out of Asia, Africa and Latin America and will eventually be destroyed by the revolutionary struggle of the peoples. The ultimate triumph of socialism and the complete downfall of imperialism are inevitable. This is an inexorable law of historical development.

All events taking place in the international arena substantiate still more clearly that US imperialism is the main force of aggression and war, the international gendarme, the bulwark of modern colonialism and the most heinous enemy of the people of the whole world.

US imperialism is the No. 1 target in the struggle of the world people. It is the primary task of the socialist countries and the Communist and Workers' Parties to enlist and concentrate the broad anti-imperialist forces in the struggle against US imperialism. Only by fighting resolutely against US imperialism can world peace be safeguarded and the revolutionary struggle of the peoples be crowned with victory.

At the present period the attitude towards US imperialism is a major yardstick to verify the position of the Communist and Workers' Parties. Communists should always hold fast to the principled position of opposing imperialism, US imperialism above all. Particularly today when the US imperialists are expanding their aggression in Viet Nam, all the socialist countries should take a still colder and tougher attitude towards US imperialism. We should never tolerate renunciation of principle and compromise with US imperialism in international affairs.

Socialist countries should not dissolve their anti-imperialist struggle into diplomatic relations with the imperialist states or weaken it, just because they maintain such relations. Socialist countries should adhere to the class principle in diplomacy, too, and should bring pressure to bear upon US imperialism, exposing and condemning its policy of aggression and war.

It is also wrong only to clamor against US imperialism without taking concrete actions to stop its aggression. Particularly, one should not put obstacles in the way of the anti-imperialist forces taking practical measures in unison to deal blows to the US imperialist aggressors. If such an act is committed, it will not only make it impossible to check US imperialist aggression, but it will also make the US imperialists more arrogant and outrageous and, eventually, will encourage their acts of aggression.

It is a principle of the foreign policy of the socialist countries to struggle against the imperialist policy of aggression and war and for world peace and security. While fighting to prevent war, however, Communists should never fear it, but should resolutely wipe out the aggressors in case of an armed attack by the imperialists. Only by adhering to the principled stand of opposing imperialism and by fighting resolutely against it, is it possible to check imperialist aggression and defend peace.

Especially, socialist countries should be alert to the fact that today the US imperialists, while refraining as far as they can from worsening their relations with big countries, are directing the spearhead of their aggression mainly to Viet Nam and trying to swallow up one by one such divided or small countries as Korea, Cuba and East Germany. Attention should be also directed to the possible maneuverings of the US imperialists to temporarily ease the situation or maintain the status quo in Europe in order to concentrate their forces on aggression in Asia.

In this case, the easing of tension on one front does not contribute to improving the general international situation; on the contrary, it provides conditions for the imperialists to intensify aggression on the other front. It, therefore, constitutes a greater danger to world peace and security.

Under the present situation, the US imperialists should be set back and their forces be dispersed to the maximum in all parts and on every front of the world—in Asia and Europe, Africa and Latin America and in all countries, big and small—and they should be tied up, hand and foot, everywhere they set foot so that they may not act arbitrarily. Only in this way can we succeed in defeating the US imperialists' strategy of destroying the international revolutionary forces, including the socialist countries, one by one, by concentrating their forces in a particular area or country.

Our Party and people will carry on an unflinching struggle against the imperialist forces of aggression and by US imperialism and strive to unite with all forces opposing US imperialism.

To defend world peace, we must fight not only against US imperialism but also against its allies. Struggles should be intensified particularly against Japanese and West German militarism.

Japanese and West German militarism are being revived rapidly under the active patronage of US imperialism, and Japan and West Germany are regenerating into new hotbeds of war in Asia and Europe. Under these circumstances, the struggle against Japanese and West German militarism must not be neglected.

It is a good thing that the socialist countries are fighting against the militarism of West Germany. Our Party and people are opposed to the revival of West German militarism and its revanchist ambition, and strongly condemn the US imperialists for their criminal act of actively encouraging it. We support the struggle of the German people and the position of the German Democratic Republic against the rearmament of West German militarism.

We must be on the lookout for the menace of Japanese militarism in Asia just as we are alert to the menace of West German militarism in Europe. Just as all the socialist countries struggle against US imperialism and its ally, West German militarism, in Europe, so in Asia they should, as a matter of course, fight against US imperialism and its ally, Japanese militarism.

Today Japanese militarism has appeared in Asia as a dangerous force of aggression. The Japanese militarist forces harbor an illusion of materializing their old dream of the "Greater East Asia Co-Prosperity Sphere" with the backing of US imperialism. Japan's Sato government, actively supported by US imperialism, has not only mapped out war plans to invade Korea and other Asian countries, but has already started stretching out its tentacles of aggression to south Korea.

In effect, a tripartite military alliance has been formed among US imperialism, the Sato government of Japan and the south Korean puppet clique, through bilateral military agreements. The Sato government is an active accomplice of US imperialism in its aggression in Viet Nam and is sending large quantities of war supplies including various kinds of weapons to South Viet Nam in compliance with US orders. Japan serves the US imperialist war of aggression in Viet Nam as a supply base, a repair station, and a launching point.

At the instigation of the US imperialists, the Sato government pursues a hostile policy towards our country and the other socialist countries in Asia. It is also intensifying its economic and cultural penetration in a number of Asian, African and Latin-American countries under the specious name of "aid", "joint development" and "economic and technical cooperation".

The struggle against Japanese militarism is a struggle to defend peace in Asia and the world and is an important part of the struggle against US imperialism. All socialist countries should attach importance to the struggle against Japanese militarism and frustrate its aggressive designs by concerted action. Especially, they should thoroughly lay bare and shatter the attempts of Japan's Sato government to disorganize the anti-imperialist front under the guise of a "friend" of the Asian, African and Latin-American peoples.

True, there exist certain contradictions between US imperialism and the Japanese ruling circles, and the socialist countries may take advantage of the contradictions in the interests of the anti-imperialist struggle, when they are aggravated in the future. But we must view all aspects of US-Japanese relations. Despite their contradictions, US imperialism and Japanese imperialism are bound in an alliance based on master-and-servant relationship for their common interests in Asian aggression and they are in league with each other politically, economically and militarily. We should not over-estimate the contradictions between the United States and Japan and underestimate their alliance in master-and-servant relationship.

We should harbor no illusion about the Japanese ruling circles and should not expect any good from them. To ignore the menace of Japanese militarism and have close ties with the Sato government is, in fact, tantamount to encouraging the overseas expansion of the Japanese ruling circles and consolidating the position of US imperialism in Asia.

Socialist countries may develop economic relations with Japan, but should make no bargaining with its ruling circles on political questions. Relations with the Sato government should in all circumstances favor the interests of the Japanese people and of the anti-imperialist struggle in general.

Today the Japanese people are fighting against US imperialism and Japanese monopoly capital in defence of the security of Japan and world peace. The struggle of the Japanese people constitutes a heavy blow to U.S. imperialist aggression in Asia and to Japanese militarism and contributes to the cause of world peace.

The Korean people emphatically condemn the aggressive schemes of Japanese militarism. The rearmament of Japanese militarism and its aggression against south Korea should be stopped decisively and the "ROK-Japan treaty" concluded under the manipulation of the US imperialists should be abrogated. Japan should free herself from US imperialist domination and develop along the path of independence and democracy. The Korean people fully support and express militant solidarity with the Japanese people led by the Communist Party of Japan in their struggle for the complete independence and democratic progress of Japan.

US imperialist aggression in Viet Nam and the struggle of the Vietnamese people against it are the focal point of the struggle between the forces of revolution and counterrevolution at the present moment.

US imperialist aggression in Viet Nam is not only directed against the people of Viet Nam; it is also an aggression against the socialist camp, a challenge to the national-liberation movement and a threat to peace in Asia and the world.

The Vietnamese people have risen as one in the sacred battle to shatter US imperialist aggression determinedly, to liberate the South, defend the North and reunify the country. They are constantly inflicting serious political and military defeats upon the aggressors, thereby driving US imperialism up against the wall. The South Viet Nam National Front for Liberation has already liberated four-fifths of the territory and two-thirds of the total population, while the North Vietnamese people are successfully repelling the barbarous bombings of US imperialist air pirates. The heroic anti-US, national-salvation struggle of the people of North and South Viet Nam affords an example to the people of the whole world fighting against imperialism for peace, democracy, national independence and socialism, and inspires them boundlessly.

On behalf of this conference, I would like to extend the warmest militant greetings and congratulations to the fraternal people of North and South Viet Nam who are achieving brilliant victories and accomplishing heroic feats in their just war of resistance against the US imperialist aggressors.

The Vietnamese people are not only valiantly struggling for the complete liberation and independence of their country, but are also shedding their blood in battle to defend the socialist camp and safeguard peace in Asia and the world.

The attitude one takes towards US imperialist aggression in Viet Nam and towards the Vietnamese people's struggle against it, is a criterion showing whether or not one is resolutely opposed to imperialism, and whether or not one actively supports the liberation struggle of the peoples. The attitude towards the Viet Nam question is a touchstone that distinguishes the revolutionary position from the opportunist position, proletarian internationalism from national egoism.

All socialist countries and peace-loving people should oppose the aggression of US imperialism in Viet Nam and render every possible support to the people of Viet Nam in their righteous war of liberation. Since the Democratic Republic of Viet Nam is suffering aggression by the US imperialists, the socialist countries should more resolutely confront and fight them, and support the people of Viet Nam in every way. There should be absolutely no hesitation or passivity on this point.

All socialist countries should pool their strength and come to the aid of the fighting Vietnamese people and should foil the aggression of US imperialism against Viet Nam by joint efforts. At present, however, the countries of the socialist camp, because of their differences, are not keeping step with each other to oppose US imperialist aggression and aid the Vietnamese people. This troubles the fighting people of Viet Nam and really grieves Communists.

Fraternal parties should not merely engage in polemics over the Viet Nam question at this time when the Democratic Republic of Viet Nam is suffering US imperialist aggression. It is the Workers' Party of Viet Nam that can decide on the Viet Nam question. No one has the last say on this question except the Workers' Party of Viet Nam. As far as the Viet Nam question is concerned, the fraternal parties should always follow the policy of the Workers' Party of Viet Nam, and support its stand. As regards the aid given by fraternal countries to the Democratic Republic of Viet Nam, too, only the Workers' Party of Viet Nam can correctly judge this issue and fraternal parties should respect its decision.

Today's situation is different from that of yesterday, when the Soviet Union was making a revolution single-handedly. Since there were no other socialist countries in the world at that time, the Soviet Union had to obtain everything including arms, by itself. But today with the existence of a powerful socialist camp, is there any reason why the Vietnamese people should not receive aid from the fraternal socialist countries in their difficult war against the common enemy? The socialist countries are duty bound to offer aid to the Democratic Republic of Viet Nam and the Vietnamese people are entitled to receive it. If the aid of the socialist countries to the Vietnamese people is used effectively in the battle against the US imperialist aggressors, it will be a very good thing and will never be otherwise. In order to defeat the US imperialists in Viet Nam, all fraternal countries should give more aid to the Democratic Republic of Viet Nam.

This, we consider, is the revolutionary stand of opposing US imperialist aggression in Viet Nam in deed and is the internationalist stand of sincerely helping the Vietnaese people.

This is not the time for the socialist countries to remain passive, extending only political support to the people of Viet Nam. They should take more positive measures to aid the Viet-

namese people. In the light of the situation where the US
imperialists are extending aggression even to the Democratic
Republic of Viet Nam by bringing in troops of their satellite
countries and puppets, every socialist country must send
volunteers to Viet Nam to defend the southeastern outpost of
the socialist camp and safeguard peace in Asia and the world.
This is the internationalist duty of the socialist countries to
the fraternal people of Viet Nam. No one can possibly object if
the socialist countries send volunteers to Viet Nam.

If all the socialist countries help the Vietnamese people to
shatter US imperialist aggression against Viet Nam, US
imperialism will decline like the setting sun and the revolutionary movements in all countries of Asia and the rest of the
world will make great headway.

The Workers' Party of Korea and the Korean people regard
US imperialist aggression against Viet Nam as one against
themselves and they regard the struggle of the Vietnamese
people as their own. Our people will be more resolute in their
struggle against the common enemy, US imperialism, and will
exert every possible effort to support the people of Viet Nam.
We are ready to send volunteers to join the Vietnamese
brothers in their battle whenever the Government of the
Democratic Republic of Viet Nam requests it.

The only just solution to the Viet Nam question is the four-
point position of the Government of the Democratic Republic
of Viet Nam and the five-point statement made by the South
Viet Nam National Front for liberation. The Workers' Party of
Korea and the Government of our Republic fully support this
just position of the Vietnamese people.

The US imperialists are now staging the fraudulent farce of
"peace talks" in an attempt to cover up another plot to
escalate the war. No amount of deceptive artifice, however,
can conceal US imperialism's foul aggressive nature. We
strongly condemn the plot of the US imperialists to extend the
war of aggression in Viet Nam, and denounce their "peace
talks" sham.

The US imperialists must immediately stop all acts of
aggression against the people of Viet Nam and must get out of
South Viet Nam without delay, taking their aggressive army,
the troops of their satellites and puppets and all the murderous
weapons with them. If the US imperialists continue to act
recklessly in disregard of the repeated warnings of the Viet-

namese people and the socialist countries and the strong condemnation of the people of the world, they will suffer a still more ignominous defeat. Ultimate victory is on the side of the Vietnamese people who have risen in the righteous cause, and the US imperialist aggressors will face inevitable ruin.

One of the important international questions today is to defend the Cuban revolution. The triumph of the Cuban revolution is the first victory of socialist revolution under the very nose of the United States; it is a continuation of the Great October Revolution in Latin America. It is a historic event that extended the socialist camp to the Western Hemisphere and brought about a new turn for the revolutionary movements of Latin America. The Republic of Cuba has become a base of revolution in Latin America.

Today, the Cuban people, under the leadership of the Communist Party of Cuba, are marching firmly ahead in the front lines of the anti-imperialist struggle, holding aloft the banner of revolution. The Cuban people are safeguarding their revolutionary gains and building socialism under difficult conditions, valiantly repulsing the incessant acts of aggression and provocation perpetrated by the US imperialists.

It is a sacred internationalist duty for the countries of the socialist camp and the Latin-American people to defend the Cuban revolution. The socialist countries should give wholehearted support to the fraternal Cuban people in their revolutionary cause, safeguard the Cuban revolution and gave positive assistance to the socialist construction of Cuba. Communists who consider the interests of the revolution to be the supreme law can never act otherwise in relation to Cuba.

It is quite natural for Cuba to receive aid from the socialist countries, and the fraternal parties and countries should be glad of it. This is demanded by the interests of the Cuban revolution and of revolution in Latin America. We should fully understand the circumstances of Cuba and the position of its Communist Party.

The Communist Party of Cuba knows the Cuban question better than anyone else, and only the Communist Party of Cuba can map out correct policies to suit the realities of Cuba. All socialist countries are only duty bound to respect the policies of the Communist Party of Cuba and support the struggle of the Cuban people. No attempt should be made to bring pressure to bear upon the Communist Party and people of Cuba and split the revolutionary forces of Latin America.

The Workers' Party of Korea has given and is giving full support to the just stand of the Communist Party of Cuba which, under the banner of revolution, is correctly leading the revolution and construction in its country and striving for the unity of the socialist camp and the cohesion of the international communist movement. Our Party and people resolutely condemn the aggressive moves of the US imperialists against Cuba and firmly support the heroic struggle of the Cuban people to defend their revolutionary gains and build socialism. We will make every effort in the future, too, to cement our friendship and solidarity with the Communist Party and people of Cuba.

Tremendous revolutionary changes are taking place in the life of the Asian, African and Latin-American peoples today. The national-liberation movement of the Asian, African and Latin-American peoples, along with the revolutionary struggle of the international working class for socialism, is a great revolutionary force of our times and a powerful factor for world peace.

Amidst the unprecedented upsurge of the national-liberation movement, many countries have attained national independence and embarked upon the building of a new life. The peoples in those countries which are still under colonialist oppression are fighting more vigorously for freedom and liberation.

But the imperialists will not leave their colonies meekly; they are maneuvering in every way to seize and dominate even an inch more of land. The imperialists suppress the national-liberation movement in Asia, Africa and Latin America and carry out subversive activities to wrest newly independent countries away from the anti-imperialist front one by one. While openly resorting to brute force, they attempt to infiltrate into the newly independent countries with "aid" as bait, to meddle in the internal affairs of those countries and disorganize them from within.

In recent years, the US imperialists have still more intensified their subversive activities and coup d'etat maneuvers against the newly independent states. By bribing and whipping up the reactionaries, the US imperialists seek to pit them against the progressive forces and sway certain newly independent countries to the Right. They maneuver in this way to make those countries suppress their revolutionary forces internally and oppose the socialist countries and disorganize the anti-imperialist forces externally.

The recent developments provide a serious lesson to all Communists. They show that the more the revolutionary forces, including the Communist Parties, grow, the more desperately foreign imperialism and domestic reactionary forces maneuver to stifle them. The Communists should keep the sharpest vigilance over this and be always ready to counter possible savage repression by the enemy, organizationally and ideologically, strategically and tactically. Revolution is complex and requires a scientific art of leadership. A revolution can emerge victorious only when the line of struggle is laid down scientifically and scrupulously and the most appropriate time is chosen to unfold a decisive fight, on the basis of a correct judgment of the revolutionary situation and an exact calculation of the balance of forces between the enemy and oneself. We should engrave on our consciousness such experiences and lessons of the international revolutionary movement and make good use of them in our own revolutionary struggle.

Much is yet to be done to abolish the imperialist colonial system in Asia, Africa and Latin America and achieve the complete liberation and independence of the peoples. The road of national liberation is a road of arduous struggle. In its course one will encounter the desperate resistance of the imperialists and reactionaries and undergo many hardships and trials.

The attainment of political independence is no more than the initial step towards the ultimate victory of the national- liberation revolution. Peoples who have won independence are confronted with the task of fighting the subversive activities of foreign imperialists and domestic forces of reaction and carrying the cause of national liberation to final completion. For this purpose, the machine of imperialist colonial rule should be destroyed; imperialism and domestic reaction must be deprived of their economic footholds; the revolutionary forces should be strengthened; a progressive socio-political system should be established; and an independent national economy and national culture should be built. Only in this way can the peoples of the newly independent countries eliminate the centuries-old backwardness and poverty left by colonial rule and construct rich and strong, independent and soverign states.

The Workers' Party of Korea and the Government of the Republic positively support the peoples of all newly independent countries in their struggle to consolidate national independence and achieve national prosperity. We shall continue to endeavor for the promotion of our relations of friendship and cooperation with the newly independent nations.

Our Party and Government consider it an important principle of foreign policy to support the struggle of the Asian, African and Latin-American peoples against imperialism, for freedom and liberation. The Korean people sharply condemn the aggressive maneuvers of the US imperialists against the Laotian people and fully support the struggle of the Laotian people for national independence. Our people support the righteous struggle of the Cambodian people against the aggression and intervention of US imperialism and its stooges, for independence, neutrality and territorial integrity. We support the Asian, African and Latin American peoples in their liberation struggles, and express militant solidarity with them.

We also support the working classes and the toiling peoples of the capitalist countries in their revolutionary struggle against the exploitation and oppression by capital and for democratic rights and socialism and express firm solidarity with them. Our Party and people will always stand firmly on the side of the peoples battling for peace and democracy, national independence and socialism and will strive to strengthen our solidarity with them.

Comrades, the socialist camp and the international communist movement have been experiencing harsh trials in recent years. Modern revisionism and dogmatism have laid grave obstacles to the development of the international revolutionary movement.

We can achieve the unity of the socialist camp and the cohesion of the international communist movement and successfully fight against imperialism by overcoming Right and "Left" opportunism and defending the purity of Marxism-Leninism.

Marxism-Leninism has developed and attained its victory in

the course of the struggle against Right and "Left" opportunism. As the experience of history shows, various deviations from Marxism-Leninism emerge in the course of revolution. This is not so surprising. It is somewhat inevitable that
as long as imperialism exists and the class struggle goes on,
Right and "Left" opportunism will appear within the working-
class movement as its reflection and a struggle will be waged
against them.

Right and "Left" opportunism are bourgeois and petty-
bourgeois ideas appearing in the working-class movement.
They distort the revolutionary quintessence of Marxism-
Leninism from both extremes and harm the revolution. We
must fight against Right and "Left" opportunism on two
fronts.

Modern revisionism revises Marxism-Leninism and
emasculates its revolutionary quintessence under the pretext
of "changed situation" and "creative development". It rejects
the class struggle and the dictatorship of the proletariat; it
preaches class collaboration and gives up fighting imperialism.
Moreover, modern revisionism spreads illusions about imperialism and in every way obstructs the revolutionary struggle of the peoples for social and national liberation.

It is true that modern revisionism has already suffered a
severe blow by the principled struggle of the Marxist- Leninist
parties and is on the decline. This, however, does not mean
that modern revisionism has been destroyed completely.
Modern revisionism still remains a big danger to the international communist movement. It finds expression above all in a
weak-kneed attitude towards imperialism and a passive approach to the revolutionary struggle of the peoples. We, therefore, cannot slight the struggle against modern revisionism.

We must fight "Left" opportunism as well as modern revisionism. "Left" opportunists fail to take into account changed
realities and dogmatically recite isolated propositions of
Marxism-Leninism; they lead people to extremist action under
super-revolutionary slogans. They also divorce the Party from
the masses, split the revolutionary forces and prevent a concentrated attack on the principal enemy.

When "Left" opportunism is allowed to grow, it may also
become as big a danger as modern revisionism to a particular
party and to the international communist movement. Without

fighting "Left" opportunism, it is impossible to unite the anti-imperialist forces to wage a successful struggle against imperialism, nor is it possible to combat modern revisionism successfully.

Thus, both modern revisionism and "Left" opportunism create tremendous obstacles to the advancement of the international revolutionary movement. It is wrong to ignore the danger represented by "Left" opportunism under pretence of opposing modern revisionism, and it is likewise wrong to ignore the danger implicit in modern revisionism for reasons of opposing "Left" opportunism. Unless Right and "Left" opportunism are overcome, it is impossible to lead the revolution and construction correctly in each country, nor is it possible to dynamically advance the international revolutionary movement.

The struggle against Right and "Left" opportunism is closely linked with the struggle for the unity of the socialist camp and the cohesion of the international communist movement. Our Party will fight against Right and "Left" opportunism and, at the same time, uphold the banner of solidarity. We should not commit the "Leftist" error of rejecting solidarity on the plea of fighting opportunism, nor should we commit the Rightist error of giving up the struggle against opportunism for reasons of defending solidarity. Our Party will do all it can to safeguard the unity of the socialist camp and the cohesion of the international communist movement, while carrying on an uncompromising struggle against Right and "Left" opportunism.

The socialist camp and the international communist movement are the determining factors in the development of the history of mankind at present. They are the most powerful revolutionary forces of our times that are confronting imperialism and all the forces of reaction. The existence of a united and powerful socialist camp and international communist movement checks the imperialist policy of aggression and war and inspires the revolutionary struggle of the peoples the world over.

The imperialists are afraid of the socialist camp and the international communist movement more than anything else. It is for this reason that the imperialists have incessantly perpetrated and are perpetrating armed aggression and subversive activities against the socialist countries. The imperialists are now attempting to devour the socialist countries one by one.

Under these circumstances, the most important thing is to defend the socialist camp jointly from imperialist aggression; for this, the socialist camp must stand firmly united as one. However, because of its internal differences, the socialist camp is not advancing as a solid block, as a united force now. This has a negative influence on the development of the world revolutionary movement and the international situation.

It is a sacred duty of every Communist to fight in defence of the socialist camp and its unity. Communists must not tolerate any act of weakening the unity of the socialist camp. Renegades of the revolution must not be drawn into the socialist camp, nor must this or that country be artificially excluded from it. Both positions will undermine the socialist camp. We cannot allow anyone to destroy the socialist camp which was built with the blood of the working classes of the whole world. This is a matter of principle that concerns the destiny of the socialist camp and the future of the international revolutionary movement.

We cannot replace the socialist camp with any community of a different character.

On the other hand, we should oppose the attempt to deny the existence of the socialist camp or to split the socialist camp and the inernational communist movement. The splitting of the˙socialist camp, of the international communist movement and of each party into two cannot be a normal, and still less a desirable thing. We must seek unity through struggle.

It is really regrettable for the Communists of the whole world that the differences between the fraternal parties have gone so far beyond ideological and theoretical bounds today that they can hardly be settled. But, however serious they may be, the differences between fraternal parties are an internal affair of the socialist camp and the international communist movement. Differences among the parties must not be developed into an organizational split, but must on all accounts be settled by means of ideological struggle guided by a desire for unity.

No socialist country must be excluded from the socialist camp and the international communist movement. No one should make an exaggerated or distorted appraisal of a fraternal country or party, and consider any of the 13 socialist countries as being outside the socialist camp or the international communist movement. We are of the opinion that utmost prudence should be used in appraising the leadership of a fraternal country or fraternal party.

The relationship between fraternal parties should in no way be identified with the hostile relations we have with imperialism. Even when the leadership of a fraternal party commits an error, Communists should offer comradely criticism and help it to return to the right path.

Meanwhile, one should not draw hasty conclusions concerning the character of a fraternal country's society from isolated phenomena that are revealed in one aspect or other of its social life. The character of a given society is determined by the class that holds power, and the form of ownership of the means of production.

We should see the difference between the socialist and the capitalist countries in the right light. There exist fundamental contradictions between the socialist and the capitalist countries which originate from the nature of their social systems. These contradictions exist objectively, independent of anyone's subjective intentions. A given measure taken by the leaders may sharpen or alleviate contradictions between the socialist and the capitalist countries, but as long as the social systems are opposed to each other, the fundamental contradictions between socialism and capitalism cannot disappear.

It is not right to class a fraternal country with the enemy or push it towards the imperialists' side even if it has some negative aspects. Communists can never allow themselves to be carried away by prejudices or subjectivity in their attitude towards fraternal parties and countries.

Our Party considers it necessary to refrain from making hasty conclusions on fraternal parties or fraternal countries in spite of differences and take our time to examine them in the course of struggle. Meanwhile, it is possible to promote unity with them on condition that they oppose imperialism, support the national-liberation movement and do not interfere in the internal affairs of fraternal parties and countries. We must adopt a positive attitude of criticizing their negative aspects and helping them to rectify them, while appreciating and supporting their positive aspects.

Our Party, with the interests of the international communist movement in view, believes it beneficial for all socialist countries to continue to advance together in the revolutionary ranks. This will increase the might of the socialist camp and make it possible to deal greater blows at imperialism.

The socialist camp is in a complex situation today because of its differences, but its existence is a hard fact of reality. No one can liquidate the socialist camp at will. Even if anyone should bring a non-socialist country into the socialist camp, it cannot thereby become a socialist country. On the other hand, if anyone should artificially exclude a socialist country from the socialist camp, it cannot cease to be a socialist country.

The socialist camp is an integral whole which is united on a common political and economic basis and knitted together by the same goal of building socialism and communism. The socialist countries make up the socialist camp, all as equal members. If the socialist camp grew by even one more country, it would be a welcome thing, and would not be a bad thing. The final victory of the world revolution will be achieved through the victory of revolution in each country and the expansion of the socialist camp.

Our Party always defends the socialist camp as a whole and is opposed to all attempts to split it. Our Party will continue to unite with all the fraternal parties and countries, while combatting Right and "Left" opportunism. We will go on fighting resolutely to defend the unity of the socialist camp and the cohesion of the international communist movement based on the principles of Marxism-Leninism and proletarian internationalism, on the revolutionary principles of the Declaration and Statement of the meetings of representatives of the fraternal parties.

The US imperialists are now taking advantage of the disunity of the socialist camp and the international communist movement to further intensify aggression and plunder everywhere in the world. Particularly, US imperialism is extending its aggressive war against the Vietnamese people by mobilizing huge armed forces.

It is true that the peace-loving people of all the continents of Asia, Africa, Latin America, Europe, etc., are now waging extensive campaigns to oppose US imperialist aggression and support the heroic struggle of the Vietnamese people. But the Communists cannot rest content with this. We must further systematize the struggle for aiding the Vietnamese people against the aggressive war of US imperialism on a worldwide scale and raise it into a higher stage. Just as the US imperialists are escalating the war of aggression in Viet Nam, so the people of the world should escalate their struggle to oppose US imperialism and aid the Vietnamese people.

Therefore, it is of the utmost importance to achieve joint anti-imperialist action and form an anti-imperialist united front on an international scale.

The achievement of joint anti-imperialist action and an anti-imperialist united front is the most urgent question of principle in the international communist movement today. It is related to the fundamental problems of whether or not the US imperialist policy of aggression and war can be checked, whether or not the socialist camp can be defended, whether or not the national-liberation movement can be stepped up and whether or not world peace and security can be safeguarded.

The materialization of joint anti-imperialist action and an anti-imperialist united front will make it possible to wage a more vigorous campaign to aid the Vietnamese people, frustrate the US imperialist policy of aggression and war and safeguard Asian and world peace. It can also provide conditions for gradually settling the differences among the fraternal parties and restoring the unity of the socialist camp and the cohesion of the international communist movement, and will make it possible to accelerate the revolutionary movement in all countries more positively. Joint anti-imperialist action is, therefore, absolutely necessary for the benefit of both the cause of peace and the cause of revolution.

As soon as US imperialism started armed aggression against Viet Nam, our Party advocated waging a joint anti-imperialist struggle to make a collective counterattack on the aggressors. A number of other fraternal parties proposed to do the same.

But the joint anti-imperialist struggle has failed to be materialized because of the differences within the international communist movement. We consider that the socialist countries and the Communist and Workers' Parties must settle this situation and pool their strength in opposing US imperialism and aiding the people of Viet Nam in their struggle.

All socialist countries have condemned the US imperialist aggression of Viet Nam, and, on a number of occasions, expressed the positions of their parties and states to support the fighting Vietnamese brothers. And they are all giving economic and military aid to the people of Viet Nam. The Communist and Workers' Parties in the capitalist countries, too, are active in their struggle against the US imperialist war of aggression in support of the Vietnamese people.

We, therefore, consider that despite the differences over a number of questions, there is an initial basis for taking joint anti-imperialist action, above all, to counter US imperialist aggression in Viet Nam and to aid the people of Viet Nam. We should not ignore this and should work actively to form an anti-imperialist united front.

Refusal to take joint action against imperialism is not an honest attitude of opposing revisionism and defending the purity of Marxism-Leninism, or of contributing to the strengthening of the unity of the socialist camp and the cohesion of the international communist movement. Nor can it be regarded as a stand of opposing US imperialism and aiding the fighting people of Viet Nam.

The basic strategy of the world revolution today is to direct the main spearhead against US imperialism. We must clearly distinguish a friend who has made an error from a foe. The foe should be attacked, but a friend who has made a mistake should be criticized and led back to the right path. We should in this way join efforts with all our friends and fight the main enemy.

In the struggle against US imperialism, we must strive to take joint action with the Communist and Workers' Parties and democratic social organization of all countries and the international democratic organizations. Although these organizations may not have the same opinion on different problems, and although their positions may differ from each other and their composition may also be complex, they still have the vast masses under them. In order to enlist still larger masses in the anti-imperialist struggle, Communists must not reject joint action with these organizations.

Communists should be alert not only to differences but also to common viewpoints; they should always view matters from all aspects, and refrain from going to extremes. If we fail to take joint action with the Communist and Workers' Parties and democratic social organizations of all countries and the international democratic organizations, the vast masses united under them will drop out of the anti-imperialist front. Without the masses there can be no revolution. Through joint action with these organizations, we can reach their masses, exert revolutionary influence on and mobilize them to take part in the anti-imperialist struggle. Refusing to take joint anti-imperialist action means divorcing oneself from the masses, becoming isolated and, in fact, it will only bring about serious consequences which will undermine the anti-imperialist struggle.

Communists should under no circumstances be narrow-minded. We must rally all anti-imperialist forces and struggle against imperialism with united efforts. It is a basic principle of the communist strategy and tactics today to win over more allies, even if they are not a consistent and steadfast force, so as to broaden the anti-imperialist front, isolate US imperialism as much as possible and hit it jointly.

The history of the international communist movement knows many instances of the Communists taking joint action with the Right-wing Social-Democrats in the struggle against imperialist wars. The united front policy pursued by the Communists in the past played an important role in mobilizing the people to the struggle against imperialist wars.

In the historical conditions of today, when the world socialist forces have grown stronger, there exist greater possibilities for carrying out joint anti-imperialist action on an international scale. Drawing on the historical experience of the international communist movement, we must exploit even the slightest possibility of waging a powerful joint anti-imperialist struggle.

It has become an international trend of today to condemn the aggressive war of US imperialism in Viet Nam and to support the Vietnamese people. Even those who turned to revisionism have found it impossible, in face of world public opinion, to refuse support to the Vietnamese people. This is a good thing and can never be a bad thing.

Of course, there can be different categories of people among those who oppose US imperialism and support the Vietnamese people. Some, repenting of their past mistakes, may condemn the US imperialist aggression and support the Vietnamese people now in order to make up for them. Others may reluctantly join the anti-imperialist struggle, under pressure from the people of their own country and the peoples throughout the world, although their fundamental position remains unchanged.

But, whatever their motives, it is necessary to enlist all these forces in the joint anti-imperialist struggle. If somebody wants to rectify his past mistakes, at least on the Viet Nam question, that is undoubtedly a good thing, a welcome thing. And even if someone reluctantly opposes US imperialism and supports the Vietnamese people, under pressure from the people, that will be also favorable and not inimical to the anti- imperialist struggle.

It is our belief that the more forces are drawn into the joint anti-imperialist struggle, the better it will be. It is necessary to induce those who shun the anti-imperialist struggle to participate in it and to encourage passive people to become active in the struggle.

Also, the joint struggle against US imperialism will draw a more distinct line of demarcation between Marxism-Leninism and revisionism. It will be clarified through actual struggle whether one's opposition to US imperialism and one's support of the Vietnamese people is real or sham. Actions are the criterion for telling right from wrong. Opportunism can also be rooted out in the actual revolutionary struggle as well as in the ideological struggle.

In carrying out joint action, Communists must always adhere to the principle of uniting while struggling and of struggling while uniting. The joint action we advocate does not mean unconditional unity or unprincipled compromise. What we mean is to take concerted action and join efforts with the anti-imperialist forces in opposing US imperialism and supporting the Vietnamese people, while abiding by Marxist-Leninist principles. In this way, we should, in the course of the joint struggle, criticize and get rid of the opportunist elements, supporting and encouraging the anti-imperialist aspects.

We consider that joint anti-imperialist action by no means conflicts with the struggle against revisionism. Rather, it is a positive form of struggle against opportunism of all shades. To realize joint anti-imperialist action and an anti-imperialist united front is a correct policy which makes it possible not only to carry on a successful struggle against imperialism but to bring about the revolutionary awakening of the masses of the people, oppose all kinds of opportunism, and safeguard the purity of Marxism-Leninism.

It is an urgent task for the Communists of the whole world today to adopt and carry out concrete measures for joint action against US imperialism in support of the Vietnamese people.

We deem it necessary for the socialist countries, first of all, to send international volunteers to assist the fighting people of Viet Nam. This will be the first step towards the realization of joint anti-imperialist action. Sending international volunteers to Viet Nam will be a powerful blow to the US imperialist aggressors and make them desist from their reckless escalation of the war of aggression in Viet Nam.

We should work hard to make sure that the international democratic organizations also take joint anti-imperialist action in their activities. The keynote of these organizations' activities should be to oppose US imperialism and give support to the fighting people. Thus, the democratic social organizations in all countries should be made to attain joint anti-imperialist action through the medium of the international democratic organizations, and all the international democratic organizations should join forces and take action together to oppose US imperialism and support the peoples of the fighting countries. Joint anti-imperialism action achieved in this way in the activities of the international democratic organizations, will display a great force.

These measures, however, cannot in themselves fully solve the question of materializing joint anti-imperialist action and an anti-imperialist united front. The most important thing is to create conditions among the fraternal parties for achieving joint anti-imperialist action. The Communist and Workers' Parties should, first of all, wage a resolute struggle against imperialism and give active support to the revolutionary movements of the peoples, each from its own position. In this process, we should gradually narrow down the differences and create an atmosphere conducive to mutual contacts. And when definite conditions are created, the fraternal parties may hold a consultative meeting to discuss the question of joint anti- imperialist action in a concrete way.

To work actively in this way to achieve joint anti-imperialist action and an anti-imperialist united front on the international scale, overcoming all difficulties, is, we believe, the way for all fraternal parties to be true to Marxist-Leninist principles and discharge their internationalist duties at the present time.

It is a matter of importance in the international communist movement that the Communist and Workers' Parties maintain their independence. Only when independence is ensured can each party successfully carry on the revolution in its own country and contribute to the world revolution, and the cohesion of the international communist movement can be also strengthened.

Independence is each party's sacred right which no one is allowed to violate, and each party is duty bound to respect the independence of other fraternal parties. Respect for independence is prerequisite and basic to the unity and cooperation of the fraternal parties. A truly voluntary, solid and comradely unity and cooperation among the fraternal parties is possible only if they all respect each other's independence.

Mutual relations of the fraternal parties should be based on the principles of complete equality, independence, mutual respect, noninterference in each other's internal affairs and comradely cooperation. This norm was defined at the 1957 and 1960 meetings of representatives of the parties of all countries on the basis of the historical experience of the international communist movement, and its correctness has already been confirmed in life. All Communist and Workers' Parties without exception must strictly observe and faithfully live up to this norm. If this norm should ever be violated, complicated problems would arise between the fraternal parties, the unity of the international communist movement would be undermined and many difficulties would crop up in the way of progress.

In recent years there have been incessant violations of the norm governing the mutual relations of the fraternal parties in the international communist movement. This has given rise to complicated problems in the international communist movement and created serious obstacles to the unity of the fraternal parties.

All parties must respect other parties on an equal footing and strive to maintain comradely relations with each other. Among the Communist and Workers' Parties, there can be neither senior nor junior parties, nor a party that leads, nor a party that is led. No party is entitled to a privileged position in the international communist movement.

In the international communist movement there is no international organization which exercises unified leadership over the activities of the parties of all countries. Times have changed, and the days are gone when the communist movement needed an international center. Ever since the dissolution of the Third International there has been no "center" or "hub" in the international communist movement. It is therefore impossible for a "hub" of the revolution to shift from one country to another. It is also impossible for any country to become the "hub of the world revolution" or for any party to become the "leading party" in the international communist movement.

The revolution in each country is being carried out with the efforts of its own people under the leadership of its own party, and on no account by any international "center" or by the party of another country. Communists accept no "hub" or "center" whatsoever in the international communist movement, because that would mean giving one party a privileged position. Then that party would occupy a higher position and would be able to give instructions and orders to other parties, which would be compelled to obey and worship the former. Should such a relationship be allowed to exist among the fraternal parties, it would deprive each party of its independence and even prevent it from carrying on the revolution and construction independently in its own country. This kind of relationship can never be tolerated in the international communist movement.

The Communist and Workers' Parties, all as equal members of the international communist movement, are contributing jointly to the development of the international revolutionary movement and Marxism-Leninism.

If they are to play the role of the vanguard detachment in the revolution, the Communist and Workers' Parties must be guided only by Marxism-Leninism. Marxism-Leninism is the most scientific and revolutionary theory tested in practice and the acme of all the progressive ideologies of mankind. It sets out general laws which must be strictly observed in the revolution and construction in all countries.

Each party, applying Marxism-Leninism creatively to the realities of its country, should work out and carry into practice its own guiding theory for revolution and construction in its own country. It cannot lead revolution and construction by using the guiding theory of another party.

Each party's guiding theory is valid only within the bounds of its country. Since actual conditions differ from country to country, the guiding theory of the party in a particular country, however excellent, cannot be applied to another country. It is therefore impossible to hold up the guiding theory of the party of one country as being valid for Communists of all lands; it must not be imposed upon other parties.

For the Korean Communists the only guiding principle is Marxism-Leninism and the lines and policies of our Party worked out through its creative application to the realities of our country. For us there can be no other guiding ideology.

Communists must under no circumstances be presumptuous or impose their views upon other parties. It is impermissible among the Communist and Workers' Parties for one party to exert pressure on the parties of other countries or interfere in their internal affairs just because they do not obey its will. In the international communist movement today, however, some parties still impose their views and lines upon other parties, bringing pressure to bear upon them and interfering in their internal affairs because they do not accept their views and lines.

The interference of certain fraternal parties in the internal affairs of the Communist Party of Japan is one such example. Even if differences exist, a fraternal party should not back up the anti-party factionalists within another party, sow confusion in it and split the democratic movement of another's country. Outside interference has brought great difficulties to the activities of the Communist Party of Japan. Despite all these difficulties, however, the Communist Party of Japan consistently opposes interference in its internal affairs and upholds its independence, and is unwaveringly leading the revolutionary struggle of the Japanese people.

Our Party, too, has had the bitter experience of interference by great-power chauvinists in its internal affairs. Needless to say, those great-power chauvinists met with rejection they deserved. At that time, we, in the interests of the revolution and out of the desire to preserve unity, settled the issue between ourselves, even though it was hard for us to bear. In the future, too, we should oppose all types of interference in our internal affairs and guard against great-power chauvinism.

In the international communist movement there is no party which has a monopoly of the right to draw conclusions at its own will on problems of principle. No party should form arbitrary conclusions on important international issues and force other parties to accept them. Communist and Workers' Parties should discuss matters of common concern and act in accordance with mutually-agreed-upon conclusions. Only then can the unity of purpose and action be guaranteed.

Each party should be careful not to fall into subjectivism in dealing with important international issues or in relation to the fraternal parties. Communists must not appraise fraternal parties hastily or harbor prejudices against them because the latter do not obey them or have different views. No party must regard fraternal parties as going against Marxism-Leninism because their positions are different from its own. Moreover, there should be no practice of arbitrarily attaching various labels to fraternal parties which maintain an independent position.

Certain people now attach the labels of "centrism," "eclecticism," "opportunism," and the like to our Party and other Marxist-Leninist parties. They allege that we are taking the "road of unprincipled compromise" and are "straddling two chairs." This is nonsense. We have our own chair. Why should we throw away our own chair and sit down uncomfortably, straddling two chairs belonging to others? We will always sit on our steady Marxist-Leninist chair. Those who accuse us of straddling two chairs when we are sitting on our sturdy chair, are themselves no doubt sitting on a chair which is crooked to the left or to the right.

The slanders against our Party merely prove that our Party not only opposes Right opportunism but also is uncompromising with "Left" opportunism, and firmly adheres only to the principled stand of Marxism-Leninism. We oppose opportunism of all descriptions because we are Marxists-Leninists.

A Communist should not act arrogantly and say that whatever he does is right and whatever others do is wrong. It is impermissible to behave like this with comrades fighting for the commom cause. Communists may have different opinions on different matters, even though they are all guided by Marxism-Leninism. But even in such cases, they must have an understanding of each other, hold sincere consultations and strive for unity. This is the rule of conduct Communists must observe.

All Communists have their own standpoint and can tell right from wrong. A party cannot be indiscriminately regarded as subscribing to the lines and policies of other parties or as taking the cue from them, just because it has connections with those parties. Regarding others with suspicion is a specific characteristic of great-power chauvinism and sectarianism. Great-power chauvinism and sectarianism suspect others for no reason and like to divide people into different sides. We will not take any "side." If someone asks us which "side" we are on, we will answer that we are on the "side" of Marxism-Leninism, on the "side" of revolution. Communists should not look at the independent activities of fraternal parties through tinted glasses and should not get too nervous about them.

The activities of all Communist and Workers' Parties cannot be fitted into any set pattern. The policies of fraternal parties cannot be the same since the actual conditions and revolutionary tasks differ from country to country. The unified line of the international communist movement by no means excludes diversity in the policies of individual parties.

Communists must check great-power chauvinism in the international communist movement. Therefore, all fraternal parties should be independent without blindly following anyone, and should reject great-power chauvinism. And all the parties should unite and prevent anyone from ruling over the socialist camp and the international communist movement, and restrain great-power chauvinism from exerting influence. If no one accepts and follows great-power chauvinism, no matter who may brandish it, it will become impotent and produce no effect. Only when great-power chauvinism disappears, can the independence of all parties be firmly assured and the relations between the fraternal parties be developed in a healthy way.

Communists must learn to hold fast to their convictions under any circumstances. A Communist, if he is a real one, cannot follow in the wake of others blindly, parroting what others say and moving in others' steps without his own conviction.

Communists are not engaged in revolution on instructions from anyone or to get into anyone's good graces. Communists make revolution out of their own faith in Marxism-Leninism, for the emancipation of the working class and the working people in their own countries and for the cause of the international working class. It is a noble trait of Communists to stick fast to and fight unyieldingly for their own convictions.

The present situation in the international communist movement demands us to maintain independence and identity more firmly. If we lack independence and identity and follow in others' steps in present-day conditions, we cannot have principle and consistency in our lines and policies. This not only will eventually do enormous harm to our revolution and construction, but will inflict a great damage to the international communist movement.

We can and will never dance to the tune of others. Based on Marxist-Leninist principles and the realities of our country, we should lay down our lines and policies and implement them by ourselves. In this way, we should vigorously advance our revolution and construction. In the sphere of international activities, too, we must maintain our independent position in accordance with our convictions.

Our Party's independent position is linked closely with the principle of proletarian internationalism. Being internationalists, we categorically reject isolationism and nationalism. We immensely treasure the international solidarity of the working class and value the unity and cooperation with the fraternal parties and countries. We deem it necessary to respect the experience of other parties and learn from each other. What we oppose is the tendency to follow others blindly, without independence, to depend wholly on others without faith in one's own strength and to swallow the experience of others in lumps instead of approaching it critically.

We should continually develop our relations with the fraternal parties and countries on the basis of a correct combination of independence and unity. We maintain that the socialist camp and the international communist movement should unite in accordance with the principles of Marxism-Leninism and proletarian internationalism, in accordance with the declaration and statement of the meetings of representatives of the fraternal parties.

To unite and cooperate on the basis of equality and independence and to maintain independence while consolidating international solidarity is the firm and steady policy consistently followed by our Party in its relations with fraternal parties and countries. This policy not only accords with the interests of the revolution and construction in our country but fully conforms to the interests of the international communist movement. It will help surmount the difficulties existing in the international communist movement at present and achieve genuine unity.

The international developments and the events in the international communist movement in recent years have once again clearly testified to the correctness of the lines and policies of our Party.

All our successes are associated with our Party's line of independence. Thanks to the line of independence, our Party has not deviated either to the Right or to the "Left" in mapping out its lines for internal and external activities and has been able to avoid errors on matters of principle.

Today the international prestige of our Party has grown and the international position of our Republic has been consolidated. We have won innumerable friends and sympathizers throughout the world. Our Party's line of independence in the. international communist movement is receiving support from more and more fraternal parties. The achievements scored by our Party in its foreign activities inspire us with legitimate confidence and pride.

As in the past, so in future too, our Party will continue to adhere to the line of independence in its internal and external activities, safeguard the purity of Marxism-Leninism against Right and "Left" opportunism, and abide by the principles set out in the Declaration and Statement of the meetings of representatives of the Communist and Workers' Parties of all countries. Our Party will strive to defend the unity of the socialist camp and the solidarity of the international communist movement based on the principles of Marxism-

Leninism and proletarian internationalism, and to oppose imperialism and carry the revolution through to the end in close unity with the people of the whole world.

2. On the Acceleration of Socialist Construction and the Strengthening of Our Revolutionary Base

Comrades,

The greatest national task confronting the Workers' Party of Korea and the Korean people at the present stage is to achieve the reunification of the country and the nationwide triumph of the revolution. To do so, we must, first, push ahead vigorously with revolution and construction in the northern half where the people have already seized power and are building a new life, and turn the northern half into a powerful base of our revolution. Socialist construction and growth of the revolutionary forces in the northern half of the Republic constitute the decisive guarantee for the reunification of our country and the triumph of the Korean revolution as a whole. By mobilizing all the forces of the Party and the people, we must further accelerate socialist construction in the northern half and more solidly build up our revolutionary base— politically, economically and militarily.

It is of paramount importance for our revolutionary struggle and constructive work today to reorganize the whole work of socialist construction in line with the requirements of the prevailing situation and, especially, to carry on the building of the economy and defenses in parallel so as to further increase our nation's defense capacities to cope with the enemy's aggressive maneuvers. This is the basic strategic line of our Party which we have carried on for several years now in view of the changed situation. In the future too, we must follow this line of the Party with all firmness and consistency and base all our work on it.

How to combine economic construction with the building of national defenses is one of the fundamental questions on which the success of the building of socialism and communism depends. We Communists should reject all kinds of deviations which may possibly appear in this respect, and settle the matter in a correct way.

It is wrong not to conduct economic construction properly, only emphasizing defense upbuilding on the ground that a war could reduce everything to rubble when it breaks out. It is also wrong not to strengthen defense potentials adequately, emphasizing only economic construction, captivated by a pacifistic mood.

Of course, the danger of war will not disappear as long as imperialism remains, and a great deal can be destroyed when a war breaks out. Yet if necessary economic construction is neglected for fear of war and its devastation, it will be impossible to increase the might of the country and improve the people's living standard, and it will be entirely impossible to build socialism and communism before the downfall of imperialism. The danger of war caused by the imperialists and a war of aggression unleashed by them may possibly delay or temporarily interrupt our economic construction, but it can never check our forward march towards socialism and communism.

In the meantime, the people can prevent war and consolidate peace by waging an energetic struggle against the imperialist policy of aggression and war. But if one merely believes that war will not break out, and fails to build up defense power properly, it will rather increase the danger of war and make it utterly impossible to protect the revolutionary gains and defend the country and the people against imperialist aggression, let alone build socialism and communism. The possibility of preventing war is no more than a possibility, and as long as imperialism remains, there can be no absolute guarantee of peace and a war may break out at any moment.

We should neither overestimate nor underestimate the danger of war and the effect of its destruction on our socialist construction. Even if there is a growing danger of war, we must energetically continue with economic construction to make the country rich and strong, to improve the people's living standard and to accelerate the forward march of socialism and communism, while further increasing the defense potentials. As our experience shows, even if a war breaks out and causes great destruction, we can build a new life again, as long as we have the Party, the Government, the people and the territory. At the same time, even if war seems not likely to break out right now, we must continue to strengthen our defense capabilities and keep ourselves always ready to protect our revolutionary gains and defend the country and the people against imperialist aggression, while stepping up economic construction vigorously. Only when our defense power is built up invincibly and we keep ourselves ready for action, will the enemy not dare challenge us and, even if he starts a reckless adventure, can we promptly administer a crushing blow to the aggressors and defeat them.

Adhering consistently to this principle, our Party assessed the trend of developments at each period and has accordingly carried out economic construction in proper combination with the upbuilding of the nation's defenses.

In recent years our Party has been compelled to direct special attention to further increasing our defense capacities in the face of intensified aggressive moves of the imperialists. As you comrades all know, the US imperialists provoked the Caribbean crisis against the Republic of Cuba in 1962, thereby challenging the entire socialist camp and making the international situation extremely tense. After that, the US imperialists set out on a still more open aggression in Asia. They provoked the Bac Bo Gulf incident against the Democratic Republic of Viet Nam, stepped up the war of aggression on a large scale in South Viet Nam and further aggravated tensions in Southeast Asia, the Far East and other areas.

To cope with this situation, our Party set forth the line of carrying on economic construction in parallel with defense building already at the Fifth Plenary Meeting of its Fourth Central Committee in 1962, and took a number of important measures for further increasing our defense potentials while reorganizing economic construction. Subsequent developments have proved that the step taken by our Party was entirely correct. By greatly boosting the defense power through our efforts to carry out the Party's decision, we have become able to defend the security of our country firmly even when the imperialists are running amuck.

Today the aggressive acts of the US imperialists are further stepped up and their plot for expanding the war is more and more undisguised. The Pak Jung Hi clique in south Korea, upon US imperialist instructions, is not only making active preparations for a new war, but has already joined directly in the US imperialists' war of aggression in Viet Nam. The situation has grown tenser and the danger of war is increasing in our country and all other areas of Asia.

Under these circumstances, we must continue to propel the economic construction of socialism and, at the same time, build our defenses more energetically. We must make our defensive might invincible and get everything ready to cope with any surprise attack by the enemy. True, this will require allocation of much manpower and materials to national defense, and it will inevitably delay the economic development of our country to a certain extent. But we should direct greater efforts to the strengthening of our defense power to make the country's defense perfect, even if it calls for some readjustment of the development rate of the national economy. This is in agreement with the fundamental interests of the revolution and construction in our country at the present stage. It is therefore necessary for us to push ahead steadfastly with both economic construction and defense building along the line set forth by the Party, and we must not neglect either sector.

The economic construction of socialism is an important revolutionary task for us today. Communists struggle to bring freedom and liberation to the people and provide them with a new happy life. We have already emancipated our people from exploitation and oppression and ensured political liberties and rights to them by carrying out democratic and socialist revolutions in the northern half of the country. By establishing an advanced, socialist system, we have opened up a wide avenue for the development of productive forces and improvement of the people's living standard. Now it is important to increase the people's material well-being by consolidating the triumphant socialist system and bringing its advantages into full play. This calls for a successful building of the economy. When economic construction is carried out successfully, it is possible to attain a high level of development of the productive forces commensurate with socialist society, make the country rich and strong and decisively raise the living standard of the people. And when the foundations of an independent economy are consolidated by forcefully stepping up economic construction, the political independence and sovereignty of the country can be assured solidly and defense potentials, too, can be strengthened.

The economic construction of socialism in the northern half of the Republic is the basic guarantee of increasing the material power of our revolutionary base. It has an enormous significance not only for the happy life of the people in the northern half but also for the reunification and future prosperity of our country. By steadily increasing the economic power of the northern half, we can clearly demonstrate the superiority of the socialist system to the people in south Korea and give an ever more powerful support to their revolutionary struggle. The building of a socialist, independent economy in the northern half is also a reliable asset for the rapid rehabilitation and development of the economy in south Korea after the reunification of the country.

It is our national and, at the same time, internationalist duty to build the economy successfully in our country. We can fortify the eastern outpost of the socialist camp and help strengthen the might of this camp as a whole only if we increase our own economic strength. Both the vitality of our socialist system and the correctness of the Marxist-Leninist lines and policies of our Party are expressed, after all, in the practical results of our socialist economic construction. Our struggle for economic construction, therefore, is a struggle to increase the might of the socialist camp and further the development of the international revolutionary movement, a struggle to blow up the slanders of the imperialists and reactionaries against the socialist system and demonstrate the true advantages of this system, a struggle to overcome revisionism and dogmatism and safeguard the purity of Marxism-Leninism in the communist movement.

Beginning shortly after liberation, our Party has done everything in its power to consolidate the economic foundations of the country and improve the material and cultural life of the people. After the war, we, acting upon the principle of self-reliance, laid the firm foundations of an independent national economy and basically solved the questions of food, clothing and housing for the people. Under the leadership of the Party, our working people have waged a vigorous labor campaign for the fulfillment of the Seven-Year Plan and achieved fresh successes in socialist economic construction over the past five years. Our heavy industry bases have been reinforced, our light industry has developed still more and the material and technical foundations of agriculture have been strengthened considerably. The towns and villages of our country have been better built and the material well-being and cultural standards of the people, too, have been improved on the whole. We must continue to push forward economic construction dynamically in order to consolidate and develop our economic achievements and carry into effect the magnificent program of socialist construction set forth at the Fourth Congress of the Party.

What is important in the socialist economic construction of our country today is to make effective use of the already-created economic foundations and radically raise the quality of products and construction in all fields. Under the leadership of the Party our people have laid solid bases for production in all fields of the national economy by carrying out a vast amount of constructive work, through a heroic struggle and creative labor, for more than ten years after the war. The bases of heavy and light industries and the socialist agriculture which we have built have immense productive potentialities. If we further readjust and reinforce those economic foundations and make effective use of them, we will be able to produce much more than now. We are now turning out an incomparably greater amount of industrial goods and farm produce than before, and have already attained a fairly high level in the output per head of the population. If we increase the variety of goods and radically improve their quality, we can satisfy the demands of the national economy and the population better, even with the present volume of production. To make the most of the economic assets we have already created and to raise quality in production and construction—this is the basic direction of the economic development of our country at the present stage, and precisely here are vast reserves for the growth of production and improvement of the people's living standard. It is in this basic direction that we must exert our main efforts to mobilize all and every reserve and potential latent in the national economy. Meanwhile, we should continuously carry out new capital construction to further expand our economic bases.

The central task in industry is to give priority to the mining and power industries and add flesh to the skeleton of industry, to improve technical management and make more technical innovations, thereby normalizing production and raising productive capacity to the highest possible level. In agriculture, grain output should be increased substantially and, at the same time, all other branches such as the production of industrial crops and vegetables, livestock breeding and fruit growing should be further developed by energetically promoting the technical revolution, improving labor administration, continuously increasing support to the countryside, and raising the level of management on the cooperative farms. The growing requirements of the national economy for transport must be satisfied in full by rapidly developing railway and other transport services, and the effectiveness of investment must be increased in all fields of the national economy by carrying out capital construction in a concentrated way and on a priority basis. An all-Party, all-people struggle must be unfolded in all fields to thoroughly establish the Taean work system and diligently build up the economic life. We must, in this way, make our socialist country richer and stronger, radically improve the material and cultural life of the people, and make preparations for still larger economic construction in the future.

Another important question in socialist economic construction is to consolidate the economic independence of the country. To build an independent national economy on the principle of self-reliance is a consistent line of our Party. We have already achieved brilliant successes in the implementation of this line. Especially, under the present situation when the aggressive maneuvers of the imperialists are more open and when complicated problems exist within the socialist camp, it is imperative for us to further consolidate the foundations of the independent economy of the country.

Of course, we will, in the future too, strive to extend and develop economic and technical cooperation with fraternal countries on the principles of complete equality and mutual benefit and of proletarian internationalism. We will develop economic ties and cooperation with the newly independent countries in Asia and Africa, and with all countries which respect our sovereignty and want to trade with us to fill each other's economic needs. This cooperation, however, should be effected strictly on the basis of building an independent national economy. Only then can our own economic power be fur-

ther increased and our cooperation with other countries be conducted effectively.

We must thoroughly carry out the Party's policy of further
strengthening the foundations of an independent national
economy. We must reinforce productive branches and enterprises and equip them perfectly, further improve the structure
of the national economy, continue to develop small and
medium enterprises side by side with large ones, distribute the
country's productive forces rationally and, especially, promote
the development of local economy. It is necessary in all fields
to bravely surmount difficulties cropping up in the way of progress and successfully solve economic and technical problems
by raising the technical levels and stepping up the struggle for
thrift and by displaying a greater revolutionary spirit of self-
reliance. We should thus make our national economy more
solid, virile and independent so that we may fully meet the
material requirements of the state and the people under any
circumstances.

While accelerating economic construction as best we can, we
must do everything to increase the country's defense power.

In order to strengthen our defensive power, it is necessary,
first of all, to firmly prepare the People's Army and the entire
people politically and ideologically.

Our People's Army is a revolutionary army, and so the basic
condition for increasing its might lies in arming our soldiers
politically and ideologically. The lofty mission and revolutionary spirit of fighting for the freedom and liberation of the
people, the comradeship between man and officer, voluntary
military discipline and close ties with the people are the characteristics and merits of a Marxist-Leninist revolutionary
army, which are nonexistent in any imperialist army of aggression. It is thanks to these political and ideological merits that
a revolutionary army is fully able to defeat an aggressive army
far superior both in technique and in number. This is proved by
the experience of the anti-Japanese armed struggle and the
Fatherland Liberation War in our country and by the experience of many revolutionary wars in the world.

The basic mission of our People's Army as the direct con-
tinuer of the anti-Japanese armed struggle and as the revolutionary armed forces led by the Workers' Party, is to serve the
Party and the revolution and defend their socialist fatherland
and people. Our People's Army is an army organized with best

sons and daughters of the workers, peasants and other sections of the working people; the superiors and inferiors are in perfect unity; and the army maintains close bonds of kinship with the people.

The organizations of the Party and the League of Socialist Working Youth in the army should conduct political and ideological work among the soldiers regularly and energetically, thus bringing home to them the lofty mission of the People's Army and arming them firmly with Marxist-Leninism and the policies of our Party, with socialist patriotism and an indomitable revolutionary spirit. It is necessary in the army to promote the traditional trait of unity between superiors and inferiors and between the army and the people and establish iron military discipline. Our military personnel should be educated to have a boundless love for their people, bear a burning hatred against the enemy and display mass heroism and valor in battle. All the soldiers must in this way be reared as revolutionary fighters loyal to the Party, the revolution and the people, and our People's Army should be turned into a match-for-a-hundred army.

At the same time, the Party organizations at all levels should take great care to assist the People's Army. The People's Army is the army of our Party, and the reliable defender of our country and people. The Party organizations should energetically conduct propaganda and education concerning the People's Army among the Party members and the working people and actively support the People's Army in every way. All our cadres, Party members and people should love the soldiers, non-commissioned officers and officers of the People's Army as if they were their own brothers and aid them with all sincerity. Thus, the men and officers of the People's Army should be able to devote themselves entirely to discharging their military duties without any worries, thanks to the profound affection, support and assistance of the whole Party and the entire people. We should make sure that in the event of war, the soldiers and the people firmly unite in a body, as true revolutionary comrades, and fight with single-hearted devotion to defend the country, sharing sweets and bitters, life and death.

We should also see to it that the soldiers and the people do not fall into a pacifistic mood but sharpen their vigilance and maintain themselves alert at all times against the aggressive maneuvers of the enemy and his possible provocation of war. Communists do not want war, but they never fear it. To be afraid of war is a manifestation of bourgeois pacifism and a revisionist ideological trend. We must strictly guard against the appearance of such an ideological virus within our ranks or its infiltration from without. We must prepare the entire army and people to bravely meet and fight any surprise enemy attack without the slightest confusion.

To strengthen our defense power it is essential to carry through the military line of our Party on the basis of equipping the army and the people politically and ideologically. Having defined it as the basic content of its military line to make our army a cadre army, modernize it, arm all the people and turn the whole country into a fortress, our Party has exerted tireless efforts to put this line into practice, and has already attained great successes in this respect. In the future, too, we should continue to abide by the Party's military line and implement it thoroughly.

Turning the People's Army into a cadre army and modernizing it constitute important guarantees for building up our army into an invincible armed force. We should steel the People's Army ranks politically, ideologically and in military technique so that in case of an emergency everyone, from the rank and file up to the generals, can undertake and perform the duties of higher rank. This will not only greatly increase the combat capabilities of the People's Army itself, but also create numerous military cadres and thus rapidly expand our armed forces in case of necessity.

When the political and ideological superiority of a revolutionary army is combined with modern military techniques, it can become a really great force. At present, military science and techniques are developing rapidly in the world, and up-to-date army and military equipment are being used in modern warfare. Our enemies are equipping themselves with newer and newer weapons. We must firmly arm our People's Army with modern weapons and combat technical equipment to counter the aggression of the enemies who are armed to the teeth, in conformity to the requirements of modern warfare. We must modernize our weapons by all possible means and make them still more powerful on the basis of the latest achievements of science and technology. Servicemen should be given energetic field training so as to enable all of them to handle up-to-date weapons skillfully and to acquire a sufficient mastery of modern military science and techniques.

In modernizing the People's Army and developing military science and techniques we must take into full account the actual conditions of our country which has many mountains and long coastlines. As the experience of the last Fatherland Liberation War shows clearly, if dogmatic errors are committed in the military sphere, it may cause serious harm to national defense. While actively endeavoring to modernize the People's Army, therefore, we must always develop and apply military science and techniques suited to the specific conditions of our country, and properly use conventional weapons along with modern ones.

The arming of the entire people and the fortification of the whole country constitute the most powerful defense system from the military strategic point of view, a system which is capable of thwarting any enemy attack. This is the way to carry out the mass line of our Party and fully effect the principle of self-defense in national defense. By arming the entire people and fortifying the whole land, we can crush the uninterrupted subversive activities of the enemy at every step and shatter all forms of armed attack by our own efforts. This defense system can be established only on the basis of the political and ideological unity of the people and the solid economic foundations of the country under our socialist system.

Along with the People's Army, we must arm the workers, peasants and all other sections of the people and build indestructible defense installations in all parts of the country, both on the front line and in the rear. We should solidly build up the ranks of the Worker-Peasant Red Guards, intensify their military and political training and see that all cadres and Party members acquire military knowledge and training and study the experience of war. In factories, the Worker-Peasant Red Guardsmen and workers should defend their factories, and in the countryside, the Worker-Peasant Red Guardsmen and peasants should defend their villages; and the entire people, holding a weapon in one hand and a hammer and a sickle in the other, should reliably safeguard our socialist homeland and continue to build socialism successfully. We should, in this way, convert the whole of our territory into an impregnable fortress so that we can completely destroy the enemies wherever they may invade our country.

Victory in modern warfare depends largely on whether man-power and material resources needed to carry out the war are fully secured for a long period. Hence, we should direct deep attention to consolidating the rear. In particular, we should effectively build up zones of military strategic importance, develop the munitions industry and create reserves of necessary materials. We should also be prepared in peacetime to immediately place the whole economy on a war footing in the event of emergency and to carry on production in wartime.

Our Party and people will thus carry out economic construction and defense building in parallel in conformity with the requirements of the current situation, and thereby translate into reality the magnificent program of socialist construction while creditably discharging the duty of defending the country at the same time.

Comrades, revolution and construction are the work of the masses themselves, and they can be carried out successfully only when the broad masses are mobilized under the leadership of the Marxist-Leninist party. Therefore, the most important question in accelerating our socialist construction and fortifying our revolutionary base is to strengthen the Party—the General Staff in revolution—educate and remold the entire people and rally them around the Party; in other words, to firmly build up the ranks of the revolution, politically and ideologically.

Our Party has tirelessly worked to consolidate itself organizationally and ideologically, to awaken the masses and win them over to the side of the revolution in the course of the practical struggle for the revolution and construction, to train all Party members as revolutionaries through the nuclear role of the Communists steeled in long revolutionary struggle and to equip all the people with the revolutionary spirit through the nuclear role of the Party members.

As a result, our Party has grown into a seasoned Marxist-Leninist Party which is closely knit together, with one mind and will and has accumulated a wealth of experience; the Party ranks have gained in scope and strength, and a large number of new revolutionaries capable of creditably carrying forward our revolutionary cause have grown up. Our people have been tempered in the thick of struggle, and their practical experience of struggle has led them to place infinite trust in the Party and unite solidly around it.

In the northern half of our country, the exploiting classes and all exploiting institutions have already been liquidated and a new, socialist system established and, on this basis, the worker-peasant alliance has been more consolidated and the political and ideological unity of the whole people achieved. In the exploiter society, class antagonism and struggle between the exploiting and the exploited classes, between the ruling and the ruled classes constitute the basis of social relationships, but in our society where the socialist system has triumphed, unity and cooperation among the working class, cooperative farmers and working intellectuals constitute the basis of social relationships. Our workers, peasants and intellectuals, for their common socio-economic positions and their common objectives and interests, are united in a comradely way and closely cooperate with each other, working together for the victory of the cause of communism under the leadership of our Party.

The political and ideological unity of the masses of the people—based on the worker-peasant alliance—and their common aspiration and enthusiasm to build socialism and communism under the leadership of the Party are the main driving force propelling the progress of our society and the decisive factor in speeding up the building of socialism. This unity is also the source of our invincible strength and the foundation of the solidity of our society.

This, of course, does not mean that there are neither hostile elements nor class struggle in our midst. Class struggle continues under socialism, too.

Class struggle under socialism is expressed, above all, in the struggle against the subversive activities of hostile elements worming in from without and of the remnants of the overthrown exploiting classes and in the struggle against bourgeois and feudal reactionary ideas and their penetration. The enemy makes every attempt to destroy our socialist system and restore its old positions. Although the hostile elements lurking in our midst are very few, we must increase our vigilance of the enemy's subversive maneuverings and crush them completely. Especially in our situation where the country remains divided and we are directly confronted with the US imperialists, the chieftain of world reaction, it acquires a greater importance to struggle against the enemy's subversive activities, sabotage and ideological infiltration, to which we should always pay deep attention.

Under socialism the remnants of the outdated ideas also persist in the minds of the working people and the struggle against these remnants is also a manifestation of class struggle in the sense that it is a struggle between working-class and bourgeois ideologies. If we weaken the struggle against the ideological vestiges of the past, bourgeois and petty-bourgeois ideas could gain ground among the working people, and this would not only create big obstacles in the way of our socialist construction but would easily play into the hands of the enemy in his subversive activities. We must not in the least slacken the struggle against the outworn ideas among the working people but must carry it on vigorously.

The struggle against the remnants of old ideas, however, is an internal affair of the working people who are advancing hand in hand to realize a common ideal; it is a task arising from the need to educate and remold all the working people and lead them to a communist society. This problem, therefore, should always be solved by means of persuasion and education, unlike suppressing the hostile elements, and in such a way as to serve the purpose of remolding the people's thinking and further cementing their unity.

We should neither underestimate nor overestimate the danger of survivals of the outdated ideas. In our society today there are no socio-economic and material conditions for engendering the outdated ideas; the predominant ideology of our working people is the revolutionary ideology of Marxism-Leninism and communist ideology. It is, therefore, quite possible for us to overcome the vestiges of outmoded ideas by persistent ideological education of the working people.

In firmly building up our revolutionary ranks it is very important to combine properly the work of cementing the unity and cohesion of the masses of the people with the class struggle against the conspiratorial maneuvers of the hostile elements. A person may commit a "Leftist" error if he emphasizes and overestimates class struggle only, forgetting

that the alliance of the working class, peasantry and intellectuals constitutes the basis of social relations under socialism.
In that case, one will tend to suspect people, treat innocent
persons like hostile elements, divorce the Party from the
masses and create an atmosphere of unrest in society. On the
other hand, one may commit a Rightist error if he sees only the
political and ideological unity of masses of the people, making
it an absolute, oblivious of the fact that hostile elements,
ideological survivals from the past and class struggle also continue to exist under socialism. In that case, vigilance against
hostile elements could be let down, the struggle against outdated ideas could be weakened, the leading role of the Party
and the working class could be paralyzed and bourgeois influence could spread widely in social life. Both Right and
"Left" deviations will, in the long run, make it impossible to
clearly distinguish friend from foe and to correctly implement
the class and mass lines, and will bring heavy losses to the
building of socialism and communism. We should oppose both
Right and "Left" deviations and steadily strengthen the unity
and solidarity of the masses of the people, while skillfully waging class struggle.

From the viewpoint of class relationship, the course of
building socialism and communism is a process in which the
working class, having seized power, transforms society after
its own pattern in all spheres of economy and culture, ideology
and morality, that is, a process of working-classization. The
historical mission of the dictatorship of the proletariat not only lies in liquidating the exploiting classes and crushing their
resistance but in remolding all the working people to working-
classize them, thus gradually eliminating all class distinctions.
In our society, where the exploiting classes have been wiped
out and the socialist system has triumphed, an important task
of the dictatorship of the proletariat is to educate and remold
the working people and working-classize the whole society.

By correctly combining the class line with the mass line, we
must isolate and crush the handful of hostile elements and, at
the same time, educate and remodel the broad masses to rally
them close around the Party. We must constantly enhance the
lead role of the working class and also revolutionize and
working-classize the peasants and intellectuals, thus cementing the political and ideological unity of our society still more.

With the progress of socialist construction in our country the ranks of the working class have grown rapidly and the standards of their ideological consciousness and their level of culture and technology have risen higher. Our working class has been doing a good job of carrying out the historical mission of transforming society and is displaying a high degree of revolutionary zeal and creativity in socialist construction.

It is not by weakening its class leadership or by dissolving itself in other sections of the people that the working class obliterates class distinctions. On the contrary, the working class holds fast to its class stand, constantly enhances its leading role, remolds the other sections of the working people on its own pattern and thereby strengthens its solidarity with them and gradually eliminates all the class distinctions. We should, therefore, elevate the leading role of the working class and increase its revolutionary influence in all spheres of social life. We should further enhance the ideology, organization and culture of the working class and build up its ranks more solidly. In this way we should make our working class a truly revolutionary and cultured class and enable it to perform its role better as the leading class.

The peasantry is the most reliable ally of the working class and one of the main detachments of our revolution. Always giving deep concern to the peasant question and pursuing a correct rural policy, our Party has successfully solved this problem. We abolished feudal relationships by carrying out an agrarian reform in the countryside shortly after liberation and, in the postwar period, we reorganized individual peasant farming into the socialist collective economy, thereby emancipating the peasants from all kinds of exploitation and oppression and transforming them into socialist working people. Through the democratic and socialist revolutions and through socialist construction, the socio-economic position of our peasants has not only changed fundamentally but a great change has also taken place in their ideological consciousness; their technical and cultural standards have also been raised speedily. On the basis of socialism, the worker-peasant alliance led by the working class has been solidified and the political and labor enthusiasm of the peasants continues to increase.

Our task is to consolidate and develop the successes already achieved in the solution of the rural question and, further, to eliminate all the backwardness of the countryside left over from the exploiter society and obliterate step by step the distinctions between town and country, the class distinctions between the working class and the peasantry. This means striving for the final solution of the peasant question. Our Party summed up our achievements and experience in rural work and elucidated the basic principles and specific ways and means for the solution of the rural question under socialism. In accordance with the correct line advanced by the Party, we should energetically push ahead with the technical, cultural and ideological revolutions in the countryside, continuously strengthen the guidance and assistance given to the countryside by the working-class party and state, and steadily bring cooperative ownership closer to ownership by the whole people, while developing the two forms of ownership in organic combination. Thus, on the basis of equipping agriculture with modern technology as we have done in industry, and of consolidating and developing the socialist system established in the countryside, we should raise the material and cultural life of the peasantry to the level of the working class, further remold the thinking of the peasants and thus revolutionize and working-classize them still more.

Intellectuals play an important role in the building of a new society. The working class which has seized power can speedily develop science and technology, literature and art and build socialism and communism successfully only when it firmly strengthens the ranks of its own intellectuals.

From the first days of its founding, our Party, taking into consideration the important role of the intellectuals in revolution and construction, has made persistent efforts to educate and remold the old intellectuals, while training a large number of new intellectuals from among the working people. It is true that the old intellectuals come mostly from rich families and served Japanese imperialism and the exploiting classes in the past. But they, as intellectuals of a colonial country, were subjected to national oppression and discrimination by foreign imperialism and, therefore, had a national and democratic revolutionary spirit. Our Party put faith in their revolutionary spirit and adopted the line of actively drawing them into the building of a new society, thus transforming them into intellectuals serving the working people. Over the past 20 years our old intellectuals, following the path indicated by the Party, have served the country and the people in good faith and performed great feats in revolution and construction. They have grown into fine socialist intellectuals thanks to the tireless education of the Party and through the trials of arduous revolutionary struggle. Meanwhile, thanks to the correct policies of our Party on education and on the training of cadres, hundreds of thousands of new intellectuals from the ranks of the working people have been trained, who now serve the revolutionary cause in all the political, economic, cultural and military fields. Thus our Party has remolded the old intellectuals and brought up new intellectuals and thereby built them into its reliable contingent of intellectuals. All our intellectuals place boundless faith in the Party, are united firmly around it and display a high degree of zeal and creativity in socialist construction. This testifies to the correctness and brilliant victory of our Party's policy towards intellectuals.

Today we are confronted with the important task of further revolutionizing the intellectuals. To revolutionize and working-classize the intellectuals means to completely eradicate the residue of outworn ideas remaining in their minds and to equip them with the revolutionary spirit of the working class, with communist ideology, thus turning them into true intellectuals of the working class, into ardent Communists.

True, the remnants of bourgeois and petty-bourgeois ideas remain, to a relatively large degree, in the minds of the intellectuals. But it is fundamentally wrong to mistrust, for this reason, the revolutionary spirit of the intellectuals, and, moreover, to distrust our intellectuals who have been remolded and tested in the flames of struggle. To suspect and reject the intellectuals is a factionalist tendency. To underestimate their role is a tendency to ignore science and technology. Such tendencies have no place in our Party's policy towards the intellectuals.

Our Party trusts its intellectuals, cherishes and loves them and highly appreciates their feats. The Party will continue to guide and assist intellectuals patiently in their ideological transformation and provide them with all conditions to serve socialist construction better, giving full play to their knowledge and talents. Our intellectuals should have pride in the fact that they are full-fledged soldiers of the Party, fighters for the working class, and actively endeavor to eliminate the survivals of outdated ideas and learn from the revolutionary spirit, organization and militancy of the working class. At the same time, the intellectuals, bearing in mind that they serve society chiefly with technique and knowledge, should do everything in their power to master their specialties and raise their scientific and technical qualifications. Our workers and peasants, on their part, should love intellectuals and learn scientific knowledge and technique from them with an open mind. Only by so doing can we successfully working-classize the intellectuals and raise the technical and cultural standards of the workers and peasants to the level of engineers and assistant engineers. Only by so doing will it be possible to strengthen the unity of the workers and peasants with the intellectuals, develop creative cooperation between them and thereby further facilitate the economic and cultural construction of the country. We will fully revolutionize and working-classize all intellectuals, old and new, and will always join hands with them in the struggle for the victory of the cause of communism.

In promoting the political and ideological unity of our society, work with people whose social and political records are complicated holds an important place. The social and political composition of the population of our country has become very complex because of the protracted colonial rule of Japanese imperialism, the partition of the country by US imperialism and the enemy's divisive schemes during the Fatherland Liberation War. This being the situation, we have to be particularly prudent in our work with various strata of the population.

The invariable principle our Party adheres to in its work with those who have complicated social and political records is that we should appraise each of them always attaching importance to his present attitude, isolate hostile elements to the maximum, and win everyone possible over to the side of the revolution. The social status and thoughts of a man are not unchangeable. Even those who committed crimes against the people in the past may repent of them and reform themselves into good people now, and even those whose social status is complicated may acquire progressive ideas as society advances and their environments change. As a matter of course, we must always firmly maintain our class stand in our work with people and must remember that the comfirmed reactionary elements from the hostile classes never desist from their subversive schemes. But such hostile elements are very few. Because we trust the masses of the people and are convinced of the superiority of the socialist system, the justness of our cause and the invincible force and authority of our Party, we do not suspect people for no reason but believe that everyone can be educated and remolded except the confirmed reactionaries. So we boldly trust and embrace even those whose social status, backgrounds and past records are complicated, and provide them with conditions for doing their work without anxiety if they support our Party and work zealously now. This policy of our Party makes it possible to shatter all the divisive maneuvers of the enemy, win over the masses of the people of all classes and strata to the side of the Party and the revolution, isolate hostile elements still further and give them no room to act in. We should, in the future, too, hold fast to this policy and apply it correctly in practice.

The policy of our Party with regard to the various classes and strata of society is a correct Marxist-Leninist policy based on its class and mass lines and is in full accord with the realities of our country. This is clearly borne out by the fact that though the social composition of our population is complex and we stand directly confronted with the enemy, the broad masses of the people are rallied around our Party and their revolutionary zeal and creative activity are ever higher. We should continue to thoroughly implement the Party's class and mass lines, so that we may further expand and reinforce our revolutionary ranks and turn the whole society into one big family closely united in an amicable, cheerful and stimulating atmosphere.

To accelerate the process of working-classization of the society and solidly build up the revolutionary ranks it is necessary to conduct political and ideological work energetically among the Party members and the working people. Socialism creates the socio-economic and material conditions for remolding the ideas of the working people and uniting them. However, the ideological transformation and unity of the people do not come of themselves simply because the socialist system has triumphed and living standards have improved.

Only by carrying on ideological work more energetically and patiently in keeping with the progress of socialist construction, can we really educate and remold the working people and unite them solidly. The complex international and internal situation we are facing today and the vast and arduous revolutionary tasks confronting us demand a further intensification of political and ideological work among the masses.

We must continue to vigorously conduct among the Party members and the working people communist education with class education as the main content in combination with education in the revolutionary traditions, and decisively intensify education in Marxism-Leninism and in the Party's policies.

The most important thing here is to increase the class consciousness of the working people and imbue them with the hatred for imperialism, landlords and capitalists. This class education should be conducted well particularly for the new generation who have not experienced exploitation and oppression or undergone the ordeals of arduous revolutionary struggle. We should bring home to the working people the aggressive nature of imperialism and the essence of the exploiting classes and the exploiting system so as to induce them to hate imperialism, hate the exploiting classes and system and fight against them uncompromisingly. We should educate the Party members and the working people in the class principle so that they may harbor no illusion about the imperialists and hostile classes, maintain sharp revolutionary vigilance against their aggressive schemes and subversive and sabotaging maneuvers, expose and crush them at every step.

In particular, US imperialism and Japanese militarism are the most dangerous forces of aggression directly confronting us and the main target of our struggle. We must instill our working people with more hatred of US imperialism and Japanese militarism and prepare them ideologically to fight resolutely against US and Japanese imperialism at any time.

We have not yet completed the national-liberation revolution throughout the country—the people in south Korea are still groaning under the oppression of the US imperialists and their stooges. To liberate south Korea and reunify the country is the national duty of the entire Korean people. We must educate the working people of the northern half in a revolutionary way to fight against US imperialist colonial rule in south Korea, against the renewed aggression of Japanese militarism and for the final accomplishment of the Korean revolution. We should see that all our working people always remember the plight of the south Korean people and the task of reunifying the country and devote themselves to all revolutionary struggle and constructive work in the lofty spirit of assisting the people in south Korea more actively.

Class education for the working people is class struggle in the ideological field. The struggle against imperialism and the exploiting classes is inseparable from the struggle against their reactionary ideas. If we do not combat the vestiges of the outmoded ideas still in the minds of the working people, it will be impossible to equip them with the working-class ideology, communist ideology. Moreover, the US imperialists and their lackeys are using every conceivable means and method to spread reactionary bourgeois ideology among us and are craftily machinating to use the backward ideological elements among our working people in their subversive activities.

We should, therefore, continue to wage an energetic struggle to prevent the infiltration of reactionary bourgeois ideology and to wipe out the old ideological survivals in the minds of the working people. We must categorically reject the reactionary bourgeois ideology, and the corrupt bourgeois morality and way of life, and oppose selfishness, liberalism and other vestiges of outdated ideas and backward ways. We must tirelessly strive for the triumph of the lofty communist ideology and morality, for the establishment of the communist tone of life. We should see to it that all our working people oppose degradation and indolence, lead a frugal life, display voluntary zeal in labor, love the collectives and organizations and fight for commom prosperity, helping each other along.

Whether or not the Communists can lead the revolutionary cause of the working class to victory depends on whether or not they hold fast to the Marxist-Leninist principles and apply them properly in their activities. For the Korean Communists and people to carry out the Korean revolution successfully, it is essential to defend and implement the lines and policies of our Party which represent the creative application of the Marxist-Leninist principles to the realities of Korea. Therefore, imbuing the Party members and the working people with the principles of Marxism-Leninism and the policies of our Party is always the central problem in our ideological work. Today when the slanders and abuses of the imperialists and world reaction against Marxist-Leninist ideology have become intensified as never before and opportunist ideological trends of all descriptions have appeared within the international communist movement, it is a still more important problem for us to educate the Party members and the working people in Marxism-Leninism and Party policies.

We must further strengthen the study of Marxism-Leninism and Party policies throughout the Party, and must repeatedly explain and propagate the principles of Marxism-Leninism among the masses and bring the lines and policies of our Party home to them. Everyone should regard self-studying and ideological training as the first and foremost revolutionary task and tirelessly endeavor to acquire the revolutionary spirit and quintessence of Marxism-Leninism, to arm himself firmly with the ideas of our Party, and to make the Party lines and policies his own unshakable conviction. We should, at the same time, lead the Party members and the working people to fully understand the nature and harmfulness of Right and "Left" opportunism, such as modern revisionism, dogmatism and factionalism and acquaint them with all their manifestations. In this way, we should make sure that all our Party members and working people are deeply convinced of the correctness of our Party's Marxist-Leninist lines and policies, support and defend them determinedly and fight to carry them through to the end. We should enable the Party members and the working people to clearly discern Marxism-Leninism from Right and "Left" opportunism, resolutely oppose opportunism and always adhere to the revolutionary principles of Marxism-Leninism.

We must, in particular, oppose factionalism and defend the unity and cohesion of the Party. Through arduous struggle, our Party rooted out the historical legacy of factionalism, achieved the unity of the communist movement in Korea and established its ideological system throughout the Party. Today our Party is closely knit organizationally and ideologically and all the Party organizations and Party members act with one mind and will. But we must by no means become complacent. Our Party members must always remember the fact that in the past, when the external and internal situation was complex and our revolution was undergoing trials, the anti-Party factionalists lurking within the Party attacked the Party in league with international sectarians. As long as opportunist and great-power chauvinist tendencies exist within the international communist movement, we cannot be certain that a similar attempt will not be made again. And under the present complex situation, waverers may appear within our ranks, too, particularly under sectarian and other opportunist influence from without. We must, therefore, always sharpen vigilance against sectarianism. We must oppose any divisive maneuvers and factional activities from within and without, designed to cause our Party members to vacillate and split our ranks, and must staunchly defend the Marxist-Leninist unity of our Party and strengthen it more.

Only when the whole Party and the entire people are firmly armed ideologically and theoretically and are closely united in this way, can they prevent opportunist ideological trends of all shades from infiltrating from outside or from appearing inside and, no matter what wind may blow, they can continue to advance triumphantly, holding aloft the revolutionary banner of Marxism-Leninism, under the seasoned leadership of the Party Central Committee.

The struggle to defend and implement the Marxist-Leninist lines and policies of our Party is closely related to the struggle to oppose flunkeyism towards great powers and establish Juche. If a person loses Juche and falls into flunkeyism, his faculty of independent thinking will be paralyzed and, as a result, he will not only be unable to display creativity but, in the end, will even become unable to distinguish right from wrong and follow others blindly and will be inclined to depend only on others for everything, losing faith in his own strength. Then he may lapse into Right or "Left" opportunism, such as revisionism, dogmatism and factionalism, and do great harm to the revolution and construction.

We must reject all manifestations of flunkeyism towards great powers and root it out completely, and establish Juche more thoroughly and promote the revolutionary spirit of self-reliance in all spheres. We should establish Juche in ideology and continue to strictly abide by the principle of independence in politics, self-sustenance in the economy and self-defense in national defense.

Education in socialist patriotism occupies a very important place in the ideological education of the working people.

Socialist patriotism is the patriotism of the working class and the working people aspiring to socialism and communism; it combines class consciousness with the spirit of national independence, love for one's class and social system with that for one's nation and fatherland. The working people, including the working class, make up the overwhelming majority of the nation, and the interests of the nation are inseparable from the interests of the working people. The road of capitalism is the road of exploitation and oppression, the road of dependence and ruin. Only socialism eradicates class exploitation and national oppression and ensures complete independence and prosperity to the nation. This is why the Communists, who fight for the interests of the working people and for socialism, are the most authentic patriots, and only the working class and the other working people who want their class emancipation and socialism can possess true patriotic sentiments.

Our socialist patriotism is based on the socialist system which has abolished exploitation and oppression and brought freedom and happiness to the working people and, hence, it should be manifested, above all, in a love for the the socialist system and the working people. We should bring home to all the working people the superiority of the socialist system established in the northern half of our country so that they can resolutely fight in defense of this system and actively endeavor to consolidate and develop it. Every one of the working people should be made to display a high degree of enthusiasm and creativity in socialist construction, deeply aware that his work is an honorable contribution to the consolidation of the socialist system and to the happiness of the working people. All the working people should be educated to value and take good care of state and social property as common assets of the people, to manage the joint economy efficiently and work hard to build up the economic life of the country assiduously.

Socialist patriotism finds expression in the love for their fatherland and nation as well as in the love for the socialist system and the working people. Those born in Korea make the revolution and build socialism and communism in Korea. The Korean revolution is the basic duty of Korean Communists and people. Away from the Korean nation and Korean soil of three thousand *ri*, it is impossible to talk about the Korean revolution. Without taking into account the history and traditions of Korea and the sentiments and customs of the Koreans, it is impossible to carry out the Korean revolution successfully. He who does not love his fatherland and nation cannot have enthusiasm for the revolution in his country nor can he devote himself to the struggle for its victory. This is why we Communists love our country and nation more ardently than anyone else does, why we fight determinedly for national independence and prosperity, treasure our national culture, all the fine heritages and traditions of the nation, and endeavor to carry them forward. Communists oppose all forms of national oppression and inequality and reject national nihilism.

We should encourage national pride and independence among the working people and urge them to fight more resolutely for the complete reunification and independence of the country and for the future prosperity of our nation. Working people should be taught to love the mountains and rivers of their country and their native places and make them more beautiful, to love their language and national culture and endeavor to develop them further.

Of great importance here is to educate the working people to take a correct attitude to the legacies of our age-old national culture and our time-honored national traditions. We must not fall into the nihilistic tendency to negate and erase all things of the past, or into the restorationist tendency to follow them blindly. These tendencies are big obstacles to creating a new, socialist culture and way of life and to equipping the working people with the idea of socialist patriotism. Only on the basis of discarding the backward and reactionary elements of our national heritage, and critically absorbing and developing all the progressive and popular elements, can we create and further develop a new, socialist culture and way of life. And only when the working people are well acquainted with the present and past of their nation and love the fine traditions and heritages of their nation, will their patriotic feeling be deepened. We should give the working people a correct and adequate education in the long history and culture of our country so that they may value all the splendid traditions and legacies of our nation, cherish its fine manners and customs, inherit and develop them to suit the new, socialist life of today.

The class interests of the working class are in themselves internationalist, and its international solidarity constitutes a guarantee for the triumph of the communist cause. Hence, socialist patriotism rejects all types of chauvinism, including bourgeois nationalism, and is closely linked with proletarian internationalism. Only a person who is boundlessly faithful to his country's revolution can remain loyal to the revolutionary cause of the international working class, and only a true internationalist can become a true patriot. The national and international duties of the working class are one and the same.

We must equip the entire working people more firmly with the ideas of proletarian internationalism, with the spirit of international solidarity with the revolutionary peoples. We should see that our Party members and working people continue their efforts to defend the unity of the socialist camp and the cohesion of the international communist movement, develop relations of friendship and cooperation with the fraternal parties and countries and strengthen solidarity with the international working class and the progressive people of the whole world. We should educate the working people to fight for the victory of the revolution in their country and, at the same time, fight for the advancement of the world revolutionary movement and always strongly support and encourage the liberation struggle of the oppressed nations and the exploited peoples. Our Party members and working people should be also made not only to prize the successes and experience gained in the revolutionary struggle in their country but also to respect the achievements made by the peoples of other countries in their struggle, and modestly learn from their valuable experience. Thus, we should see that the entire people, holding high the banner of proletarian internationalism, under the leadership of our Party, unite with the peoples of the fraternal countries, with the progressive people of all countries, and fight for peace and democracy, national independence and for the triumph of the common cause of socialism, supporting, encouraging and learning from each other.

We should also educate the working people in the spirit of looking forward to the future, in revolutionary optimism.

Ours is a lofty cause of bringing happiness and prosperity not only to the people of our generation but to all future generations; it is the great cause of communism, the idea of mankind. We must deeply convince all working people of the justness of their cause and the important mission devolving on their generation, so that they will strive with all devotion to bequeath a better life to the posterity, for a radiant future of communism.

It is particularly important to teach the working people faith in the victory of communism. Imperialism is an old force which has outlived its days and communism is a new force that represents the future of mankind. The road to communism may be beset with innumerable difficulties and obstacles, twists and turns, but no force can hold back the law-governed process of the development of history in which imperialism falls and communism triumphs. Although the imperialists are now stepping up aggressive maneuvers and making noisy anti-communist campaign, this is nothing but the frenzy of the doomed. And although the international communist movement is now undergoing serious trials, they are only temporary obstacles to its onward march. This cannot change the laws of the development of history nor blot out the great idea of communism. On the basis of Marxist-Leninist theory and historical facts, we must bring home to the working people the inevitability of the downfall of imperialism and the triumph of communism and the truth of communism. We should thereby see to it that all our working people march forward vigorously with a burning aspiration for and a firm faith in a communist future, surmounting all difficulties and obstacles under any circumstances.

We will energetically conduct political and ideological work among the Party members and the working people and thereby arm them more firmly with Marxist-Leninist ideology, communist ideology, and rally them more closely around the Central Committee of our Party. When we train our Party members into ardent communist revolutionaries, educate and remold the broad sections of working people in the revolutionary communist spirit and further cement the unity of the Party and the people, our revolutionary ranks will be invincible.

In this way, we will steadily expand and reinforce the revolutionary ranks, and will thereby further accelerate socialist construction in the northern half of the Republic and fortify our revolutionary base as firm as a rock politically, economically and militarily.

LET US DEVELOP REVOLUTIONARY FINE ARTS: NATIONAL IN FORM AND SOCIALIST IN CONTENT

Talk with Workers in the Fine Arts on the Occasion of the Ninth National Art Exhibition, *October 16, 1966*

Many fine works of art are displayed at the Ninth National Art Exhibition. It is very gratifying that our artists have succeeded in representing the arduous but dynamic path of revolution which our Party has traversed and the heroic struggle of our people. They have made great progress not only in the content of their work but also in the technique.

Many of the pictures on exhibition are of high quality, particularly the oil entitled, *On the Road of Advance* and the Korean brush, ink, and color paintings *Old Man on the Rakdong-gang River* and *Women of Namgang Village*.

Among the people in *On the Road of Advance* there are a small young soldier, an elderly commanding officer and a young nurse. Some are smiling whereas the others are serious and preoccupied. They have come a long way through hard battle; but each face is optimistic, expressing unconditional loyalty to our Party and a firm conviction in the victory of the revolution.

Old Man on the Rakdong-gang River presents one impressive scene from the Fatherland Liberation War: our People's Army and the masses, united as one force, fight bravely against the enemy. The canvas portrays exceptionally well both the emotions of an old man helping soldiers of the People's Army, despite the danger, and the determination of those soldiers carrying out their combat mission with sharp vigilance and burning hatred for the enemy.

Then there is the *Women of Namgang Village.* How lifelike and full of fighting spirit the picture is! Its characters are the very image of the resourceful, fearless women of Korea who fought at home as heroically as the men on the front, making any sacrifice necessary to win victory in the Fatherland Liberation War. Even the oxen they are driving seem to be filled with spirit.

In addition, *On the Way to the South* and *The Wrath of Sinchon*, both fine paintings. The Korean painting, *On the Way to the South,* portrays the traditional unity between army and people well—the People's Army rely on the masses in their fight for the country and the people, and the people, in turn, wholeheartedly support the soldiers of the People's Army and love them as their brothers. *The Wrath of Sinchon*, an oil, vividly represents the indignation of the people, looking over the bloodbath of the enemy and making a grim vow, "We'll take our revenge on those beasts."

There are several fine canvases in the exhibit which graphically show the true nature of the exploiter society; thus, they make an effective contribution to the class education of our younger generation. Among others, *Daughter, At a Mill,* and *The Day When the Daughter Is Sold* are worthy of mention. *Daughter* is an oil which eloquently shows with what wickedness and craftiness the landlords used to torment the peasants. Every detail is painted with great skill: the pitiable looks on the faces of the mother and daughter grief-stricken at the forced separation; the crying child and the haughty air of the steward, the landlord's agent. Anyone standing before this canvas is filled with hate for the classes that exploit them. Our children must be shown many pictures like this. They know very little about traffic in human beings, about the sorrow and humiliation their parents suffered in the past under the oppressive hand of the landlords and capitalists. Show them many pictures of this kind and they will come to see vividly the true nature of an exploitative society and can better appreciate the happy life they know today under socialism.

You have produced many good canvases. Some deal with the brilliant revolutionary traditions of our glorious anti-Japanese armed struggle, with the proud struggle of our working people actively engaged in socialist construction, and with the happy life of the people under the socialist system we have established in our Republic. Others represent the save-the-nation struggle against US imperialism of the people in the southern half of the Republic.

Aside from paintings, there are many excellent examples of art for the stage and the cinema, sculpture, industrial art and embroidery.

All this is strong evidence that our fine arts are developing soundly under the correct guidance of our Party. I warmly congratulate all you Party workers in art and literature who have created so many excellent works of art, upholding the Party's literary and artistic policy and struggling energetically to see that it's carried out.

I would like to avail myself of this opportunity to speak to you about some problems concerning the continued development of our fine arts.

Our arts must be truly popular ones that respond to the sentiments of our people; they must be revolutionary ones that serve the interests of the Party and the revolution. Therefore, our fine arts must be national in form and socialist in content in every way.

To achieve this end our most essential task is to develop our fine arts on the basis of the splendid national traditions of Korean painting.

Korean painting is an artistic form peculiar to Oriental painting. It is characterized by forcefulness, beauty and elegance. The canvases by An Gyon and Kim Hong Do, Li dynasty artists, not only reflect life truthfully but reveal a touch that is forceful and beautiful. They say that Sol Go, the celebrated ancient artist, painted pine trees on a wall so dexterously that birds outside mistook them for real ones and tried to perch there, flying into the wall and banging down.

Since we have this unique, wonderful form of art, why imitate others? To slight Korean painting and value only Western painting shows a tendency towards flunkeyism and national nihilism.

They say that in imperialist and capitalist countries of the West abstract paintings, which are puzzles to viewers, are very much in vogue. We must struggle resolutely to prevent this degenerate trend in bourgeois artistic taste from penetrating the fine arts of our country.

This in no way means, however, that you should only produce Korean paintings from now on, rejecting positive artistic forms from other countries. We should continue to develop oil painting and various printing techniques. Oil can be an excellent medium for art when it is used to portray the lives of our people in simple, clear and delicate brushstrokes that harmonize with Korean sensibility. In other words, in the fine arts as in all other fields, we must thoroughly establish Juche and develop the art of our country on the basis of indigenous forms.

When we say that the development of our fine arts should be based on Korean painting, we do not mean that everything from the past should be imitated in a mechanical, restorationist way. First we must study the art of drawing characteristic of Korean painting, noteworthy for its clarity and simplicity, and then develop it to meet the needs of our time. Korean painting is a valuable artistic expression. However, this classical art form has many shortcomings, a major one of which is the lack of color. Canvases were done mostly in black and white. We must completely overcome this and similar defects in Korean painting in our time, transforming it to suit our contemporary sensibility.

As well as developing and perfecting national forms in Korean art, we should also work actively to transform it into genuinely revolutionary fine art with socialist content.

The most important thing here is the correct choice of subject.

One important component of a work of art should be its power to educate the people in revolutionary consciousness and inspire them to revolutionary struggle. Without this element a work does not really deserve to be called revolutionary art. In the past, Korean painters exclusively depicted nature—beautiful landscapes, attractive birds and other animals; they rarely did figurative paintings which portrayed the daily life and struggle of the people. Such paintings, however skillfully done, cannot touch the hearts of our people and have any educational value today in the midst of our dynamic struggle for revolution and construction. Our painters ought to produce canvases that serve to educate the masses in communism and compel them forward in their efforts to carry on the revolutionary struggle and work of construction.

Your first task, then, is to create many works of art which present our people's glorious revolutionary struggle. Specifically, you must produce more works depicting the infinite loyalty of the anti-Japanese guerrillas to the revolution, their dedication to the people and country, their firm confidence in the victory of the revolution and indomitable fighting spirit, and their lofty sense of revolutionary comradeship. This is very important today in arming our people with our Party's revolutionary ideas. At the same time, more works of fine art representing the immortal exploits of our People's Army and countrymen during the Fatherland Liberation War as well as the revolutionary struggle of the south Korean people should be produced. Battle, however, should not be the only theme. The people's heroic struggle to construct socialism and communism and scenes of their happy life today under the socialist system deserve attention. Our artists should also continue to create many works which expose the true nature of the old, exploiter society.

Thus, if you develop the indigenous form of our fine arts and then use it to depict the achievements of the masses in their everyday struggle and stimulating lives, our fine arts will become truly revolutionary ones. The canvases at the exhibition prove that our painters have worked hard to improve our fine arts. Many paintings in the style of traditional Korean art show an adequate handling of color already and express different aspects of our people's lives and struggle in a very realistic way. Artists should draw from these positive experiences and persist in their efforts to develop our fine arts.

In addition to painting, fine arts for the cinema and the stage, industrial art, sculpture, embroidery, crafts, etc., should continue to be developed on the basis of traditional Korean forms suitable to the emotions and aspirations of builders of socialism.

For our fine artists to create genuinely popular and revolutionary works of art which are national in form and socialist in content, it is important that they faithfully depict reality in all its variety and in different forms, adhering closely to the method of socialist realism.

The fine arts of capitalist society are based exclusively on subjectivism, formalism and naturalism, divorced from real life; they are removed from the daily lives of the people and fail to win their love. The reverse is true of our fine arts—specifically geared to serve the masses of the people and develop in the midst of their love. Korean artists have an honorable task: to create a large number of works so popular that all our people will return to them again and again, works which portray men and women devoted to the struggle for our revolutionary cause and socialist construction, that is, works which breathe the same air as the masses and march alongside them in the age of revolution.

Workers in the fine arts must necessarily penetrate vibrant reality if they are to produce works of high quality which satisfy the Party's demands and win the people's love.

An artist who fails to recognize the vibrant substance of life or understand the thoughts and feelings of the masses can never produce a work of value, no matter how great his artistic talents may be. Such a person is likely to paint pictures which are out of touch with present-day needs and which falsely beautify and idealize life. Paintings that do not meet the demands of the times will never earn the people's admiration. When art grossly exaggerates reality, no one will believe it. It will fail to have any influence on people.

Artists must themselves go to factories and villages and scrutinize the real conditions. They must work with the workers and peasants and study their lives deeply. Only then can they grasp the true feelings and thoughts of the population. Only then can they produce lifelike works of art that will serve our revolution and enjoy the love of the people.

We must popularize the creations of our fine arts and train a large reserve of talented fine artists.

Painting, making objects for industrial art and sculpting are not mysteries limited to a handful of specialists. Workers, peasants and even young people, children and students can do all these things. We should see to it that the broad masses participate actively in the creation of the fine arts. We should carefully tend the new buds that grow and give them every possible chance for development. The results will be innumerable works of fine art and a rapid increase in the ranks of our artists. Since painting does not involve physical exertion, I think it would be good to train many women as artists. The state should always be deeply concerned with the systematic training of artists and provide them with all the necessary conditions for their creative activities.

We must effectively organize work to show the excellent product of our fine arts to a wide public. High quality paintings should appear in illustrated magazines, they should be reproduced extensively in other media and then be sent to factories, enterprises, cooperative farms and to the People's Army, to say nothing of educational and cultural institutions. It is also advisable to display excellent examples of sculpture in our children's palaces, Young Pioneers' camps, club houses and other places where children and working people gather.

Furthermore, all the paintings in the National Art Exhibition should be reprinted and made into an album. This is the only way we can preserve the products of our fine arts and locate any picture easily whenever we need it.

I hope you can train yourselves as better Red literary and art workers of the Party and create more and more excellent works of fine art in the future.